Periodicals and Journalism in Twentieth-Century Ireland 2

PERIODICALS AND JOURNALISM IN TWENTIETH-CENTURY IRELAND 2

A Variety of Voices

Mark O'Brien & Felix M. Larkin

EDITORS

FOUR COURTS PRESS

Set in 11.5 pt on 13.5 pt Centaur MT for
FOUR COURTS PRESS LTD
7 Malpas Street, Dublin 8, Ireland
www.fourcourtspress.ie
and in North America for
FOUR COURTS PRESS
c/o IPG, 814 N Franklin St, Chicago, IL 60610

A catalogue record for this title is available
from the British Library.

ISBN 978-1-84682-862-1

Printed in England
by CPI Antony Rowe, Chippenham, Wilts.

Contents

Contributors   7

Introduction   11

1   Mirrors of a changing Ireland: *The Bell's* series
'The Fourth Estate', 1944–5   18
Felix M. Larkin

2   *The Leader*, the *Irish Press* and the 1953–4 libel action over
Professor T.D. Williams' 'A Study in Neutrality': 'the bloody
borderland of contemporary history'   36
Michael Kennedy

3   'Friendship of the intelligent few and hostility of the
unimaginative many': the business of publishing periodicals
in Dublin, 1930–55   60
Sonya Perkins

4   *Fortnight*: a voice of reason and moderation in Northern
Ireland's 'Troubles'   82
Andy Pollak

5   Inside stories and outsider opinions: *The Phoenix*   102
Joe Breen

6   *Honesty* and *Publicity*: two periodicals, one man's war on cant
in the Irish Free State   122
Anthony Keating

7   The *Church of Ireland Gazette* and the twentieth century:
'a Church paper for Church people'?   135
Ian d'Alton

8   Political capital: *In Dublin*, advocacy and opinion, 1976–83   155
Martina Madden

9   Writing from the margins: *In Touch, Identity, Out* and *GCN*   173
     Mark O'Brien

10   *Status*: a feminist news magazine, 1981   190
     Pat Brennan

11   'The mouthpiece of the ordinary woman': empowering
     women through the *Irish Housewife* magazine   203
     Sonja Tiernan

12   Irish-produced women's magazines in the 1950s and '60s   220
     Caitriona Clear

13   *Combar*, a post-revival case study of Irish-language publishing:
     'inné, inniu agus amárach'   237
     Regina Uí Chollatáin and Aoife Whelan

14   The *Catholic Bulletin*, 1911–39: battle of civilizations or
     long revolution?   258
     Patrick Maume

15   Influencing the influential: Irish Jesuit periodicals   277
     Declan O'Keeffe

Index   296

Contributors

JOE BREEN is a former managing editor at the *Irish Times*. He has lectured in University College Dublin and Dublin City University. He co-edited, with Mark O'Brien, *The Sunday papers: a history of Ireland's weekly press* (Dublin, 2018).

PAT BRENNAN is a journalist and former news editor and deputy editor of the *Sunday Tribune* (1985–91), having previously worked as a reporter and feature writer for the *Irish Press* and *Magill*. She was a producer and television programme editor for RTÉ news from 1991 to 2016. She is co-author, with Gene Kerrigan, of *This great little nation: the A–Z of Irish scandals and controversies* (Dublin, 1999).

CAITRIONA CLEAR lectures in nineteenth- and twentieth-century European history at NUI Galway. She has published on women religious, women's household work, Maura Laverty, and oral history. Her latest book, *Women's voices: Irish women's magazines in the 1950s and 60s* (London, 2016), is on the history of popular print media. She is currently researching Irish popular reading in the 1940s and 1950s, and is committed to recovering the often-overlooked, non-dramatic 'everyday' working and social life of those decades.

IAN d'ALTON is an historian of Southern Irish Protestantism and co-editor of *Protestant and Irish: the minority's search for place in independent Ireland* (Cork, 2019). A recipient of the Royal Historical Society's Alexander Prize (1972), he has been an honorary senior research fellow at the University of Liverpool (2011–12) and a visiting fellow at Sidney Sussex College, Cambridge (2014). He is the author of *Protestant society and politics in Cork, 1812–1844* (Cork, 1980), and of twenty book chapters. He is currently a visiting research fellow in Trinity College Dublin.

ANTHONY KEATING is an independent scholar based in the north-west of England where, prior to his recent retirement, he held a senior lectureship and led the BSc (Hons) in psychosocial analysis of offending behaviour at Edge Hill University. He completed his PhD at Dublin City University in 2002, defending a thesis that explored the cultural and communicative aspects of child abuse in Ireland between 1922 and 1972, supervised by Professor John Horgan. He has published widely on this subject and more latterly on radical journalism in the regional press of the Irish Free State.

MICHAEL KENNEDY is the executive editor of the Royal Irish Academy's Documents on Irish Foreign Policy (DIFP) series. He has published widely for over twenty-five years on Irish diplomatic, political and military history. His most recent books include *The Emergency: a visual history of the Irish Defence Forces, 1939–1945* (with Comdt Daniel Ayiotis and Dr John Gibney) (Dublin, 2019) and *Ireland: a voice amongst the nations* (with Dr John Gibney and Dr Kate O'Malley) (Dublin, 2019). Michael also appears on radio and television, and talks regularly to a wide variety of audiences on aspects of modern Irish history.

FELIX M. LARKIN is a co-founder and former chairman of the Newspaper and Periodical History Forum of Ireland. He is the author of *Terror and discord: the Shemus cartoons in the* Freeman's Journal, *1920–1924* (Dublin, 2009) and co-editor, with Mark O'Brien, of *Periodicals and journalism in twentieth-century Ireland: writing against the grain* (Dublin, 2014). A collection of his occasional writings, *Living with history*, will be published in 2021. He is a contributor to each of the three volumes of *The Edinburgh history of the British and Irish press* (2020 & forthcoming).

MARTINA MADDEN is a communications and public relations coordinator who has worked in the non-profit sector in Ireland for more than a decade. A social sciences graduate of the University of Glasgow, she completed an MA in political communication at Dublin City University in 2018.

PATRICK MAUME is a graduate of University College Cork and Queen's University Belfast, where he passed many idle hours with the QUB library set of the *Catholic Bulletin*. Since 2003 he has been a researcher with the Royal Irish Academy's *Dictionary of Irish biography*. He has published biographies of Daniel Corkery and D.P. Moran, a survey of early twentieth-century Irish nationalist political culture, and numerous papers on nineteenth- and twentieth-century Irish cultural and political history with particular reference to print culture.

MARK O'BRIEN is associate professor of journalism history at Dublin City University. He is the author of *The fourth estate: journalism in twentieth-century Ireland* (Manchester, 2017), *The* Irish Times: *a history* (Dublin, 2008) and *The truth in the news? De Valera, Fianna Fáil and the* Irish Press (Dublin, 2001). His co-edited works include *Politics, culture, and the Irish American press, 1784–1963* (New York, 2021), *The Sunday papers: a history of Ireland's weekly press* (Dublin, 2018) and *Periodicals and journalism in twentieth-century Ireland: writing against the grain* (Dublin, 2014). He is a co-founder and former chairperson of the Newspaper and Periodical History Forum of Ireland.

DECLAN O'KEEFFE is college historian at Clongowes Wood College, where he also edits *The Clongownian*. He took an MA in history (UCD) with a dissertation on Matthew Russell, SJ and the *Irish Monthly* and has continued to research and publish on the role and influence of Jesuit publications in Ireland in order to examine the intellectual mission of the Society of Jesus and the process by which it was established, developed and propagated. He has been published in 'A *different discipline': revisiting Canon Sheehan of Doneraile (1852–1913)* and *Engendering Ireland: new reflections on modern history and literature*, as well as in several issues of *Studies*.

SONYA PERKINS holds a PhD and MPhil from Trinity College Dublin. The title of her PhD thesis is 'In search of a cultural republic: intellectual and literary periodical publishing in Dublin 1930–55'. She is a former chief executive of the *Irish Arts Review* and worked in magazine publishing in Ireland and the UK for many years. She is the author of 'Where and what is Ireland?' in *Periodicals and journalism in twentieth-century Ireland* (Dublin, 2014) and 'Father Senan Moynihan' in the Royal Irish Academy's *Dictionary of Irish biography*.

ANDY POLLAK was editor of *Fortnight* from 1981 to 1985, while working in the Belfast office of the *Irish Times*. He was later *Irish Times* religious affairs correspondent, education correspondent and assistant news editor. In 1992–3 he coordinated the Opsahl Commission, an independent inquiry into ways forward for Northern Ireland, and edited its report, *A citizens' inquiry* (Dublin, 1993). Between 1999 and 2013 he was founding director of the Centre for Cross Border Studies in Armagh, and secretary of several all-Ireland education networks. He is co-author of a biography of Revd Ian Paisley (Dublin, 1986) and a memoir by Seamus Mallon (Dublin, 2019).

SONJA TIERNAN is the Éamon Cleary Chair of Irish Studies and co-director of the Centre for Irish and Scottish Studies at the University of Otago, New Zealand. She has held fellowships at the National Library of Ireland, Trinity College Dublin, the Keough-Naughton Institute of Irish Studies at the University of Notre Dame, the School of Irish Studies at Concordia University and the Moore Institute at NUI Galway. She has published widely on modern Irish and British women's history. Her most recent monograph, *The history of marriage equality in Ireland: a social revolution begins*, was published by Manchester University Press in 2020.

REGINA UÍ CHOLLATÁIN, head of the UCD School of Irish, Celtic Studies and Folklore, has published widely on Irish-language revival, media and print culture. Recent publications include chapters in *The Edinburgh history of the British and Irish press* vols 2 & 3 (2020) and *Saothrú na Gaeilge scríofa i suímh uirbeacha na hÉireann, 1700–1850* (co-editor, 2017). She was awarded the Nicholas O'Donnell Fellowship, Melbourne University (2019) and ICUF senior visiting professor (2011–12). A regular panellist on Irish broadcast media, she is a former board member of TG4; a member of the National Academic Advisory Board of the Museum of Literature of Ireland (MoLI) and the National Folklore Commission; former chair of the National Newspaper and Periodical History Forum of Ireland (2015–18); and president of the Global Irish Diaspora Congress, which she co-founded in 2017.

AOIFE WHELAN is head of Irish Studies and also lectures in Modern Irish in the UCD School of Irish, Celtic Studies and Folklore. She is co-editor (with Richard Allen and Oliver O'Hanlon) of *Freedom of speech in the press in times of conflict: historical perspectives from Ireland and Europe* (Bern, Switzerland, 2021). She was appointed deputy editor of the Revolution Papers in 2016 and was an invited curator of the online exhibition 'Treasures of the Oireachtas Library' commemorating the centenary of Dáil Éireann in 2019. She is currently publications officer for the Newspaper and Periodical History Forum of Ireland.

Introduction

In *The Edinburgh history of the British and Irish press*, Martin Conboy defines the contribution that the periodical press has made to British and Irish culture in the twentieth century as 'reporting and reflecting on current events as well as pushing for social and political change, and beyond all else establishing spaces within their publications for the creation of communities of taste, opinion, political orientation and lifestyle'.[1] The great importance of that contribution is the justification for this volume, the second collection of studies on periodicals and journalism in twentieth-century Ireland that we have edited and Four Courts Press has published. The first volume was published in 2014. In these two volumes we have sought to address a gap in the field of Irish press history in the twentieth century; as we observed in the introduction to the first volume, 'the work that has been done to date on Irish periodicals has tended to concentrate on the journal as literary miscellany rather than as a vehicle for news and commentary'.[2]

The periodicals or journals that feature in this volume all contributed to Irish culture in one or more of the ways listed by Conboy, and some continue to do so. Nine of the fifteen chapters that follow are about individual titles, while three survey a number of periodicals with a common purpose and/or the same target audience; none of the publications in question was considered in the earlier volume. The first two chapters are, however, each concerned with a particular series of articles that appeared in periodicals – *The Bell* and *The Leader* – that were the subject of general essays in the first volume. The articles in *The Bell*, discussed by Felix Larkin, were published in 1944 and 1945 under the umbrella title 'The Fourth Estate'. They are significant, and relevant to the theme of this volume, because of the light they shine on Irish newspapers and periodicals at that time – 'a vital component of Irish society that was otherwise immune from the scrutiny of the Fourth Estate', as Larkin points out. Michael Kennedy, author of the chapter on the articles in *The Leader*, writes that those articles – about Ireland's Second World War neutrality, and published in 1953 – were 'illuminating in the absence of serious scholarship on the history of Irish foreign policy for the following decade and a half'; they are worthy of attention because of that and because of the celebrated libel action that followed their publication. The third chapter in this volume, by Sonya

1 Martin Conboy, 'Concluding comments' in Martin Conboy & Adrian Bingham (eds), *The Edinburgh history of the British and Irish press*, iii: *Competition and disruption, 1900–2017* (Edinburgh, 2020), pp 660–3 at p. 663. 2 Mark O'Brien & Felix M. Larkin, 'Introduction' in Mark O'Brien & Felix M. Larkin (eds), *Periodicals and journalism in twentieth-century Ireland: writing against the grain* (Dublin, 2014), pp 9–15 at p. 9.

Perkins, is a commentary on the business of publishing periodicals in Ireland in the period 1930–55. It was often a messy business. Perkins reminds us that, notwithstanding the editorial accomplishments of the periodicals, they were generally produced in the face of 'grinding commercial pressures ... to sell advertising, increase distribution, promote subscriptions and solicit patrons'.

The chapters referring to individual periodicals or groups of periodicals cover a wide spectrum of Irish life and opinion in the twentieth century. Conboy's definition of the contribution of periodicals to our culture suggests a convenient – if somewhat crude – means of categorizing them. Thus, four of the chapters are about periodicals whose *raison d'être* was or is essentially 'reporting and reflecting on current events'. Perhaps the most remarkable of these was *Fortnight*, the Belfast magazine published – with one brief interruption – between 1970 and 2011 and committed, as stated in Andy Pollak's chapter on the magazine, to 'working to make Northern Ireland a functioning society based on democracy, human rights and equality for all'. Its aim, according to Pollak, was to provide 'a reasoned, "neither unionist nor nationalist" analysis of that conflicted society, while opening its pages to writers of all points of view'. Pollak, editor of *Fortnight* from 1981 to 1985, notes with satisfaction 'the influence some of its analysis and proposals had on political developments in Northern Ireland'.

The others in the 'reporting and reflecting' category are *The Phoenix*, *Honesty* and the *Church of Ireland Gazette*. Joe Breen, in his chapter on *The Phoenix*, describes it as having charted 'a dissenting or alternative history of contemporary Ireland which, invariably, tested the boundaries of what was considered journalism, not least by established journalists'. Its forthright investigative journalism is leavened with satirical humour, especially in its provocative covers; Breen argues that satire 'is an important part of the magazine's identity and story'. *Honesty* was an earlier radical journal – published between 1925 and 1931, the organ of one James W. Upton – and it was similar to *The Phoenix* in consciously situating itself 'as separate and distinct from mainstream Irish journalism', to quote from Anthony Keating's chapter about it. Keating argues that *Honesty* was 'by far and away the most socially radical journal published in the [Irish] Free State, exposing what it viewed as Ireland's sordid underbelly and the cant of its political and journalistic classes'. The *Church of Ireland Gazette* is, in contrast, unapologetically an establishment organ – a newspaper for Church of Ireland laity throughout Ireland. In the words of Ian d'Alton in his chapter on the *Gazette*, its role is to keep 'the minority well-informed about itself and the wider world'. Founded in 1856, it has required significant financial support from the Church of Ireland to survive since 1963. The Church's determination to keep the *Gazette* going is, in d'Alton's view, evidence of 'the acute sensitivity of Irish Anglicanism (and, indeed, a wider Protestantism) to its identity and history'; the *Gazette* is seen as integral to both. Originally published in Dublin, the *Gazette* is now published in Northern Ireland. *Fortnight* is the only other periodical in this volume published outside Dublin.

Four chapters discuss periodicals that fall into the category of 'pushing for social and political change'. The first of these, by Martina Madden, considers *In Dublin* magazine. Launched in 1976 as a 'what's on' listing guide, Madden explains that it soon 'evolved to become a features-led magazine that included a significant quantity of social affairs and political content focusing on issues of local politics, planning and development, and social issues, including the gay rights movement and feminist activism'. She sees *In Dublin* in its early years as 'the voice of a new generation' on the issues of contraception, divorce, homosexuality and abortion – as well as the perennial problems of unemployment and emigration. In his chapter, Mark O'Brien reviews the various publications that served the gay community from the late 1970s onwards – *In Touch, Identity, Out* and *Gay Community News* (*GCN*) – and demonstrates their role in the gay rights movements in Ireland; he writes that they 'cannot be separated from the various movements that emerged in the 1970s, the personalities involved, the priorities that different individuals felt should be pursued and the legal challenge to the law [criminalizing homosexual acts]'. They provided solidarity to those engaged in these movements, but O'Brien also emphasizes that 'they sought to give a voice to the formerly voiceless and to disrupt the idealised image of Irishness that then prevailed and which was based on the long-term symbiotic relationship between nationalism, heteronormativity and religiosity'.

Pat Brennan's chapter looks at the short-lived *Status* magazine, described by her as 'a news magazine for women ... squarely focused on women's rights'. She writes that it 'began life [in 1981] hoping to be a force for change, holding government to account on women's issues'. It ceased publication after ten months because of its failure to attract sufficient advertising, but Brennan comments that 'it is arguable that the glossy magazine format was never right for a feminist periodical in the small Irish market'. The *Irish Housewife*, the subject of a chapter by Sonja Tiernan, was an earlier and longer-lived crusading feminist journal. Founded in 1946, it was the organ of the Irish Housewives' Association – and Tiernan writes that 'the magazine used the term housewife in the title in order to politicise housewives and portray these women as powerful consumers who could in turn become significant political lobbyists'. She notes that 'many feminist campaigns and campaigners can be traced through the articles published in the *Irish Housewife*'. It should be seen as in the tradition of the *Irish Citizen*, the Irish suffragist newspaper, about which Tiernan wrote in our first volume of studies on periodicals and journalism.

The remaining four chapters are about periodicals in the third category of 'establishing spaces within their publications for the creation of communities'. Caitriona Clear notes in the opening paragraph of her chapter that 'women's magazines have been almost completely ignored by historians of Irish media', and she remedies this deficiency by providing an overview of a number of such magazines produced in Ireland in the 1950s and 1960s. The most successful of these, according to Clear, was *Woman's Way* – launched in 1963 and described by her as modelled on the British women's magazine format, but 'self-consciously and proudly Irish'. She concludes that *Woman's Way*, and the other magazines she discusses, 'contributed to Irishwomen's emancipation by enabling them to publicise their doings, communicate with each other, trade with each other, and confide their worries' – a less radical, and less overtly political, approach than that followed by *Status* or the *Irish Housewife*.

Likewise, *Comhar* has been 'a forum for many Irish-language writers to develop their craft in post-revival Ireland' for over eighty years – to quote from the chapter on that journal by Regina Uí Chollatáin and Aoife Whelan. They describe it 'as a monthly journal in which literature, debate, analysis and current affairs among other themes are discussed' – but they point out that much of its work, being in the Irish language, is not universally accessible and so 'may not have reached general journalistic discourse'. Their chapter gives a flavour of 'the wealth of material in … the fountain of its archive'. The *Catholic Bulletin*, published between 1911 and 1939, was a very different kind of Irish-Ireland publication: Patrick Maume, in his chapter, observes that it has had 'a long afterlife in Irish cultural historiography, usually as a quotable compendium of extreme expressions of Catholic Irish-Ireland ideology derived from the early twentieth-century Gaelic Revival'. He argues that 'the conflicts of which the *Catholic Bulletin* was part can be traced back, in terms of the self-perception of the participants, to the Land War and earlier struggles over the decline of Protestant Ascendancy', and on this basis he hypothesizes that 'the break between nineteenth- and twentieth-century nationalism has been overestimated'.

As outlined by Declan O'Keeffe in his chapter, the mission of the Jesuits in Ireland from the late nineteenth century onwards has been 'to influence the influential in society and to gradually change the system from within'. They have pursued this aim through, *inter alia*, the publication of a wide range of periodicals – most notably, the *Irish Monthly*, *Studies* and the *Irish Messenger* (the last two of which are still going strong). O'Keeffe's chapter guides us through the history of these periodicals, covering the period from 1873 to the present day. Some of them have enjoyed remarkable longevity; and O'Keeffe tells us that *An Timire*, the Irish-language companion journal to the *Messenger* launched by the Jesuits in 1910, is the oldest Irish-language magazine still in print. The quarterly *Studies*, founded in 1912, remains today 'a quiet force and influence in intellectual life in Ireland' — so described in 1966 by its then editor, as quoted by O'Keeffe in his chapter.[3]

O'Keeffe raises the pertinent question of the future — 'where now?' — for periodicals such as *Studies* in the digital age, and this is an issue for all extant periodicals of the kind considered in this volume and for print media generally. Martin Conboy is sadly correct when, in *The Edinburgh history of the British and Irish press*, he suggests that 'writing the history of the press in the twentieth century … is implicitly requiring us to consider the potential loss of such an engine of public opinion'.[4] Periodicals struggled to survive in twentieth-century Ireland, 'littered as it was with the corpses of fine journals, from *Shan Van Vocht* through the *Irish Statesman* and *The Bell* to *Hibernia* and *Dublin Opinion*' — to quote from Ian d'Alton's chapter in this volume; and Sonya Perkins' chapter particularizes what she calls 'the prosaic commercial realities of periodical publishing'. The advent of the digital age exacerbates the problem. Contemplating the future, we can surely echo John Horgan's observation in his *Great Irish reportage*: 'Writing about current events will have been transformed by the rise of digital media in ways we can only guess at.'[5] It is at any rate hard to envisage that it will be possible — or profitable, in intellectual or any other terms — for historians of the future to compile two volumes on twenty-first-century Irish periodicals like we have done on the twentieth-century ones.

Curiously, Horgan's *Great Irish reportage*, an anthology of journalism since 1922, includes pieces from only three of the periodicals — *The Bell*, *Hot Press* and *Magill* — that were the subject of chapters in the first of our two volumes. Bryan Fanning referred to this in a most generous and perceptive review of that volume, and he speculates that Horgan had concluded 'that much of the best Irish journalism appeared in the mainstream newspapers'. Fanning seems to endorse that view when he writes that the periodicals covered in our first volume 'are mostly interesting for the doctrines they espoused', rather than for their journalism.[6] This is fair comment: the first volume did concentrate on periodicals that provided an outlet for those writing against the grain of

---

3 The editor in question was Roland Burke-Savage, SJ   4 Conboy, 'Concluding comments', p. 662.   5 John Horgan, 'Introduction' in John Horgan (ed.), *Great Irish reportage* (Dublin, 2013), pp xiii–xv at p. xv.   6 Bryan Fanning, 'Partisan reviews' in Bryan Fanning (ed.), *Irish adventures in nation-building* (Manchester, 2016), pp 130–7 at p. 137; previously published in the *Dublin Review of Books*, Jan. 2015.

mainstream Irish society, thereby creating 'a space for diversity of opinion not available in national newspapers or in the provincial press'.[7] In contrast, the periodicals featured in this volume are mainly organs of important communities within Irish society – not always mainstream, but significant communities nonetheless that would not otherwise have a voice in Irish media. The emphasis in this volume is on presenting 'a variety of voices' (to quote the subtitle of the volume), not just dissenting voices – and so in the pages that follow are heard the voices of women, the young, the gay community, religious interests and the Irish-Ireland movement. *The Phoenix* and *Honesty* are the only avowedly dissident journals to feature in this volume, though what Joe Breen describes in his chapter on *The Phoenix* as its 'solidly green republican sympathies' may be less outside the mainstream of Irish society today than they once were. Also, the canvas in this volume has been extended to Northern Ireland, with the chapters on *Fortnight* and the *Church of Ireland Gazette*; no Northern Irish periodicals featured in the first volume.

It is necessary to record here that, despite this volume's wider focus, no piece from any of the periodicals other than *The Bell* and the *Standard* that are discussed in it appears in Horgan's *Great Irish Reportage*. Does this confirm that the best Irish journalism is indeed to be found in mainstream newspapers? The chapters in this volume would indicate otherwise – in which case the most likely explanation for the paucity of periodical journalism in Horgan's anthology is that, when it was compiled in 2013, the periodical was still seen more 'as literary miscellany than as a vehicle for news and commentary'.[8] Our aim in editing two volumes on periodicals and journalism has been to change that perception – while, more generally, advancing the understanding and appreciation of an important aspect of Irish press history. Both volumes were produced with the support – financial and otherwise – of the Newspaper and Periodical History Forum of Ireland which, since its inception in 2008, has served the cause of press history in Ireland through annual conferences and through the publication of volumes of collected studies such as this one; this is the seventh collection that the Forum has facilitated.[9] Members of the Forum have also contributed to the two volumes of *The Edinburgh history of the British and Irish press* published to date, volumes that will be an invaluable source of information on the history of the press in these islands in the nineteenth

7 O'Brien & Larkin, 'Introduction', p. 10.   8 Ibid., p. 9.   9 The others are: *Irish Communications Review*, 12 (2010); Kevin Rafter (ed.), *Irish journalism before independence* (Manchester, 2011); Mark O'Brien & Kevin Rafter (eds), *Independent newspapers: a history* (Dublin, 2012); Mark O'Brien & Felix M. Larkin, *Periodicals and journalism in twentieth-century Ireland: writing against the grain* (Dublin, 2014); Ian Kenneally & James T. O'Donnell, *The Irish regional press, 1892–2018: revival, revolution and republic* (Dublin, 2018); Joe Breen & Mark O'Brien, *The Sunday papers: a history of Ireland's weekly press* (Dublin, 2018).

and twentieth centuries for some time to come. A third volume, covering the pre-1800 period, is eagerly awaited.[10]

The editors gratefully acknowledge the grants towards publication of this volume from the Newspaper and Periodical History Forum and from the Faculty of Humanities and Social Sciences Publication Fund at Dublin City University. We thank the contributors for sharing their scholarship with us and for their patient cooperation with the editorial process. Thanks also to our friends at Four Courts Press for their courage – or foolhardiness – in agreeing to publish a second volume on periodicals and journalism, and for their work in bringing it to fruition. Four Courts Press have a reputation for producing handsome volumes, and this one is no exception.

Mark O'Brien & Felix M. Larkin

---

10 Nicholas Brownlees (ed.), *The Edinburgh history of the British and Irish press*, i: *Beginnings and consolidations, 1640–1800* (Edinburgh, forthcoming); David Finkelstein (ed.), *The Edinburgh history of the British and Irish press*, ii: *Expansion and evolution, 1800–1900* (Edinburgh, 2020); Martin Conboy & Adrian Bingham (eds), *The Edinburgh history of the British and Irish press*, iii: *Competition and disruption, 1900–2017* (Edinburgh, 2020).

1 / Mirrors of a changing Ireland: *The Bell*'s series 'The Fourth Estate', 1944–5

FELIX M. LARKIN

> It is part of the regular policy of *The Bell* to open as many windows as possible on the lives of as many people as possible, so that we may form a full and varied picture of modern Ireland.
>
> —Seán O'Faoláin (1944)[1]

One of the windows opened by *The Bell* under Seán O'Faoláin's editorship was on Irish newspapers and periodicals, in a series of six articles that appeared under the general title 'The Fourth Estate' in successive issues of the magazine between December 1944 and May 1945. Mark O'Brien, in his essay on *The Bell* in the earlier volume on periodicals and journalism that he and I co-edited, argues that '*The Bell* represented a dramatic intervention in the journalism of mid-twentieth century Ireland.'[2] For *The Bell* to have trained its sights on fellow newspapers and periodicals – and indeed on itself in the final article of the series – was certainly a 'dramatic intervention' in that it broke the convention that the press did not hold itself to account, at least not in the public sphere. Thus Hugh Oram, in his foreword to *The newspaper book*, published in 1983, could say: 'Irish newspapers have been chronicling the passing of time for over three centuries. By contrast, they have been singularly slight in recording their own progress for posterity.'[3] This reticence was less the product of modesty about their role in Irish society than of a recognition that freedom of the press was a delicate thing – always under threat in subtle and not-too-subtle ways – and that, while it was fair game to comment on and criticize anything that was published in another newspaper or periodical, to dig deeper into the affairs of other organs might delegitimize the status of the press generally, diminish its

I am grateful to Ian d'Alton, Peter Lacy and Mark O'Brien for their comments on earlier drafts of this essay. In quotations from *The Bell*, I have retained capital letters and italics as they appear in the original. 1 Introductory note by O'Faoláin to an article by Revd Matthew Bailey, 'What it means to be a Presbyterian', *The Bell*, 8:4 (July 1944), 298 – quoted in Kelly Matthews, The Bell *magazine and the representation of Irish identity: opening windows* (Dublin, 2012), p. 1. 2 Mark O'Brien, 'Other voices: *The Bell* and documentary journalism' in Mark O'Brien & Felix M. Larkin (eds), *Periodicals and journalism in twentieth-century Ireland* (Dublin, 2014), pp 158–72 at p. 158. 3 Hugh Oram, *The newspaper book: a history of newspapers in Ireland, 1649–1983* (Dublin, 1983), foreword.

influence and give ammunition to those wishing to circumscribe its freedom. There was also a certain *esprit de corps* within the press, notwithstanding often fierce competition between individual newspapers and periodicals – a sense of 'dog doesn't eat dog'.

O'Faoláin's purpose in commissioning a series of articles on 'some typical papers and periodicals' was 'to see what, if anything, they [the newspapers and periodicals] reflect from the bright (or dirty) face of this New Ireland',[4] and in a long note preceding the first article he introduced the series as follows:

> Here we start another new series. We have called it 'The Fourth Estate'. It might have been called 'Tutors of the Nation', following the famous statement attributed to Napoleon: 'A journalist is a grumbler, a censurer, a giver of advice, a regent of sovereigns, a tutor of nations. Four hostile newspapers are more formidable than a thousand bayonets.' It is our hope that an analysis of six typical periodicals and papers of the day may cast some further light on that mysterious entity, the Irish Character.[5]

In the second article of the series, the *Irish Times* is described as 'this mirror of a changing Ireland'.[6] All the newspapers and periodicals featured in the series are treated as mirrors of the changing Ireland of the 1940s, and for O'Faoláin the changes that he observed in the Ireland of that time were not welcome. He had fought in the War of Independence and later took the republican side in the Civil War; but, as Declan Kiberd has written: 'Having said "revolution or death" in 1921, he was by 1940 confronted by the death of the revolution.'[7] In June 1943, he expressed his disillusionment in what is probably his own most searing piece in *The Bell*, entitled 'The Stuffed Shirts', as follows: 'The final stage of the Revolution was – and is to this day – a middle-class *putsch*. It was not a society that came out of the maelstrom. It was a class.'[8] That was the 'face of this New Ireland' that *The Bell* saw reflected in the newspapers and periodicals – not bright, but dirty.

The organs featured in the series were the leading ones of the day: three daily newspapers – the *Irish Times*, *Irish Independent* and *Irish Press*; the Catholic press – principally, the *Irish Catholic* and *The Standard*; and two monthly periodicals – *Dublin Opinion* and *The Bell*. All were published in Dublin, though all had a countrywide circulation and were addressed to an audience that was not

---

4 Introductory note by O'Faoláin to the second article in the series 'The Fourth Estate', *The Bell*, 9:4 (Jan. 1945), 290. 5 *The Bell*, 9:3 (Dec. 1944), 209. 6 *The Bell*, 9:4 (Jan. 1945), 297. 7 Declan Kiberd, *After Ireland: writing from Beckett to the present* (London, 2017), p. 30. 8 *The Bell*, 6:3 (June 1943), 187. Regarding 'The Stuffed Shirts', see Maurice Harmon, *Seán O'Faoláin: a life* (London, 1994), pp 140–1.

limited to the Dublin urban elite that guided their fortunes. To that extent at least, they could validly be regarded as reflecting the 'face of this New Ireland'. Moreover, as Malcolm Ballin has remarked in his *Irish periodical culture, 1937–1972*, 'although most journals in Ireland during the twentieth century were published in Dublin, the regional affiliations of editors ... ensured that metropolitan domination was not unchallenged'.[9] O'Faoláin – a native of Cork city, born in 1900 – was typical of the editors to whom Ballin referred. He had, however, spent most of the period 1926–33 in America and in London; and only when he returned to Ireland did he settle on the east coast – at first, in Co. Wicklow; and then in Killiney, Co. Dublin. Kiberd has suggested that one of the reasons *The Bell* was so influential – and why it survived in the difficult circumstances of the period of O'Faoláin's editorship, 1940–6 – was that 'he was one of the "risen people" himself, the son of humble parents in Cork, and therefore not perceived as greatly "above" the people to whom he addressed his journal'.[10]

To write these articles on newspapers and periodicals, O'Faoláin recruited two recent graduates of Trinity College Dublin, Vivian Mercier and Conor Cruise O'Brien – both of whom would later become respected literary critics and, in the case of O'Brien, distinguished in other fields as well. Both seem to have shared O'Faoláin's disappointment with 'this New Ireland'. O'Brien was already serving in the Irish department of external affairs and to preserve his anonymity, as was required of civil servants at that time, his articles were published under the nom de plume 'Donat O'Donnell'. He contributed two of the articles, those on the *Irish Independent* – for which his father, Frank Cruise O'Brien, had worked unhappily in the last years of his life[11] – and on the Catholic press. The other four were written by Mercier, with O'Brien adding a rider to Mercier's article on *The Bell* in which he deftly parodied the magazine's style and content. For both Mercier and O'Brien, it was their first time being published outside a student milieu. Mercier's article on *Dublin Opinion* – the first of the articles to be published – prefigures in some respects his most significant book, *The Irish comic tradition* (1962), in which he argued that comedy is the central tradition of Irish and Anglo-Irish literature and can be traced back to oral Gaelic roots in the ninth century. He identified the elements of this tradition as 'a bent for wild humour [and] a delight in witty word play'.[12] All the articles in the series, but most especially Mercier's, display that 'delight in witty word play'. Self-evidently the authors, and maybe the editor too,

9 Malcolm Ballin, *Irish periodical culture, 1957–1972: genre in Ireland, Wales and Scotland* (New York, 2008), p. 33. 10 Kiberd, *After Ireland*, p. 30. 11 Donald H. Akenson, *Conor: a biography of Conor Cruise O'Brien* i: *Narrative* (2 vols, Montreal & Kingston, 1994), p. 68. 12 Vivian Mercier, *The Irish comic tradition* (Oxford, 1962), p. ix.

had some fun in doing them – although they are serious and well researched pieces. Mercier and O'Brien were lifelong friends, having roomed together in Trinity[13] – and one has the impression when reading the articles that they were competing with one another in wit as well as insight, an amiable rivalry that probably stretched back to their undergraduate days. In his article on the *Irish Press*, Mercier refers to O'Brien as 'my fellow-sniper' – and that catches the overall tone of the articles.[14]

O'Brien did not include either of his articles in the compilation of occasional essays that he published as *Writers and politics* in 1965, and nor did *Dublin Opinion* feature in Mercier's *The Irish comic tradition* – though it deserved to be recognized as an important part of that tradition. We can only wonder why they did not wish to revisit their earliest published work. Did they consider the articles too ephemeral, too rooted in the Ireland of the 1940s? My contention in this chapter is that the essential importance of these articles is the fact of their appearing at all in the Ireland of the 1940s. Nevertheless, as I hope to demonstrate in the remainder of the chapter, the articles have inherent and lasting value for the student of 'that mysterious entity, the Irish Character' – and, more specifically, for any historian of Irish newspapers and periodicals. I will now consider the articles individually in the order in which they were published, before concluding with a brief observation on O'Brien's essay, 'The parnellism of Seán O'Faoláin', which first appeared in *Irish writing* in July 1948 and was later included unchanged in his seminal book, *Maria Cross: imaginative patterns in a group of modern Catholic writers* (1952).[15]

'*DUBLIN OPINION*'S SIX JOKES', VIVIAN MERCIER, DECEMBER 1944[16]

'The best jokes are made, not born.' So Mercier asserts at the start of this article. He then suggests that *Dublin Opinion*'s jokes 'of its own native manufacture', by which he means jokes specific to Ireland and indicative of the state of the country, fall into six categories.[17]

The first is the Civil Service Joke, a job in the civil service being – in Mercier's words – 'regarded by most of *Dublin Opinion*'s readers as the fulfilment of their highest ambition for their most brilliant children'.[18] (Was this a side-swipe at O'Brien, now ensconced in the department of external affairs?) Mercier points out that the Civil Service Joke is also the Cork Joke – for, he

13 Patrick Maume, 'Vivian Herbert Samuel Mercier' in James McGuire & James Quinn (eds), *Dictionary of Irish biography* (9 vols, Cambridge, 2009) – hereafter, *DIB*. 14 *The Bell*, 9:6 (Mar. 1945), 475 15 Akenson, *Conor*, p. 507, n. 23. 16 *The Bell*, 9:3 (Dec. 1944), 209–18. 17 Ibid., 209–10. 18 Ibid., 218.

says, 'if you took away the Corkmen, where would the civil service be? And if you took away the Civil Service, where would the Corkmen be?'[19] The second category is the Where Were You In 1916 Joke, ridiculing those who, often with scant justification, boasted of their involvement in the Easter Rising and subsequent War of Independence when politically expedient to do so. The third is the Irish Navy Joke, aimed at the miniscule size of the Irish navy – just two ships; Mercier notes that *Dublin Opinion* always mentioned only one of the two ships on the principle that 'to have one ship is more than twice as funny as to have two'.[20] The fourth is the New Ireland Joke, a 'back-handed cut at the more absurd manifestations of the Gaelic Revival'.[21] The fifth is the Ourselves-As-Others-See-Us Joke, which is 'usually located in Hollywood, and pigs in the kitchen generally figure in it somewhere'.[22] The final category is the Farmer Joke, depicting the archetypal Irish farmer 'filling up forms, submitting to inspection, resisting inspectors, selling his cattle, giving them away when the price goes to hell, trying to buy land, being evicted – everything, in fact, except making a decent living'.[23] This is the picture of Ireland in the 1940s that Mercier builds up from the pages of *Dublin Opinion*, and he presents it as a subject worthy of humour – and perhaps worthy of nothing else.

Dublin Opinion was, Mercier says, 'one of the most political funny papers in existence' – and it 'has succeeded in drawing its readers from men of all parties'.[24] He explains this remarkable achievement in an era when Civil War divisions in Ireland were still very raw, as follows:

> The real secret of *Dublin Opinion*'s impartiality, I believe, is that its sympathies were with the losing side [in the Civil War]. It could not attack those in power, who then had the majority of the people behind them. At least, it could not if it wished to keep its circulation, or even, perhaps, some freedom of speech. On the other hand, it had no desire to persecute the unhappy Republicans.[25]

As further evidence of the magazine's impartiality, he recalls that 'in its very first number, published early in 1922, when the Civil War was already on the horizon, it called for peace ... [The] cover drawings and political cartoons hammered home this one idea for months.'[26] Mercier assures us that 'on the whole, *Dublin Opinion*'s fun lacks bitterness'.[27] That is fair comment, but it is not offered by Mercier as an unalloyed mark of approval. He criticizes the

19 Ibid., 212. 20 Ibid., 213. 21 Ibid. 22 Ibid., 214 23 Ibid. 24 Ibid., 214–15. 25 Ibid., 215. 26 Ibid. 27 Ibid.

magazine for failing to address such issues as unemployment and the Dublin slums, and he writes:

> When Arthur Booth was editor (he died in 1926) there was a stronger vein of sympathy with the underdog running through both drawings and prose than there is now … Unemployment was a theme rarely absent from his covers in the post-Civil War years. When C.E.K. (Mr C.E. Kelly, one of the present editors) began to draw the covers, a more playful – and at the same time original – spirit appeared in them. Arthur Booth's Cassandra-like prophecies of war and famine are the commonplace of cartoonists, whereas C.E.K.'s humour is all his own. He has, moreover, stamped his personality on *Dublin Opinion* and, through it, on Ireland.[28]

In Mercier's analysis, Kelly – despite the originality of his work – had turned *Dublin Opinion* into a middle-class organ, aimed at readers in 'the new and rapidly growing middle-class of Ireland';[29] and he claims that '*Dublin Opinion's* portrayal of the poor aims at arousing pity – when not arousing simply laughter – and pity, we know, is a *bourgeois* virtue, implying some degree of condescension'.[30] The Irish middle-class, Mercier reminds us, 'had just made a successful revolution, and could afford to laugh'[31] – and he concludes with the plainly sarcastic observation that 'if the future historian wants to find out what we [the people of Ireland] made of our victory, what sort of spiritual climate it brought about in us, he will be little good at his job if he ignores the evidence provided by the files of *Dublin Opinion*'.[32]

'*THE TIMES* (IRISH)', VIVIAN MERCIER, JANUARY 1945[33]

The stilted title of this article is not explained by its author (nor by the editor), but it is a bizarre formulation since nobody ever refers to the *Irish Times* as '*The Times* (Irish)'. *The Times* of London is sometimes, for purposes of clarity, styled '*The Times* (London)' – so is *The Bell* here trying to draw a subtle parallel between the two newspapers, the implication being that the *Irish Times* is a pale green imitation of the London *Times*? Unlikely, since the article does not discuss any such parallel. Or is the title just a 'witty word play' on the Latin adage – incidentally, quoted in Joyce's *A portrait of the artist as a young man*[34] – with which Mercier concludes his article and which, he says, the *Irish Times* 'is never

28 Ibid., 215–16. 29 Ibid., 217–18. 30 Ibid., 218. 31 Ibid. 32 Ibid. 33 *The Bell*, 9:4 (Jan. 1945), 290–7. 34 Harry Levin (ed.), *The essential James Joyce* (London, 1963), p. 123.

tired of saying': *Tempora mutantur et nos mutamur in illis*, meaning 'the times are changing, and we change in them'.[35]

Change is the theme of Mercier's article – the changes forced upon the *Irish Times* as it adapted to the new Ireland emerging 'out of the maelstrom' of revolution. Over twenty years after 'the final stage of the Revolution',[36] the newspaper was still perceived by the plain people of Ireland as – or so Mercier claims – 'a dyed-in-the wool, dry-as-dust, dead-in-the-last-ditch Ascendancy organ, the sworn enemy of the Irish people'.[37] He dismisses this view of the newspaper as 'fantasy'.[38] He argues that 'the *Irish Times* is now, and perhaps to a certain degree always was, the newspaper of the Protestant professional classes rather than of the landowners',[39] and that over the previous twenty years it had served the Protestant middle class well by 'finding for it compromise formulae, which have made the passage from Unionist to "ex-Unionist" to Fine Gael supporter to Fianna Fáil supporter seem natural and honourable instead of a hideous betrayal of tradition'.[40] He writes:

> The Clergy, the Lawyers, the Doctors, the Artists and the Professors were the true 'people of Burke and of Grattan' ... And their allegiance belonged in the end not, as the landowners' did, to England, the country which preserved their power, but to Ireland, the country which employed their talents. There are Vicars of Bray to be found in other professions besides the Church. If the State secures their livelihood, all the professions will sooner or later come to support the State, with reservations.[41]

Likewise, the *Irish Times*' allegiance was ultimately to Ireland – where it plied its trade, and found much of its news and most of its readers – and it made the changes necessary for survival. Mercier concludes that 'it may be that one of its attractions is that it alone presents the public with the spectacle, in its own reincarnations, of the Protean nature of modern Irish life – subject, of course, to the limitations which a heritage is said to present to rebirth'.[42] The extent of the changes by 1945 were such that Mercier could say that 'slowly but surely it is becoming the organ of the entire professional class, Protestant and Catholic'[43] – and that process would, of course, continue apace in the following years. He concedes, however, that 'a great many of its Protestant readers must follow it a little breathlessly as it boxes the compass, ever moving a few points farther away from the true or fixed North of Unionism. They must frequently be shocked by its liberalism.'[44] He thus, very obliquely, alludes

---

35 *The Bell*, 9:4 (Jan. 1945), 297. 36 See n. 8 above. 37 *The Bell*, 9:4 (Jan. 1945), 290–1. 38 Ibid., 291. 39 Ibid., 292. 40 Ibid., 293. 41 Ibid. 42 Ibid., 296. 43 Ibid., 293. 44 Ibid., 294.

to the growing differences in *mentalité* – which were, however, always there – between Southern Irish Protestants and the Northern variety.

Mercier characterizes the politics of the *Irish Times* as 'on the left'[45] – but he qualifies this by saying that it had 'its own particular brand of conservative progressivism', and that its policies were wholly consistent with the approach favoured by the greater part of Irish society, which, 'whatever extreme name it may call its politics, was ... not much more than conservative progressive'.[46] He comments: 'It has been maliciously said that the *Irish Times*, in its anxiety not to appear Green, has turned more than a little Pink – if some readers do not positively see Red.'[47] He judges that its journalism, like its politics, is 'ten times more alive than its rivals in the newspaper world ... always ready with a campaign, a controversy, or an appeal'.[48] It had a freedom that its rivals, being closely identified with political parties and/or business interests, did not have. He adds that 'the other papers must envy the *Irish Times* its fun, if not its circulation'.[49] Mention of circulation touched a raw nerve, for daily sales of the *Irish Times* in 1945 amounted to a meagre 27,000 copies;[50] the equivalent figures for the *Irish Independent* and *Irish Press* were approximately 140,000 and 110,000, respectively.[51]

'THE *IRISH INDEPENDENT*: A BUSINESS IDEA', CONOR CRUISE O'BRIEN (WRITING AS DONAT O'DONNELL), FEBRUARY 1945[52]

O'Brien, quoting Fr Stephen Brown, SJ, declares that 'the *Irish Independent* was first and foremost a commercial undertaking' – or, as the title of his article proclaims, 'a business idea'.[53] He links its launch by William Martin Murphy in 1905 to the success of Lord Northcliffe's *Daily Mail* in Britain: that success 'showed all enterprising businessmen ... that the newspaper industry was a serious proposition, provided one thought in terms of low selling prices, big circulation and high advertising charges'.[54] The similarities between the two newspapers, as itemized by O'Brien, were not 'confined to such matters as bold headlining and short editorials'.[55] Both were organs 'of business interests' and were 'in themselves great businesses', and neither could 'afford the luxury, which, say, the *Manchester Guardian*, or to a lesser degree the *Irish Times*, may permit themselves of admitting, *in camera* as it were, that the business classes or their spokesmen may, in some instance, be wrong'.[56]

45 Ibid.   46 Ibid., 296.   47 Ibid., 294.   48 Ibid., 295.   49 Ibid.   50 Mark O'Brien, *The* Irish Times: *a history* (Dublin, 2008), p. 107.   51 *The Bell*, 9:4 (Feb. 1945), 393.   52 Ibid., 386–94.   53 Ibid., 386. The quotation is from Stephen J. Brown, *The press in Ireland: a survey and a guide* (Dublin, 1937), p. 40.   54 Ibid., 386.   55 Ibid., 389.   56 Ibid.

The *Independent*, however, 'was a *Daily Mail* with a difference' – for, as O'Brien explains:

> The English mass circulation papers, with their industrialised and on the whole irreligious market, can cater fairly directly for the more primitive emotions. Ecclesiastics may condemn, say, an undue emphasis which certain newspapers lay on sexual crimes, but the circulations of the newspapers grow and the flocks of the ecclesiastics decline. In Ireland, obviously, the situation is far different. Not that the Irish have no appetite for lurid journalism – the huge and expanding Irish circulations of certain English newspapers in the 'twenties, while competition was still free, are proofs to the contrary – but that the Church whose authority most of them accept is strong enough to prevent any Irish newspaper from gratifying this appetite.[57]

The phrase 'while competition was still free' is a reference to the restrictions which successive Irish governments in the 1930s had imposed on imported newspapers – in O'Brien's words, 'some were banned; the rest taxed' and so 'the tide of cultural invasion was rolled back'.[58]

Not surprisingly, O'Brien – future author of the highly regarded study, *Parnell and his party* (1957) – alludes to the *Independent*'s antecedents in the Parnell 'split', before its acquisition by William Martin Murphy. As to the newspaper's then current politics, he notes that 'although, as it proudly maintains, "tied to no political party", it has strong historical and sentimental connections with a party [Fine Gael] whose repeated defeats at the polls are bad for the prestige of its backers' – including, presumably, the *Independent* itself.[59] He points out that 'in the General Election of 1932, faced by what it no doubt genuinely believed to be a threat to the established order in the rise of the Fianna Fáil party, and by the certainty of dangerous competition from the newly founded *Irish Press*, it reacted with spirit and skill' – by emphasizing the threat of communism everywhere and associating it with the rise of Fianna Fáil, against 'a flame-coloured backdrop of world chaos'.[60] This campaign failed to stop Fianna Fáil's success, but O'Brien comments: 'Occasional political failures or miscalculations matter very little to such an enterprise when weighed against commercial success.'[61]

Unlike the previous articles in the series, this one discusses the outlook for the future and, while O'Brien is certainly insightful in his analysis, he perhaps indulges too much in some wishful thinking about the possible decline of an organ that he clearly has little respect for. He writes:

57 Ibid., 387.   58 Ibid., 392.   59 Ibid., 393.   60 Ibid., 389–90.   61 Ibid., 391.

> The *Independent* has not, now, as of old, any advantages in price over
> its principal competitor, and the other factor which brought it success,
> a good news service, matters less, now that the radio 'scoops' all the
> papers every day. In giving more space to news and advertisements than
> its rivals, the *Independent* has left itself little room for 'features' ... and this
> is notoriously a bad circulation policy. Middle-class Catholic families
> who were reading the *Independent* ten years ago are reading the *Irish Times*
> today – it was a bad day for the *Independent* when the *Irish Times* quietly
> dropped the invidious 'Roman' before 'Catholic' – and there is always the
> great post-war danger that the *Irish Times* might cut its price to 1d. and
> exploit 'sensations' that the *Independent* cannot mention.[62]

He concludes, however, by observing that 'the *Independent* can be trusted to
react vigorously against all these dangers' – as indeed it did. One way that
O'Brien anticipates it might react is by using 'its commanding financial position to get better features than the other papers can afford',[63] and the irony is
that eventually among those 'better features' would be a weekly column by the
author of this sardonic critique of the newspaper.[64]

'THE *IRISH PRESS*', VIVIAN MERCIER, MARCH 1945[65]

In a short introduction to this article, O'Faoláin reminds his readers – though
most would not have needed reminding – that the *Irish Press* 'was founded by
Mr de Valera before he came to power and ... he is still the chief shareholder'.
He then states that 'the Opposition [in Dáil Éireann] refers to it ... as the
Government organ, but members of the Government have denied any official
connection – which is quite accurate without being wholly true'.[66] That final
comment is gloriously mischievous – for, in the Ireland of the mid-1940s, de
Valera and the government were so inextricably intertwined that to claim any
real distinction between them was otiose. O'Faoláin was, however, technically
correct: the *Irish Press* was de Valera's newspaper – not the government's, not
even Fianna Fáil's.

   In the article itself, Mercier emphasizes the scale of the task de Valera
faced in establishing the *Press*. He points out that 'to found a big modern
newspaper like the *Irish Press*, and to win a circulation for it against the competition of its two securely established rivals, was a remarkable achievement'.
He continues:

62 Ibid., 393. 63 Ibid., 393–4. 64 Akenson, *Conor*, p. 458. 65 *The Bell*, 9:6 (Mar. 1945), 475–85.
66 Ibid., 475.

Its founder required an unusual combination of vision and practical ability. No one denies that Mr de Valera possesses the former: there are still a number of people foolish enough to believe that he is deficient in the latter ... Nothing could be further from the truth. Where the welfare of his country, his party, or his policy is involved, Mr de Valera is – to borrow Harpo Marx's definition of Alexander Woollcott – 'just a big dreamer with a good sense of double-entry book-keeping'. His financing of the *Irish Press* would be pointed out as a landmark in the career of any mere businessman – but his biographers have so far chosen to ignore it altogether. A number of good Irishmen, who had refused to cash their Republican Bonds when the Cosgrave Government endeavoured to redeem the loan made to the Irish Republic, were persuaded by Mr de Valera to exchange their bonds for shares in Irish Press Ltd. At the time they certainly did so with no hope of gain.[67]

Mercier's criticism of de Valera's biographers was characteristically cheeky, for Seán O'Faoláin had himself published two biographies of de Valera – one in 1932, the other in 1939.[68] O'Faoláin was an indulgent editor, willing to let a young author have his fun.

Mercier argues that 'there was much idealism behind the starting of the *Irish Press*'[69] and he pronounces its policy, as set out in its first editorial, 'at least as sincere as any such manifesto can be'. He quotes: 'In national affairs, we stand for independence, for that greatest temporal blessing a nation may enjoy, the full liberty of all its people ... Our ideal, culturally is an *Irish* Ireland.'[70] Moreover, he points out that the first issue had a photograph of Mrs Pearse starting the printing machinery – 'intended to symbolise the *Irish Press*' continuity with the great tradition of 1916'[71] – and he observes that 'this crusading spirit, this "Irish Ireland" afflatus, can be found even on the sports page'.[72]

The idealism of the early years did not, however, last – and Mercier charts its decline. He records that the founding editor, Frank Gallagher, gave up the editorship in 1934, and he says he has 'the impression, though I may be wrong, that the old spirit left the *Irish Press* for good then'.[73] De Valera and Fianna Fáil had, by 1934, won two successive general elections and were well settled into government, and he explains that the role of the *Press* had therefore become 'that of a weapon of defence rather than of attack'[74] – and 'it is always far easier to write an editorial in attack than in support'.[75] The change, in his view,

---

67 Ibid., 476. Alexander Woollcott (1887–1943) was a well-known America critic, notably with the *New Yorker* magazine. 68 *The life story of Éamon de Valera* (Dublin, 1932); *De Valera* (London, 1939). 69 *The Bell*, 9:6 (Mar. 1945), 475. 70 Ibid., 477–8. 71 Ibid., 478. 72 Ibid., 479. 73 Ibid., 482. 74 Ibid., 481. 75 Ibid., 484.

was complete by 1939; what he calls 'the paper's carefree days' were over,[76] and it could now justifiably be described as 'the Government organ'[77] – though, as we have seen, the editor expressed a reservation on that last point. Mercier further asserts that, by virtue of some of the luminaries that sat on the *Press*' board of directors, it was now also 'almost as closely linked with the new Big Business of Ireland as the other two daily papers'.[78]

The article ends on a positive note. Mercier suggests that the *Press* is 'mainly read on its merits as a newspaper rather than on any political count – by those who prefer Roddy the Rover's folksy column, smelling of turf smoke and homespun, to the *Independent*'s "Spectator" column which is European and personal; or by those who consider its Sports columns superior to the other papers'.[79] He declares its magazine page 'much better than anything the *Independent* attempts'.[80] In these circumstances, he foresees for it 'a profitable, a respectable, even a pious future, but it is not likely to expand on the mystical semi-revolutionary lines of its opening years'.[81]

'THE *CATHOLIC PRESS*: A STUDY IN THEOPOLITICS', CONOR CRUISE O'BRIEN (WRITING AS DONAT O'DONNELL), APRIL 1945[82]

Donald Harman Akenson, O'Brien's biographer, has written of this article that O'Brien did a 'very reined-in review of the Catholic press. No witticism here; Conor seemed afraid to say what he really thought.'[83] It is indeed the most sober of the articles in this series, and it is the longest; but it is also the one that most confounds our expectations. That capacity to surprise – the happy result of turning what O'Brien elsewhere called 'the suspecting glance' upon a subject and upending conventional thinking about it[84] – is the hallmark of the very best of O'Brien's writings throughout his long and prolific career. It is evident in embryo in this article.

He briefly surveys a number of Catholic publications, but it is those 'most frequent in issue, the two weekly newspapers, the *Irish Catholic* and the *Standard*', that largely command his attention.[85] The initial task he sets himself is to explain the 'theopolitical' background to these newspapers as he perceives it. He writes that 'the real importance of Ireland [is] as an arsenal in the war-potential of the Church Militant'.[86] He tells us: '[Ireland] contains the

76 Ibid., 482. 77 Ibid., 481. 78 Ibid., 485. 79 Ibid., 484. 80 Ibid. 81 Ibid., 485. 82 *The Bell*, 10:1 (Apr. 1945), 30–40. 83 Akenson, *Conor*, p. 119. 84 Conor Cruise O'Brien, *The suspecting glance* (London, 1972), pp 9–12, 63. 85 *The Bell*, 10:1 (Apr. 1945), 33. 86 Ibid., 31.

principal deposits of faith from which the Great Powers can be influenced towards Catholicism, or at least away from Materialism. Witness, to take the most obvious examples, the great bridgeheads of the Faith at Boston and Liverpool, Glasgow and New York.'[87] This is the context in which he judges the two newspapers: they are 'weapons in a world battle, the latest phase of the Counter-Reformation',[88] and 'part of a world idea and a world organisation'.[89] Their function is 'a double one: first, defensive, to preserve Ireland as a Catholic bastion in the centre of Anglo-Saxony; second, offensive, to keep up the spirits of those in the field, Irish Catholic laymen and missionaries'.[90] O'Brien is emphatic that the newspapers should not be seen 'as "reflections of Irish Catholic opinion", which they certainly are not'.[91] They 'are militant in their origin and in their nature',[92] whereas he feels 'the Catholicism of the ordinary Irishman, in Ireland, is neither demonstrative nor aggressive'.[93] He elaborates as follows:

> Protestant England has two hundred and thirty Catholic periodicals against our twenty. It is as obvious that the Catholic Press stands in a direct relation to the power of infidelity as that the demand for anti-aircraft guns fluctuates with the demand for war-planes. The *Irish Catholic* and the *Standard* are strong-points on an ideological frontier, and the average Irishman not feeling the frontier to be menaced, nor much desiring to put it forward, is not particularly interested in them. Their direct influence on Irish life is therefore at present small.[94]

Instead of lampooning, as he might have been tempted – and encouraged – to do, the 'spiritual jingoism ... with which the two papers, in varying degrees, have been afflicted',[95] O'Brien simply dismisses both as a side show in the Ireland of the 1940s. This was a strikingly unusual – even eccentric – perspective, but one that hinted at a more nuanced understanding of Irish Catholic culture at that time than was, or is, common. Contrary to how Akenson appraised this article, I believe that O'Brien was saying here precisely what he thought.[96]

He outlines the history of the newspapers. The *Irish Catholic*, the older of the two, was founded in 1888 by T.D. Sullivan – described by O'Brien as 'a Home Rule MP, a Land Leaguer, a member of the Bantry Band, and most famous perhaps as the author of *God save Ireland*'.[97] The 'Bantry Band' was a

---

87 Ibid.   88 Ibid.   89 Ibid., 32.   90 Ibid.   91 Ibid., 31.   92 Ibid., 40.   93 Ibid., 31.   94 Ibid., 38–9.   95 Ibid., 40.   96 Christopher Morash has described O'Brien's article as 'a particularly astute analysis of the Catholic press' – Christopher Morash, *A history of the media in Ireland* (Cambridge, 2010), p. 146.   97 *The Bell*, 10:1 (Apr. 1945), 33.

group of Irish Party MPs who had roots in west Cork or were otherwise linked to the Sullivan dynasty, Tim Healy being its most prominent member.[98] William Martin Murphy, later of the *Independent*, was also part of it – and he was the source of the start-up funding for the *Irish Catholic*. The Bantry Band was rabidly anti-Parnell in the 'split', and the *Irish Catholic* became, in O'Brien's words, 'correspondingly ferocious'.[99] He argues that 'it was in these days that the *Irish Catholic's* character and policy were definitively formed … In that crisis [the "split"] everything which was radical, everything anti-clerical, everything that was left of the old freethinking Fenians, grouped itself around Parnell. The *Irish Catholic* in denouncing him was doing more than condemning adultery.'[100] It adopted, and had retained, 'the doctrine of Conservative Nationalism' – and so 'an association developed with the growing indigenous ruling-class'.[101]

The *Standard* began in 1928, and O'Brien remarks that it employed 'for a religious end the sensationalist techniques of modern profane journalism, and in this … it was far ahead of the *Irish Catholic*'.[102] In the late 1930s, it came under the influence of Professor Alfred O'Rahilly, of University College Cork (who would be ordained a priest in 1955, at the age of 71). O'Brien gives us a very colourful pen-portrait of him:

> Professor O'Rahilly probably does not write all of the *Standard* every week, but it would be feeble merely to say that he has impressed his personality upon it. It is he who has given it a social policy, consisting of his own monetary theories, he who fights its battles with H.G. Wells and others, he who orients its attitude to science and philosophy and life. Under his occupation the *Standard* shifted to something that might almost be described as the Left.[103]

O'Brien regards the *Irish Catholic* as 'lagging behind the *Standard* in social policy and lacking the benefits of Rahillization',[104] but the two newspapers have this in common: 'by their extreme sensitivity to all shades of red and pink, the principal Catholic papers tended to promote an attitude of suspicion, almost of paranoia, among some Catholics'.[105] He concedes, however, that 'the *Standard* at least has shown signs of realising that it is less important to pursue imaginary Bolsheviks than to translate the Social Encyclicals into concrete Irish terms'[106] – that, presumably, is what he meant by its shift to 'something that might almost be described as the Left'.

---

98 Regarding the Bantry Band, see Felix M. Larkin, 'Double helix: two elites in politics and journalism in Ireland, 1870–1918' in Ciaran O'Neill, *Irish elites in the nineteenth century* (Dublin, 2013), pp 125–36 at pp 129–32. 99 *The Bell*, 10:1 (Apr. 1945), 34. 100 Ibid. 101 Ibid. 102 Ibid., 36. 103 Ibid., 38. 104 Ibid. 105 Ibid., 39. 106 Ibid., 40.

The other publications that O'Brien references in this article – albeit
briefly – are 'the short-lived *Catholic Penny Magazine* (1834) and *Duffy's Fireside
Magazine* (1851–54)'; the *Irish Ecclesiastical Record* and the *Irish Monthly* – founded,
he notes, in 1864 and 1873, respectively; and 'the high-brow *Studies* ... [and] the
popular *Irish Messenger*, published by the Jesuits'. He comments that, while these
periodicals cover 'a very wide range, culturally', their 'ideological range is much
narrower than what orthodoxy tolerates in other lands. We have nothing quite
so rootedly conservative as the English *Tablet*, and nothing nearly as liberal as
the American *Commonweal*.'[107]

'VERDICT ON THE BELL', VIVIAN MERCIER, MAY 1945[108]

That *The Bell* was included among the organs featured in these articles is, as
Kiberd has observed, 'a measure of O'Faoláin's liberalism';[109] and, despite
Mercier's protestations that he hadn't 'the moral courage to tell the Editor all
those dreadful things I've been thinking about him', he renders his verdict without pulling his punches.[110] Of O'Faoláin himself, he says: 'I have never met a
man so in love with the written word – provided he himself has written it.'[111] In
fairness, he balances this barb by acknowledging that he is 'the most stimulating Editor one could hope to find';[112] and, in support of this contention, he
instances O'Faoláin's engagement with this series of articles: 'He suggested it; he
indicated the subjects for the various articles; he discussed each one individually
with me or Donat O'Donnell, giving a very clear idea of what he was after; the
only trouble was, he would not stop there: he wanted to write the darn things.'[113]
In other words, O'Faoláin 'is not just a figurehead – he is the magazine';[114] and,
though this would not have been news to regular readers of *The Bell*, he explains
that O'Faoláin 'writes his own Editorial, all 3,000 words of it; he usually has
another piece – a lecture, short story or what not – under his own name; [and]
he writes the little blurb in italics at the head of most *Bell* contributions'.[115]

Mercier is, however, duly appreciative of the magazine. Noting that it 'has
remained what it described itself as on its first cover – A Survey of Irish
Life',[116] he assesses its importance in terms that might be considered extravagant if his article were not otherwise so relentlessly critical:

It fulfils for Ireland the functions which in England, e.g., are carried out
by a multiplicity of periodicals – some monthly, some weekly. *The Bell* is

107 Ibid., 32, 38   108 *The Bell*, 10:2 (May 1945), 156–64.   109 Kiberd, *After Ireland*, p. 34.   110 *The Bell*,
10:2 (May 1945), 157.   111 Ibid.   112 Ibid.   113 Ibid.   114 Ibid.   115 Ibid.   116 Ibid., 158.

to Ireland a sort of *Horizon, New Statesman and Nation, John O'London's Weekly* and *World Review* all rolled into one. The American equivalents would be, say, *Partisan Review, The New Republic, The Saturday Review of Literature* and *Harper's Magazine*. Even that, probably, does not exhaust the list. Some of its reportage is on the same level of interest as that of *Life* or *Picture Post* – if you omit the photographs.[117]

The first of Mercier's many criticisms is of O'Faoláin's habit of comment-ing on the work of his contributors in notes preceding the pieces that he publishes. Mercier suggests that 'if the punters out there … cannot see for themselves that such-and-such a poem is good, bad or indifferent, there is no use climbing up on a pedestal to cast pearls before swine'.[118] Second, he accuses *The Bell* of 'Editorial condescension'; he writes that 'its readers like to think. They are, if you wish, small-town intellectuals … and I know their virtues and limitations. One of the latter is *not* that they cannot think for themselves.'[119] Third, he feels that it covers the arts 'rather scrappily', with 'book reviews … most capriciously treated of all'.[120] As regards short stories – a staple of *The Bell* – he claims that '*The Bell* seems to have made no new Irish reputations in this field. It has been suggested … that one reason for this is that the Editor has too many preconceived ideas of what a short story should be, and does not allow the individual imagination enough scope.'[121] Fourth, he criticises *The Bell*'s role as political commentator:

> Now, the Editor's heart is in the right place. He is agin the Government, as every intellectual should be in a capitalist country. And his basic approach to the historical situation is sound. Ireland has, as he is never tired of saying, merely achieved her bourgeois revolution … The Philistine [aka Goliath] is rampant in Ireland, and Seán is ever ready to play David against him. But his ammunition is always the same old set of well-worn pebbles – half-a-dozen generalities, one or other of which has done duty for every editorial in the past four and a half years.[122]

Finally, and perhaps most importantly, he complains that *The Bell* 'diffuses from its Editorials too blighting an atmosphere of pessimism – as unjustifi-able in its own way as an equal overdose of optimism would be'. Mercier feels that 'there *are* hopeful symptoms about the Ireland of today', one of them being that '*The Bell* has been able to win and keep a public for itself'.[123]

117 Ibid., 159. 118 Ibid., 158. 119 Ibid., 159. 120 Ibid., 161. 121 Ibid., 162. 122 Ibid., 163. 123 Ibid., 163–4.

O'Brien, as already noted, added a rider to this article – an accomplished piece of satire in two parts, a mock trailer for the next issue of *The Bell* and a 'Speech from the Dock, by the Editor' in response to 'Comrade' Mercier's verdict on his magazine.[124] Akenson opined that, in allowing the rider to appear, 'O'Faoláin went beyond licensing self-criticism and crossed to virtual masochism.'[125] O'Brien would later offer his own straight but highly critical verdict on *The Bell*, in an article about *Horizon*, the British magazine of literature and art, published in *The Bell* in 1946 – in the penultimate issue under O'Faoláin's editorship: 'In its caution, its realism, its profound but ambivalent nationalism, its seizures of stodginess and its bad paper, it [*The Bell*] reflects the class who write it and read it – teachers, librarians, junior civil servants, the lettered section of the Irish petty bourgeoisie.'[126]

CONCLUSION: O'FAOLÁIN AS CONTROVERSIALIST

In his essay 'The parnellism of Seán O'Faoláin', O'Brien (still writing as Donat O'Donnell) described O'Faoláin as 'parochial' and his novels and stories as 'free from all taint of generality'.[127] He elaborated as follows:

> He [O'Faoláin] neither affirms nor denies anything of universal importance … His stories are illuminating about Ireland; an anthropological entertainment to the curious foreigner, an annoyance and a stimulus to the native. To Ireland, the stimulus is of great value; in a time of sleepy simulation Mr O'Faoláin's irascible and dissenting temperament has struggled, not without success, to preserve some honest intellectual life among his people.[128]

This, like O'Brien's verdict on *The Bell*, is an unkind assessment – especially since O'Faoláin was the person who, to quote Akenson, had given O'Brien 'his first important sequence of publications'[129] – but time has shown it to be essentially correct. Writing in 2015, almost twenty-five years after O'Faoláin's death, Kiberd noted that only one of the many volumes he produced – short stories, novels, biographies, travelogues – remained in print.[130] Curiously, that was his life of Hugh O'Neill, earl of Tyrone (1550–1616) – which O'Brien

124 *The Bell*, 10:2 (May 1945), 164–7. **125** Akenson, *Conor*, p. 120. **126** *The Bell*, 11:6 (Mar. 1946), 1030–8 at 1030. **127** Donat O'Donnell [Conor Cruise O'Brien], *Maria Cross: imaginative patterns in a group of modern Catholic writers* (London, 1953), p. 113. **128** Ibid., pp 113–14. **129** Akenson, *Conor*, p. 118. **130** Declan Kiberd, 'Lost umbrellas', review of Paul Delaney, *Seán O'Faoláin: literature, inheritance and the 1930s* (Dublin, 2014), *Times Literary Supplement*, 27 Mar. 2015, 27.

dismissed as a work of 'historical introspection', redolent of O'Faoláin's 'half-mystical ideas of the nation'.[131]

O'Faoláin is therefore remembered today – if at all – not for his literary output, but as the controversialist who edited *The Bell* in its glory days and so preserved 'some honest intellectual life' in Ireland at a time when such was in short supply. The journalism of *The Bell* under his stewardship – including those long editorials that Mercier decried – opened 'many windows' that the establishment in independent Ireland would have preferred to keep shut, and the articles reviewed in this chapter are particularly revealing of O'Faoláin's achievement insofar as they cast light on a vital component of Irish society that was otherwise immune from the scrutiny of the Fourth Estate – namely, itself. In the words of O'Faoláin's biographer, Maurice Harmon, 'all of this was revolutionary; it was new … it had the dynamism of change'.[132] Yet, like the other newspapers and periodicals that Mercier and O'Brien discussed in these ground-breaking articles, *The Bell* was an organ of the Irish middle class that O'Faoláin and his two young authors despised – the incorrigibly conservative Irish middle class that, as Mercier remarked, 'had just made a successful revolution, and could afford to laugh'.[133] The idea linking all six articles is that the Fourth Estate was accordingly complicit in the stagnation that followed that revolution.

131 Seán O'Faoláin, *The Great O'Neill: a biography of Hugh O'Neill, earl of Tyrone, 1550–1616* (London, 1942); O'Donnell [Cruise O'Brien], *Maria Cross*, pp 106, 108. For an insightful critique of O'Brien's view of O'Faoláin's *The Great O'Neill*, see Akenson, *Conor*, p. 123. 132 Maurice Harmon, 'Seán O'Faoláin', *DIB*. 133 See n. 31 above.

2 / *The Leader*, the *Irish Press* and the 1953–4 libel action over Professor T.D. Williams' 'A Study in Neutrality': 'the bloody borderland of contemporary history'[1]

MICHAEL KENNEDY

I

In July 1953 professor of modern Irish history at University College Dublin (UCD) Robin Dudley Edwards confided to his diary that his colleague, professor of modern history Desmond Williams, was 'purring'.[2] Williams' landmark articles on Ireland's Second World War neutrality had just appeared to acclaim in the widely read national daily *Irish Press* newspaper. Titled 'Neutrality!' they were a revised version of his earlier series, 'A Study in Neutrality', which had appeared anonymously in the fortnightly newspaper *The Leader*.[3] Though anonymous, 'A Study in Neutrality' was widely known to have been Williams' work. Williams was particularly satisfied, Edwards added, that no reader of either paper had discerned his most secret source.

Based on British and American wartime sources, classified captured German diplomatic documents and off-the-record discussions with Irish officials, 'Neutrality!' and 'A Study in Neutrality' provided the first insights into the secret world of neutral Ireland's wartime diplomacy. Williams praised taoiseach and minister for external affairs Éamon de Valera for his conduct of foreign policy from 1939 to 1945. He contended that de Valera had 'skilfully accepted the advantages with which circumstances provided him' during the conflict.[4] Republishing 'A Study in Neutrality' as 'Neutrality!' in the *Irish Press*, the newspaper de Valera had founded, Williams hoped he could convince the

---

1 Jack White, *The devil you know* (Dublin, 1970), p. 14, a reference to the research of lead character Dr Myles Keating, whose fictional exploits are loosely styled on those of Williams. 2 R.D. Edwards, journal entry, 14 July 1954 (University College Dublin Archives Department (hereafter UCDA), LA22/36). Thomas Desmond Williams (1921–87), professor of modern history, UCD (1949–83). See Michael Laffan, 'Williams, (Thomas) Desmond' in James McGuire & James Quinn (eds), *Dictionary of Irish biography* (Cambridge, 2012) – hereafter, *DIB*. 3 The articles in the *Irish Press* appeared during June and July 1953 and those in *The Leader* from Feb. to Apr. 1953. 4 Williams to MacWhite, 23 Feb. 1953 (UCDA, P194/637).

taoiseach to grant him access to closed Irish diplomatic archives so that he could next write a major history of Ireland and the Second World War.[5] In the 1950s major works on contemporary Irish history rarely ventured beyond the Civil War of 1922 to 1923, so this would be a career-defining achievement for the 32-year-old professor.

The Leader had been founded by D.P. Moran in 1900. His barbed style and Irish-Ireland agenda coloured the paper until his death in 1936.[6] Moran's daughter Nuala, a civil servant, who had been writing for *The Leader* in her spare time, resigned her government position to take over from her father as editor of the paper. After 1936 *The Leader* was less belligerent, though under Nuala Moran's proprietorship it remained strongly Catholic, and took more interest in social and cultural current affairs issues. *The Leader* became a fortnightly in the 1940s. In 1951 Williams became involved in its editing, ensuring that it reached 'an exceptional level of sophistication on both national and international affairs'.[7] *The Leader* entered a second heyday in the 1950s, due in part to Williams' editorial input. It was a natural home for 'A Study in Neutrality'. Yet the series brought the newspaper some controversy through a successful 1954 libel action taken against its author, *The Leader* and the *Irish Press*, because of the way Williams, at times a somewhat injudicious writer, had cast the wartime activities of Leopold Kerney, Ireland's Minister to Spain from 1935 to 1946 in both series.[8] It was the first of two libel actions that the periodical lost in quick succession, the second being by the poet and author Patrick Kavanagh in 1954–5.[9] The action over 'A Study in Neutrality' thus marks a significant moment in the 1950s revival of *The Leader*.

From conversations with senior Irish officials Williams had learned of high-level wartime suspicions in Dublin about Kerney's actions in Madrid. These suspicions, centring on whether Kerney's contacts with German agents had been contrary to Ireland's national interests, resonated with inferences Williams made from captured German diplomatic documents he had seen while working with the British foreign office as an official historian in the late 1940s. Seeking to convey his sense of Kerney's wartime actions in his articles in the *Irish Press* and, earlier, in *The Leader*, Williams turned hearsay into history.

5 Williams to Aiken, 28 July 1953 (National Archives of Ireland (hereafter NAI), DFA 305/14/192/1).   6 See Patrick Maume, 'Irish-Ireland and Catholic Whiggery: D.P. Moran and *The Leader*' in Mark O'Brien & Felix M. Larkin (eds), *Periodicals and journalism in twentieth-century Ireland* (Dublin, 2014), pp 47–60.   7 Joseph J. Lee, *Ireland, 1912–1985: politics and society* (Cambridge, 1990), p. 606. Williams had been a founding editor of the *Cambridge Journal* with Michael Oakeshott in 1947.   8 Leopold Harding Kerney (1881–1962), Irish consul, Paris (1919–22), Irish republican envoy in Paris (1923–5); commercial secretary, Paris Legation (1932–5); Irish minister to Madrid (1935–46).   9 An anonymous profile of Kavanagh by poet/diplomat Valentin Iremonger led to Kavanagh taking a successful action against *The Leader* in 1954–5.

He suggested that Kerney had acted without authority from Dublin and that, in doing so, he had endangered Ireland's national interests by misrepresenting de Valera's intentions to the German agents.

This chapter focuses on how shortcomings in Williams' style as an historian hampered how he wrote about the suspicions he picked up concerning Kerney's conduct. It does not deal systematically with Kerney's activities in wartime Madrid. Despite a number of detailed assessments and a full biography, until Kerney's private papers are made available and a thorough search made of international archives it remains impossible definitively to appraise his conduct.[10] It is a diplomat's job to meet individuals of all persuasions, particularly when representing a neutral state in wartime. Yet some of those who observed Kerney were left with suspicions. For example, a British agent in Madrid who knew Kerney spoke of Kerney's discretion, but made the telling point that Kerney 'is usually talked of as neutral, but he seems always to be included with the Axis people on government invitations and I myself, although we have never talked about the matter, would be inclined to regard him as more pro-Axis than pro-British'.[11] Why Kerney generated such suspicions in Madrid, London and Dublin, and whether they were justified, has not yet been satisfactorily resolved.

When Kerney read Williams' articles he believed that, though not directly named in either series, he was identifiable, and that Williams had made damaging personal allegations against him. Kerney contended that he had acted in Madrid only as was expected of him by the department of external affairs, and that his reputation had been diminished by how Williams had represented him in *The Leader* and in the *Irish Press*. Kerney moved to restore his reputation, as he saw it, through the courts. Williams was unable to mount a persuasive defence as he could neither divulge the confidential manner by which he learned of the suspicions about Kerney nor produce the documentary evidence he used. He was thus obliged to concede publicly that there were errors in his account of Kerney's activities in Madrid. This chapter examines how Williams came to write 'Neutrality!' and 'A Study in Neutrality' and how pre-existing weaknesses in Williams' approach to writing history appear to have foreshadowed the events leading to the libel action.

10 See Eunan O'Halpin, *Defending Ireland: the Irish state and its enemies since 1922* (Oxford, 1999), Dermot Keogh, *Ireland and Europe, 1919–1989: a diplomatic and political history* (Cork, 1989), Barry Whelan, *Ireland's revolutionary diplomat: a biography of Leopold Kerney* (Notre Dame, IN, 2019) and leopoldhkerney.com, created by Kerney's son Éamon. Kerney's private papers remain in family possession.   11 Unsigned letter to Jones, 4 Sept. 1942 (The National Archives, Kew, London (hereafter TNA), HS 9/834).

II

By the time he came to publish 'A Study in Neutrality' in 1953, Williams had developed close connections with the department of external affairs, particularly with former secretary of the department, Ireland's then ambassador to Britain, Fred Boland. He knew retired ambassador to Italy Michael MacWhite from Dublin academic connections and was a neighbour of, and knew socially, the Defence Forces' director of military intelligence (G2), Colonel Dan Bryan, who worked closely with external affairs during the Second World War.[12] Williams also had social connections with many of the up-and-coming generation of post-war Irish diplomats, including Conor Cruise O'Brien, Tommy Woods and Valentin Iremonger.[13] He was well-placed to pick up insights into the conduct of Irish foreign policy.

Williams also had access to another significant source on Irish foreign policy. This had come about following a mishap in his academic career. After a notable undergraduate performance at UCD,[14] and an MA dissertation on the rise of National Socialism that left external examiner Sir Herbert Butterfield persuaded that 'its "anarchic" character' displayed 'great promise for the future', Williams left Dublin in 1943, on a travelling studentship for Cambridge.[15] As a doctoral student of Butterfield's at Peterhouse researching 'Pan-Germanism in Austria from 1898 to 1902', Williams was doing 'excellent historical work', Butterfield thought.[16] Yet Butterfield's influence had not improved Williams' writing style. Butterfield told Williams it remained 'ragged and untidy'; Williams had yet to produce 'an absolutely finished piece of work, all the writing polished up, and all the proof correcting done'.[17] By 1947 Butterfield felt he had made progress with Williams' writing style; he also sensed that Williams had convinced others in Cambridge of 'his first class quality'.[18] In July 1947 Williams was recommended for a bye-fellowship. Master of Peterhouse Professor Paul Vellacott controversially vetoed the award because of Williams' involvement in a college prank.[19]

Distancing himself from Peterhouse, in October 1947 Williams took a foreign office post in Berlin as an assistant editor on the Allied Documents on German Foreign Policy (DGFP) project, which was publishing captured

12 Writing to Boland, Bryan referred to 'my friends in the History department UCD Williams and Edwards' (NAI, DFA London Embassy, Boland papers, 11 Nov. 1955). 13 They also wrote for *The Leader*. 14 A first-class BA in history and German and six other subjects. 15 Michael Bentley, *The life and thought of Herbert Butterfield: history, science and God* (Cambridge, 2011), p. 167; 'anarchic' referred to the writing style and dissertation structure. 16 Butterfield to Williams, 25 June 1946 (Cambridge University Library (hereafter CUL) BUTT/531/W197). 17 Ibid. 18 Butterfield to Williams, 15 July 1947 (CUL, BUTT/531/W199). 19 See Bentley, *Butterfield*, p. 241 and Butterfield to Vellacott, 10 July 1947, and Butterfield to Williams, 15 July 1947 (ibid.).

German diplomatic records.[20] The position was low-ranking and at a level where vacancies were filled by word of mouth from within the Oxford and Cambridge academic communities. Williams decided to lie low in Berlin until he had 'achieved satisfactory published results' and the storm over the bye-fellowship had subsided.[21] He was unhappy as a government historian, writing to Butterfield that DGFP was a 'barbaric outfit' producing politicized state-sponsored history lacking academic integrity.[22]

While in Berlin, and from the autumn of 1948 at DGFP's British base at Whaddon Hall near Bletchley in Buckinghamshire, access to wartime communications between Berlin and the German legation in Dublin gave Williams unparalleled access to classified material on Irish-German relations. He gained insights into wartime Irish foreign policy known only to the serving and retired officials in Dublin with whom he was in contact. Journalist Kees van Hoek suggested that DGFP gave Williams access to 'riches so abundant as seldom to fall into a modern historian's lap'.[23] He could not quote openly from what he had seen, but he now knew the questions to ask, and he knew who in Dublin to ask them of.

III

Williams had turned down a junior lectureship at UCD in 1947 in the wake of his bye-fellowship failure. The chair of history was his 'objective'.[24] The death, in February 1948, of professor of history John Marcus O'Sullivan created the necessary vacancy. O'Sullivan's chair was divided into new chairs of medieval and modern history. Edwards, incoming professor of medieval history Aubrey Gwynn and newly elected president of UCD Michael Tierney ensured the chair of modern history went to Williams.[25] Gwynn explained to Butterfield that 'two young students of Modern Irish History are thinking of going against him ... But we want European, not modern Irish history.'[26]

While Butterfield believed in Williams' exceptional promise and advocated his professorial appointment, he also flagged his former student's weakness

20 No evidence has emerged to further Dermot Keogh's suggestion that Williams worked for British intelligence while at Cambridge or afterwards, and his Peterhouse record shows no break in his studies. See Keogh, *Ireland and Europe*, p. 171; letter from Dr Roger Lovatt, archivist, Peterhouse to the author, 24 Oct. 2016. 21 Williams to Butterfield, undated, but spring 1948 (CUL, BUTT/531/W202A). 22 Williams to Butterfield, 17 July 1949 (CUL, BUTT/531/W207A). 23 *Irish Times*, 2 July 1949. 24 Williams to Edwards, 18 July or 18 Sept. 1947 (UCDA, LA 22/919). 25 Gwynn to Butterfield, 14 Mar. 1948 (CUL, BUTT/531/G79). 26 Gwynn to Butterfield, 1 May 1949 (CUL, BUTT/531/G87).

as a writer. Gwynn, acknowledging that there was 'much force' in objections to entrusting 'so big and important a chair to so young a man, without any previous experience of his quality as a teacher, examiner or colleague', hinted there were doubts as to what Williams might achieve.[27] He realized Williams' appointment was a gamble. Gwynn and Edwards chose to ignore one telling warning: Butterfield's otherwise glowing reference for Williams contained the notable comment that 'his ability and experience as a writer have not so far quite kept pace with his power as an historian'.[28] Williams was 28, and, with a 'certain ruggedness' to his style of writing, as Butterfield put it, had no notable academic publications and no doctorate.[29] Butterfield's biographer Michael Bentley uncharitably concluded that 'Williams couldn't write' and his appointment was 'preposterous'.[30] But to the academics seeking to have him return to UCD, Williams had great, though as yet unsubstantiated, promise. Appointments at professorial level without a doctorate or substantial publications were not that unusual at the time, and so, as Gwynn wrote to Butterfield, 'we have finally decided to act on your advice, take a plunge boldly and appoint him at once to the new Professorship of Modern History'.[31] The point here is not whether Williams was or was not a good choice for the chair of modern history, but to highlight, in light of what was to happen over 'A Study in Neutrality', that the difficulties Williams encountered when putting pen to paper were known.

In the autumn of 1949, Williams returned to UCD 'trailing clouds of Cambridge glory', as his future student Joe Lee would later memorably put it.[32] Williams immersed himself in Dublin intellectual life with 'demonic energy'[33] and showed 'initiative, imagination and energy' as a lecturer and teacher at UCD.[34] Contemporary newspapers attest that the young professor was an active public intellectual.

During a conversation with Bryan some months after his return to Dublin, Williams 'intimated' that he had learned from his former foreign office colleagues that a forthcoming DGFP volume was likely to contain 'rather sensational revelations as to the part played by certain Irish officials during the war', but he coyly added that to give details would be 'a breach of confidence' as he remained bound by the Official Secrets Act.[35] Dublin had been worried about possible revelations and external affairs had scoured new volumes for references to Ireland. There was, Guy Liddell of MI6 wrote to the Cabinet

27 Gwynn to Butterfield, 2 Mar. 1948 (CUL, BUTT/531/G83). 28 Typescript reference by Butterfield, 4 May 1949 (CUL, BUTT/531/W207). 29 Bentley, *Butterfield*, p. 167. 30 Ibid., p. 241. 31 Gwynn to Butterfield, 18 June 1948 (CUL, BUTT/531/G86). 32 Lee, *Ireland*, p. 590. 33 Ibid. 34 Laffan, *DIB*. 35 'Note by the DDG on his visit to Dublin, 5th–6th September 1950' (TNA, KV4/281). My thanks to Professor Eunan O'Halpin for a copy of this document.

Office in London, 'considerable nervousness' in official circles in Dublin about DGFP.[36] Bryan, aware of how 'certain officials' had acted during the war, sought an advance copy so that he might warn the Irish government before publication.[37] With information on the future contents of the DGFP series, as well as what he knew about Ireland from his time with DGFP, Williams built up his value to Bryan. The information at his disposal was a commodity tradable with the director of military intelligence.

Through the early 1950s Williams remained in close contact with the department of external affairs. Minister Frank Aiken 'vetted' Williams in mid-October 1952 for a lecture Williams was to give on NATO. Williams told Edwards that Aiken was 'slow and brash but extremely pleasant and anxious to learn'.[38] At the same time Williams was in touch with Boland in London. In one letter he told Boland that William Langer's recently published book on American foreign policy, *The challenge to isolation*,[39] contained 'very exact references' from state department files on Irish-American relations in the summer of 1940.[40] With Langer's book, his lecture on NATO, and his own forthcoming articles in mind, Williams wrote in *The Leader* in late 1952 that Irish 'administrators have steadfastly refused to consider publications which would throw light on the execution of neutrality.'[41] He was now about to do just that.

IV

'A Study in Neutrality' first appeared in eight parts in *The Leader* through spring 1953.[42] It was later judged to show Williams' knowledge of documentary material and 'sureness of touch in decoding the meaning of that material'.[43] It was an important piece of historical analysis, but it was 'not without traces of hasty composition',[44] suggesting that the author had not attended to Butterfield's early advice that 'there is too great a discrepancy between your power of improvisation and writing at speed on one hand, and your concern to produce a finished piece of literary work'.[45] As the series progressed, the gap between Williams' analytical abilities as an historian and his practical skills as a writer became evident.

---

36 Liddell to Gwyer, 6 Oct. 1950 (ibid.).   37 The reference in the memorandum was to the spy Herman Görtz.   38 Edwards, journal entry, 13 Oct. 1952 (UCDA, LA22/35).   39 William L. Langer and S. Everett Gleason, *The challenge to isolation; the world crisis of 1937–1940 and American foreign policy* (Washington, DC, 1952).   40 Williams to Boland, 8 Oct. 1952 (NAI, DFA London Embassy, Boland papers).   41 *The Leader*, 25 Oct. 1952.   42 Ibid., 31 Jan. 1953 to 25 Apr. 1953.   43 Lee, *Ireland*, p. 590.   44 Ibid.   45 Butterfield to Williams, 1 Mar. 1945 (CUL, BUTT/531/W203).

After the third instalment, which looked at Irish-American relations, questions were being asked.[46] Matt Feehan of the *Sunday Press* asked Boland how he could access the documents Williams used.[47] Boland could offer no assistance, though he revealed he had known from Williams about the material since the late 1940s and also from an unnamed friend in the State Department 'who gave me a rough outline of the contents of the documents in the strictest confidence'. Williams was 'the only person in Ireland' who had seen the documents. There were eighty pages on Ireland, mostly German Minister to Ireland Edouard Hempel's despatches to Berlin, 'but the chance of anyone getting access to the documents before they are published is simply nil'.[48] Boland was favourably inclined towards what Williams had so far written. He thought the articles 'very good apart from one or two minor blemishes. His analysis and judgements are shrewd and accurate.'[49] Williams felt that the only people in Ireland likely to comment publicly on the series, 'and who are competent to do so, are precluded by virtue of their position. And writers find it difficult to have themselves corrected in public or their version revised, which after all is what is needed.'[50] In making this prophetic statement he did not consider the reactions of retired civil servants such as Kerney nor how he himself might react to being corrected in public.

As the series progressed Williams argued that in 1942 Kerney, though he remained unnamed in the text, had contacts with Nazi agent SS Standartenführer Edmund Veesenmayer and his representative Helmut Clissmann, which could have imperilled Irish neutrality.[51] Resident in Ireland prior to 1939 Clissmann had connections with the IRA. Also, he was married to a friend of Kerney's, Elizabeth 'Budge' Mulcahy, who was from a prominent Sligo republican family. Through Kerney's friendship with Budge Mulcahy he had first met Clissmann in the pre-war years. Clissmann, working for German intelligence during the Second World War, suggested contacting Kerney to Veesenmayer.

Williams believed that Kerney 'certainly told the Germans that de Valera, if his hands were forced, would co-operate in German action that appeared likely to be successful'.[52] He maintained in *The Leader* that the two Germans reported to Berlin that, in Kerney's view, de Valera saw a German victory as the only chance of ending the partition of Ireland and that if Germany could provide Ireland with arms Ireland might, after a German defeat of Russia, cease to be neutral, coming in with Germany. Williams argued that Kerney acted without instructions in meeting the Germans and apparently conveying

46 *The Leader*, 28 Feb. 1953.   47 Feehan to Boland, 11 Mar. 1953 (NAI, DFA London Embassy, Boland papers).   48 Boland to Feehan, 12 Mar. 1953 (ibid.).   49 Ibid.   50 Williams to Boland, 14 Mar. 1953 (ibid.).   51 *The Leader*, 28 Mar. and, primarily, 11 Apr. 1953.   52 Williams to MacWhite, 23 Feb. 1953 (UCDA, P194/637).

this opinion. He gave no sources, adding that the Germans might have misinterpreted or misrepresented the Irish diplomat.

Was there any evidence to back up what Williams wrote? Privately he knew
that the 'reports from Kerney to Dublin and the German reports made by
Kerney's intermediary are very different'.[53] Williams had specific knowledge
of Kerney's reporting to Dublin and the line he believed Kerney had taken
with the German agents. The relevant Irish files were closed, and Williams
made no reference to how he gained this information. He evidently knew
there were differing accounts of what Kerney said, but he never mentioned
this in print.

Kerney's account to Dublin of meeting Veesenmayer, which was made public in 1991 when the archives of the department of foreign affairs were opened,
shows he told Dublin he wished to leave Veesenmayer 'without any doubt as
to Ireland's position of very decided neutrality'.[54] He also told Veesenmayer
that the 'public declarations of the Taoiseach proved clearly that Ireland would
resist the violation of her neutrality by Americans, English or Germans'.
However, when it came to achieving Irish unity one opaque phrase that stands
out in Kerney's report is that 'no opportunity would be lost to secure in the
most practical and in the least costly way the unity of Ireland'. Kerney did not
develop this point.

Wartime Irish diplomatic records do show that Kerney was held in suspicion by the department of external affairs and G2 for his activities in
Madrid. He came to the attention of MI6 for his activities in Madrid and
consequently appeared on a British intelligence blacklist.[55] The secretary of
the department of external affairs, Joseph Walshe, who harboured a longstanding personal dislike of Kerney, felt Kerney had deceived external affairs,
an action he later called 'the Madrid betrayal'.[56] External affairs believed that
in 1942 and 1943 Kerney was 'in almost constant touch' with the Clissmanns
'and it was Helmut who suggested the meeting with Veesenmayer'.[57] He was
investigated by G2 and was brought back to Dublin in 1943 for debriefing by
Walshe on his contacts in Madrid. He was admonished by de Valera and by
Walshe, particularly for his use of the diplomatic bag for third-party correspondence, including by Budge Mulcahy. Though they came with caveats
about the dulling of his memory, Boland, who had been Walshe's second-in-
command during the war, recalled external affairs' wartime 'uneasiness about
Kerney on security grounds':

53 Ibid.   54 Kerney to Walshe, 24 Aug. 1942 (Documents on Irish Foreign Policy (hereafter DIFP) VII,
No. 218).   55 See below p. [XX].   56 Walshe to Nunan, 6 July 1953 (DIFP X, No. 208).   57 Nunan
to Walshe, 10 Mar. 1954 (NAI, DFA/10/A/47).

He appeared to be in touch with Frank Ryan and others considered dangerous to the State, but there was a feeling that the information he furnished to the Department about these contacts lacked amplitude and candour. Warnings about Kerney's discretion and contacts also reached us from Dan Bryan. We had reason to think that Kerney was misusing the diplomatic bag in a way likely to become obvious to belligerent security services.[58]

Irish diplomatic records thus show that Kerney was distrusted in Dublin for maintaining connections with individuals who did not support the interests of the Irish state, including German intelligence agents, yet they do not specifically back up Williams' 1953 allegations as to what Kerney apparently said to Veesenmayer and Clissmann.

A 1954 interview between Conor Cruise O'Brien and a former German intelligence officer provides further details on the Kerney-Veesenmayer/Clissmann meetings that run counter to Williams' account. Dr Kurt Haller, who worked with Veesenmayer, explained that the reason for making contact with Kerney was that the German foreign office 'could get "nothing out of the then Chargé d'Affaires in Berlin" and that they hoped to learn more about Irish official thinking and, in particular, the attitude of Mr. de Valera through Mr. Kerney who was, of course, already known to Mr. Clissmann'.[59] Haller told Cruise O'Brien 'that he saw Mr. Veesenmayer's report on his visit and that it was, from the German point of view, "disappointing". Mr. Kerney had simply adopted the formally correct attitude of a neutral head of mission and declined to hold out any hope that Ireland would be likely to come in on the German side, or at all.'

After reading the sections of Williams' *Leader* articles concerning Veesenmayer immediately on their publication, Boland felt that 'unless the German emissary told his authorities very tall stories indeed, our friend Dom Leopoldo has a good deal of explaining to do. I am afraid that … he was one of those people who always thought he knew better than his instructions.'[60] Walshe, Ireland's Ambassador to the Vatican since 1946, was also suspicious of what Kerney had apparently said to Veesenmayer, but 'found it very hard to believe that he would have gone so far'.[61] Neither diplomat considered that Williams might simply have made mistakes in his account.

---

58 Boland to Nunan, 3 Mar. 1954 (ibid.).   59 Secret annex to report by Cruise O'Brien, 29 Sept. 1954 (DIFP X, No. 310). The Irish diplomat in question was William Warnock.   60 Boland to Walshe, 14 Apr. 1953 (NAI, DFA London Embassy, Boland papers).   61 Walshe to Nunan, 21 May 1953 (DIFP X, No. 203).

V

The last episode in 'A Study in Neutrality' appeared in *The Leader* in late April 1953. In late June 1953, the *Irish Press* announced its publication of Williams' *Leader* articles as a new series, 'Neutrality!'. 'Meticulous in detail ... this is the story Ireland has been waiting for', they promoted the upcoming series.[62] On 27 June, the first article, '1939', appeared. The secretary of the department of external affairs, Seán Nunan, wrote to Boland that Aiken wanted Boland to immediately forward 'any inaccuracies or misstatements they contain'.[63] Nunan explained to Walshe that Aiken wished, once the series was complete, 'to publish an official correction in regard to any points which might appear erroneous'.[64]

Almost two weeks into the series, published daily in the *Irish Press*, Boland sent his assessment to date to Nunan. There was 'so far not much in the way of actual *misstatement* in Professor Williams' articles ... the *interpretations* he puts on events are, of course, another kettle of fish'.[65] The account was 'very general' and based 'mainly' on United States and German documents. Boland questioned Williams' reliance on these as

> a great many things happened in the period which never found their way into the documents at all. Where Professor Williams goes wrong, it is usually a question of false emphasis rather than of actual misstatement, the reason being his 100 per cent reliance on the documentary sources available to him to the exclusion of everything else.[66]

This was not the praise of a few weeks previously. Boland felt that Williams failed to give adequate weight to virulent anti-Irish press campaigns in Britain and the United States and to the British economic squeeze on Ireland during the winter of 1940. He felt Williams did not account for the strong pro-neutrality sentiment in Irish public opinion. Boland noted factual inaccuracies, including confusion over the location of the Donegal air corridor, errors over the German offer of arms captured at Dunkirk to the Irish Defence Forces and Hempel's alleged advice to de Valera to make closer contacts with pro-German elements in America. Additionally, Williams did not mention 'one of the sharpest crises of the war' when in December 1940 Germany tried to fly in additional staff for its legation to Dublin and the Irish authorities refused their admission.

62 *Irish Press*, 25 June 1953.   63 Nunan to Boland, 2 July 1953 (NAI, DFA 5/305/14/192/1).   64 Nunan to Walshe, 2 July 1953 (ibid.).   65 Boland to Nunan, 10 July 1953 (ibid.). Misstatements such as the date of establishment of Irish Shipping (Williams said 1942 instead of 1941) and the cause of death of Seán Russell, citing drowning instead of toxaemia.   66 Ibid.

Walshe too was critical of Williams, but understood the problems facing him. Having read the articles published to 4 July, Walshe pointed out that

> Williams, not knowing the whole story, and, particularly, our part of it, is bound, sometimes, to fall into error when he ventures to pass judgement or to come to conclusions not immediately related to his documents. He is no more perfect than any other historian in this respect.[67]

This was what was to happen when he came to cover Kerney. Where he did have direct documentary evidence, Williams was for Walshe 'too forbearing in passing judgement'. In the case of the confiscation of the German legation radio transmitter by the Irish security services, there was 'a blurring of detail, almost to the point of changing the historical significance of the event'. But there were no glaring errors. Walshe felt Williams had 'done an immense service to the country':

> for the first time a qualified historian, trained in England and, therefore, more likely to be accepted as impartial in this matter, writes what is, on the whole, a serene, impartial, concrete and really splendid account of the policy of neutrality as conceived and executed by the Taoiseach during the war.

He thought there was no other work like this, no 'serious, impartial, intellectual apologist of this most vital phase of Irish history'. He hoped external affairs would assist with corrections and Williams' work would appear as a book. Williams was 'so patently honest, so concrete in his judgements when he has all the material, and so clear minded (if only his style were equally clear)'. This was the praise and assistance that Williams wanted from external affairs. Yet Walshe was writing before Williams dealt with Kerney and wartime Madrid. Walshe and Boland had noticed Williams' 'blurring of details' and 'false emphasis', his errors when passing judgment and his coming to conclusions 'not immediately related to his documents'. How he dealt with Kerney would be a further test of his skills as an historian.

External affairs dissected the *Irish Press* articles alongside the earlier *Leader* series 'with a view to comparing references in them to the Irish diplomat who negotiated during World War II with Herr Ribbentrop's confidential officer, Veesenmayer'.[68] Writing to Nunan of the first five *Irish Press* articles, Walshe, looking back to 1942 and the 'ugly business' in wartime Madrid, felt that

67 Walshe to Nunan, 9 July 1953 (ibid.).   68 Joachim von Ribbentrop (1893–1946), German foreign minister (1938–45).

we shall have to go extremely carefully about corrections. The Madrid betrayal, so far, has been glossed over. It would be a pity to have the whole ugly business brought on to the tapis just now. Have you spoken to Dan Bryan? He will remember the recurrence of the name in question in the British black list, and the fact that the two chief British agents insisted on showing it both to him and to me.[69]

In a 1954 letter to Nunan marked 'secret and highly combustible', Walshe clarified that it was Kerney's name.[70] He told Nunan to ask Bryan to recall when Guy and Cecil Liddell of MI6 'showed us a list of suspected contactmen, of whom Kerney was one. I remember feeling thoroughly humiliated, especially because I was in complete ignorance of his machinations.' This was not Walshe speculating, this was Walshe remembering. He and Bryan both saw Kerney's name on the British blacklist and it stung both men.

Looking back again to the Second World War, Walshe wrote in more detail to Nunan of his 'impressions, all vague, highly libelous, and uncharitable' about Kerney. Kerney came into Walshe's 'picture of the war years as the one person we were never sure of ... [He] never felt that he belonged to the Department. He acted on his own and told us very little. I don't remember his ever talking to me about secret matters.'[71] Summing up Kerney's attitude 'based on pure surmise', Walshe felt that 'Kerney was always a megalomaniac. He had the superiority attitude towards the mere Irish which so many of our more shallow-minded countrymen acquire after too long a residence abroad'. He continued:

> After his first accidental contacts with the Germans he began to be convinced that they were invincible and were bound to win. ... Kerney then decided that he had a major role to play in the world, and most probably made and maintained, for a brief period at any rate, contacts with the IRA in Ireland. In other words ... he ceased to be a servant of the State for that phase of his activities.

This was Walshe at his most damning. Walshe told Nunan that these were 'just impressions, they may be all wrong; only it is strange that we did not feel that way about any other official of the Department'.

Williams had picked these suspicions up during conversations in Dublin and was about to raise the 'ugly business' in Madrid in the *Irish Press*. The 10

---

69 Walshe to Nunan, 6 July 1953 (DIFP X, No. 208). The agents were Guy and Cecil Liddell of MI6. 70 Walshe to Nunan, 15 Mar. 1954 (NAI, DFA Holy See 14/75). 71 Ibid.

July *Irish Press* instalment, 'Germans Get Uneasy on IRA Possibilities', was followed by 'German Talk with a Diplomat'. Williams had revised his text slightly for the *Irish Press*, removing some references to the unnamed Kerney, including one to the indiscreet nature of his contacts with Veesenmayer. Yet he still made the same allegations that he had made in *The Leader* that in meeting Veesenmayer Kerney had acted in a manner contrary to Ireland's national interests.

VI

On seeing how he had been portrayed in the *Irish Press*, Kerney acted. He tried first, through the director of the government information bureau, Frank Gallagher, to protest directly to the *Irish Press* that Williams was wrong. But Gallagher knew that *Irish Press* editor-in-chief Vivion de Valera had passed the articles.[72] Kerney felt hurt professionally; here was an attack on his reputation as a diplomat. He also felt personally aggrieved as, a lifelong supporter of Éamon de Valera, he was being tarnished in the paper set up by his mentor and in which he, Kerney, was one of the first shareholders. On 13 July he wrote to external affairs that in Williams' articles

> an attempt is made to besmirch the reputation of an Irish diplomat who represented Ireland on the Continent ... it is evident that the person so attacked is myself. I shall be guided by legal opinion in deciding whether to take an action for libel against Mr. Williams and the *Irish Press*.[73]

Kerney called for his report to Dublin on his meeting with Veesenmayer to be published by external affairs in the public interest to 'clarify the position by setting matters in their true light' as this 'might dispense me from the necessity of taking legal proceedings'. He also looked for an apology from Williams and from both papers.[74] Kerney privately noted that Williams had used the *Irish Press* 'for the purpose of practically branding me as a traitor'.[75]

Aiken planned to come to Kerney's support. A draft press statement from late July 1953 explained that his notice 'had been drawn to allegations,

---

72 Edwards, journal entry, 14 July 1953 (UCDA, LA22/36). According to Eamon Kerney, his father had not immediately seen the articles in *The Leader* and Williams had not contacted him in advance (email correspondence, 2016). 73 Kerney to Nunan, 13 July 1953 (NAI, DFA 10/A/47). The letter was hand delivered by Kerney. 74 Whelan, *Revolutionary diplomat*, p. 260. 75 Memorandum, 'Mr Kerney's attitude towards defendants', 29 Oct. 1954, in Kerney's private papers. Quoted in Whelan, *Revolutionary diplomat*, p. 262.

reflecting on the official conduct of an Irish diplomat during the last war'.[76] The minister wished 'to assure the public that his Department was not concerned with the writing of these articles and that the allegations in question are not supported by the evidence of his Department's wartime records and reports'. It further added that

> all Irish diplomats then serving abroad loyally represented the Government's policy of unqualified neutrality on which policy the entire people at home were united. All our representatives abroad, without exception, kept the warring Powers and the other neutral States constantly aware of Ireland's determination to remain at peace unless and until she were attacked, and, in that case, to resist her attackers, whoever they might be.

This document would never be issued.

The *Irish Press* wanted Williams to republish his series immediately as a pamphlet. Williams planned first to seek access to Irish archives and he awaited the release of further German wartime documents. Unaware of Kerney's complaint, Williams wrote to Aiken in late July 1953 that he intended to lengthen his articles into a pamphlet or a book. DGFP volumes for 1940 were soon to be published and Williams inquired whether it would be possible to secure Aiken's consent to look at some of the relevant files in external affairs covering aspects of Irish foreign policy during the war years. Williams knew this might be impossible, but he hoped that, with other states making their documents available and because the topic was 'now more remote and "historical" than it was hitherto', access might be granted.[77]

The internal Iveagh House response was blunt: 'No – but correct any mis-statement in *Irish Press* articles'.[78] It was deemed not to be in the public interest to make the material available. The same day as Williams wrote to Aiken, Aiken answered a Dáil question from Fine Gael TD Oliver J. Flanagan on whether, in light of Williams' articles, a white paper based on official documents outlining Irish diplomatic contacts with the belligerents during the Second World War might be published.[79] Aiken was definite: there would be no white paper. It was a goal of his ministries that the conduct of Ireland's external relations be kept beyond public view. 'A Study in Neutrality' and 'Neutrality!' would not bring Williams the access he sought to Irish records.

76 Draft press release (NAI, DFA 5/305/14/192/1). 77 Williams to Aiken, 28 July 1953 (ibid.). 78 Note on Williams to Aiken, 28 July 1953 (ibid.). 79 Dáil Éireann, vol. 141 (5), 28 July 1953.

External affairs' reply to Williams took time to draft. It went through many versions, each containing less information, and in the end the reply was scrapped on Aiken's orders. Williams was, on Aiken's further instruction, invited by phone to call to Iveagh House to meet Legal Adviser Michael Rynne who would 'endeavour to assist' him 'to complete and correct certain points' in both series.[80] Rynne was the most senior officer from the war years still in Dublin and he was also a German scholar, having studied in Berlin and Heidelberg in the 1920s. Rynne and Williams talked 'about small points of factual detail' for two hours in the late afternoon of 26 August 1953.[81] A note for Rynne explicitly stated that 'The "Veesenmayer story" has not been reviewed by either Mr Walshe or Mr Boland as it came later in the series.'[82] Rynne's notes of his conversation with Williams show that the Veesenmayer story was the only real issue of importance for external affairs. Rynne corrected errors in Williams' other articles based on Walshe's and Boland's comments and dealt with what Rynne described as general 'mainly "legal" questions' put by Williams. He noted that 'nothing of political importance, or even bordering on the "secret and confidential", was discussed' and no documents were shown to Williams. No reference was made by either to Veesenmayer. Thanking Rynne for his 'kindness in talking so freely and informatively', Williams hoped that when rewriting his articles Rynne's 'criticisms and remarks' would prove 'of great value'.[83] There matters seemed to rest. Iveagh House was content that Williams had been shown the error of his ways without getting access to any confidential sources and Kerney seemed not to be pursuing his legal action.[84]

VII

But he was. On 22 October Kerney's legal representative served writs on Williams, the *Irish Press* and *The Leader*. Two months later his statement of claim was delivered. Kerney was looking for combined damages of £20,000. He believed that Williams' 'youth, recklessness and cocksuredness have placed him in an unfortunate position. He has to be taught a lesson.'[85] Williams was going to end up in court.

80 Note by Rynne on draft of reply to Williams, 25 Aug. 1953 (NAI, DFA 5/305/14/192/1). 81 'Note re Conversation with Professor Williams concerning Neutrality', 26 Aug. 1953 (ibid.). 82 Memorandum, 'Professor Williams' Articles on Irish Neutrality', 26 Aug. 1953 (ibid.). 83 Williams to Rynne, 27 Aug. 1953 (ibid.). 84 Nunan to Walshe, 6 Oct. 1953 (NAI, DFA Holy See Embassy 14/75). 85 Memorandum, 'Mr Kerney's attitude towards defendants', 29 Oct. 1954, in Kerney's private papers. Quoted in Whelan, *Revolutionary diplomat*, p. 261.

In February 1954, as the first mention of the case in the high court approached, Williams' solicitor, Alexis FitzGerald, requested a meeting with Cabinet Secretary Maurice Moynihan. FitzGerald explained to Moynihan that Williams had three options. He could settle with an apology and a money payment; let the case proceed, adopting an apologetic attitude in the hope of moderating any damages; or fight the case fully, pleading that the references to Kerney were faithfully based on German reports and that those reports represented truthfully statements made by Kerney to Veesenmayer. Williams' counsel was taking this last approach, and he and his client felt that the government might have an interest in the matter. It might be in the public interest to clarify that the statements alleged to have been made by Kerney did not represent de Valera's attitude or that of his government. Moynihan promised to find out if the government desired to express any views.

On 19 February, the case came before Mr Justice Kevin Haugh, who gave the defendants two weeks to file their defence. Moynihan's blunt response to FitzGerald arrived the following day: 'I am directed by the Taoiseach to inform you that the Government do not think that the public interest requires that they should express any views on this matter.'[86] Williams and his defence team would have to look elsewhere for material to support their case. They had to file their defence by 5 March. The trial was to begin in the late summer or in early autumn of 1954.

Williams next wrote to Kenneth Duke, a former colleague at the foreign office, seeking the release of a small number of still-classified German documents. He had not referred to these in his articles, but he explained that he had 'information "off the record", from certain Irish and British officials' that would be substantiated by them.[87] In seeking this second strand of evidence to back up his argument, Williams explained that he believed that Kerney 'co-operated in discussions with German agents on the possibility of bringing about a German invasion of southern Ireland, directed against the British forces in Ulster'.[88] He was looking for the release of a small number of documents 'in relation to this precise issue' to support his case.

Recourse to the foreign office was a long shot in increasingly desperate circumstances. It followed, almost exactly, advice Butterfield and philosopher Michael Oakeshott had given Williams in 1950 when he was at loggerheads with journalist and historian Elizabeth Wiskemann after writing a scathing review of her book *The Rome-Berlin axis*. Like Kerney three years later,

---

86 Moynihan to FitzGerald, 20 Feb. 1954 (NAI, DFA 5/305/14/192/1). 87 Williams to King, 20 Feb. 1954 (TNA, FO 370/2380). 88 Williams to Passant, 23 Feb. 1954 (ibid.).

Wiskemann thought Williams had 'impugned her professional competence and indeed her character' and sought redress.[89] Williams refused to apologize. Discussing the simmering controversy, Butterfield explained to Oakeshott that Williams was 'ungracious in manner sometimes, and he has never learned to write as well as he can talk'.[90] Oakeshott told Williams simply 'to substantiate what he wrote'.[91] In 1954 Williams acted on the advice he had received in 1950: he would try to substantiate what he had written.

Duke passed Williams' list of documents to E. James Passant, head of the German section in the research department at the foreign office library. The list included ten German foreign ministry documents dating from May 1941 to January 1943. Williams also sent Passant copies of *The Leader* articles containing the alleged libel. Passant felt that the passages Kerney objected to 'appear to be based mainly on the record of conversations between Kerney and Helmut Clissmann in Madrid' recorded in four documents.[92] He sought clearance for Williams to obtain copies of these documents from Margaret Lambert, editor-in-chief of DGFP. She asked whether 'any of the German documents support the allegations made by Mr Williams?' and deplored the possibility of 'helping one private person to attack another with German documents which we hold for the purpose of objective historical study'.[93] Exceptions over unpublished documents had been made in favour of governments, but no exception had been made in favour of an individual. Passant and Lambert were noticeably unhelpful to Williams. Their cool attitude towards their former colleague and their distaste at his actions reciprocated Williams' 'contempt' for Lambert and his feeling that Passant was 'selectively honest' as an historian.[94]

Having looked through the documents Williams sought, Passant 'was very doubtful whether they would, in fact, support [Williams'] plea of justification'.[95] He felt Williams was 'certainly not' entitled to publish materials from captured German archives.[96] Having signed the Official Secrets Act when he joined the foreign office, Williams had 'committed a gross breach of trust' and Passant ventured that 'the documents did not justify the construction based upon them in the articles, so that Mr Kerney may be expected to win his case'.[97] The foreign office thought the documents unexceptionable: 'Mr.

89 Brogan to Williams, 15 June 1950 (CUL, BUTT/531/W208). 90 Butterfield to Oakeshott, 20 July 1950 (CUL, BUTT/531/O4). 91 Oakeshott to Butterfield, 6 July 1950 (ibid.). 92 Clissmann to Woermann, 5 Dec. 1941 and Veesenmayer to Woermann, 29 Jan. 1942 regarding Kerney-Clissmann meetings and 'Note for Fuehrer Sonnleithner', 5 Oct. 1942 and Veesenmayer to Woermann, 'Ireland', 26 Jan. 1943. 93 Minute by Lambert, 24 Feb. 1954 (TNA, FO 370/2380 LS 9/13). 94 Williams to Butterfield, 15 July 1949 (CUL, BUTT/531/W207A) and 6 June 1961 (CUL, BUTT/531/W322). 95 Memorandum by Passant of meeting with Williams, 27 Feb. 1954 (TNA, FO 370/2380 LS 9/15). 96 Minute, Sedgewick to Liesching, quoting a conversation with Passant, 8 Mar. 1954 (TNA, DO 35/5431). 97 Ibid.

Kerney's attitude, in the conversations he had had with the emissaries from Germany, seemed to him to have been cautious and perfectly proper in every way'.[98] On 27 February 1954 Williams learned that the foreign office would produce the documents he sought, 'on the request of the Court – but not of the parties to the action'.[99]

Williams could not mount a successful defence with off-the-record material. Neither could he now rely on captured German material to support his case. Thanking Passant, he put on a brave face: 'we shall be putting in a request to the Court that it authorise an approach to His Majesty's Secretary of State'.[100] Writing to Butterfield, Williams seemed upbeat: 'life goes pretty well here, despite libel actions' and 'two war criminals are arriving shortly in Dublin to give evidence on my behalf!'[101] Williams was in fact 'very doubtful' whether Clissmann 'would prove a reliable witness', wondering if, under cross-examination, 'he might not prove more of a liability than an asset'.[102] Indeed Clissmann provided Kerney with a detailed report for use in court rebutting Williams' points.[103]

VIII

External affairs had also been preparing its position. Nunan knew there was 'no knowing how this action will develop or what will be brought to light when it comes up ... it is well that the Department should be prepared for the worst!'[104] Not only was Clissmann to give evidence, now Veesenmayer would tell his story from prison in Germany, and captured documents were possibly being made available by the foreign office.

Informed that the foreign office would release the documents required by Williams if asked to do so by the court, Boland read them and had no objection to their production. Only one referred to Kerney directly and Boland informed Dublin that 'what Mr. Kerney said to Mr. Clissmann, according to this report, seemed to me quite unexceptionable. If Professor Williams is relying on these four documents to substantiate the suggestions he made in his articles, I doubt whether he will find them of very much use to him'. Boland recalled that Williams had told him in 1948 about his findings in the German foreign office archives about Kerney:

---

98 Boland to Nunan, 23 Mar. 1954 (NAI, DFA 10/A/47).   99 Minute by Passant, 25 Feb. 1954 (TNA, FO 370/2380 LS 9/13).   100 Williams to Passant, 23 Mar. 1954 (ibid.).   101 Williams to Butterfield, 3 Apr. 1954 (CUL, BUTT/531/W234).   102 Memorandum by Passant of meeting with Williams, 27 Feb. 1954 (TNA FO 370/2380 LS 9/15).   103 See Whelan, *Revolutionary diplomat*, pp 263–8.   104 Nunan to Walshe, 10 Mar. 1954 (NAI, DFA 10/A/47).

he referred to statements by Mr. Kerney which don't appear in the four documents at all and which he apparently made the basis for his criticisms of Mr. Kerney in his published articles. The only explanation of this … is that the four documents which the British Foreign Office have picked out are not the particular documents which Professor Williams had in mind at all.[105]

Boland advised against getting drawn into the case. The department of external affairs claimed privilege over pertinent Irish official material.

In the week before the trial opened, recognizing that he was unable to produce any evidence to back up his allegations about what Kerney had allegedly said to Veesenmayer, Williams accepted defeat. Edwards recorded that 'a deep depression settled on me, partly after listening to TDW's explanation of why he thinks he is unlikely to succeed in the action Leopoldo Kerney has taken against him over the neutrality articles'.[106] Edwards did not go into detail, but an insight emerges from the quote from Edwards with which this account started. The full sentence reads: 'TDW purring that no one has suspected he was able to keep straight by having read (though he dared not quote) Dan Bryan's records.' Colonel Dan Bryan, the former director of G2, was indeed Williams' most secret source.[107]

The widespread assumption was that Williams had used captured German documents without permission. The 'captured documents' ruse was a cover for Williams' other sources. However, Passant's notes show that Williams' source concerning Kerney turned out not to be the captured German documents he now sought but 'conversations with various Irish officials – including the head of the Irish Intelligence Service'.[108] Edwards, Williams and Bryan were close, and it is no surprise that Bryan and Williams should have spoken. But Edwards' suggestion was that Williams had not only spoken with Bryan, but had also read G2 records, or at least Bryan's personal papers, on matters concerning Irish wartime diplomacy. Bryan, in 1954 commandant of the military college at the Curragh, was a still serving and highly respected senior officer. He had, it would seem, while director of intelligence, let Williams see papers in his possession closed to public scrutiny. It was a complete breach of confidentiality. It explains Williams' take on the Kerney-Veesenmayer meetings and why nothing Williams sought would support his case. It also explains

105 Boland to Nunan, 23 Mar. 1954 (ibid.).   106 Edwards, journal entry, 28 Oct. 1954 (UCDA, LA22/37).   107 A portion of Bryan's private papers was accidentally destroyed after his death. It is unclear what Williams might have seen. The remaining papers, held at UCDA (P71), contain sporadic references to Kerney.   108 Memorandum by Passant of meeting with Williams, 27 Feb. 1954 (TNA, FO 370/2380 LS 9/15).

why Williams could not argue, when challenged by Kerney, that he had written in good faith with supporting evidence. 'A Study in Neutrality' conveyed how Bryan felt about Kerney, but it conveyed suspicions, not hard evidence. Williams unwisely wrote hearsay as history, a methodological mistake leading to flawed interpretations.

On 4 November the high court sat to hear the case. Justice Haugh granted an adjournment while the parties consulted. After the court reconvened, Kerney's legal team announced a settlement. Kerney would receive an apology in court, *The Leader* would pay £5 damages and the *Irish Press* £500. Kerney's team stressed he had not departed from his duties in Madrid and Williams had 'caused Mr Kerney great pain and must have created considerable curiosity and comment amongst the public, to whom he was well known'. Counsel for the *Irish Press* emphasized that Williams was a 'well-known and reputable historian, and they assumed that the information contained in the articles was factual and accurate'. Williams had admitted that the passages about which Kerney had complained 'were not true statements of fact', and 'they now desired to express to Mr Kerney their regret that these untrue statements should have received publication in their newspaper, and that they had caused him distress and anxiety'. Williams 'wished to withdraw unreservedly the imputations of Mr Kerney and to state that any such imputations were based on statements now proved to be wrong'. He 'accepted Mr Kerney's account and regretted the imputation and apologised for them'. It was over quickly and none of the promised drama unfolded.

The British embassy had been watching the proceedings. Counsellor Leonard Walsh-Atkins voiced

> a private suspicion that something more has been going on behind the scenes than is disclosed by the terms of the settlement. I thought myself that Desmond Williams had perhaps been imprudent in using his inside knowledge of the archives as a basis for his articles in advance of publication of the archives. On the other hand, he is a locally eminent historian and one is bound to raise one's eyebrows at his admission that the statements complained of were 'completely unfounded' and 'now proved to be wrong'.[109]

Was Williams simply looking for an exit as he could not reveal Bryan to be his secret source and accepted it was easier to draw a line under the episode and move on?

109 Walsh-Akins to Harrison, 9 Nov. 1954 (TNA, DO 35/5431).

Edwards wondered if, now that Butterfield was master of Peterhouse, Williams would be 'spirited off' to Cambridge.[110] Williams was the 'most energetic and influential member' of the UCD History Department, and Bentley argues that after the 1954 judgment 'the Dubliner's professional star had now begun its downward trajectory'.[111] Williams had it all in academic terms before the libel action: the acclaim, the access to information and the opening to publish a ground-breaking account of Irish wartime foreign policy. Now he had stated in court that sections of his major work since returning to Dublin contained serious errors. He had not marshalled his facts rigorously and could not substantiate his argument about Kerney's actions in Madrid with available verified sources. Williams had been warned by Butterfield on their first meeting in Dublin in 1943 that 'you must never on any account present an uncorrected proof or a typescript full of mistakes to any historian'.[112] Williams had not listened and it had returned to haunt him. Butterfield always felt that he could turn Williams into an accomplished writer.[113] It was not to be. Edwards' 18 January 1955 diary entry is thus revealing:

> The achievement of six years in publication has failed to substantiate H[erbert] B[utterfield]'s case that here was a promise of historical ability without an equal in decades. This is not the time to discuss it with Williams but if Williams can see it as simply as that, then he should be induced to publish his [Cardinal] Morone in Germany and Anglo-Polish crisis articles to be followed by the books on National Socialism origins, Trent and the Vatican.[114]

Writing to Butterfield in December 1954 Williams opened by saying that his health, always poor, had declined for several months and after the trial he was confined to bed for ten days.[115] The trial took a further toll on Williams in one very evident way: 'A Study in Neutrality' never advanced beyond 'Neutrality!', its summer 1953 *Irish Press* version.

Williams published an article on Anglo-Polish relations in 1956 only after a thorough critique of its structure and methodology by Butterfield.[116] Returning to a familiar theme, Butterfield felt that Williams had

> not taken sufficient trouble and given yourself sufficient training to get the best out of your ideas and to turn into artistry a number of points that

110 Bentley, *Butterfield*, p. 277. 111 Ibid. 112 Butterfield to Williams, 1 Mar. 1945 (CUL, BUTT/531/ W203). 113 Butterfield to Williams, 15 July 1947 (CUL, BUTT/531/W199). 114 UCDA, LA22/38. 115 Williams to Butterfield, 1 Dec. 1954 (CUL, BUTT/531/W236). 116 T.D. Williams, 'Negotiations leading to the Anglo-Polish Agreement of 31 March 1939', *Irish Historical Studies*, 10:37 (Mar. 1956), pp 59–93.

really call for artistry … [Y]our style is rather ragged … [Y]ou don't put a sufficiently microscopic eye upon single words in order to hit the appropriate one … [Y]our proof correcting in the typescript itself is rather bad, even in the cases where you are transcribing English documents.[117]

Butterfield was also worried that Williams was facing into a libel action for his Anglo-Polish relations article from historian Sir Lewis Namier and journalist and author Ian Colvin. While the article did not produce this response, Butterfield's 1955 assessment of the text shows that Williams had not modified his methodology and writing style in response to Kerney's action over 'A Study in Neutrality' and 'Neutrality!'.

IX

In *The Leader* and the *Irish Press*, Williams had publicly questioned how Kerney had conducted his affairs in Madrid. Skilled in assessing power relationships in history, Williams misinterpreted his power relationships with officialdom, and with his own oral and written sources, when writing 'A Study in Neutrality' and 'Neutrality!'. The settlement against Williams, *The Leader* and the *Irish Press* publicly called into question Williams' abilities as an historian at a time when he was a well-known public intellectual in Ireland. This had a detrimental effect. His plans to remould 'A Study in Neutrality' into a major work on Ireland and the Second World War unravelled, and he never gained open access to Irish diplomatic archives. Williams' *Times* obituary was headed 'distinguished historian who wrote too little'.[118] Contemporaries sensed that this was an outcome of Kerney's legal action.

Williams had tripped himself up in his use of confidential information. He could not show that Kerney had really overstepped the mark, as he alleged. Kerney's case highlights Williams' lack of precision as a writer. It shows his difficulty in meticulously revising and correcting a draft. It emphasizes his casual manner dealing with classified sources and sensitive information, a manner that led to critical weaknesses in 'A Study in Neutrality' and 'Neutrality!'. These tendencies had been flagged early in Williams' academic development by Butterfield. Williams discovered, through Kerney's reaction to his writings, that there were those who took the impact of the written word very seriously. It was not enough never to explain and never to apologize, as was his strategy with Wiskemann in 1950.

117 Butterfield to Williams, 12 May 1955 (CUL, BUTT/531/W245).   118 *The Times*, 21 Jan. 1987.

Williams' career achievements were not to be in academic writing but in teaching and building up the Department of History at UCD. The clash with Kerney did not diminish his influence. If anything, it added to his aura. He continued to fascinate as a teacher and colleague. Michael Laffan summed up in his *Dictionary of Irish biography* entry for Williams that 'his first two decades in UCD were characterised by initiative, imagination, and energy. He was a man of cosmopolitan mind and interests, and he helped to internationalise what had been an insular university'. His eccentricities, including being the defendant in a libel action, are still spoken of with eyebrows cheerfully raised. Kerney might have won the battle, but he did not win the war. He cleared his reputation in 1954 but sources, some quoted above, released since 1990 show that more research is needed to fully assess his wartime career, to explain why he incurred the suspicions that Williams sensed and to assess if they were warranted.

Williams continued to write for the *Irish Press* and *The Leader*, but writing was never to be his strong point. His low level of published academic output did not matter; it was an age before research metrics. 'A Study in Neutrality' still holds enduring ideas about Ireland's wartime external relations. The series was illuminating in the absence of serious scholarship on the history of Irish foreign policy for the following decade and a half after its publication. It formed the basis of many future substantial accounts of Ireland's foreign policy. Works by Williams' students – J.J. Lee, Ronan Fanning and Dermot Keogh in particular – built on 'A Study in Neutrality' to thoroughly analyze Ireland's external relations.[119]

Williams needed tangible written evidence to back up his arguments about Kerney's intent in meeting Veesenmayer. That he did not have. Hearsay is not proof, and feelings are not evidence. Butterfield had warned Williams, 'you are never as tactful in writing as you can be in conversation and you are still chiefly at fault because you do not sufficiently cultivate the literary graces'.[120] When tackling the Kerney-Veesenmayer meeting, rigorous accuracy was required at a level of precision Williams was unable to attain in the written word. In his coverage of events in wartime Madrid, Williams ventured outside the realms of academic history into a high-stakes real-life situation and he was snared by it. Kerney did not win because he could stand over his actions in Madrid, he did not have to. He won because, in writing about them, Williams could not stand over his own actions as an historian.

---

119 For details, see the bibliography in Michael Kennedy & J.M. Skelly (eds), *Irish foreign policy, 1919–1966* (Dublin, 2000).   120 Butterfield to Williams, 26 June 1950 (CUL, BUTT/531/W209).

3 / 'Friendship of the intelligent few and hostility of the unimaginative many': the business of publishing periodicals in Dublin, 1930–55[1]

SONYA PERKINS

The prosaic commercial realities of periodical publishing may have received rather less attention than the enticing editorial content of individual journals, but distribution data and business records provide rich nuance to Irish periodical publishing history. These records help to unravel the various revenue streams that made publication possible, for a time at least, but they also illuminate the ambitions of the editors, and the overlapping spheres of influence – cultural and commercial – in Dublin in the early twentieth century, and they test received wisdoms that have been based rather more on anecdotes and editorial hyperbole than on hard data.

Dublin Magazine, the *Capuchin Annual, Motley, Ireland To-Day, Commentary, The Bell* and *Envoy* were published in Dublin between 1930 and 1955. These periodicals were commercial operations as well as cultural and journalistic projects: there were bills to be paid, and financial implosion was the catalyst for the demise of more than one of them. *Envoy* editor John Ryan's harried correspondence with J.P. Dunleavy on the eve of the periodical's launch in 1949 illustrates the financial anxieties:

> I am beginning to get worried as to whether or not you are still interested in the magazine ... I have had to pay out of my own pocket almost £100 to meet our commitments and am facing the prospect of having to pay out another £200 before the first issue comes out. The two subsequent issues will need £160 apiece bringing the capital which this company must have on hand within the next three months to £500. This is a hell of a lot of jack as you can understand, and as time is running on I would be grateful if you would let me know soon if you are still willing to put up the amount which you mentioned.[2]

1 This article is drawn from my doctoral thesis, 'In search of a cultural republic: intellectual and literary periodical publishing in Dublin 1930–55', Trinity College Dublin, 2019.   2 John Ryan to J.P. Donleavy, 5 Oct. 1949 (Southern Illinois University Carbondale: Special Collections Research Center, Morris Library, *Envoy* records, MS 43-7-2).

Eason & Son (Dublin) dominated newspaper and magazine distribution in Ireland throughout the 1930s and 1940s, and beyond,[3] though there were of course regional distributors such as News Brothers in Cork and Porters in Derry. Extant distribution data recorded by Eason's from 1934 to 1948 reveals an Irish periodical publishing market that was crowded and competitive. In February 1934, Eason & Son recorded that it distributed more than 160,000 copies of 190 individual Irish and imported periodicals in that month alone.[4] In a memo dated 6 November 1935, Eason's analyzed the proportion of imported to 'home' magazines across various categories (film, educational, agricultural, juvenile and others). This was a market dominated by domestic religious periodicals and imported 'women's interest' magazines (table 1).

Table 1. Periodicals distributed by Eason's in Dublin in February 1934[5]

	Irish	Imported
Religious	59,026	1,014
Humorous*	22,500	1,885
Women's interest**	9,165	57,022

* The Irish figure relates exclusively to *Dublin Opinion* **Fashion/ladies and fiction/home categories.

The market dominance of religious titles is hardly surprising. The 1926 census recorded that 92.6 per cent of the Free State's population was Catholic[6] and 1 million people attended Mass in the Phoenix Park at the culmination of the Eucharistic Congress in Dublin in 1932.[7] The *Irish Messenger of the Sacred Heart* was the most widely distributed religious periodical: 11,280 copies of this 2d. periodical were distributed by Eason's in February 1934, and it maintained its dominance throughout the 1930s and 1940s – by 1948, distribution through Eason's had risen to 13,296.[8] The *Irish Messenger* was published by the Apostleship of Prayer, from 5 Great Denmark Street in Dublin. The editorial content was aimed at the entire family – the January 1935 issue, for example, carried articles on managing small children, the 'Young Crusaders' Corner' for children, accounts of the missions in China and two short stories. One of the more unique features was several pages dedicated to 'Thanksgivings' from readers,

3 L.M. Cullen, *Eason & Son: a history* (Dublin, 1989).   4 Report, Feb. 1934 (EAS/A1/6/1/4).   5 Ibid. 6 Cited in Terence Brown, *Ireland: a social and cultural history 1922–2002* (London, 2004), p. 20.   7 Brian P. Kennedy, *Dreams and responsibilities: the state and the arts in independent Ireland* (Dublin, 1990), p. 23.   8 News circulation figures 1868–1965 (EAS/A1/6/1/4).

such as: 'Able to give up life of sin'; 'Two cousins enter convent'; and 'Wife able to leave mental home'.[9]

'Women's' magazines were the other dominant sector in the publishing market and the majority of these titles were imported from England: for example, Weldon's had a stable of titles in this category, including *Weldon's Bazaar* (4*d.*), *Weldon's Good Taste* (4*d.*) and *Weldon's Journal* (6*d.*). It was, however, an Irish publication that claimed the distinction of being the most widely distributed woman's periodical in the 1930s and 1940s. *Model Housekeeping* was produced by Grafton Publishing in Dublin, and according to Eason's records, 7,020 copies were distributed in February 1934.[10]

Distribution figures for *Model Housekeeping* held steady throughout the 1930s and 1940s. The (unnamed) editor of *Model Housekeeping* claimed in 1934 that:

> The success of *Model Housekeeping* has proved beyond yay or nay that Ireland can hold its own in open competition with the publishing houses of any other country. *Model Housekeeping* is in fact the biggest 3*d.* woman's magazine in Great Britain or Ireland. It is an exclusively Irish enterprise edited and printed in its entirety in Dublin, controlled and financed by Irish nationals.[11]

Priced at 3*d.* and available by subscription at 6*s.* for one year, *Model Housekeeping* was a professionally produced publication that carefully nurtured its readership ('our loyal family'[12]) and the subtitle on the front cover proclaimed it to be 'Ireland's National Woman's Magazine'. Articles were generally well-written and illustrated, but it was the volume of advertising that was most impressive. Full-page advertisers in 1934/5 included Wills's Gold Flake Cigarettes, Sunbeam Silk Stockings, Pim's Department Store, Atkinsons Poplin Ties, Jacobs, Ovaltine, Hoover, Blue Band Margarine, Pond's Cream and Cunard White Star Cruises. Potential advertisers were often the subject of flattering editorial articles – for example, C. Powell Anderson's 'Who's Who' social diary in March 1934 included an item on Mr J.T. Molloy, managing director of Clery's.[13] In June 1934 it was noted that Miss S. McKenna, manager of Arks Advertising, could 'tell advertisers of all classes how to advertise to reap the best results from their expenditure'. Miss McKenna had, the writer added, 'a cool competent bearing combined with natural charm' as well as blue eyes and fair hair.[14]

---

9 *Irish Messenger*, Jan. 1935, 42.   10 News circulation figures 1868–1965 (EAS/A1/6/1/4).   11 *Model Housekeeping*, May 1934, 359.   12 'Our Monthly Chat' in *Model Housekeeping*, Nov. 1934, unpaginated. 13 *Model Housekeeping*, Apr. 1934, 305.   14 Ibid., June 1934, 422.

The Eason's report in February 1934 records that 22,500 copies were distributed in the domestic 'humorous' category. This figure relates entirely to *Dublin Opinion*, the monthly illustrated satirical magazine, priced at 3*d*. and published from 67 Middle Abbey Street in Dublin from 1922 to 1968.[15] It was founded by cartoonists Arthur Booth and Charles E. Kelly and the writer Tom Collins. The masthead for *Dublin Opinion* included the tag line 'The National Humorous Journal of Ireland'. The tone was funny but with serious intent. Kelly later remarked: 'true humour is not idle words … but has a useful function as a corrective of folly, pomposity and injustice'.[16] *Dublin Opinion* was very successful at securing advertising, which ran on the inside front and back covers, the back cover and throughout the magazine. Full-page advertisements for Kennedy's Bread, Ovaltine, Nugget Boot Polish, Wills's Gold Flake Cigarettes, Poplins Ties, Jacobs, and Clery's featured throughout 1935. The published advertising rates indicate the importance of this revenue stream – £18 for a full-page advertisement in black and white (the addition of two colours increased the rate to £22, and a three-colour advertisement carried a rate of £30).[17] Undoubtedly, the primary reason for the success of the advertising effort was its circulation. The April 1935 edition of *Dublin Opinion* included a half-page advertisement, with the headline 'See How We've Grown!' The advertisement claimed a circulation of 3,000 copies for its first issue in 1922, which, by December 1934, had risen to 41,130.[18] In the July 1935 edition, the entire inside front cover was allocated to a similar advertisement, with the tag line: 'Sound reasons why you should advertise, guaranteed net sales of 41,130 – the largest circulation of any monthly journal in Ireland'.[19] This was not an instance of publisher hyperbole. The advertisement states that these 'net-paid-for sales' were guaranteed by the Audit Bureau of Circulations (ABC) in London.[20] And, indeed, they were: the ABC records confirm these sales.[21]

Given the market dominance of women's magazines, it was hardly surprising that the publishers of *Dublin Opinion* saw an opportunity to extend into a new market. In January 1935, an advertisement was published in *Dublin Opinion* announcing a new periodical to be published from March. *Modern Girl and Ladies Irish Home Journal* would be the rather cumbersome title of this

15 *Dublin Opinion* is comprehensively considered by Felix M. Larkin in his chapter 'Humour is the safety valve of a nation': *Dublin Opinion, 1922–68*' in Mark O'Brien & Felix M. Larkin (eds), *Periodicals and journalism in twentieth-century Ireland: writing against the grain* (Dublin, 2014), pp 123–42. 16 Charles E. Kelly, 'May we laugh please?' in *The Furrow* 4:12 (1953), 697–705 at 701, cited in O'Brien & Larkin (eds), *Periodicals and journalism*, p. 124. 17 *Dublin Opinion*, Apr. 1935, p. 36. 18 Ibid. 19 Ibid., July 1935, inside front cover. 20 Ibid., Apr. 1935, 36. 21 Net sales of *Dublin Opinion* 1930–57 provided by the ABC by email to this writer, 31 July 2014.

new periodical and the advertisement promised a guaranteed circulation of 50,000.[22] An advertisement in the March issue of *Dublin Opinion* declared that *Modern Girl* was on sale: 'The journal for which every feminine reader in Ireland has been waiting. The happenings of the moment from the Feminine angle.'[23] Articles on sport, hobbies, careers, art and literature as well as 'frocks, frills, femininities', home, health and happiness were promised, and all for a cover price of 3*d.*, which positioned it in direct competition with *Model Housekeeping*.

The publishers of *Dublin Opinion* did not explicitly claim ownership of this new periodical. However, the office address published in *Modern Girl* was 67 Middle Abbey Street, the address of *Dublin Opinion*. A note in *Eason's Monthly Bulletin* in January 1935 announced the imminent arrival of *Modern Girl*, noting that it would be published from the *Dublin Opinion* offices and that 'the publishers are confident that there will be a very big demand'.[24] In format and design *Modern Girl* bore a striking resemblance to *Dublin Opinion* – a full-page colour illustration graced the front cover of the first issue, the design of which was credited to Sean Coughlin, one of the regular illustrators for *Dublin Opinion*. A full page was entitled 'About Ourselves' and the publishers chose to introduce the magazine in verse (a notable editorial device in *Dublin Opinion*):

> Of health and home, of fireside clime
> Of tables laid with tea-ware blue
> Must introduce itself in rhyme
> A Magazine for home and You.[25]

And it was surely more than coincidental that several of the advertisements in the inaugural March issue of *Modern Girl* also appeared in the March issue of *Dublin Opinion*. The Electricity Supply Board's (ESB's) All-Electric Installations at 37 Merrion Square, and the National University of Ireland each ran identical advertisements in both periodicals. The first issue of *Modern Girl* also included advertisements for Gaeltacht Industries Depot, Dublin Gas Company, Hiltonia Mattresses and the National Spa and Hydro at Lucan. However, the absence of major advertisers such as Sunbeam Silk Stockings, Hoover and Pond's Cream (all of which advertised in *Model Housekeeping*) was ominous.

The editor was not named and the editorial vision was unremarkable. This was, after all, 'the journal for which every feminine reader in Ireland has been waiting'. It may be assumed, then, that the reader turned with bated breath to one of the first articles in the inaugural issue, entitled 'Ideas for Sandwiches',

---

22 *Dublin Opinion*, Jan. 1935, 403.   23 Ibid., Mar. 1935, 2.   24 *Eason's Monthly Bulletin*, Jan. 1935, 5.   25 *Modern Girl and Ladies Irish Home Journal*, Mar. 1935, 4.

which advised the reader to 'Pound the contents of a small tin of lobster to a paste with a little melted butter. Season with salt and pepper. Spread between two buttered slices of bread.'[26]

Modern Girl could not match the editorial proficiency of *Model Housekeeping* nor the exclusivity of *Irish Tatler and Sketch*, the other leading women's magazine. There was not a single reference to circulation figures throughout 1935. In the November issue a full-page advertisement was given over to promote bound volumes of *Dublin Opinion* as an ideal Christmas gift. The December issue did not appear, and in January 1936 *Eason's Monthly Bulletin* confirmed that '*Modern Girl* is discontinued'.[27]

How, then, did intellectual and literary periodicals operate financially in such a crowded publishing market in an era before the Arts Act and the belated state acknowledgment of its role 'to stimulate public interest in, and to promote the knowledge, appreciation, and practice of, the Arts'?[28] Analysis of periodicals categorized by Eason's as 'Literary & Review' and distributed by Eason's throughout the 1930s and 1940s indicates that between the behemoths of Catholic periodicals and imported magazines, there was a niche market for intellectual publishing, based in Dublin. It was a modest market, as the distribution data illustrates, but it was consistent and it was well served.

In April 1937 Eason's recorded its distribution of thirty-nine periodicals categorized as 'Literary & Reviews': 40 per cent were Dublin-based periodicals and 50 per cent were published in London.[29] The imported periodicals were among the leading literary periodicals published in England at the time. For example, in February 1934 Eason's in Dublin distributed fifty-four copies of *Blackwood's Magazine*, fifty-two copies of *Cornhill Magazine* and twenty-two copies of *Fortnightly Review*.[30] The Second World War sounded the death knell for literary magazines in London, and *The Criterion*, *Cornhill Magazine* and *London Mercury* all closed within a few months of each other. *Horizon*, founded in 1940, was the notable exception, though again the market in Ireland was modest – Eason's distributed just twelve copies in 1941. The number soared in 1942, with eighty-four copies distributed in April that year, a consequence perhaps of a surge in interest occasioned by the 'Irish Number' of *Horizon*, published in January that year.[31]

This, then, was the market in which the *Capuchin Annual*, *Dublin Magazine*, *Motley*, *Ireland To-Day*, *Commentary*, *The Bell* and *Envoy* operated. These periodicals are notable for the dominant editorial visions that sustained each of them, the

---

26 Ibid., 10.   27 *Eason's Monthly Bulletin*, Jan. 1936, 6.   28 Arts Act 1951, Irish Statute Book (www.irishstatutebook.ie). The Act sought to stimulate public interest in and promote the knowledge, appreciation and practice of the Arts. It also established the Arts Council which was permitted to fund matters relating to the Arts.   29 News circulation figures 1937–48 (EAS/A1/6/1/4).   30 Report, Feb. 1934 (EAS/A1/6/1/4).   31 *Horizon* (Irish number), Jan. 1942.

diversity of content, publication of original writing and consistent engagement with contemporary culture. They were clustered in Dublin, and the
editors navigated the competitive and fluid cultural and commercial spheres
with some aplomb.

Dublin Magazine was the grand survivor. Seumas O'Sullivan launched the
title as a monthly in 1923 and was the editor until his death in 1958. O'Sullivan
was born James Sullivan Starkey on 17 July 1879 in Ranelagh, Dublin. By
the time he launched *Dublin Magazine*, he was already a well-regarded poet.
Dublin Magazine was priced at 2s. 6d. (with one-year subscriptions at 10s. 6d.).
Circulation within Ireland was undoubtedly modest, but its very survival
when peer periodicals imploded around it should be regarded as a significant achievement. However, longevity is not the only reason for re-assessing
Dublin Magazine. It provided a respected medium for the work of Patrick
Kavanagh, W.B. Yeats, Padraic Colum, James Stephens and Frank O'Connor.
The received wisdom is that *Dublin Magazine* under O'Sullivan was apolitical,
conservative and self-regarding. Certainly, O'Sullivan did not choose to publish impassioned editorials on the topics of the day. His editorial style was
as measured as his poetry, but in providing a platform in *Dublin Magazine* for
other views and other impassioned voices, he was arguably anything but apolitical. In 1936, he published a twelve-page article by Seán O'Faoláin, which
excoriated Daniel Corkery for his particular brand of nationalism, arguing
that Corkery's *Hidden Ireland*, with minimal alteration, 'would equally well
trumpet encouragement to all Nazis, Fascists, Communists and any other
type of exclusivist for whom the essential test of literature is a political, racial
or religious test'.[32] Also in 1936, O'Sullivan published a review of Francis
Hackett's *The green lion*: 'This book is important for all Irishmen. There is
a phase of Irish life unrolled in it whose full value, perhaps, will be realized only in the far future.'[33] The book was banned that same year, and in
the October–December edition, O'Sullivan published 'A muzzle made in
Ireland', Hackett's damning indictment of censorship.[34]

O'Sullivan printed, on average, 550 copies of each issue of *Dublin Magazine*
and the earliest distribution data records that seventy-two copies were distributed by Eason's in Dublin in February 1934.[35] Data recorded in April each year
between 1937 and 1948 shows that supply from Eason's in Dublin rarely exceeded
eighty copies of each issue. O'Sullivan supplied *Dublin Magazine* directly to some
bookshops and he may have distributed through one of the other distributors,

32 *Dublin Magazine*, Apr.–June 1936, 61.   33 Ibid., 90–1.   34 Ibid., Oct.–Dec. 1936, 8–18.   35 A series
of invoices and statements from the printer Alex Thom to *Dublin Magazine* from 14 Dec. 1942 to 3 Apr.
1947 record print runs of 500–550 copies (TCD, Seumas O'Sullivan/Estella Solomon Collection). News
circulation figures 1868–1965 (EAS/A1/6/1/4).

but it is unlikely that retail distribution accounted for the entire print run. The evidence suggests that subscriptions accounted for the bulk of *Dublin Magazine*'s circulation. Several international subscription agencies acted on its behalf, including the Moore-Cottrell Subscription Agencies in New York[36] and Continental Publishers and Distributors in London.[37] Subscription orders were also sent directly to O'Sullivan in Dublin. Several distribution lists survive, and it is likely that these were of subscriber copies. Many of the same names recur from list to list – for example, Sir Alfred Beit in Blessington, Mrs le Brocquy in Dublin, Sean O'Casey in Devon and James Guthrie in Glasgow. In some cases, names are scored through and 'cancel' is written alongside, or the address is updated.[38]

Income from subscriptions was obviously crucial to the survival of these periodicals – the December 1947 issue of *The Bell* included an editorial appeal for new subscribers[39] and in April 1950 Ryan allocated a full page to an appeal for new subscribers: '*Envoy* needs your support'.[40] Father Senan Moynihan appealed to Irish men and Irish women everywhere to join the association of patrons of the *Capuchin Annual*, which he edited, and the success of the scheme may by judged by the fact that the names of the subscribers ran over twenty pages of the 1943 edition and numbered more than 2,000.[41]

The evidence indicates that O'Sullivan assiduously dispatched *Dublin Magazine* to editors of peer periodicals worldwide. One undated memo records that it was sent to the editors of seventy-nine periodicals, including *The Spectator* and *Cornhill Magazine* in London; *Edinburgh Review* in Dundee; *Atlantic Monthly* in Boston; *The Bookman* and *Dial* in New York; and the *Sunday Times* in Sydney.[42] O'Sullivan also arranged exchange advertisements with international peers – for example, *Dublin Magazine* included three full-page advertisements for *Poetry* (the iconic Chicago journal founded by Harriet Monroe in 1912) from 1933 to 1935 and, in turn, *Poetry* included three full-page advertisements for the *Dublin Magazine* in its December 1933, February 1934 and May 1934 issues. From his office on Crow Street in Dublin, and despite his meagre resources, O'Sullivan

36 Note from the Moore-Cottrell Subscription Agencies, North Cohocton, New York, enclosing a cheque for 7s. 6d. for a subscription for Fordham University Library, New York, 14 Apr. 1942 (TCD, Seumas O'Sullivan/Estella Solomon Collection, MS 4638/1904a).   37 Subscription order from Continental Publishers and Distributors, London, renewing a subscription from Radio Free Europe in Germany, 23 Aug. 1951 (TCD, Seumas O'Sullivan/Estella Solomon Collection, MS 4640/2545).   38 The inclusion of Padraic Fallon on a distribution list of 148 names and addresses helps to date that document. Fallon's address at 7 Rowe Street, Wexford, was crossed out and a new address at Prospect House, Clonard, Wexford, was hand written beside his name. Fallon moved from Dublin to Wexford in 1939, but at least one biographer has dated his move to Prospect House as 1948.   39 Cited in Frank Shovlin, *The Irish literary periodical, 1923–1958* (Oxford, 2003), p. 124.   40 *Envoy*, Apr. 1950, 94.   41 'The Association of the Patrons of the Capuchin Annual', *Capuchin Annual* (1943), 513–33.   42 Distribution list, undated (TCD, Seumas O'Sullivan/Estella Solomon Collection, MS 4648/4213).

positioned *Dublin Magazine* among an international network of intellectual peri-
odicals, and for the readers of those periodicals, *Dublin Magazine* reflected 'the
best of Ireland's creative spirit'.[43] It was a model carefully replicated by Ryan at
Envoy more than a decade later – exchange advertisements were arranged with
Points in Paris, *The Wind and the Rain* in London, *Meanjin* in Melbourne and the
Sewanee Review, America's 'oldest literary quarterly'.

The *Capuchin Annual* was published in Dublin by the Irish province of
the Capuchin Franciscans from 1930 to 1977. It was edited by Father Senan
Moynihan from 1930 to 1955. Born in Meenascarthy, Camp, Co. Kerry on 24
November 1900,[44] he entered All Hallows in Dublin in October 1918, but he
stayed for only six months before joining the Capuchin order in 1920. Under
his editorship, the *Capuchin Annual* became, as Patrick Kavanagh described
it, 'an amazing phenomenon of modern political Catholic Ireland'.[45] Father
Senan was an extraordinary character: he was acknowledged for his generous patronage of writers and artists; he counted among his closest friends
Thomas McGreevy, Maud Gonne, Margaret Pearse and Eleanor Lady Yarrow;
he moved in the same social circles as John Betjeman and Seán O'Faoláin,
encompassing Jammets and the Clarence hotel; he organized the Jack B. Yeats
exhibition at the National College of Art; he was on the board of National
Gallery; and he was suggested as a member of the first Arts Council. The
first edition of the *Capuchin Annual* in 1930 was priced at 1s., but the cover price
rose rapidly: by 1940 it was priced at 5s. and by 1949 the price had reached the
princely sum of one guinea. The *Capuchin Annual* was distributed by Eason's in
Dublin through its books division. Father Senan claimed that the first edition
of the *Capuchin Annual* sold out,[46] though the print run is unknown, and there
is at least one claim that the second edition also sold out.[47] However, Father
Senan later took the unusual step of publishing signed declarations of print
runs. In 1934 he claimed that '15,000 copies are being printed',[48] with further
signed declarations of print runs of 20,000 copies in 1936,[49] 21,000 in 1937[50]
and 25,000 in 1940.[51]

Motley was launched in 1932 as a publicity vehicle for the Gate Theatre. It
was edited by Mary Manning, who was born on 30 June 1906 in Dublin. Her
maternal aunt was Louie Bennett, the suffragist and trade unionist. Manning
studied acting at the Abbey school, and her first play, *Youth's the season?*, directed
by Hilton Edwards at the Gate in 1931, was hailed as one of the most accomplished first plays ever seen in Dublin – the silent character of Egosmith was

43 Press notice from the *Manchester Guardian*, quoted in the advertisement for the *Dublin Magazine*, in the
Southern Review, July 1935, xii. 44 1901 census (http://www.census.nationalarchives.ie/). 45 *Irish Times*,
10 Jan. 1942. 46 *Fr Matthew Record*, xxiii, no. 8, 300–1. 47 *Irish Press*, 9 Dec. 1932. 48 *Capuchin Annual*
(1934), 309. 49 Ibid. (1936). 50 Ibid. (1937). 51 Ibid. (1940).

included at the suggestion of her lifelong friend, Samuel Beckett.[52] *Motley*'s first edition was priced at 6*d*. and carried an illustration on the front cover by Micheál Mac Liammóir. Its brief and irregular run ended in 1934 and it might be summarily dismissed as a marketing tool were it not for the fact that under the editorship of Mary Manning it provided an outlet for Irish writers, introduced film criticism and was an often caustic critic of cultural life in the Free State: as Manning described it, Ireland was 'becoming more and more like a crazy musical comedy (words by Lewis Carroll, music by Stravinsky) with new parties forming and unforming and new armies marching and counter marching fortnightly'.[53] Manning published contributions from Mainie Jellett, Blánaid Salkeld, Padraic Colum and Irene Haugh, and theatre and cinema reviews from Owen Sheehy Skeffington in Paris and W.J.K. Mandy in London. *Motley* was, as would be expected, sold from the Gate Theatre, but it also had broader circulation through Eason's in Dublin – with 100 copies distributed in February 1934[54] – and in London, at Beaumont booksellers on Charing Cross Road.[55]

James (Jim) O'Donovan was the editor of *Ireland To-Day*, which was launched in June 1936, with a cover price of 1*s*. and one-year subscription at 14*s*., and it ran to seventy-eight pages. The first issue declared that it was the first lay monthly magazine to deal with social, economic, national and cultural matters.[56] O'Donovan was born on 3 February 1896 in Castleview, Co. Roscommon, and attended University College Dublin, where he was recruited into the Irish Volunteers by his chemistry professor. He opposed the Treaty and served as IRA director of chemicals during the Civil War. He was imprisoned for two periods in the early years of the Free State but then secured employment with the ESB. Incredibly, while employed there, he launched *Ireland To-Day* and managed to maintain his anonymity as editor (and keep his job) for the duration of that periodical's publication. Contributors included Owen Sheehy Skeffington on foreign affairs, Liam O'Laoghaire on film, Seán O'Faoláin on books and Eamonn Ó Gallcobhair on music. There were literary contributions from Padraic Gregory, Francis Hackett, Frank O'Connor and Lennox Robinson. Initially, it seemed to have hit on a winning formula, and by February 1937 Eason's was distributing 1,040 copies. However, by February 1939, *Ireland To-Day* had ceased publication. O'Donovan's son, the journalist Donal O'Donovan, later recalled that Eddie Toner, *Ireland To-Day*'s business manager, had claimed that Owen Sheehy Skeffington's articles had precipitated a 'whispering campaign' in Dublin, advertising sales had dried up and

52 Bridget Hourican, 'Manning, Mary Howe' in *Dictionary of Irish biography* (http://dib.cambridge.org/) – hereafter, *DIB*. 53 *Motley*, Sept. 1932, 9. 54 News circulation figures 1868–1965 (EAS/A1/6/1/4). 55 *Motley*, Feb. 1933. 56 *Ireland To-Day*, Jan. 1937, 3.

newsagents had been told to 'take that red rag off the shelves'.[57] However, in his letters to subscribers to announce the closure of the journal, O'Donovan attributed the cause to financial difficulties: 'There has not proved to be sufficient financial support for such a venture in Ireland and means of making up the constant monthly deficit have proved unavailing.'[58]

The year 1940 heralded the era of *The Bell*, the most researched and acclaimed Irish twentieth-century periodical. It was launched in October 1940, priced 1s., by Seán O'Faoláin and Peadar O'Donnell. O'Faoláin requires little introduction, as he has been the subject of more scholarly research and popular attention than all the other editors in this group combined.[59] By the time *The Bell* was launched in October 1940, O'Faoláin was an established writer – his published work included *Midsummer night madness* (1932), *Bird alone* (1936) and *King of the beggars* (1938).[60] O'Donnell was the co-founder of *The Bell* and edited the periodical from 1946 to 1954. He was born on 22 February 1893 in Donegal. A schoolteacher by training, he was active in the IRA in Donegal during the War of Independence and opposed the Treaty. While interned for long periods in the early 1920s, he began to write and, like O'Faoláin, he had been published – his works included *Islanders* (1928), *Ardrigoole* (1929) and *On the edge of the stream* (1934).[61]

Much has been made of the claim that the first issue of *The Bell* in October 1940 sold out on the day of publication. It has been described as 'a runaway success, its circulation figures reaching at least 5,000 copies',[62] and increasing to 5,500 copies by February 1943.[63] The source for those claims, however, was O'Faoláin himself. Eason's distribution data for the April reporting period for each of the years 1941–7 reveals a different picture: 1,607 copies of *The Bell* were distributed in April 1941 and, following a price increase from 1s. to 1s. 6d., 1,183 copies were distributed in April 1942; 1,261 copies in April 1943; 1,534 copies in April 1944; 2,067 in April 1945; 1,924 copies in April 1946; and 1,500 copies in April 1947.[64] In addition, Eason's supplied 160 copies to Belfast in October 1945 and 109 copies in October 1947.[65] It has been claimed that as many as 1,000 copies of *The Bell* may have been 'sent abroad'.[66] But to whom were they sent? Terence Brown has concluded that the print run of *The Bell* was probably 3,000 copies each month and this seems more accurate.[67]

57 Donal O'Donovan, *Little old man cut short* (Bray, 1998), p. 16.   58 National Library of Ireland, James L. O'Donovan papers, MS 21,987 (I) 3593, letter from the editors to W.S. Armour, 11 Mar. 1938.   59 For example, Niall Carson, *Rebel by vocation: Seán O'Faoláin and the generation of* The Bell (Manchester, 2016) and Paul Delaney, *Seán O'Faoláin: literature, inheritance and the 1930s* (Celbridge, 2014).   60 Maurice Harmon, 'O'Faoláin, Seán', *DIB*.   61 Fearghal McGarry, 'O'Donnell, Peadar', *DIB*.   62 Carson, *Rebel by vocation*, p. 50.   63 'Memo for businessmen', *The Bell*, July 1941, 54.   64 News circulation figures 1868–1965 (EAS/A1/6/1/4).   65 Ibid.   66 Matthews, The Bell, p. 38.   67 Brown, *Ireland*, p. 191.

Commentary was launched in November 1941, priced at 6d., by Sean Dorman, who was born c.1910 in Kinsale, Co. Cork.[68] His maternal uncle and godfather was Lennox Robinson, who exerted a defining influence on Dorman's literary aspirations. Commentary was born out of Dorman's ambition to 'have a magazine of my own!'[69] In the December 1941 issue, Dorman claimed that the November issue had sold out. In April 1942, he claimed that the previous two issues had sold out: 'Our circulation now ranks above that of a number of well-known Dublin literary periodicals.'[70] However, as Dorman gleefully recalled some years later: 'No mention of which periodicals or how we knew what their circulations were! Perhaps just a piece of sharp salesmanship in the blessed days before the Trade Descriptions Act.'[71] In April 1945 Eason's recorded that it distributed 1,131 copies of Commentary and this increased to 3,107 copies in the April reporting period in 1947, making Commentary more widely distributed than The Bell for that period.[72] However, Eason's report in April 1948 does not include any distribution figures for Commentary. It followed the trajectory of Motley. Launched primarily as a publicity vehicle for Dorman's Picture Hire Club (which offered paintings for sale on a hire-purchase basis), Commentary broadened its remit under Dorman's editorship but his presence became ever more prominent and, not content to limit himself to editor's letters, he also contributed lengthy articles, included numerous photographs of himself, and gradually increased the prominence given to his name on the front cover. Despite the editorial ego running apparently unchecked, Commentary is particularly notable for its coverage of modern Irish artists and for developing an audience, however short-lived, that was more extensive than The Bell's.

Envoy carried the tag line 'An Irish Review of Literature and Art' and was launched in December 1949 by John Ryan, born on 19 February 1925 in Camden Street, Dublin. Though only 24 years old, he managed to harness the unpredictable genius of Patrick Kavanagh and the tireless promotional efforts of James Hillman, who would move on from Envoy to a remarkable career as a psychologist, academic and Pulitzer-nominated author. On 28 December 1949, a statement from Envoy to the printer Cahill & Co. recorded that 2,500 copies of the first issue had been printed.[73] Of this initial print run, Eason's took 1,500 copies.[74] There is no record of Eason's returns of the first issue, so it is possible that all 1,500 copies supplied to Eason's sold

68 A stained glass window in memory of Dorman's parents, Nora and Stewart Dorman, and his uncle Lennox Robinson is in St John the Baptist Church in Kinsale, Co. Cork.   69 Sean Dorman, Limelight over the Liffey (Fowey, Cornwall, 1983), p. 112.   70 Commentary, Mar.–Apr. 1942, 16.   71 Dorman, Limelight, p. 118.   72 News circulation figures 1868–1965 (EAS/A1/6/1/4).   73 Unsigned letter to Cahill & Co., 28 Dec. 1949 (SIU Carbondale, Envoy, MS 43-7-2).   74 Eason & Son to John Ryan, 23 Nov. 1949 (SIU Carbondale, Envoy, MS 43-6-3).

out – *The Bell* and *Commentary* had, after all, made similar claims. Ryan also engaged regional distributors: News Brothers in Cork grudgingly took 300 copies of the December 1949 issue, but 130 copies were returned and supply for the January issue was reduced to fifty copies.[75] Efforts to distribute through Porters were even less successful – on 18 April 1950, Porters cancelled supply of *Envoy*.[76] Distribution through Eason's declined dramatically. A statement dated 19 September 1950 records that, of a reduced provision to Eason's of 1,000 copies of the June and July issues, almost half had been returned unsold.[77] This is, of course, the peril of retail distribution: the supply of copies on a sale or return basis means that unsold copies will eventually be returned to the publisher and their cost deducted from the original sale. Ryan alluded to the problem of returned copies in his memoir, recalling that he 'finally wheedled the Red Cross' into taking many of them. He vividly recalled Patrick and Peter Kavanagh's strategy for returned issues of the short-lived *Kavanagh's Weekly*:

> The answer was to *burn*. Soon the flat in Pembroke Road came to resemble the stokehold of the *Ile de France*, as Paddy and brother Peter, stripped to the waist, fed a seemingly inexhaustible supply of returned *Weeklies* to the fireplace. Though heat and smoke were intolerable stoke they must, though bale followed bale, as the newspaper remorselessly continued to arrive at the door.[78]

The market, then, for intellectual periodicals was limited and retail sales revenue therefore modest, further constricted by the requirement to provide the distributor with a discount off the retail price of the periodical.[79] The editors had to look elsewhere for financial support. As Patrick Kavanagh so memorably raved in *Kavanagh's Weekly*: 'What about giving us an ad? We bawled.'[80]

If they could not compete for advertisement support based on circulation, then these periodicals would have to differentiate themselves by the quality of their readership. We see, then, in 1932, Mary Manning declaring that the Gate audience, and by extension the readers of *Motley* were 'highly intelligent ... drawn from all classes and all ages of people'.[81] In 1937, in a letter to a prospective contributor, James O'Donovan requested an article that

75 News Brothers Ltd to John Ryan, 29 Dec. 1949 (SIU Carbondale, *Envoy*, MS 43-6-6).   76 C. Porter & Co. Ltd to Messrs Envoy, 18 Apr. 1950 (SIU Carbondale, *Envoy*, MS 43-6-6).   77 Statement from Eason & Son to Envoy Publishing, 19 Sept. 1950 (SIU Carbondale, *Envoy*, MS 43-7-2).   78 John Ryan, *Remembering how we stood* (Dublin, 1987), pp 102–3.   79 Seumas O'Sullivan paid Eason's 33% of the sales revenue to distribute *Dublin Magazine*.   80 'Sinn Féin', *Kavanagh's Weekly*, 21 June 1952, p. 1.   81 *Motley*, Sept. 1932, 2.

would be appropriate for the 'intelligent lay readers' of *Ireland To-Day*.[82] Seumas O'Sullivan suggested his readers were visionaries 'who shared our faith in the cultural future of this country'.[83] John Ryan claimed that the readership of *Envoy* was 'a really discerning one and not merely the kind who simply buys a magazine to while away an idle hour'.[84] In July 1941, *The Bell* declared that it 'has found its Public, a discriminating Public'.[85] Father Senan declared that the *Capuchin Annual* 'has the enthusiastic approval not of the clique or the few but of the people everywhere and in all walks of life'.[86]

Securing and retaining advertising support was critical, a fact acknowledged by the editors across these periodicals as they thanked advertisers and encouraged readers to support the companies that supported the periodical. O'Sullivan gave advertisers equal prominence alongside contributors, subscribers and readers when he thanked all those 'who have enabled us to carry on our work' and said that 'strong in the certainty of their continued support, we look forward with confidence to the future of this journal'.[87] A full-page 'Memo for Businessmen' published in *The Bell* in July 1941 reported that *The Bell* had carried sixty pages of advertising in the first six issues and declared that 'leading Industrialists and Business men are now satisfied that the magazine is here to stay':

> We sincerely thank those firms who made our success possible ….We are glad to be able to say to advertisers generally that *The Bell* has reached a stage where Good Will Advertising in *The Bell* is just Good Advertising.[88]

The inside back cover of *The Bell* in January and February 1942 was given over to listing its advertisers – though the failure to actually sell that page to one of those listed advertisers struck an ominous note. *Ireland To-Day* declared: 'Our advertisers are supporting *Ireland To-Day*. Kindly give them your preference.'[89] In his first editor's note in the *Capuchin Annual* (1934), Father Senan thanked all those who had helped with the *Annual*, noting that 'special gratitude is due to the provincial and metropolitan advertisers, whose patronage makes the *Annual* possible'.[90] In 1936 he urged his readers to study the advertisements:

> They are a guide to firms of repute. We must point out that in patronising our advertisers you are gaining for us their continued support

82 James O'Donovan to Father Martindale, 14 Jan. 1937 (NLI, James O'Donovan papers, MS 21,987 (X)). 83 *Dublin Magazine*, July–Sept. 1943, 1. 84 John Ryan to Miss S.E. Nicholson, 8 Nov. 1949 (SIU Carbondale, *Envoy*, MS 43-7-4). 85 'Memo for Businessmen', *The Bell*, July 1941. 86 *Capuchin Annual* (1943), 513. 87 *Dublin Magazine*, July–Sept. 1943, 1. 88 'Memo for Businessmen', *The Bell*, July 1941. 89 *Ireland To-Day*, June 1936 and Nov. 1936. 90 *Capuchin Annual* (1934), 309.

– without which it would be impossible to publish the Annual. AND
THAT WOULDN'T DO, WOULD IT?[91]

Who, then, were these advertisers? Dublin companies dominated the advertising pages of these periodicals. Just as publishing centred on Dublin, so too
did commercial life. Even the extraordinarily successful *Ireland's Own*, though
based in Wexford since 1902, had an advertising office and manager on Lower
Ormond Quay in Dublin.[92]

Commentary has been criticized for catering for a 'small elite … an affluent,
self-consciously modern, European-oriented readership'.[93] It attracted advertising from Brown Thomas and Jammets restaurant, which might appear to
support this thesis, but these companies also chose to advertise in *The Bell*.
The first issue of *Ireland To-Day* featured advertisements from Kennedy and
McSharry, who assured readers of the quality of their 'flawlessly cut' shirts,
and from Dodge, who offered 'cars of distinction for the discriminating'.[94]
The readership of *Dublin Magazine* has been described as 'a highly educated
subset of the Irish middle and upper classes'[95] and, indeed, its regular advertising clientele included Barnardo Furriers, Fitzpatricks Shoes and Royal Bank
of Ireland, but all three also advertised in *The Bell* and the *Capuchin Annual*. The
picture is further complicated by less lofty consumer brands such as Kennedy's
Bread, which advertised in *The Bell*, *Ireland To-Day* and *Envoy*. Throughout 1946
Kennedy's Bread also ran a series of advertisements in *Dublin Magazine*, entitled 'Why I Buy Kennedy's', which profiled typical customers, among them a
docker who declared there was nothing like hard work and fresh air to give a
man an appetite.

Dublin Magazine carried advertising for Trinity College's *Hermathena*, *Irish
Historical Studies* and, in 1940, the limited edition *Dublin Theatres and Theatre Customs*
by La Tourette Stockwell PhD (which was priced at 16s.), but it also included
advertising from the Carlton Cinema. In 1948 O'Sullivan published a list of
some of the contributors to *Dublin Magazine*, among them Samuel Beckett,
Francis Hackett, Æ, and Liam O'Flaherty. Below this stellar roll call there
appeared a half-page advertisement for Carlton Cinema, which announced
Slave Girl, 'introducing Lumpy the Talking Camel'.[96] *Envoy* could delight in an
advertisement for *Points*, the French magazine 'for young writers of all nations',
breathlessly noting that it was 'printed in Paris in French and English', in the
same issue as advertisements for the considerably less glamorous Weatherwell

91 Ibid. (1936), 29.   92 Email correspondence with Gerard Breen, former editor of *Ireland's Own* (26
Sept. 2015).   93 Clair Wills, *That neutral island: a cultural history of Ireland during World War II* (London, 2007),
p. 285.   94 *Ireland To-Day*, June 1936.   95 Matthews, *The Bell*, p. 39.   96 *Dublin Magazine*, July–Sept. 1948.

Plaster Boards and J.F. Keating Painting, Building and Plumbing. *Envoy* carried regular advertisements for Dublin's public houses, including John McDaid's 'where the elite meet'.[97]

The *Capuchin Annual* had a dedicated advertising salesman, Larry Egan, which may help to explain the astonishing volume of advertising pages – in 1932 it carried eighteen pages of advertising at the front and twenty-six pages of advertising at the back of the 334-page book; by 1942 this had increased to forty-eight pages of advertising at the front and eighty-six pages of advertising at the back of the 706-page book. The *Capuchin Annual* drew substantial advertising from beyond the Pale. For example, Frank Corr's Chemist in Newry, Tully Drapers in Drogheda, Cleeves Toffees in Limerick and Stephen Faller's Opticians in Galway. From May to December 1954, the income from advertising in the *Capuchin Annual* was recorded at almost £3,000.[98] Little wonder then that Larry Egan was singled out for particular thanks on the editor's page by Father Senan: 'and then Larry – need I tell any advertiser of ours or indeed any reader of the annual that his second name is Egan?'[99] A full-page photograph of 'the one and only Larry' was also published in the 1946–7 edition of the *Capuchin Annual*.[100]

Efforts were made to attract national brands, and there were some notable insertions – Cantrell & Cochrane Minerals, Lemon's sweets and the Electricity Showrooms in *Ireland To-Day*; Lemon's mints and MacBirney's in *Dublin Magazine*; Kennedy's Bread and Goodall's in *The Bell*; and Tullamore Dew and Batchelors Canned Foods in *Envoy*. In a letter dated 7 February 1950, Ryan wrote to the advertising manager at D.E. Williams & Co., thanking him for the half-page advertisement for Tullamore Dew: 'Our special position as a literary magazine makes the task of finding advertisements not an easy one and we are, therefore all the more appreciative of your gesture.'[101]

Many of the leading brands were managed by the rapidly expanding advertising agencies in Dublin – by 1945 it has been estimated that there were nineteen advertising agencies in Dublin, with a combined turnover of £750,000.[102] Arks, for example, had the accounts for the Sweepstakes, Cantrell & Cochrane Minerals, Fruitfield Jams and Punch & Co. (manufacturers of boot polish).[103] The increasing dominance of advertising agencies is illustrated by *Envoy*. In January 1951, a letter was sent from *Envoy* to 'our advertising agencies in the city' to advise them of advertising rate increases.[104] Clearly the

97 *Envoy*, Dec. 1949 and Jan. 1950.   **98** 'Publications Payments June 1954–June 1963' (Capuchin Archive, Dublin, uncatalogued collection).   **99** *Capuchin Annual* (1948), 599.   **100** Ibid. (1946–7), 206.   **101** John Ryan to the advertising manager, D.E. Williams & Co. Ltd, 7 Feb. 1950 (SIU Carbondale, *Envoy*, MS 43-7-6).   **102** Hugh Oram, *The advertising book: the history of advertising in Ireland* (Dublin, 1986), p. 113.   **103** Ibid., pp 69–86.   **104** Letter to advertising agencies Jan. 1951 (SIU Carbondale, *Envoy*, MS 43-7-1).

agencies did not respond with sufficient bookings and in his final editor's letter in July that year, Ryan singled out the agencies for specific opprobrium: 'We have known the misfortune of encountering the power-drunk moguls of big-business, and experienced the ordeal of enduring that contemporary har-row – the advertising agency.'[105]

The origin of some advertisements was occasionally rather more opaque than might appear at first glance and lines between editorial and commercial activities could be fluid, to say the least. Was there a connection, one wonders, between Eileen O'Faoláin's effusive six-page feature on the Galway Hat Factory in the January 1941 issue of *The Bell* and the subsequent placement of several full-page advertisements from Les Modes Modernes, the business name for the factory, later that year? It has been noted that *The Bell* was fortunate to have a few faithful advertisers, among them radio retailer Pye Radio, 'whose adverts covered nearly every back cover of the magazine' and whose principal, J.P. Digby, contributed articles on inland fisheries to *The Bell*.[106] Pye Radio was established in Ireland in 1936 by C.O. Stanley, who was also involved with the founding of Arks Advertising in Dublin in 1930.[107] Digby was a 'lead-ing authority on Irish fisheries'[108] and contributed several articles to *The Bell*, where O'Donnell would have been particularly receptive to his views on the neglect of Irish fisheries to the detriment of the fishermen. In 1951, Browne and Nolan published Digby's book, *Emigration: the answer* and *The Bell* allocated six pages in the December 1951 issue to a review that concluded: 'Mr. Digby is to be congratulated on writing so stimulating a book and creating such wide vistas for Irish endeavour.' Digby's connection with another major advertiser in *The Bell* should also be noted. The board of Pye Radio included the Cork business magnate William Dwyer, owner of Dwyer & Co. and its offshoot Sunbeam Wolsley Hosiery. Sunbeam Wolsley took regular full-page advertise-ments in *The Bell*, at times taking the inside back cover when Pye Radio was placed on the outside back cover.

The origin of the major advertisements in *Envoy* is particularly notewor-thy. Full-page advertisements for Monument Creameries ran in every issue of *Envoy*, and usually on the premium inside front cover. Monument Creameries was owned by John Ryan's parents, Agnes and Seamus. They were staunch republicans who had provided aid, funds and shelter to the IRA during the War of Independence, although Agnes became disillusioned and embittered by the Civil War and did not share her husband's enthusiasm for Éamon de Valera. Seamus, who was elected as a Fianna Fáil senator in 1931, died suddenly

105 *Envoy*, July 1951, 7.   106 Matthews, *The Bell*, p. 68.   107 Mark Frankland, *Radio man: the remarkable rise and fall of C.O. Stanley* (London, 2002), p. 242.   108 *The Spectator*, 20 Apr. 1956, 31.

in 1933 and Agnes ran the business thereafter. The first Monument Creamery had opened on Parnell Street in Dublin in 1918 and by the 1940s the Ryans had twenty-six shops, two bakeries, two tearooms and a pub. Agnes was also a patron of the arts, collecting the work of Jack B. Yeats and commissioning Sean O'Sullivan to paint portraits of her children.[109] It is then hardly surprising that she would support her son's endeavours with *Envoy*, by placing advertisements for Monument Creameries in each issue.

Mitchelstown Creameries, Ireland's most successful cooperative, was the other major and regular advertiser in *Envoy*, and it took the outside back cover in most issues. The manager of Mitchelstown Creameries was Eamonn Roche, who had served as an IRA quartermaster during the War of Independence and had been imprisoned in England. He served as TD for Kerry and Limerick West, siding with de Valera and voting against the Anglo-Irish Treaty. Roche was also a longstanding friend of Ryan's father, Seamus, and the pair were related by marriage – Roche was married to Agnes' sister Alice.[110] John Ryan apparently had no qualms about capitalizing on family relationships to support *Envoy*. On 5 October 1949, Ryan wrote to 'Dear Uncle Eamonn':

> You may remember that I mentioned the matter of an advertisement for *Envoy*, the new magazine which myself and some friends are bringing out in the near future. The ad is a two-colour back page for the twelve months … The cost of an insertion is £10 per issue but the cost for the twelve months is only £100. By ordinary standards this is not excessive. I would be very grateful to you if you could let Arks know about it and I will send our man around to them to collect the order and the block.[111]

'Uncle Eamonn' was apparently true to his word and regular full-page advertisements for Mitchelstown Creameries were placed in *Envoy*. In her memoir of her mother, Agnes, Íde Ni Riain recalled a family quarrel about *Envoy* when Patrick Kavanagh was deemed to have gone 'too far' in his diary: 'It's not so much that I mind', Mrs Ryan said to the editor, 'but you needn't expect your Uncle Eamonn to give the magazine any more advertisements, *or the Monument*'.[112]

Just as Ryan apparently had no qualms about leveraging family support, on at least one occasion it seems that the lines between commercial and editorial concerns at *Envoy* were, to say the least, blurred. On 20 January 1950, Ryan

109 Íde M. Ní Riain, *The life and times of Mrs. A.V. Ryan (née Agnes Harding) of the Monument Creameries* (Dublin, c.1987). 110 Terry Clavin, 'Roche, Eamonn', *DIB*. 111 John Ryan to Eamonn Roche, 5 Oct. 1949 (SIU Carbondale, *Envoy*, MS 43-7-5). 112 Ní Riain, *Mrs. A.V. Ryan*, pp 111–12.

wrote to G. Byrne of Byrne's Public House at Galloping Green in Stillorgan, Co. Dublin, thanking him for the cheque and advertisement, before continuing:

> I showed the poem to Patrick Kavanagh, the reigning Irish Poet Laureate, and he suggested that it should go like this:

> *On the new Dublin-Bray Autobahn*
> *Gerry Byrne's is still your best man.*
> *At Galloping Green,*
> *The Best people are seen.*
> *Come out till we fill up your can!*

> If you like this better, as I'm sure you will, you might let me know.[113]

The connection of Joseph McGrath with several of these periodicals is noteworthy. McGrath shared with O'Donovan, O'Faoláin and O'Donnell a history of involvement with the Irish Volunteers, though O'Donovan subsequently took a dramatically different course – he opposed the Treaty and later drew up the S-Plan for the bombing campaign in Britain and became the IRA's chief liaison officer with the Nazis. McGrath served as the pro-Treaty government's director of intelligence during the Civil War and was closely linked with Oriel House and its shadowy campaign of violence against suspected republicans. He was a co-founder of the Irish Hospitals Sweepstakes in 1930.[114] The Sweepstakes was a grassroots organization, so it would be expected that it would advertise in mass circulation newspapers and, indeed, it sponsored a popular nightly programme on Radio Éireann for thirty years. It has been argued that McGrath had few interests outside horseracing,[115] and yet the Sweepstakes supported several of these periodicals. It took regular double page spread advertisements in the *Capuchin Annual*, although given the annual's impressive circulation and McGrath's devout Catholicism that was, perhaps, unsurprising. However, McGrath's rationale for supporting O'Donovan at *Ireland To-Day* is less clear. On 15 February 1937, Dr Patrick McCartan (former IRB member and Sinn Féin deputy) wrote to O'Donovan urging him to approach McGrath for financial support.[116] O'Donovan acted on this advice despite McGrath's activities during the Civil War, of which O'Donovan was

113 John Ryan to G. Byrne, 20 Jan. 1950 (SIU Carbondale, *Envoy*, MS 43-7-1).   114 See Marie Coleman, *The Irish Sweep: a history of the Irish Hospitals Sweepstakes 1930–1987* (Dublin, 2009) and Damian Corless *The greatest bleeding hearts racket in the world: Irish Hospitals Sweepstakes* (Dublin, 2010).   115 Marie Coleman, 'McGrath, Joseph (Joe)', *DIB*.   116 Patrick McCartan MD FRCSI to James O'Donovan, 15 Feb. 1937 (NLI James O'Donovan papers MS 21,987 (IX)).

all too aware, as indicated in his note of 27 February 1932: 'Joe McGrath (now the Hospitals Sweepstakes king) is by his own admission ingloriously associated with and deeply implicated in the murder activities of 1922–1924.'[117]

Nonetheless, McGrath approved O'Donovan's request for support – on 29 October 1937, he signed a letter to O'Donovan on Hospitals Trust-headed paper, enclosing a cheque for £200 'as agreed'. A handwritten note on this letter records that O'Donovan sent two letters of thanks – a formal covering note to McGrath at the Hospital Trust at 13 Earlsfort Terrace and a second note, thanking McGrath personally, to his home at Cabinteely House.[118] Two years later, the oligarch McGrath provided the staunch socialist Republican Peadar O'Donnell with £1,000 to support the establishment of *The Bell*.[119]

The Sweepstakes also placed advertisements in *Envoy*. Here again, the Ryan family's impeccable Republican credentials may have been a factor and there is a suggestion that *Envoy*'s secretary, Tony McInerney, was a former IRA gunrunner.[120] However, what is less obvious is the motivation and commercial justification for the Sweepstakes advertising in *Dublin Magazine* throughout the 1930s and 1940s. A series of full-page Sweepstakes advertisements placed in *Dublin Magazine* in 1947–8 is notable too because the style of the advertisements was markedly different from the standard style of Sweepstakes advertisements. The series celebrated 'Irish Craftsmanship' (the Irish-language translation was also included) and each advertisement featured an aspect of Irish cultural heritage, with a tag line across the bottom: 'with the compliments of Hospitals Trust Ltd Dublin'. The first in the series highlighted 'Illumination and Writing – Annals of the Four Masters' declaring that 'Their art represents a climax never since reached.'[121] Other instalments in the series celebrated Irish metalwork, pottery, lace and crochet. The average print run of the *Dublin Magazine* from 1944 to 1947 was 550 copies, so the Irish Sweepstakes' advertising campaign could hardly have been justified on commercial grounds, and a broader commercial patriotism may have been an influencing factor.

Patronage was also sought among the Irish diaspora, as the editors struggled to maintain financial solvency. O'Donovan looked to New York and appealed to John Caldwell-Myers at the American-Irish Historical Society, who donated $50 in 1937, while Patrick McCartan gave £105 for five subscriptions and £100 for 'stock' in *Ireland To-Day*.[122] O'Sullivan sought the help of

117 Cited in David O'Donoghue, *Devil's deal: the IRA, Nazi Germany and the double life of Jim O'Donovan* (Dublin, 2010), p. 70.   118 Joseph McGrath to James O'Donovan, 29 Oct. 1937 (NLI, James O'Donovan papers, MS 21,987 (IX)).   119 Carson, *Rebel by vocation*, p. 81.   120 Dick Russell, *The life and ideas of James Hillman* (New York, 2013), p. 240.   121 *Dublin Magazine*, Apr.–June 1947, ix.   122 Dr Patrick McCartan to James O'Donovan, 15 February 1937, NLI, James O'Donovan papers, MS 21,987 (IX).

Julia Feely in New York; Ryan called on Leslie Daiken in London; O'Donnell's thwarted tour of the US was designed to drum up a thousand subscribers; and Father Senan, naturally, called on Irishmen and Irishwomen everywhere to support his work.

By the end of the 1950s *Commentary, Ireland To-Day, The Bell* and *Envoy* had closed. Financial difficulty was not the sole cause in each case, of course, but it undoubtedly played a significant role. O'Donovan reflected wearily as he faced the imminent closure of *Ireland To-Day:*

> We have done our best, we are apparently on the verge of failure, no better after all than all the other failures that have gone before us … if Ireland cannot support even one magazine of our type, then unfortunately, all our efforts to bridge the deficit having failed, we can only face the inevitable end with the deepest reluctance and regret.[123]

By 2 July 1951 the Envoy Publishing Co. Ltd was overdrawn by £761 2s. 6d.[124] In his editorial in the final issue that same month, Ryan reflected:

> One may suppose that for a literary magazine to survive for such a period without official or private patronage, is in itself an achievement. No effort was spared to make the journal a financial success … Here at home we enjoyed the friendship of the intelligent few and the hostility of the unimaginative many.[125]

In the case of the *Capuchin Annual*, its spectacular financial implosion (the debt at Capuchin Periodicals on 1 May 1954 was approximately £71,234, of which £62,416 19s. 6d. was due to the bank)[126] hastened Father Senan's resignation. He left the Capuchin order in 1958 and departed Ireland for Australia in 1959,[127] and the cultural tour de force that was the *Capuchin Annual* declined in his wake, though it continued to be published until 1977. Anthony Cronin later recalled of the demise of *The Bell*: 'I think Peadar was a bit fed up. It was a constant struggle to keep it alive.'[128]

Foregrounding the business operation of these periodicals embeds them in the broader publishing environment and illuminates the grinding commercial pressures and the dogged determination of these editors to sell advertising, increase distribution, promote subscriptions and solicit patrons. To consider

---

123 James O'Donovan to Dr Patrick McCartan 12 Feb. 1938 (NLI, James O'Donovan papers, MS 21,987 (VII)). 124 Envoy Publishing Accounts (SIU Carbondale, *Envoy*, MS 43-7-7). 125 *Envoy*, July 1951, 7 126 Day Book (ledger) May 1954–Feb. 1978 (Capuchin Archive, uncatalogued collection). 127 *Irish Times*, 21 Aug. 1959. 128 Anthony Cronin, cited in Matthews, *The Bell*, p. 101.

these editors only in terms of their editorial accomplishments does them a disservice.

In 1956, O'Faoláin was appointed the second director of the Arts Council, and during his tenure the first grants (or 'guarantees against loss') were given to periodicals, namely *Studies*, *Irish Writing* and *Dublin Magazine*.[129] A new era in Irish periodical publishing beckoned.

---

129 Sixth Annual Report of the Arts Council, 1957–8.

4 / *Fortnight*: a voice of reason and moderation in Northern Ireland's 'Troubles'

ANDY POLLAK

Fortnight magazine, which started publication in September 1970 and closed in January 2012, virtually 'book-ended' the Northern Ireland 'Troubles'. Whether fortnightly, monthly or (for two short periods) two-monthly, it provided a reasoned, 'neither unionist, nor nationalist' analysis of that conflicted society while opening its pages to writers of all points of view. In the words of one of its later editors, John O'Farrell, it was 'totally pluralist yet maintaining a liberal ethos'. It tried to reflect Seamus Heaney's belief that 'the mind is a bigger place than the region'. It was remarkable for its longevity: few small, impecunious, left-of-centre magazines have survived as long in the late twentieth and early twenty-first centuries in major European countries, let alone in remote provinces not known for their intellectual sophistication. It was also notable for the fact that almost every significant political and literary figure in Ireland wrote for it during that time; and for the influence some of its analysis and proposals had on political developments in Northern Ireland.

The magazine was started by an *engagé* academic lawyer, Tom Hadden, who worked at Queen's University Belfast for most of the forty-two years of *Fortnight*'s existence. Hadden, the son of a liberal unionist family in Portadown, had gained a taste for running a small magazine when he co-edited the *Cambridge Review*, a cultural journal for academics, during his time as a postgraduate researcher at Emmanuel College, Cambridge, in the mid-1960s. He was lecturing at the University of Kent when the first serious violence broke out in Northern Ireland in 1969 and quickly decided to return to his native province. He started working to set up a local magazine of politics and the arts soon after he arrived in Belfast that autumn to teach at Queen's, recalling that he 'spent quite a lot of time wandering around the Falls and the Shankill trying to get a handle on what was going on'.[1] He made an arrangement with a printer in Lurgan and the first edition appeared in September 1970.

Hadden noted that even in those early days nobody involved in *Fortnight* expected any instant solutions to Northern Ireland's problems of institutionalized discrimination against Catholics, sectarian division and violence over

---

1 Interview with Tom Hadden, 29 Oct. 2019.

the two communities' clashing versions of national self-determination. 'There is no future for any of us in a policy of absolutes', opined one early editorial; 'Those of us who stand in the centre on either side have a plain duty to join in fending off the threat from those committed to violent non-solutions.'[2] The magazine had lesser and more attainable goals: 'One was to give space to contributors from all sides, with the aim of recognising and then working to accommodate our differences by rational discussion rather than military – or media – confrontations.'[3] The first of those aspirations was triumphantly achieved: with one major exception, Democratic Unionist Party (DUP) leader Ian Paisley, the list of contributors over the next four decades could have served as a political and cultural *Who's who* for Northern Ireland (and, to a lesser extent, for Ireland as a whole).[4] The range of early contributors ran from the unionist hard right (Captain Lawrence Orr on why Stormont had prevented unrest for fifty years) to the nationalist far left (Bernadette Devlin on building a workers' union).

The stated aims were accuracy, impartiality and inclusiveness: 'One of the main functions of *Fortnight* is to present the facts so that people can make up their own minds. We make no apology for not taking a committed line on every issue, or for allowing our contributors to make their own conflicting judgements. There is rarely a single correct interpretation of the facts.'[5] Yet the tone of the magazine's editorials in those early days was reformist and liberal unionist. The British Army was urged 'to re-establish what respect it can' among the people of the Falls Road and it was argued that 'we have got the makings of a new civilised police force' following the limited reforms brought in following the Hunt Committee's report (including the disbandment of the notoriously sectarian B-Specials).[6]

There was also a desire to support those elements, particularly in culture and the arts, which continued to struggle to maintain as much as possible of a normal society. Some of these were cosmopolitan outside voices, which *Fortnight* worked hard to include throughout its existence. In the 1971 post-internment issue, as killings and bombings ratcheted up to unprecedented levels, George Thompson of the Ulster Folk Museum pleaded for more awareness of a joint heritage that transcended sectarian divisions in a society 'on the brink of social disintegration', while Louis Muinzer, an Italian lecturer at Queen's University who wrote for the magazine for thirty years, spoke in a review of 'the heartbreaking and heartbroken time at which this book has appeared'.[7]

2 *Fortnight*, editorial no. 23, 3 Sept. 1971, 3. 3 Robert Bell, Robert Johnstone & Robin Wilson (eds), *Troubled times:* Fortnight *magazine and the Troubles in Northern Ireland, 1970–91* (Belfast, 1991), p. 3 4 Ibid. 5 *Fortnight*, editorial no. 3, 23 Oct. 1970, 2. 6 *Fortnight*, editorial no. 1, 25 Sept. 1970, cover & editorial no. 2, 9 Oct. 1970, 2. 7 *Fortnight*, no. 23, 3 Sept. 1971, 20.

The brilliant cartoons of Martyn Turner, an Englishman who would go on to become the scourge of official Ireland over four decades of cartooning for the *Irish Times*, were one of the magazine's selling points. Typical of Turner's scepticism about Irish republican 'freedom fighters' was a 1972 cartoon of a barrister pleading for his IRA clients in a Dundalk courtroom, with the words: 'The case for the defence, your honour, on this ludicrous arms charge, is that if you commit them for trial, they'll blow your brains out.'

The magazine also became a vehicle for Hadden – later joined by his long-time collaborator, Kevin Boyle, former civil rights activist and soon to be a distinguished human rights law professor at the universities of Galway and Essex – to develop serious proposals for the reform of the law, security policy and government in Northern Ireland. Hadden remained as editor until 1976, but continued as an influential member of the editorial board and a frequent contributor of major articles throughout *Fortnight*'s existence. For example, after internment in August 1971 he proposed an eight-point 'Peace Plan', including the release of all 'political' internees; a special tribunal to hear charges against those alleged to be involved in violence; an urgent report on ill-treatment of internees; a referendum on the link with Britain and the participation of rep-resentatives of the nationalist community in an interim government elected by PR.[8] It was the first of many lengthy and carefully considered policy proposals in the magazine's columns, indicative of Hadden's concern to undermine sup-port for the IRA by working to make Northern Ireland a functioning society based on democracy, human rights and equality for all.

It is perhaps notable that until the mid-1990s editors of *Fortnight* came largely from Northern Protestant backgrounds, with the brief and unsuccess-ful exception of Ciaran McKeown of the Peace People in 1976–7. However, they were completely untypical of that community in that they were secu-lar, liberal and social democratic. So while the magazine tended to argue for rational, 'middle-way' solutions between unionism and nationalism – includ-ing power-sharing government, strong human rights safeguards and increased North-South links – it also espoused left-wing economic policies such as state-driven planning and investment, and redistribution of income to poorer people. Integrated education was another cause it championed, with regular contributions from Chris Moffat, Hadden's partner.

As the North descended into near Civil War in the early 1970s, *Fortnight*'s tone became, if anything, more measured. However, in the most violent year, 1972, it allowed itself to contemplate some more dangerous ideas. For example,

8 Ibid., cover & 3.

after Bloody Sunday in January of that year, it ran a cover story entitled: 'After Derry: A New Partition' in which it commented:

> The two communities are if anything more further apart than ever. The Protestants have sadly remained largely unconcerned by the deaths of 13 men last week. Many of them regard the affair as a just recompense for the equally terrible IRA shootings of policemen and reservists. All the passion that the South can muster cannot alter the fact that the determination of the Protestants not to be gunned or bombed into unification is as stiff as it ever was.

However the magazine expressed doubt that Derry would ever accept British rule, and urged that any new proposals should 'contain serious consideration of the right of the people of Derry, Strabane and the area around Newry to opt out of any [internal] settlement'.[9]

Not surprisingly, the magazine gave strong support to the short-lived 1974 power-sharing government between the Ulster Unionist Party (UUP), the Social Democratic and Labour Party (SDLP) and the Alliance Party, although it was critical of UUP leader Brian Faulkner as a 'reluctant liberal, a power-sharer because that is the only way he can get any power'.[10] When that experiment collapsed in the Ulster Workers' Council strike, it ran an editorial proposing independence for Northern Ireland. It listed five options – the effect of one of these, a unilateral British withdrawal, was 'likely to be unpleasant even if it doesn't lead to civil war' – and came down in favour of an 'autonomous Ulster'. This would be a compromise between Irish nationalism and what it saw as the rising 'Ulster nationalism' of unionists disillusioned with Westminster, and would lead to a semi-independent statelet with a lower standard of living than Britain, similar to places like Malta and Gibraltar.[11] Hadden later recalled that this unlikely idea, abandoned by him and Kevin Boyle in their various submissions to the Irish government in the 1980s, was probably a 'product of despair'.

Fortnight had its own problems in those most violent of years. In 1971 the Lurgan printers made it clear that they did not want to continue to print the magazine after an issue came out strongly against internment. For a few issues the magazine was typeset by the *Irish Times* in Dublin until a consignment of galley proofs was seized at Connolly Station because the required export permits were lacking. The new co-editor, Martyn Turner, a recent Queen's

9 Ibid., editorial no. 33, 9 Feb. 1972, 3.   10 Ibid., editorial no. 75, 11 Jan. 1974, 3.   11 Ibid., editorial no. 84, 7 June 1974, 3–6.

graduate and editor of student magazines, arranged the purchase of a venerable rotor printer (which had to be winched by crane into the magazine's
James Street South fourth-floor offices) and a studio camera, a monstrosity on
rails featuring several hundred thousand volts of oxyacetylene lights. Hadden
and Turner then quickly had to learn new skills: every second Tuesday Turner
made up the aluminium plates of the typeset pages and Hadden spent the
whole night printing 2,000 copies of the magazine.

In 1973 bombs were left outside the Belfast offices of three middle-of-
the-road organizations — *Fortnight*, the Alliance Party and the New Ulster
Movement — on the same day. There was a warning, but Hadden stayed in
the office anyway and, despite a shower of glass as the windows came in,
escaped unhurt. Hadden later asked, only semi-jokingly: 'Was that the IRA
or the security forces pretending to be the IRA?' In that year *Fortnight* won a
press award sponsored by its Dublin equivalent, *Hibernia* magazine. The cita-
tion read: 'Bravely entitled "an independent review for Northern Ireland" …
the co-editors have managed to keep their cool while the passions of conflict
have raged all around them.'

Fortnight was never afraid to dip its foot into those conflicted waters if it
felt it could be of some use. In November 1974 it published a four-page feature urging an end to internment without trial, which was also submitted to
the British government's Gardiner Committee examining this hugely controversial policy. During a follow-up oral submission to that committee, Hadden
and Kevin Boyle were asked what they thought the IRA would think of their
proposals. Hadden responded by suggesting that Lord Gardiner's group might
ask that illegal organization themselves. When this outlandish proposal was
rejected, he decided to follow his own advice. Through the intercession of an
IRA woman prisoner — Hadden was a prison visitor at the time — Boyle and
Hadden arranged to meet leading republicans Seamus Loughran and Maire
Drumm in a pub in the south Belfast suburb of Finaghy. Hadden made a
detailed note of this unlikely meeting ('they were as surprised about it as we
were') and submitted it to Loughran for amendment. This amended note was
submitted to the Gardiner Committee and then, with Loughran's consent,
published in the next edition of the magazine. Not everyone in the IRA was
happy with this initiative. Shortly afterwards Loughran was removed from
the IRA Army Council and ended up in a low-profile role in the Twinbrook
housing estate.[12]

In 1976 the magazine took a temporary detour after Ciaran McKeown,
an *Irish Press* journalist who was prominently involved with Betty Williams

12 Interview with Tom Hadden, 29 Oct. 2019.

and Mairead Corrigan in the Peace People, became its editor. Hadden made it a condition of McKeown's employment that the magazine had to be kept entirely separate from that high-profile peace organization. However, the tone of the magazine over the next year was very different, often with a strong spiritual underpinning, and after a year he asked McKeown to step down. The magazine was then handed to an editorial committee consisting of – at different times – Sarah Nelson, a writer on Ulster loyalism; Michael McKeown, a schoolteacher who also wrote about the casualties of the Northern conflict; the poets Robert Johnstone and Douglas Marshall; and voluntary sector worker and future SDLP chairman Jonathan Stephenson. This proved not to be a successful combination. In February 1978 the magazine ceased publication. A year later Hadden came back from Vancouver, where he had gone to the University of British Columbia to teach law on a short-term contract, and managed to restart the magazine, with it initially appearing every two months. In October 1981 the editorship passed to this writer – then a journalist working on a freelance contract in the *Irish Times*' Belfast office. In December 1982 *Fortnight* returned to monthly publication.

Like so many daily newspaper journalists who contributed to it, I valued *Fortnight* for the opportunities it gave to use controversial material that I could not publish in a more risk-averse national broadsheet newspaper. For example, the March–April 1982 issue contained hitherto unreported information about William McGrath, the housefather at the Kincora boys home in east Belfast, who had been convicted of raping and grossly abusing boys in his care the previous December. He was close to Ian Paisley and other senior political and military figures, and also headed his own small, very strange loyalist paramilitary grouping, Tara. I also asked ten 'unanswered questions' about the Kincora home that any public inquiry into the affair should address.[13] Another example of investigative journalism was a whistle-blower's account of the Fair Employment Agency's inadequacies.[14]

The magazine I inherited had become rather stale and unimaginative. I introduced more 'Sidelines', pointed and sometimes scurrilous short items on politics, paramilitaries, the security forces and other matters, which were eagerly read in a gossipy, news-hungry and conflict-ridden small society (and introduced the pseudonymous James McKnight, named after a nineteenth-century radical Presbyterian journalist, as their author). As a daily journalist at a time when the *Irish Times* coverage of Northern Ireland was leading the field under superb Northern editors like David McKittrick and Ed Moloney (with whom I worked particularly closely), I was privy to all

13 *Fortnight*, no. 186, Mar.–Apr. 1982, 4–5. 14 Ibid., no. 188, Oct. 1982, 8–11.

sorts of 'inside' stories, some of them on very sensitive topics. A typical 1984 'Sideline' read:

> I hear that around the time of the Sinn Féin *ard fheis* last month an order went out from the Provisional IRA's 'Belfast brigade staff' to all units to stop using hurley sticks to inflict punishment beatings. Apparently 'cultural reasons' were cited, meaning that it was giving the GAA a bad name in its centenary year. So for the next couple of beatings the Provo punishment squads managed to find baseball bats from somewhere to break young men's arms and legs in a fashion less offensive to the pure Gaelic soul of nationalist Ireland.[15]

It is extraordinary that over four decades *Fortnight* only received a handful of solicitors' letters about issues raised by this and other columns, and only once had to pay out significant money to a disgruntled public figure: £6,000 to Ian Paisley Jnr for a piece on his alleged behaviour during a peace conference in South Africa in 1997.

I also revamped and smartened up the magazine's dull layout, and tried to introduce some humour into its mix. Belfast's two best cartoonists, Ian Knox and Brian Moore (the latter with the Provisionals' *Republican News*), combined as Kormski to produce the anti-clerical 'Dog Collars' cartoon strip, which was both barbed and hilarious, and was a favourite of both republican and loyalist prisoners in the Maze (where *Fortnight* was to become the most popular magazine sent in by relatives, and was occasionally seized by the authorities). In 1983 we ran a competition to find the Northern Ireland Assembly's worst politician to go forward to represent the North in what we called the 'General Galtieri Perpetual Trophy' for the world's worst politician (this was a year after the Falklands War). A cross-section of journalists covering the Assembly surprisingly chose the prominent UUP barrister Robert McCartney (later to become an independent unionist MP for North Down), whose arrogance and self-regard had probably alienated many of them, for this dubious honour.

The improvements in the magazine – as well as its twelve years of sturdy and outspoken survival – were recognized in the award of the 1982 Ewart-Biggs Memorial Prize for promoting greater understanding between the people of Britain and Ireland. The widow of the former British ambassador to Ireland, murdered by the IRA in 1976, Lady Jane Ewart-Biggs, said: 'It was such a relief to be reading about Ulster in Ulster's language, forthright and tough-minded, if sometimes a little forlorn. What *Fortnight* does is to provide information and

15 Ibid., no. 211, 17 Dec. 1984–20 Jan. 1985, 30.

opinions from the centre of events – not filtered through the preconceptions of editorial offices in London or Dublin'.

The range of contributors continued to be wide and their contributions sharp and insightful. To name only a few in the early to mid-1980s: Ed Moloney on the Provisional IRA (he would come to be recognized as the leading journalistic authority on that ultra-secret armed organization); James Molyneaux on why Catholics should join the Ulster Unionist Party; John Hume on the New Ireland Forum; Gerry Adams on republicanism and socialism; Danny Morrison, Sinn Féin's propagandist-in-chief, on why Britain's will to stay in Northern Ireland would be broken; Conor Cruise O'Brien on Cardinal Tomás Ó Fiach's ambivalence (as he saw it) about republican violence; Peter Robinson on a Northern Ireland Assembly European affairs committee; Sammy Wilson on the DUP's left-wing leanings (as he saw them); the distinguished *Observer* and *Irish Times* journalist Mary Holland on the 1983 abortion referendum in the Republic; the *Guardian*'s Ireland correspondent David Beresford (a South African) on the parallels between Northern Ireland and South Africa; *Irish Times* editor Douglas Gageby on the Orange Order; the BBC *Panorama* journalist Peter Taylor (the best British TV reporter on Ireland) on the extradition of terrorist suspects from the Republic; Professor Padraig O'Malley (the Irish-American author of the best book about the first decade of the 'Troubles')[16] on the 1985 Anglo-Irish Agreement; and Bishop (later to become Cardinal) Cahal Daly on Northern Ireland's insecure Protestants. There were also interviews with Royal Ulster Constabulary chief constable Sir John Hermon, UDA commander Andy Tyrie and former UVF leader Gusty Spence. It was an impressive, if excessively male-dominated, list.

Tom Hadden and Kevin Boyle were continuing to use the magazine to put forward important ideas about Northern Ireland's future and then to lobby politicians to take action on them. The most dramatic example of this was at the Chequers summit meeting between Margaret Thatcher and Garret FitzGerald in November 1984, after which the British prime minister made her infamous 'out, out, out' comments about the Irish government's proposals. These were based on the three options from the New Ireland Forum report earlier that year: a unitary state, a federal/confederal state, or joint authority. Hadden and Boyle had also been critical of these, arguing that there was no evidence whatsoever that Northern Protestants would give their consent to any of them and that both communities in the North had to be accorded equal legitimacy. In long articles in *Fortnight* and elsewhere (including in a book, *Ireland: a positive proposal*), they argued that the way forward should be the

16 Padraig O'Malley, *The uncivil wars: Ireland today* (Belfast, 1983).

acceptance and recognition by all parties of the differing identities and loyalties of the two communities within Northern Ireland; extension of this acceptance and recognition in the context of relationships between the UK and the Republic; the protection of majority and minority rights on a political level within Northern Ireland; and the protection of communal and cultural rights through law for both communities within Northern Ireland and the Republic.

According to Boyle, at the Chequers summit Thatcher had taken a copy of the core paper containing these proposals, 'plonked it down on the table, saying something like "On this we can do business"'. Much of its thinking found its way into the Anglo-Irish Agreement the following year.[17]

Some prominent politicians and journalists preferred to write for the magazine under pseudonyms. Calvin McNee was an ever-present unionist-minded columnist for most of the magazine's long life. Sometimes he was a prominent liberal journalist, sometimes he was David Trimble. Tom Hadden, a colleague of Trimble's in the Queen's University law school in the 1980s, remembers that he would put a note in his pigeon hole asking for a thousand words, and Trimble would put the article in a brown paper envelope in Hadden's pigeon hole. Around that time, McNee's nationalist 'brother', Columbanus, started appearing, and he was eventually joined by no fewer than seventeen other McNees, with views ranging from the ultra-loyalist to the radical feminist. Another journalist with an intimate knowledge of the dangerous world of loyalist paramilitaries preferred to write under the alias John Douglas.

And there were dangers for a *Fortnight* journalist. A well-known playwright, stung by a mildly critical mention by Columbanus McNee in the course of a piece on the Belfast Festival, publicly accused the magazine – and particularly this writer – of supporting the INLA. Martin O'Hagan, a former Official IRA prisoner from Lurgan, who walked in off the street and asked for a job in 1982, investigated the activities of an East Belfast slum landlord who then initiated legal proceedings, which were later abandoned (we launched a public *Fortnight* Fighting Fund to contest the case). In September 2001, as an intrepid, muckraking *Sunday World* reporter, O'Hagan would be murdered in his home town by the Loyalist Volunteer Force. In September 1986 I wrote in the magazine about being beaten up by loyalist band members in Pomeroy, Co. Tyrone, while listening to a speech by Ian Paisley as part of research for a book about the DUP leader.[18]

17 Mike Chinoy, *Are you with me? Kevin Boyle and the rise of the human rights movement* (Dublin, 2020), p. 203.   18 Ed Moloney & Andy Pollak, *Paisley* (Dublin, 1986).

The books and arts pages were as lively as the political pages. *Fortnight* was particularly adept at seeking out little-publicized lectures by key cultural figures, such as Seamus Heaney's 1983 John Malone lecture on the English and Irish languages in Ireland and the roles of the artist and educator in Northern Ireland. Heaney was joined by Michael Longley, Derek Mahon, Tom Paulin, Sam McAughtry, Paddy Devlin and others in a feature on 'The Beauty of Belfast', whose literary reflections on that less-than-beautiful city were somewhat spoiled by the greyness of the photos used to illustrate it. There were no such problems with the December 1984 edition, the first time the magazine had returned to fortnightly publication since the mid-seventies, which was in full colour and featured a lead book review by Cardinal Ó Fiach (who had generously forgiven the magazine for publishing Conor Cruise O'Brien's broadside against him less than two years earlier).

The best contemporary Irish poets were published in *Fortnight:* Heaney, Longley, Mahon, Paulin, John Montague, Paul Muldoon, John Hewitt and James Simmons (all Northerners). In November 1995 poetry editor Medbh McGuckian, a major poet herself, met Seamus Heaney at a Queen's University dinner to celebrate his winning of the Nobel Prize for Literature the previous month, and came away with several unpublished poems. Book reviewers included the likes of the poets Eiléan Ní Chuilleanáin and Gerald Dawe, the novelist John Banville, the political scientists John Whyte and Paul Arthur, the sociologist Frank Wright, the literary critics Edna Longley, Terence Brown and Declan Kiberd, and the socialist journalist Eamonn McCann. Literary controversies were a staple ingredient. For example, in December 1985 books and arts editor Robert Johnstone (himself a well-regarded poet) took Kiberd to task for his highly critical review of a book by Longley and Dawe on the Protestant imagination in modern Ireland.[19] Johnstone wrote:

> It seems to me that there is a wilful deafness from anti-unionist, anti-British writers towards genuine attempts in the North to open up debate, to encourage self-questioning among Protestants, to try to work out who we are, and whether what we are, as a whole, might be made more humane than under the unionist Stormont. These are not reactionary, sectarian things to do.[20]

Fortnight did not only feature recognized authors. In the same issue, the magazine published a fine article by a young Derry Protestant, Richard Boggs,

---

19 Gerald Dawe & Edna Longley (eds), *Across the roaring hill: the Protestant imagination in modern Ireland* (Belfast, 1985). 20 *Fortnight*, no. 230, 2–15 Dec. 1985, 19–20.

about his very British upbringing and schooling in that divided city. He concluded it as follows:

> At university in England I discovered that I was Irish, more or less. I read
> Irish writers for the first time. I read Yeats: my mind coloured with the
> blue and dim and dark cloths of his words. I read Synge: wave upon wave
> of his liquid words broke upon my mind. I read Heaney: I sank into the
> soft bogland of his words, the centre bottomless. I read Joyce: I hoarded
> his words in my memory. I found the Citizen still asking: 'What is your
> nation?' and the Wandering Jew's reasonable, almost convincing answer. I
> treasure it: 'Ireland, I was born here. Ireland'.[21]

Boggs would go on to become a well-reviewed travel writer and photographer
and author of books on Lebanon, Syria, Yemen and Sudan.

We also liked to enjoy ourselves. In a valedictory piece in a 1991 compilation, *Troubled times*, I wrote: 'I think we can say that for a few years we let
loose a little light and fun and understanding in the ugly, violent, lovable old
shitheap that is Belfast.' From January 1984 on, the main public outlet for that
fun was the annual *Fortnight* party, started to celebrate the magazine's 200th
issue, which was a noisy, well-attended late night gathering in Belfast's Europa
Hotel which it liked to claim was 'the social event of the year'. Future editor
Malachy O'Doherty remembers *Fortnight* being a 'cool brand' around Belfast
at that time. As in all small magazines, securing paid advertisements was a
challenge, partly met at this point by persuading shops, political parties and
voluntary organizations to take out 'small ads' to congratulate *Fortnight* on its
longevity. In the late 1970s Tom Hadden and Martyn Turner had been invited
to dinner in the Europa by a senior Guinness manager only to be told that
the brewing company felt it would sell fewer pints in both communities if it
advertised in the magazine!

I left the magazine in November 1985 to research the Ian Paisley book,
jointly written with Ed Moloney, and eventually to move to work for the *Irish
Times* in Dublin. There was a brief interlude during which *Fortnight* was edited
by a Canadian radio producer, Leslie Van Slyke, who was there when the handsome if ramshackle Lower Crescent building in the university area which Tom
Hadden had shrewdly purchased to house its offices was burned down by a
homeless man sleeping in its porch.

The following autumn Robin Wilson, a *Belfast News Letter* sub-editor and
political and cultural studies tutor at the Ulster People's College, took over.

---

21 Ibid., 17–18.

Wilson remembers being interviewed for the job by Hadden and printer Noel Murphy in a burnt-out shell of a building, in a room full of rubble, and wondering 'What have I got myself into?'[22] For the first few months Wilson and Martin O'Hagan had to work in an office with no electricity, heat or running water. Despite this inauspicious start, *Fortnight*, under Wilson's editorship, was about to enter probably its most serious and thought-provoking phase, just in time for the beginning of the Northern Ireland peace process. In his 1993 book of interviews, the celebrated oral historian Tony Parker talked to a local university lecturer who said 'almost all our intellectual output about our problems is only to be found in a magazine called *Fortnight*'.[23] It might be said that the most interesting thing about the magazine up to his departure in 1995 was that Wilson, almost alone among the journalists covering it, was largely sceptical about that peace process. He recalled that during this period the magazine continued to editorialize that

> universal norms such as democracy, human rights and the rule of law would have to prevail. We pointed out that what was happening was that the British government was moving from repressing the IRA led by Adams and McGuinness to talking with the IRA led by Adams and McGuinness, and not what should have happened – which was a genuine break with the past that had been characterised by endless abrogations of human rights and the rule of law to a democratic dispensation underpinned by both those things.[24]

Wilson was a humanist, socialist and internationalist and these flavours strongly influenced the magazine's tone. An editorial in January 1990 summed up his view of Britain, Ireland and the world after the fall of the Berlin Wall. He looked forward to a forthcoming Labour government in London (which would take another seven years to arrive) and a turning away from the old, narrow identity politics in Northern Ireland. For example, he praised the Peace Train initiative, which saw a range of politicians and ordinary citizens from both jurisdictions filling a Belfast-Dublin train to protest against the IRA's bombing of the line between Ireland's two major cities. He wrote warmly that

> the easy relationship between the humanitarians, the liberals and the socialists from North and South who shared the carriages was a tantalising glimpse of a post-Provo 'new Ireland' ... an Ireland united *in the*

22 Interview with Robin Wilson, 4 Nov. 2019.   23 Tony Parker, *May the Lord in his mercy be kind to Belfast* (London, 1993), pp 125–6.   24 Interview with Robin Wilson, 4 Nov. 2019.

human sense wouldn't be a nationalist 'goal' ... more a realisation that *we are Europe too* – and that our conflict has become literally meaning-less.[25]

He went on to quote the distinguished Belfast journalist David McKittrick, who had noted that that the two governments now had the same analysis of, and almost identical interests in, Northern Ireland:

> Britain is not thinking of moving out and the Republic is not thinking about moving in. What both want is better management of the problem. They differ on the details of how to achieve this – the British think in security terms, the Irish would like to see a more political thrust on 'confidence issues' – but both are concerned to control the violence and encourage the two sides in Northern Ireland to get on better.[26]

This was entirely consistent with the editorial line set by Hadden twenty years earlier, that the two problematic communities in the North had to be recognized and respected through appropriate democratic and human rights measures, while being carefully managed by the two governments. The main weakness in Wilson's argument was his forecast of the future prospects for Sinn Féin, stating his belief that for the party of the IRA 'there was no way out of the 1% ghetto in which they are stuck in the Republic'. Wilson's strong anti-IRA posture was sometimes a barrier to him understanding the genuine changes that were taking place in the republican movement. He was also critical of John Hume for adopting Sinn Féin's 'language of national self-determination', quoting the Norwegian human rights lawyer, Torkel Opsahl, that 'the concept of self-determination, which is the design behind so much death and destruction in the former Yugoslavia at the moment, is not a help-ful one, particularly in a divided society like Northern Ireland'.[27] Following the August 1994 IRA ceasefire, Wilson warned that 'between now and the year end loyalists will do enough murdering for both sides'. He was wrong: less than two months later the loyalist paramilitaries declared their own ceasefire. He later explained that his fears had been dispelled by the 'complete character' of the IRA's action and the 'journalism-defying speed' at which events were moving.[28]

On the other hand, the Queen's University political scientist Adrian Guelke, a regular columnist (and another South African), got it right when

25 *Fortnight*, editorial no. 280, Jan. 1990, 5. 26 Ibid., no. 280, Jan. 1990, 11. 27 Ibid., editorial no. 321, Oct. 1993, 5. Opsahl was to chair the UN War Crimes Commission in Yugoslavia before his early death in 1993. 28 *Fortnight*, editorial no. 332, Oct. 1994, 5 and editorial no. 333, Nov. 1994, 5.

he warned that, unlike its South African equivalent, the Northern Irish process, by concentrating on securing and sustaining 'ceasefires by paramilitary
actors at the margins', could actually make the situation more difficult by
freezing in place 'a Cyprus-type bloodless conflict'. He warned that making
self-determination hinge on whether nationalists or unionists hold a majority
would do nothing to combat the sectarian divide and risked 'placing a political premium on the maintenance of community solidarity and offering no
incentives for cross-community cooperation'.[29] Over twenty-five years on, with
Belfast divided by nearly a hundred 'peace walls' and related structures, some
might say that was prophetic.

Between 1993 and 1995 Wilson frequently referred to the recommendations
of the 1993 report of the independent Opsahl Commission into ways forward
for Northern Ireland, an innovative 'citizens inquiry' of which he was one of
the originators and which had attracted submissions from 3,000 people.[30] In
an editorial in February 1994 he listed some of the Opsahl recommendations
as an alternative to the 'conflicting self-determinations' which appeared to be
at the heart of the talks that had taken place between John Hume and Gerry
Adams, and which had led to the December 1993 Downing Street Declaration
by the two governments, the real beginning of the peace process. Thus he
urged the British government to introduce a raft of measures that would
secure the 'empowerment of nationalists (without disempowering unionists)',
including new political institutions 'to entrench equality, not just majoritar-
ian power-sharing'; giving 'legal recognition to nationalism so that Northern
Ireland no longer enshrined unionist cultural dominance'; new North-South
structures so that relationships on the island were between Irish men and
women alone; a Bill of Rights and the repeal of emergency legislation; phased
withdrawal of the British army, initially to barracks; a review of policing with
a view to 'establishing a service which no longer entailed the majority policing
the minority'; the social and economic reconstruction of ghetto areas; and the
phased release of paramilitary prisoners.[31] Much of this, of course, appeared a
few years later in the 1998 Good Friday Agreement.

Politics in this epoch-changing period was treated by the magazine with
deep seriousness, and not only by politicians and journalists. For example, it
dealt with the Downing Street Declaration in two issues: the first bringing
together ten analysts, ranging from the business leader Sir George Quigley
to the contrarian republican Anthony McIntyre; the second gathering no
fewer than thirty-five prominent historians, writers, film-makers, poets,

29 Ibid., no. 325, Feb. 1994, 12–15. 30 Andy Pollak (ed.), *A citizens' inquiry: the Opsahl Report on Northern Ireland* (Dublin, 1993). 31 *Fortnight*, editorial no. 325, Feb. 1994, 5.

critics, theatre directors and arts administrators – from Seamus Heaney to
Roy Foster – to comment on the Declaration.[32] Later in 1994 Tom Hadden
and Kevin Boyle contributed a weighty summation of their most recent
book *Northern Ireland: the choice,* the choice being between a society based on
separation (as between the Israelis and the Palestinians) or sharing (on the
model of post-apartheid South Africa).[33] The writers came down on the side
of a combination of internal power-sharing between the two communities
and external shared authority between the British and Irish governments.
They stressed that the issue of self-determination could not be ignored:
'The idea of self-determination for the people of Ireland linked to that of
consent by unionists to any new structures is an essential element both in
the Hume-Adams plan for peace and in the Downing Street Declaration'.
Boyle and Hadden proposed a 'preferendum' with four options for people
to vote on: continued direct rule; power-sharing with joint North/South
institutions; separate institutions for the two main communities; and joint
authority.[34] The preferendum, refined and promoted by Belfast man Peter
Emerson, another *Fortnight* contributor, may yet re-emerge as an alternative
to a blunt 'border poll' vote on Irish unity as laid down by the Good Friday
Agreement.

The magazine in these years was bigger than ever, and the range and quality
of the contributors was unprecedented. Wilson was particularly keen to attract
women writers, with the monthly political column (the magazine was now
monthly again) being penned by two heavyweight commentators, the up-and-
coming Suzanne Breen in Belfast and the outstanding Emily O'Reilly (later to
become the EU Ombudsman) in Dublin. Anne Maguire, a young journalist
from Fermanagh who was beginning to make her name in the *Irish Times,* was
another regular until her tragically early death in a road accident. Others who
were contributing at this time were former Taoiseach Garret FitzGerald (who
had been a strong supporter from the start), the Booker Prize-winning novelist
Anne Enright; two of the *Irish Times'* top journalists, Conor O'Clery and Fintan
O'Toole (the former first contributed when a Queen's student back in 1970;
the latter would join the editorial committee); Robert Fisk of the *Independent;*
Will Hutton of the *Guardian;* Kevin Cullen of the *Boston Globe;* Jimmy Burns
of the *Financial Times;* Ed Gorman of the *Times;* Queen's University professor
of politics Paul Bew (soon to become one of Ulster Unionist Party leader
David Trimble's closest advisors); lawyer and former civil rights leader Michael
Farrell; and Fred Halliday, professor of international relations at the London

32 Ibid., nos. 325 and 326, Feb. and Mar. 1994.   33 Tom Hadden & Kevin Boyle, *Northern Ireland: the choice*
(London, 1994).   34 *Fortnight,* no. 328, May 1994, 16.

School of Economics. It was rare for any journalist or academic in Ireland or Britain to say 'no' when asked to write for *Fortnight.*

The poet Damian Smyth joined the magazine in 1989 as books and arts editor and then deputy editor. Both Wilson and Smyth believed that politics and the arts were inter-connected and overlapping, and were strong supporters of Edna Longley's thesis that Northern Ireland could be a 'cultural corridor' connecting Britain and Ireland, with the North 'open at both ends'. Smyth was not afraid of taking on the big guns of the Field Day theatre and publishing company (Brian Friel, Stephen Rea, Seamus Heaney, Seamus Deane et al.): he took particular exception to the exclusion from the voluminous *Field Day anthology of Irish writing* of the eighteenth-century Ulster Protestant working-class Weaver Poets, who wrote in Scots.[35] 'Trying to open up a "landing place" where Protestant unionists and Catholic nationalists could find a common language was a particular challenge,' he recalled, citing the writing of Longley and Roy Foster on this topic. 'There was no other platform for those voices in Ireland.'[36] Smyth also corrected the imbalance of far too many male poets in earlier periods by publishing many of the new generation of women poets, such as Sinead Morrissey, Vona Groarke and Leontia Flynn.

Wilson also brought in some key technical innovations. Apple's MacIntosh computers were purchased to do typesetting and page design 'in house' before a disc was sent to the printers. This led to an improvement in the magazine's appearance, with a cleaner and classier layout fitted into a new template from the well-regarded Belfast designer Wendy Dunbar. The 'Dublin Letter' was dispensed with in favour of more extensive coverage from the Republic using some of the most talented journalists in that jurisdiction. There was even some talk – in the end idle because it was deemed not feasible without a move to Dublin – of turning *Fortnight* into an all-Ireland magazine, given the absence of any serious political and cultural equivalent south of the border following the demise of *Magill.* During Wilson's period in charge the number of subscriptions doubled from 600 to 1,200, a vital lifeline for a magazine for which the total circulation probably never rose above 3,000. However, Tom Hadden emphasizes that the magazine in the early 1970s, early 1980s and early 1990s was selling more copies per head of population in Northern Ireland than the *New Statesman, New Society* and the *Spectator* put together were selling in the UK. The Irish department of foreign affairs was a longstanding supporter, with its order of a copy for every Irish embassy around the world.

35 Seamus Deane (ed.), *The Field Day anthology of Irish writing* (Derry, 1990). 36 Interview with Damian Smyth, 28 Nov. 2019.

In spring 1995 Robin Wilson stepped down in order to found the Belfast-based Democratic Dialogue 'think tank'. He was replaced by John O'Farrell, a young left-wing Dubliner who had recently completed a master's degree in European integration at Queen's University, and admits to having had little journalistic experience before he started writing articles for *Fortnight*. He identi-fied Perry Anderson, editor of the *New Left Review*, as his journalistic inspiration, 'aiming at the intelligent common reader – neither academic nor avant-garde – who can follow relatively complex stuff'. The commissioning logic of the magazine was similar to that eminent London journal: 'the reputation of the author, the urgency of the topic, the direction of the argument'.[37] Like most *Fortnight* editors O'Farrell was keen to broaden the centre ground in Northern Ireland, but also wanted to engage with republicans more than Wilson. He claims to have given Sinn Féin director of publicity Danny Morrison his first piece of paid work, an interview with visiting South African politicians Cyril Ramaphosa and Rolf Meyer, when he got out of prison in 1995. He also pub-lished former IRA prisoners like Anthony McIntyre and Tommy McKearney who were critical of the peace process and Sinn Féin's role in it. O'Farrell noted that he and his main political columnist, Suzanne Breen, 'understood that Sinn Féin and the IRA were moving away from fundamental positions, away from physical force/violence towards constitutionalism. We covered the peace process as if there was probably going to be a deal, which turned out to be what happened.'[38]

In an editorial in September 2000 to mark the magazine's thirtieth anni-versary, O'Farrell summed up the secret of *Fortnight*'s success. Rejecting the sneering words of some critics that it was 'the house journal of a small coterie of south Belfast liberals', he emphasized that if that was the case it would not have lasted so long nor had such an impact:

> *Fortnight* exists on the indulgence of unpaid contributors, underpaid staff and patient subscribers. Few of its writers are working journal-ists.[39] Many others are ordinary workers in specialised fields, forced to rise above the deadpan language of reports and free of the jargon of Voluntary Sector speak.

He then went on to list those who had contributed to this anniversary issue: 'Trainee and experienced journalists, eminent professors and hungry young academics, published poets, a novelist and film-maker, a retired senior public

37 Interview with John O'Farrell, 4 Nov. 2019. 38 Ibid. 39 The point about few of the magazine's writers being working journalists was not the case under my or Robin Wilson's editorships.

servant, a jobbing actor, a gallery photographer, a psychotherapist and the long-est surviving hunger striker. That mix is *Fortnight*'s contribution to debate about life and politics.' He concluded by thanking the magazine's funders, including the Arts Council and the European Union (through the Northern Ireland Voluntary Trust), for respecting 'what we most cherish – independence'.[40]

O'Farrell likes to point out that three successive Irish presidents – Mary Robinson (something of a *Fortnight* icon), Mary McAleese and Micheal D. Higgins – had written for the magazine. One of its successes, particu-larly under Wilson and O'Farrell, was persuading academics to write about important subjects in accessible language for ordinary people. Thus, in 2000, political geographer Peter Shirlow (later to become director of the Institute of Irish Studies at Liverpool University) wrote graphically and depressingly about the continuing deep divides – based on survey research – between work-ing-class communities in Belfast. They rarely used the same shopping and leisure facilities as their sectarian opposite numbers ('80% will not shop in a place dominated by the opposite religion'); in some areas people travelled ten times further than the nearby 'other side' to access such facilities; and 43 per cent of unemployed people surveyed would not work in a place dominated by the other religion. Shirlow concluded: 'From Shankill Road loyalists trying to whip up inter-community violence in north Belfast through to Sinn Féin cynically staging the evacuation of Catholics from Protestant areas, the desire to promote sectarianism is still a feature of this "new peaceful society"'.[41]

In 2002 O'Farrell was replaced by the prominent freelance journalist and writer Malachi O'Doherty, best known at that point for his BBC Radio Ulster *Talkback* commentaries and a well-reviewed book on the IRA.[42] O'Doherty, a liberal and occasional Alliance Party supporter, was cut from the mould of *Fortnight* editors. However, he found it difficult to maintain the magazine's cir-culation at a time of both relative peace and political inactivity as the Northern Ireland institutions went into storage (from 2002 to 2007). The endless talks and breakdown of talks as the DUP and Sinn Féin manoeuvred to upstage their more moderate counterparts, the Ulster Unionists and the SDLP, while the two governments desperately tried to sweet-talk the extremist parties into agreement (which they finally did at St Andrews in autumn 2006), did not make for political engagement from the small magazine-reading public.

Clearly the magazine had to extend its coverage into other, non-political areas. 'I said at one editorial meeting I would be as comfortable with a cover feature on jazz as one on politics', O'Doherty recalled. He included more

40 *Fortnight*, editorial, no. 388, Sept. 2000, 6–7. 41 *Fortnight*, no. 388, Sept. 2000, 38. 42 Malachi O'Doherty, *The trouble with guns: republican strategy and the Provisional IRA* (Belfast, 1997).

articles about religion, a particular interest of his. To his embarrassment, one of the controversies of his time was a picture of a woman's breast on the cover, to illustrate an article from the rising young feminist journalist Fionola Meredith. He continued the more frequent coverage of international topics (such as the Iraq war) that Wilson had begun and O'Farrell had continued. However, he conceded:

> *Fortnight* was still important. But I think it was more important in the 1970s and 1980s, because then it provided an alternative to the polarised local press of those years. By the time we reached the 2000s the Belfast papers had an unprecedented spread of political analysis and commentators from a wide range of viewpoints. The reason we had that spread was not because the local media had become converted to a higher level of comment and analysis – it was just that paying an occasional columnist was cheaper than paying a daily reporter.[43]

In 2000 Hadden had managed to pay off much of the magazine's significant debt by selling the building in Lower Crescent for a tidy sum. This was probably the only time in *Fortnight*'s history when it was fully solvent. For much of the earlier period it was kept alive by substantial grants from the British charity the Joseph Rowntree Reform Trust. The Northern Ireland Arts Council also provided grants to support the arts and culture pages. This was supplemented by the sale of voting and non-voting shares to individual supporters, by fundraising parties and campaigns, and by subventions and loans from Hadden when all else failed. Despite this, and in keeping with his strong belief in cooperative ownership, Hadden made sure that although he and Rowntree held the largest number of shares in the company, the rest of the fifty or so shareholders – including all the editors, to whom he gave shares – could always outvote him, although it never came to that. In the 1990s there was a further major grant from the related Joseph Rowntree Charitable Trust to a new charity, the Fortnight Educational Trust. This published series of supplements – edited by Damian Smyth, Chris Moffat and others – on a wide range of subjects from Irish and Ulster-Scots, through the Education for Mutual Understanding schools programme, to writers and philosophers like Samuel Beckett, Stewart Parker, John Hewitt and Francis Hutcheson. In the run-up to the Good Friday Agreement a number of separately funded opinion polls and supplements were published on people's attitudes to separation or

---

43 Interview with Malachi O'Doherty, 28 Nov. 2019.

sharing in Northern Ireland, and to a range of constitutional and political options for the region.

Despite the new (if temporary) solvency, in 2005 the money ran out to pay O'Doherty's full-time salary – the first time in over thirty years the editor had been paid a living wage – and he moved on. By this time the magazine was starting to look rather threadbare, with weaker cover stories and fewer 'big name' contributors. The much-cited daily 'Troubles Chronology', over which Linenhall librarian Robert Bell and Robin Wilson had laboured long and hard, disappeared with the end of the regular violence. There were still occasional gems: a political column by the distinguished Queen's University political scientist Richard English, author of the most authoritative book on the IRA, stressing the enormity of the republican movement's change from violence to demography and electoralism as the way towards Irish unity;[44] and, in stark contrast, an anguished 'level Stormont to the ground' cry of betrayal from that tragic and irreconcilable figure, former IRA bomber Dolours Price. Neither had it lost its humour: after the police had raided Sinn Féin's Stormont offices in October 2002, bringing the political institutions crashing down, Newton Emerson recorded Gerry Kelly informing 'a sniggering media that "this office deals in human rights, equality and justice" (racketeering, drug dealing and punishment beatings are handled by a sub-contractor)'.

However, overall it was clear that after thirty-five years the magazine was running out of steam. The end of the Northern Ireland conflict and the advent of social media, spelling the death knell for small, radical print publications everywhere, provided the broader international context. It limped on for another six years with a falling circulation under Rudie Goldsmith, who had been O'Doherty's deputy editor, becoming bi-monthly again at the end. The 'final souvenir issue' in December 2011–January 2012 signalled a transition from relative harmony to a wider disruptive environment in the future with a cover cartoon (by Martyn Turner) featuring Peter Robinson and Martin McGuinness singing from the same hymn sheet over a story on the 'North/South Euro Crisis'.[45]

POSTSCRIPT: *Fortnight*, under founding editor Tom Hadden, resumed publication as a quarterly in September 2020.

44 Richard English, *Armed struggle: the history of the IRA* (London, 2003). **45** *Fortnight*, no. 478, Dec. 2011–Jan. 2012, cover.

5 / Inside stories and outsider opinions: *The Phoenix*

JOE BREEN

When John Mulcahy died aged 86 in September 2018, his obituarists faced a small but telling dilemma. How should they balance the most outstanding achievements of a rich journalistic life? Was he the patrician champion of the arts for the manner in which he had guided the *Irish Arts Review* to prosperous waters in the 'noughties', or the fearless and imaginative editor at *Hibernia* in the 1970s, or the bold and innovative figure who launched and edited the first version of the *Sunday Tribune*, or a scurrilous muckraker enmeshed, as his detractors would say, in cheap gossip, innuendo and caricature at *The Phoenix*, the magazine he launched in the early 1980s after he left the *Tribune*?

The writer of the *Irish Times*' un-bylined obituary had no doubts.[1] Mulcahy 'was one of the most significant journalists and publishers of the last half century in this country. In a career, and a life, characterized by a combination of resilience, professionalism, innovation and sheer courage with few, if any, peers in his generation, he was a trailblazer for investigative journalism, holding up a mirror constantly to power.' In particular, the writer praised Mulcahy's work at *The Phoenix*, where he 'gave his new venture a lighter tone, employing its by-now trademark ridicule and satire to afflict the powerful, although retaining a hard, investigative edge'.[2] Liam Collins, in the *Sunday Independent*, was more circumspect. Mulcahy 'was regarded by some as a muckraking publisher and by others as an editor who exposed the Irish elites to well-deserved scrutiny'.[3] Collins cited *Modern Irish lives*: 'Over the years, *The Phoenix* has subjected Ireland's business, political, media and artistic circles to a great deal of unwanted attention, and has reported their affairs in a satirical, sometimes outrageous fashion.'[4] But in the *Irish Independent*, the previous day, Kim Bielenberg had captured perfectly the paradox at the heart of Mulcahy's life and work. He had 'liked to cock a snook at the establishment, while, at the same time, being very much a part of it'.[5]

It was not surprising that journalists, particularly those at Independent News and Media (INM), felt some ambivalence in assessing Mulcahy's legacy. *The Phoenix* and INM titles, notably the *Sunday Independent*, had been exchanging

---

1 Articles in the *Irish Times*' obituary page on Saturdays, as per house style, are not bylined.   2 *Irish Times*, 22 Sept. 2018.   3 *Sunday Independent*, 9 Sept 2018.   4 Louis McRedmond, *Modern Irish lives: a dictionary of twentieth-century Irish biography* (Dublin, 1996), p. 220.   5 *Irish Independent*, 8 Sept. 2018.

disparaging comments for some time. This was predictable. It was bread and butter for a satirical/investigative magazine to slice into the soft underbelly of the state's biggest-selling Sunday newspaper and, in turn, that newspaper was not known for turning the other cheek.[6] The *Irish Times*, the *Irish Independent*, RTÉ and other media producers were also targeted but they rarely rose to the bait with the same enthusiasm. There was no hesitation or qualification in the four-page tribute in *The Phoenix*. Mulcahy's protégé and successor as editor, Paddy Prendiville, said that his former boss would be remembered as 'the gatekeeper' of Irish investigative journalism:

> His legacy, built up over more than half a century in publishing, exists despite his rejection of the cult of the by-line as embraced by other media 'personalities'. For John, the work, the story, the uncovering of reality in politics, business and other power centres, was primary – delivered usually in a mocking style designed to puncture the self-important egos in public life.[7]

Barry J. Whyte, in the *Sunday Business Post*, was also effusive about his former boss:

> At *The Phoenix*, the old rules didn't just apply, they were the guide-ropes to help us chart a course through the bullshit ... I have vivid memories of the four days before publication when he [Mulcahy] sat at the boardroom table, red biro in hand, going through every line of every story on every page, striking out anything that displeased him, and inserting little Mulcahyisms where he felt the story was insufficiently vinegary. More important than Mulcahy's relentless red pen was his vigorous interrogation of every single article to make sure it was factually and legally accurate. If *The Phoenix* looked like a lark and read like a joke, it was neither to Mulcahy: it was deadly serious.[8]

This chapter seeks to understand the role *The Phoenix* has played in Irish journalism. But the story of the magazine also, in many ways, charts a dissenting or alternative history of contemporary Ireland which, invariably, tested the boundaries of what was considered journalism, not least by established journalists. Inevitably, it centres on John Mulcahy and his successor Paddy

6 Two examples would be 'No *Phoenix* vitriol for the ed's brother', *Sunday Independent*, 25 Mar. 2007 and '*Phoenix*'s story turns into ashes', *Sunday Independent*, 10 Nov. 2002.   7 *The Phoenix*, 21 Sept. 2018.   8 *Sunday Business Post*, 9 Sept. 2018.

Prendiville, the men who have guided the magazine for almost forty years. Malcolm Ballin's observation that a periodical is 'produced by a guiding editorial intelligence, seeking to project an identity' is apt.[9] The wrath of *The Phoenix* was personal; when, for radio ads, Mulcahy performed the character of 'Goldhawk', the fictitious compiler and disseminator of rumours good and bad, of stories controversial and provocative, he did it with cartoonish intensity and theatrical relish. At the time he launched the magazine, in early 1983, he was smarting from a number of reverses. *Hibernia*, the moribund monthly periodical he had bought in 1968 and transformed into a 'lively, irreverent and often well-informed magazine' finally closed in 1980, a victim of overreach in its move to a weekly publishing schedule and a string of legal actions, some particularly damaging.[10] But, as Brian Trench notes, it had created a distinct place in the Irish media landscape: 'It offered consistently critical perspectives on the conventional media agenda and it extended that agenda to include voices and experiences that were generally excluded.'[11]

Mulcahy's next project was an attempt to continue *Hibernia's* dissenting journalism in another guise. The *Sunday Tribune* was an 'unlikely partnership' between Mulcahy and Hugh McLaughlin, the commercial magazine publisher and co-founder of the *Sunday World*.[12] And so it proved. Although Mulcahy promised that the *Sunday Tribune* would 'aim to hold an independent line in politics and a liberal one in economic and social affairs', his business partner was saying that the new paper would not be a *Hibernia* redux.[13] As noted by Brennan and Trench, 'Some months in, Mulcahy was finding the relationship difficult and he soon left, becoming perhaps the only person, through the sale of his shares to the Smurfit Group, to make a capital gain from the *Sunday Tribune*.'[14] And so the scene was set for his comeback. Caroline Walsh, interviewing him for the *Irish Times* on the eve of publication of the first issue of the *Phoenix*, framed this publishing miracle accordingly: 'From his desk, made appropriately enough in Calcutta by C. Lazarus and Company, veteran journalist John Mulcahy was busy yesterday launching his new fortnightly magazine … which he suggests will be more irreverent and iconoclastic than anything we have had yet.'[15] Mulcahy acknowledged that the magazine was similar in many ways to the British magazine, *Private Eye*, particularly the weight afforded

9 Malcolm Ballin, *Irish periodical culture, 1937–72: genre in Ireland, Wales and Scotland* (Basingstoke, 2008), p. 2   10 John Horgan & Roddy Flynn, *Irish media: a critical history* (Dublin, 2017), p. 110.   11 Brian Trench, 'Hibernia: voices of dissent 1968–80' in Mark O'Brien & Felix M. Larkin (eds), *Periodicals and journalism in twentieth-century Ireland* (Dublin, 2014), pp 187–202 at p. 201.   12 Pat Brennan & Brian Trench, 'The Tribune's turbulent times' in Joe Breen & Mark O'Brien (eds), *The Sunday papers: a history of Ireland's weekly press* (Dublin, 2018), pp 161–81 at p. 162.   13 *Sunday Tribune*, 1 Nov. 1980.   14 Brennan & Trench, 'The Tribune's turbulent times', p. 162.   15 *Irish Times*, 7 Jan. 1983.

by the latter to investigative journalism. 'Yes,' Mulcahy said. 'There is going to be a strong emphasis on investigative journalism in sensitive areas – broadly speaking in the political and financial areas, and within those two areas in our first issue we are dealing with the judicial inquiry into interference with the Gardaí, the phone-tapping probe, Kincora and the British intelligence connection, and land deals.'[16] These general themes of corruption, political chicanery, neutrality, Northern Ireland and sharp business deals and dealmakers would become anchor tenants in the magazine. Cant, particularly in the media, would also be mercilessly highlighted.

The origins of these stories were also hinted at by Mulcahy. Walsh explained that partly because much of it was written by freelance contributors, *The Phoenix* had reverted to the old journalistic style of not using bylines or the names of its reporters. Mulcahy said this suited 'many of the contributors who wouldn't want their names known and who can have more scope by writing anonymously'.[17] Mulcahy had honed this technique in *Hibernia* by using the nom de plume 'Tom Luby' to byline short news and comment pieces.[18] As if to underline the connection between *Hibernia* and the new venture, Mulcahy used the 'Tom Luby' byline on many of the pieces in the magazine's first edition. Mulcahy also outlined his politics. He was, he said, consistently critical of the establishment because the society it controls has such glaring inequalities and deprivations and scandals within it. He added that his interest in the Northern situation was as keen as ever. He greatly regretted that British policy was not even pointed in the direction of what must be the ultimate solution to the Northern problem, 'which is that people on this island can determine the constitutional structure for the future government of the island, something that has been denied them since the Union'. He was, he said, deeply republican, explaining that one of the reasons for the magazine title was the Fenian-associated magazine of the same name launched in New York in the mid-nineteenth century. Another reason was the Egyptian myth of the bird rising from the ashes. And finally there was the appeal of a link to the Phoenix Park: 'The Phoenix Park is terribly central to Dublin and I want the magazine to be as Dublin-orientated and as Irish-orientated as possible.'[19]

Paddy Prendiville, who joined the magazine in late 1983, shared many of his editor's sympathies. Both had attended the elite Clongowes Wood school

16 Ibid.   17 Ibid. The insiders who contributed content would have been appalled to see their names in print as much as their employers would have liked to identify the sources for these stories.   18 'Tom Luby' was presumably a reference to the journalist and author Thomas Clarke Luby (1822–1901), who was a founding member of the Irish Republican Brotherhood.   19 *Irish Times*, 7 Jan. 1983.

— not, given the gap in their ages, at the same time — both had lived abroad, Mulcahy in many places, Prendiville primarily in England, and both were 'republican with a small r', with a strong belief in social justice.[20] Prendiville had been press officer with the 'Troops Out' movement in Britain before joining *Hibernia*. Subsequently, he worked as foreign editor at the *Sunday Tribune*, where he clashed with new editor, Vincent Browne, after Mulcahy exited. He then joined Mulcahy's new venture and was appointed editor after a short time. However, though notionally Mulcahy had stepped back into the role of managing editor, in practice he remained effectively the editor-in-chief, with Prendiville content to devote himself to writing and reporting.[21] Browne obviously left his mark on Prendiville and the latter has since done his best to do likewise — Browne was regularly featured in *The Phoenix*. This prompted Liam Fay in a *Hot Press* interview to ask Prendiville about coverage of Browne: 'There's a danger for any journalist in getting obsessive about various issues,' said Prendiville. 'I know I have now and again, but usually you'll find that your colleagues or boss will point this out. Vincent Browne gets a lot of coverage because he does some pretty zany, exciting and eminently publishable things, as any of his staff will tell you, if only in private.'[22]

It should be remembered that the Ireland of 1983 was in a fraught state, knee-deep in economic mire and political instability and chicanery. In 1982, there were two general elections, with Garret FitzGerald's Fine Gael/ Labour coalition giving way in March to the minority government of Charles Haughey's Fianna Fáil, supported by independent TDs Tony Gregory and Niall Blaney and three Workers' Party TDs. This flimsy arrangement collapsed the following November and FitzGerald returned to power. Against a backdrop of violence in the North and penury in the South, the Republic staggered from crisis to crisis. The smell of corruption was rife. This was the fetid mess from which *The Phoenix* rose.

'PUNCHING SIDEWAYS'

Although it has been published for almost forty years, *The Phoenix*, in spite of its critical, confrontational and often controversial framing of Irish life and governance, has, surprisingly, attracted little direct scholarly attention. The standard Irish reference works on modern Irish media, Horgan and Flynn's *Irish media: a critical history*, O'Brien's *The fourth estate: journalism in twentieth-century*

20 Paddy Prendiville interview with the author, 28 Sept. 2020.   21 Ibid.   22 Liam Fay, 'By the time I get to *The Phoenix*', *Hot Press*, 20 Sept. 2002.

Ireland and Morash's *A history of the media in Ireland,* are sparing in their references to the magazine. Horgan and Flynn, after recounting in brief John Mulcahy's career in *Hibernia* and the *Sunday Tribune,* noted that the magazine was modelled to some extent on *Private Eye* and resembled *Hibernia* in its provision of high-grade business and company news stories. They described the content as a mix of information, scandal and gossip and stated that the magazine was selling over 20,000 copies within ten years of its launch and had doubled its pagination to forty-eight pages. 'Its articles were anonymous – high-profile bylines were at this time becoming the staple of Dublin journalism – and despite an annual bill for libel settlements and costs of between £50,000 and £100,000, it has never succumbed to a really successful defamation action.' Horgan and Flynn also note that attention to legal care in the prepublication process ensured that the magazine was handled by orthodox wholesalers and appeared on newsstands.[23] Morash also noted that *The Phoenix* was modelled to some extent on *Private Eye* and observed that it would be all but unintelligible to a reader who did not live on a rich, intense diet of news and current affairs. 'If nothing else, its early circulation figures of 20,000, and its continued survival in the volatile magazine market, are a reminder that a small, but nonetheless sizeable, percentage of the Irish population live in an intensely media-saturated environment.'[24]

O'Brien, in the *Fourth estate,* takes a different approach, relating, as part of a narrative, the magazine's role in a number of important stories. He outlines the magazine's brave decision to reveal in 1983 that Fianna Fáil leader Charles Haughey owed Allied Irish Banks (AIB) over £1 million. O'Brien also recalled that the magazine had also stated that Haughey had received £1.4 million in a land sale disguised through the transactions of a multitude of companies owned by his associates. The story was subsequently fleshed out by *Evening Press* journalist Des Crowley, which led to AIB issuing a statement dismissing the report as being 'outlandishly inaccurate'.[25] Despite what O'Brien describes as persistent and determined attempts by numerous journalists to identify the source of Haughey's wealth, it was the fallout from a freak incident involving retail magnate Ben Dunne in 1992 that ultimately led to Cliff Taylor revealing in the *Irish Times* in December 1996 that Dunne had given money (£1.1 million) to a Fianna Fáil politician. It fell to *The Phoenix* to identify that politician as Charles Haughey.[26] This was the culmination of a long campaign by the magazine.

23 Horgan & Flynn, *Irish media,* pp 160–1. 24 Christopher Morash, *A history of the media in Ireland* (Cambridge, 2010), p. 190. 25 Mark O'Brien: *The fourth estate: journalism in twentieth-century Ireland* (Manchester, 2018), pp 194–5. 26 Ibid., p. 196.

These were brave and consequential revelations in Irish public life that sat easily with the magazine's caustic satirical commentary. Yet when Larkin addresses satirical journalism in a chapter in the third volume of *The Edinburgh history of the British and Irish press*, there is no mention of *The Phoenix*.[27] This omission may be due to pressure on space, given the enormous historical landscape he had to cover, and a perception that the focus in *The Phoenix* is more on investigative journalism than satire. However, Larkin makes many telling points that could apply to the magazine. For instance, he states that *Dublin Opinion* was modelled on a similar British magazine, *London Opinion*. This echoes Mulcahy's decision to base his new magazine on *Private Eye*.[28] And, dealing with the 'effusion of satire in Britain in the 1960s', he is perceptive when he states:

> What distinguishes the satire of this period from what comes before and after is that it arose from *within* the establishment rather than from below. It was not 'punching up', but 'punching sideways' through the work of young, disillusioned, upper- or middle-class people revolting against their parents and their parents' values, both political and social.[29]

The generational reference might have been appropriate when *The Phoenix* was first published, but the magazine has consistently 'punched sideways'. As previously stated, both Mulcahy and his successor Paddy Prendiville were raised in middle-class homes. Though the magazine's solidly green republican sympathies found little encouragement from within the establishment during the Troubles, its stories on politics, business, media, the arts and sport reveal a ready stream of insider information, even if, arguably, not always accurate. Sometimes, it was suspected that informants, particularly in the media arena, were deliberately planting incorrect details to obscure their identity. As such, perhaps *The Phoenix*'s apparent lack of scholarly attention may be a result of the magazine not being perceived as serious journalism, more a forum for speculation, gossip and satire. Then Tánaiste Dick Spring was reflecting the view of the establishment when, after an article in the magazine was raised in the chamber, he told the Dáil in 1983: 'Fianna Fáil are really going into the depths when they quote from something which I would not consider an oracle.'[30]

Understandably, as *The Phoenix* tends to reserve particular venom for the world of politics, politicians have not been averse to publicly dismissing it. However, judging by the content, politicians are also not averse to contributing

27 Felix M. Larkin, 'Satirical journalism' in Martin Conboy & Adrian Bingham (eds), *The Edinburgh history of the British and Irish press*, iii: *Competition and disruption, 1900–2017* (Edinburgh, 2020), pp 556–71. 28 Ibid., p. 559. 29 Ibid., p. 565. 30 Dáil Éireann, vol. 334 (10), 8 July 1983.

to the magazine in private, landing little punches in the soft belly of colleagues' political ambition and performance. And some politicians have even praised the magazine, including Mr Spring, who, eight years after his initial dismissive reference, quoted a *Phoenix* article at length in the Dáil in October 1991:

> We have had some mention of the Telecom scandal. The scandal itself was bad enough. I do not know what people are thinking about a country where one can make that kind of money fast, without any risk of exposure. One of the consequences of that scandal was that economic pressure was applied to the task of suppressing a substantial article in relation to this scene. That article was originally to have appeared in *Phoenix* magazine. I do not hold any brief for *Phoenix* magazine but I do take a serious view of arbitrary censorship imposed by virtue of the fact that one is economically and politically strong. I must ask what the people behind the suppression were afraid of in that article, a copy of which I have.[31]

The article in question – about a complex but lucrative property deal involving secret investors including businessmen Dermot Desmond and Michael Smurfit – had been pulled from the magazine when Smurfit Web Press refused to print it.[32] This resulted in the magazine featuring three clear pages where the article was due to appear.[33] For *The Phoenix*, the blank pages were badges of honour. Mulcahy distributed the text to the newspapers and to opposition politicians, which led to then Labour leader Spring reading out the full text under Dáil privilege, meaning newspapers could cover his speech without fear of legal repercussion.

SATIRICAL CRITICISM AND INVESTIGATIVE JOURNALISM

In *Media discourse*, his seminal study in 1995, Norman Fairclough stated that media discourse should be regarded as the site of complex and often contradictory processes, including ideological processes:

> Media texts do indeed function ideologically in social control and social reproduction; but they also operate as cultural commodities in a competitive market, are part of the business of entertaining people, are designed

31 Dáil Éireann, vol. 141 (2), 17 Oct. 1991.   32 Paddy Prendiville, 'John Mulcahy, a journalist for all seasons', *The Phoenix*, 21 Sept. 2018.   33 *Irish Times*, 3 Oct. 1991.

to keep people politically and social informed, are cultural artefacts in their own right informed by particular aesthetics; and they are at the same time caught up in – reflecting and contributing to – shifting cultural values and identities.[34]

The Phoenix is a complex, contrarian and often contradictory publication and, whether one approves of it or not, is most definitely a cultural artefact in its own right informed by particular aesthetics. It seeks to entertain, tease, provoke, critique, criticize, investigate and question and it employs ridicule, parody and satire, along with robust analysis and opinion, expressed forcefully, to get its message across. It is also, as Mulcahy stated in the _Irish Times_ interview before the launch, ideological, particularly in its desire for a more socially just society and a united Ireland.

Since the template for Mulcahy's magazine was _Private Eye_, many of Sharon Lockyer's incisive observations on the British publication arguably can be applied to the Irish magazine.[35] In her survey of the literature she recalls Alvin Kernan's argument that satire exploits humour in order to make a serious point and that humour is used as the 'sugar-coating of the moral pill'.[36] She states that 'satire facilitates the transgression of social norms and mores, allows the journalist to engage in risk-taking and to push at the boundaries of acceptability'.[37] Lockyer adds that although satirical humour and investigative journalism may at first appear distinct due to their discrete modes of address, 'these two types of journalistic techniques do have elective affinity'.[38] Citing David Murphy, she states that the aim of investigative and satirical journalism is to question 'what is routinely taken for granted – the factual reliability of official spokesmen and the institutions they represent' – who are news sources for the mainstream press. Thus, she argues, typical news sources for satirical and investigative journalists include disgruntled police officers, politicians and journalists.[39]

To that list in _The Phoenix_'s case could be added resentful financiers, embittered social butterflies, spiteful legal eagles – indeed a panorama of Irish life, united in its scepticism if not its churlishness. Lockyer argues that this combination of satirical criticism and investigative journalism may be successful because both techniques appeal to the judgment and suspicion that there is large-scale corruption and wrongdoing in politics, public institutions and large corporations that both journalist and reader do not know

---

34 Norman Fairclough, _Media discourse_ (London, 1995), pp 47–8. 35 Sharon Lockyer, 'A two-pronged attack? Exploring _Private Eye_'s satirical humour and investigative reporting', _Journalism Studies_, 7:5 (2006), pp 765–81. 36 Ibid., p. 766. 37 Ibid., p. 767. 38 Ibid. 39 Ibid., p. 768; David Murphy, _The Stalker affair and the press_ (London, 1991), p. 18.

about and that 'they' (politicians and public figures) do not wish us to know. 'It is this approach to politics and public life that connects the two techniques'.[40] That said, Tony Harcup warns that investigative journalism, while achieving notable results such as exposing the source of Charles Haughey's wealth, might be seen as 'perpetuating a myth that society is divided into a large number of fundamentally good people and a smaller number of fundamentally bad people'. Where is the investigative journalism into structural forces in society? he asks. 'Largely notable for its absence. Instead, particularly on television, we tend to have personalised stories of goodies, baddies and heroic reporters.'[41]

The Phoenix has little time for 'heroic reporters' or any other lionized figures in the public sphere such as business people, celebrities of any hue or, of course, politicians. This is as it should be for a satirical/investigative publication. But *The Phoenix*'s attitude to mainstream media seems particularly hostile, being characterized by a scepticism which sometimes bleeds into contempt. The feeling would appear to be mutual given the magazine's lack of profile in mainstream media. 'They hate us', said Paddy Prendiville. 'We are effectively blacked from other media.' He compares the hostile attitude in Ireland to *The Phoenix* with the relative affection in Britain for *Private Eye* – 'and they are much more extreme than us'. He sees *The Phoenix*'s approach to Sinn Féin as 'rebalancing the coverage', believing the magazine to be 'more objective' on this subject than the broad mass of mainstream media. 'At least we admit our bias.'[42] Perhaps this hostility in Ireland is born of closeness, both laying claim to the high moral ground of journalism, of objective truth and honesty. Matt Carlson sees these struggles over journalism as often struggles over boundaries:

> Basic questions of definition – who counts as a journalist, what counts as journalism, what is appropriate journalistic behaviour and what is deviant – are all matters that can be comprehended through the perspective of 'boundary work' ... Contests over journalism's boundaries are symbolic contests in which different actors vie for definitional control to apply or remove the label of journalism.[43]

Here work on the concept of fields by French sociologist Pierre Bourdieu is useful. Sue Robinson notes that one way to think about journalistic boundaries is to call upon Bourdieu's conceptualization of journalism as a field

---

40 Ibid., p. 771.   41 Tony Harcup, *Journalism: principles and practice* (London, 2009), pp 99–100.   42 Interview with author, 28 Sept. 2020.   43 Matt Carlson, 'Introduction' in Matt Carlson & Seth C. Lewis (eds), *Boundaries of journalism: professionalism, practices and participation* (New York, 2015), pp 1–18 at p. 2.

made up of actors who manoeuvre for position as influential information disseminators:

> To be considered members of the profession (and the field), all journalists must follow the rules of objectivity and other professional tenets. These could be considered the field agents' *habitus*; in field theory, an actor's *habitus* incorporates his or her background, norms, values, and belief system that guides what they do according to their positions in the field.[44]

According to Rodney Benson and Erik Neveu, 'in the ongoing struggle that is society, two forms of power, or what Bourdieu terms "capital", are crucial: economic and cultural'. Economic means simply money or assets that can be turned into money. Cultural capital covers such things as educational credentials, technical expertise, general knowledge, verbal abilities and artistic sensibilities. The social world is structured around the tension between these two forms of power.[45]

It is obvious that *The Phoenix*'s economic power is limited, but its cultural capital is much more abundant. And it is more than happy to flaunt it, to assert its superiority, mocking, ridiculing, satirizing, investigating, revealing, commenting, critiquing, revelling in its self-appointed role as an arbiter of truth, publishing 'the inside stories on what's really going in Ireland', as it states on its website.[46] Robinson cites Berkowitz's argument that when journalists publish criticism of those who deviate from the accepted norms of the field, they protect their authority as information disseminators by undermining those who step outside the community standards.[47] Some mainstream journalists and public figures generally would argue that *The Phoenix* flouts journalistic norms, that its work cannot be trusted, that it is mere gossip, hearsay, entertainment, that it is politically biased in favour of the left, and particularly Sinn Féin. As such, it would follow that *The Phoenix*'s journalism lacks the authority of the mainstream press and does not warrant being considered part of the journalistic field or, at best, should be seen as on the periphery. It is an outsider. However, Robinson cites Bourdieu as making the important point that when interlopers enter the field and commit challenging acts on a consistent basis, they can shift the boundaries if they are 'listened to'. The success, notes Robinson, of an interloper hinges on Bourdieu's statement about

---

44 Sue Robinson, 'Redrawing borders from within: commenting on news stories as boundaries work' in *Boundaries of journalism*, pp 152–8 at p. 154. 45 Rodney Benson & Eric Neveu (eds), *Bourdieu and the journalistic field* (Cambridge, 2009), p. 4. 46 www.thephoenix.ie/about-us/. 47 Robinson, 'Redrawing borders from within', p. 155.

being 'listened to'. 'Without influence', states Robinson, 'a new agent has little chance of changing anything. That said, once an actor attains authority, he or she can force some field movement. As Bourdieu wrote: "The boundary of the field is a stake of struggles".'[48]

This issue of being an interloper or an outsider in the journalistic field is further complicated by the fact that often *The Phoenix* is seen to be biting the hand that feeds it, in that it specializes in insider stories. So no matter in what field of Irish life a particular story is situated – racing, theatre, books, television, business – it is clear that the tipoff is frequently from within. On its website the publication states: 'Goldhawk seeks to supply the Inside Stories from sensitive areas and his discerning readers are often the best source of information, which can be provided anonymously on the hot line.'[49] Insider information can be loaded information as well as shining a necessary light on nefarious practices. The provider may have a motive other than a belief in freedom of information. Anonymous sources can be a mixed blessing for all media, but a magazine such as *The Phoenix* which trades on such titbits is vulnerable to manipulation. Prendiville is awake to that vulnerability and states, in response, that all information provided by sources is fully checked out for accuracy.[50] Former *Phoenix* journalists attest to this insistence on stringent verification. That said, those who see themselves as victims of *The Phoenix*'s spotlight would no doubt think differently.

It is also worth noting that the many of the magazine's news stories and commentaries are in line with standard news values, as outlined by Harcup and O'Neill. The categories include:

- *Exclusivity*: Stories generated by, or available first to, the news organization as a result of interviews, letters, investigations, surveys, polls, and so on.
- *Conflict*: Stories concerning conflict such as controversies, arguments, splits, strikes, fights, insurrections and warfare.
- *The power elite*: Stories concerning powerful individuals, organizations, institutions or corporations.
- *Relevance*: Stories about groups or nations perceived to be influential with, or culturally or historically familiar to, the audience.
- *Celebrity*: Stories concerning people who are already famous.
- *News organization's agenda*: Stories that set or fit the news organization's own agenda, whether ideological, commercial or as part of a specific campaign.[51]

48 Ibid. **49** www.thephoenix.ie/about-us/. **50** Interview with author, 28 Sept. 2020. **51** Tony Harcup & Deirdre O'Neill, 'News values revisited (again)', *Journalism Studies*, 18:12 (2017), pp 1470–88.

COVERS AND SECTIONS

Magazine covers are important statements of editorial and cultural identity and also help to drive sales. Jenkins and Tandoc state that the impact of magazine covers reflects the sociocultural influence of magazines as a mass medium; they are also 'cultural markers' reflecting the social and cultural reality in which they are produced.[52] American journalism academic Ted Spiker says that like no other medium, magazines rely on this singular page to do two crucial things: one, send a message about the personality and voice of the magazine; and two, sell issues.[53] Though the fight for journalism's soul is constantly contested in the pages of *The Phoenix*, the real target through its history has been what it perceives as the shallow, hypocritical and even venal nature of institutions and public figures, particularly church, state and business, but not exclusively so. The primary visual platform for this frame is the image-based cover with balloon caption, frequently dialogic, tied to a current news topic. This balloon caption concept was a straight lift from *Private Eye*, which continues the practice to this day. The concept arguably can be traced to the Situationists International, a small group of French cultural and political revolutionaries in the 1950s and 1960s who built a movement around their critique of mass media and advertising aimed at undermining what they saw as capitalism's totalitarian influence. It involved taking a found object, for instance an anodyne handout image of leading politicians, and subverting its meaning with a clearly fake balloon caption. The Situationists called this 'détournement', 'the excision of an item of culture (whether image, text or object) from its normative context and its subsequent juxtaposition with another fragment in order to establish an analogical relationship between the two'.[54]

An example would be *The Phoenix* cover of 4–17 October 2019, which, under the headline 'Brexit Countdown', showed then minister for foreign affairs Simon Coveney and then Taoiseach Leo Varadkar, with Coveney's bubble caption stating, 'We're just as prepared as the rugby team', and Varadkar replying, 'So we're kicking to touch'. It is both humorous and strong commentary, mashing up the disappointing Irish rugby team's performance in the World Cup with the government's Brexit strategy. Another, earlier, example would be issue of 15 July 1988, in which then Fianna Fáil TD Ben Briscoe is

52 Joy Jenkins & Edson C. Tandoc Jnr, 'The power of the cover: symbolic contests around the Boston bombing suspect's *Rolling Stone* cover', *Journalism*, 18:3 (2015), pp 281–97.   53 Ted Spiker, 'The magazine cover: the craft of identity and impact' in David Abrahamson, Marcia R. Prior-Miller & Bill Emmott (eds), *The Handbook of magazine research* (New York, 2015), pp 377–91.   54 Adrienne Russell, *Networked: a contemporary history of news in transition* (Cambridge, 2011), p. 5.

pictured embracing his leader, Charles J. Haughey. Haughey's bubble caption states, 'I love you, Terry'; Briscoe 'replies': 'Sober up, Boss'. This cover alluded to Haughey's affair with celebrity journalist Terry Keane, an open secret in media circles. Three years later, in the issue of 17 May 1991, the magazine used on the cover a photograph of Keane and Haughey together at a social occasion. Haughey's caption stated: 'There'll be no groping of journalists in the Dáil'; Keane's caption: 'Where do you suggest, then?' It would be another eight years before Keane publicly confirmed the relationship. Haughey was a regular on the cover, though very rarely, if ever, to his benefit. In 1991 alone he was featured in ten of the twenty-four covers.

Laddish sexual innuendoes were a staple, particularly in the early years. Women were rarely featured in their own right. An exception was then President Mary Robinson, who was pictured with her husband Nick in the edition of 29 June 1991. Her caption: 'Haughey's trying to shut me up' and his: 'He's a better man than I am'. By 1993, the magazine was celebrating '10 years on the boil' and Mrs Robinson was featured on the cover (4 June 1993) with the UK's Queen Elizabeth at Buckingham Palace. It was another cover loaded with sexual innuendo, this time with shades of homophobia. Mrs Robinson's caption: 'How's the queen?' Queen Elizabeth: 'Edward's fine, thank you'. There was also much pointed social commentary: the cover of 11 April 1986, under the headline 'Divorce Crisis', shows two members of the Catholic hierarchy in conversation with their backs to the camera. One caption states: 'Our position on marital breakdown is clear …' and the other caption replies: '… we're turning our backs on it'. Later that month, the first divorce referendum was defeated.

Considering the impact of the Troubles, North and South, the covers are notable for the scant reference to the bloodiness of the IRA's armed campaign. In explanation, Paddy Prendiville states that it is a rule that the cover never makes light of tragedy or violence.[55] But there have been references to the armed campaign, such as the cover of the 7 November 1986: under the black-bordered headline 'Dearly Departed' Sinn Féin president Gerry Adams is pictured with Ruairí Ó Brádaigh as the latter inspects a silver tray. Ó Brádaigh had split with Sinn Féin to form Republican Sinn Féin that year. Adams' caption reads: 'And this is a farewell gift'; Ó Brádaigh's caption: 'When does it go off?' Black humour also informs another Adams cover, dated 20 October 2006. In what appears to be a doctored image – occasionally the magazine exercises artistic licence and inserts cut-outs of personalities into images – he

---

55 Interview with author, 28 Sept. 2020. Prendiville added that the IRA was not alone in committing atrocities.

is seen with the Democratic Unionist Party leader Ian Paisley. Paisley's caption is: 'Will you recognise the police?'; Adams' caption: 'Sure we've photos of most of them!' But generally the Sinn Féin leader, though frequently featured, unsurprisingly given the magazine's republican sympathies, gets off lightly. There is even a note of admiration in the 'Goodbye Grizzly Adams' cover of 9 February 2018, in which his successor Mary Lou McDonald shares a humorous moment with him. McDonald's caption is: 'So you're finally decommissioned Gerry'; Adams' caption: 'I haven't gone away you know.'

There also could be an element of cruelty and public shaming in the way the cover amplified personal issues in scoring political points. The edition of 20 May 1994 featured former Progressive Democrats leader Dessie O'Malley at a party conference with Pat Cox, who had recently lost the leadership election to Mary Harney. O'Malley's caption is: 'The party is bigger than any one man'; Cox's caption: 'So is Mary Harney'. And, of course, they could also be very funny and biting at the same time. The 13 March 2009 cover features Bono and his U2 comrade the Edge. Bono's caption is: 'We can still hold the high notes'; The Edge: 'Safe in a Dutch bank account'. Bono was a regular target, but compared to Bertie Ahern he got off lightly.

The former Fianna Fáil leader and taoiseach was featured many times on the cover as well as being the inspiration for one of the magazine's long-running series, 'De Diary of a Nortsoide Taoiseach' (a mocking reference to his broad Dublin accent), in which his frequent use of mixed metaphors and other linguistic adventures were ruthlessly pilloried. Ahern, famously described by Charles Haughey as the 'the most devious, and the most cunning of them all', is often framed as such in the covers, though he is also depicted as a 'chancer' or a somewhat hapless victim of his very public relationship with Celia Larkin.[56] His description of himself as a socialist inspired the memorable cover of 3 December 2004 in which he is depicted as Che Guevara with a single-word caption: 'Venceremos!'. While Ahern has been a favourite target, all taoisigh have received the cover treatment; it goes with the job. Indeed, the first taoiseach to receive a cover was Fine Gael's Garret FitzGerald, in the edition of 18 February 1983. It was a very clever and apposite commentary on the government's position on the proposed amendment to the proposed wording for the constitutional amendment on abortion. FitzGerald's coalition government with the Labour Party, elected towards the end of 1982, had inherited the wording of a proposed amendment from the outgoing Fianna Fáil administration. Alongside a heading 'Amendment Aborted', a photograph of an emollient FitzGerald carried the caption: 'It wasn't MY baby.'

---

56 See *Irish Independent*, 26 Apr. 2008 for context of the Haughey quote.

The covers were mostly aimed at making a serious point through humour, and *The Phoenix*'s catalogue of strip cartoons, pocket cartoons and visual satire was equally primed to take advantage of a left-leaning view of current affairs. Cartoonists through the years have included Graeme Keys, Aidan Dowling, Paul Keane and John Chambers (responsible for the rueful 'Adventures of Festy O'Semtex'), Niall Murphy and Sean Lennon. Given space constraints it is not possible to address this work in depth, but it is an important part of the magazine's identity and story. Nor is it possible to track all the stories, hits and misses, since 1983. However, leading journalist Miriam Lord, referring to the magazine's thirtieth anniversary, was correct when she stated that 'while *The Phoenix* may not always get everything right, the magazine has broken more than its fair share of scoops over the years'.[57] These included the aforementioned revelation that it was Charles Haughey who had received £1 million from Ben Dunne (4 Dec. 1996); the pension of €27.6 million paid to Irish Nationwide's Michael Fingleton, known as 'Fingers' to its readers (27 June 2008); the fact that celebrity cleric and 'moral custodian' Michael Cleary had fathered a child with his housekeeper (14 Jan. 1994) and the revelation that Anglo-Irish Bank was 'technically bankrupt' (12 Dec. 2008). Prendiville described this as the 'quintessential example of Goldhawk's ongoing tussle with the rich and powerful'.[58]

From the start the fortnightly magazine was printed in A4 size and the cover used colour with *The Phoenix* masthead rendered in red. Up until 1994 the images had been mainly monochrome. As press colour images became more widely available, *The Phoenix* followed suit. It is remarkable, however, how little the magazine has changed over the years. It has expanded, of course, in pagination and range of content and it is now a very slick, professional production. But the core of the magazine remains as in the first edition of 7 January 1983. The masthead remains exactly the same, including *The Phoenix* logo, which was drawn by cartoonist Tom Mathews; Mathews also drew the logos for the various sections, according to Paddy Prendiville.[59] The cover price was 60p, a little less than €1 in today's terms. The first cover featured a former minister for justice, the late Seán Doherty, under the heading 'Bugging Probe'. His balloon caption states: 'Bugger off.' About 25 per cent of the thirty-two pages were advertisements. And they were quality advertisements from the likes of semi-state companies and banks, i.e. companies that would pay their bills and might include *The Phoenix* in future ad campaigns. Mulcahy's connections to the business world were paying off. And so it remains. The edition of

57 *Irish Times*, 18 May 2013. **58** Prendiville, 'A journalist for all seasons', *The Phoenix*, 21 Sept. 2018. **59** Interview with author, 28 Sept. 2020.

13 March 2020 features full-page ads for the likes of the ESB and Volvo, plus a six-page advertising feature for Environmental Ireland with Coillte and the Dublin Port Company among its main contributors. The addition of advertising features into the editorial mix is a strange and uncomfortable fit. But as income tightens for all print products, the need to create new forms of revenue forces hard decisions.

The sections such as 'Affairs of the Nation', 'Fit to Print', 'Bird's Eye View' and 'Pillars of Society' were in place in the first edition, as were 'Moneybags', 'High Society' and the 'Sport of Kings'. In time they have been augmented by the likes of 'The Last Refuge', 'The Young Bloods' and 'Northwind', the latter covering the North. The North was well represented in the first edition, with a long feature on 'Sodom and Kincora', the east Belfast boys' home scandal. *The Phoenix* followed this story of institutional child abuse keenly. It had many of its favourite ingredients: allegations of British intelligence involvement, cover-ups and nefarious loyalists. Another favourite, Charles Haughey, also turns up in round one of the magazine's long fight focusing on the source of his then mysterious wealth: 'C.J. bags £1.4 million in secret land deal'. By the end of 1983, the spine of the magazine was essentially settled. The pagination would range from thirty-two to forty-eight pages; the lower figure when ads were light and the higher figure when business was booming. The standard size was forty pages. There are twenty-four editions each year, plus an annual published for the Christmas market, which is essentially a bumper edition.

While Mulcahy and Prendiville have been the guiding journalistic lights, people familiar with the magazine state that deputy editor Paul Farrell, who joined in 1990, is both hugely influential and prodigiously productive. 'Paul is just a bulldog', said one former insider in admiration, 'and he is not ideological'.[60] Prendiville and Farrell essentially divide the magazine between them – the front half, politics, media etc., is mainly written by Prendiville, while the back end, the 'money end', i.e. business and finance, is Farrell's preserve. They are now the only full-time journalists, but in the magazine's heyday there would have been up to five full-time journalists. As the edition deadline nears they are assisted by two part-time production journalists: a design editor and a sub-editor. Freelance writers are engaged when needed. And, most important, a solicitor arrives into the office shortly before the magazine goes to press to check every line for legal issues. Following that regime has helped the magazine avoid major and costly legal actions though the nature of the magazine's content, rightly or wrongly, is an invitation to take offence. One freelance journalist recalled apologizing to Mulcahy in his office over an error that had

60 Interview with author, 8 Oct. 2020.

led to a legal issue. Mulcahy replied that 'for God's sake I'm the boss here' – it was his responsibility to shoulder. He then opened a press to reveal bundles of legal documents: 'These are all libel writs over which I've had many sleepless nights … we must always check, check and check again.'[61] Some lawsuits succeeded, particularly in the early years, but given the controversial nature of the content it is remarkable that the magazine suffered few really damaging actions, with the exception of when the MEP Avril Doyle was awarded a six-figure sum in costs and damages in 1995.

There have, of course, been controversies. One of the most bitter centred on journalist and Church of Ireland rector Stephen Hilliard, who was killed on 9 January 1990, during a robbery at his home in Rathdrum, Co. Wicklow. Shortly after his death, *The Phoenix* alleged that earlier in his life Hilliard had been a member of the IRA. This prompted an angry response from his family and his former colleagues in the *Irish Times*.[62] The latter tried to get the National Union of Journalists to censure *The Phoenix* journalists. Initially they succeeded but that decision was overturned on appeal. Hilliard's wife Betty also sought leave in the high court to begin a criminal prosecution for the publication of a libel in the magazine. Mr Justice Sean Gannon stated that because of the state of the law he had to refuse the application. But, describing the article as scurrilous and contrived, he added that it was difficult to believe that either Mulcahy or Prendiville could stoop so low as to present or adopt such 'a mean, spiteful and wounding attack upon a deceased under the guise of a commentary on his funeral'.[63] Prendiville remains adamant that *The Phoenix* was right to publish, citing the fact that the NUJ cleared the magazine of any wrongdoing.[64] He added that the story was sourced from IRA figures angry that Hilliard's involvement was being airbrushed, notably by the *Irish Times*.

If investigative journalism can backfire, satire and ridicule is also high-wire discourse. In perfect pitch it can be funny, revealing and telling; get it wrong and it can seem mean-spirited, cruel and hurtful. 'Obviously, there have been times when I've felt sorry for people we've written about', Prendiville told *Hot Press* in 2002:

> But you've got to just treat a subject of a story as part of the trade, like a doctor looks at a leg and treats it as part of a body … I'm never quite sure what's meant by a private life. Most of the people whose so-called

---

61 Interview with author, 12 July 2020. 62 The author was a member of the *Irish Times* National Union of Journalists chapel (branch) at the time. 63 *Irish Times*, 3 Mar. 1990. 64 Interview with author, 28 Sept. 2020.

private lives would be of interest are very prominent personalities, who normally project their private lives onto the public through public relations profiles of themselves, their family, their social lives and so on. What they mean by their private lives is that part of their private life that they don't want you to read about.[65]

In business terms *The Phoenix* has seen better days. John Mulcahy's son, Aengus, now owns the magazine through the company Penfield Enterprises Ltd. Unlike his father, it is believed he has no editorial role. Although Prendiville states that up to 2,000 digital subscribers have been added in 2020, the magazine was still advertising its 2018 circulation of 11,710 copies as late as summer 2020.[66] Given the difficult trading conditions during the COVID pandemic of 2020 and the general downward trend of print publications, it is very unlikely that future audits will improve on that figure. While times look uncertain, *The Phoenix* is not the only print publication facing a difficult future.

CONCLUSION

In a way everything in *The Phoenix* is a rebuke to mainstream media, not just the stories, speculation and satire about the media and its journalists, but the stories and speculation that the media does and doesn't cover in politics, the law, entertainment, business and sport; without the mainstream media and its journalism, *The Phoenix* would be devoid of an essential foil. It frames this as a classic David vs Goliath battle. Its unwavering belief in its self-appointed mission to inform, investigate and comment as it sees fit, to subvert the established narrative at every twist and turn, has fuelled the magazine in its reporting and its satire for almost forty years. When the magazine was launched in 1983, the country was in disarray, its politics and its economy reeling from repeated crises – perfect territory for a magazine fired with real journalistic zeal and attitude and unafraid of the consequences. Today, it is a much different place. In recent years *The Phoenix* has broken fewer major stories. Is this because Ireland is now less corrupt, is now a more open society? No, says Prendiville, 'they have just become better at hiding it'.[67]

Perhaps. Or maybe the magazine's best days are behind it. Certainly the energy that infused it at its peak seems in shorter supply these days. Hamstrung by fewer staff, there seem to be fewer original stories – not just fewer major stories. Commentary/reviews are more pervasive, often coloured by a tone of

---

65 *Hot Press*, 20 Sept. 2002.   66 Interview with author, 28 Sept. 2020.   67 Ibid.

bitter frustration, the cloak of the outsider. The sense is that its power and influence are on the wane.

It is also notable that with the rise of social media, where people play fast and loose with facts, rumour and innuendo, *The Phoenix* has lost some of its traction. Indeed, the internet generally has not been good to the magazine. Prendiville agrees that the magazine is playing catch-up in the digital space – the bulk of the material on its website is from its print edition. News and opinion travel so fast these days that a fortnightly magazine can seem out of date before it even hits the shops. And there is a sense that its satire, once so sharp and savage, now lacks the edginess and immediacy of the online *Waterford Whispers* for example.

That sense of decline may be correct, or this fallow period could be just that, a low point. But it should not, whatever the future holds, detract from the remarkable impact this little magazine has had on the chattering, political and business classes through its history. Without doubt, it has made mistakes, exercised poor judgment, encouraged more enemies than is healthy and lost more friends than is wise. But equally it has been true to Mulcahy's original aims to expose corruption, highlight political chicanery, defend neutrality and advocate for a united Ireland.[68] Readers didn't have to buy into every aspect of this ideology to appreciate the edgy scepticism, the racy insider stories and speculation, the irreverent/mocking tone and the frequently well-aimed cartoons. The magazine's contrarian DNA also encouraged it to ferret out stories of national importance such as Haughey's finances. Against that the magazine's relatively soft ride for Sinn Féin must have irritated many.

But perhaps John Mulcahy's influence will live on not in what he did but how he did it. Barry J. Whyte, in his tribute after his former boss' death, stated: 'While *The Phoenix* may give the impression that it's a cynical, chip-on-the-shoulder scandal rag that's interested only in the bad news and the sordid gossip about well-known figures, it was actually an incredible place for a young journalist to learn how to write news stories … Mulcahy had a sense that teaching proper scepticism – as opposed to mere cynicism – was a vital part of education of the next generation of Irish journalists.'[69]

---

68 *Irish Times*, 7 Jan. 1983.   69 *Sunday Business Post*, 9 Sept. 2018.

6 / *Honesty* and *Publicity*: two periodicals, one man's war on cant in the Irish Free State

ANTHONY KEATING

Between 1925 and 1931 the socialist-republican editor James W. Upton sequentially edited two radical journals, *Honesty: A Weekly Journal of Independent Criticism* and the very short-lived *Publicity: Ireland's National Weekly Review*. These publications were both characterized by Upton's commitment to attack 'cant' and advocate for the oppressed sections of the Irish Free State's population. They thus represent in effect one publication, under one editor and three different owners. *Honesty* was published between February 1925 and February 1931, and was initially part of the Gaelic Press stable owned by Upton's close friend and collaborator Joseph Stanley. It had had a brief prior existence, with Stanley as owner and Upton as editor, from October 1915 to April 1916.

Stanley sold his interest in the Gaelic Press in March 1929. At this point *Honesty*'s ownership was transferred to a collection of businessmen with whom Upton was quickly to fall out, as they attempted to control the editorial direction of the journal in order to increase advertising and circulation – a development that Upton viewed as corrupting the core ethos and editorial standards of the journal. Upon Upton's resignation, the owners of *Honesty* planned to do away with the name and to replace it with a new title, *Nationality*, but there is no evidence this publication was ever produced. The decision to change the name of the journal was indicative of the owner's desire to rebrand what was, by this stage, a failing publication that Upton had moulded in his own image and had been blacklisted by the very organization, Fianna Fáil, from whose membership and supporters *Honesty* had drawn a large section of its readership. Three months after his departure from *Honesty*, Upton launched *Publicity*, which he owned and edited, leaving him free of any interference from owners who did not share his vision, or placed profit over what Upton viewed as the mission of journalism: to speak truth to power, irrespective of the personal or business cost. While the title had changed, *Honesty* and *Publicity* shared the same strapline, a quotation much loved by Upton, from Shakespeare's *Henry VIII* (which is also carved onto Upton's headstone), 'Be Just and Fear Not'. This philosophy ensured that *Publicity* was short-lived. Just as Upton transferred his journalistic vision, he also transferred his commercial weaknesses. *Publicity* ceased publication in January 1932, the date that Upton's distinguished career as an editor also ended. This chapter explores Upton's journey to the editorship of these journals and his tenure as their editor, arguing that his journalistic legacy, notwithstanding his lack of business acumen, is one of considerable importance, speaking truth to power in the contested terrain of the first decade of the Free State.

JAMES W. UPTON

Upton was born in Waterford in 1872 and attended Mount Sion Christian Brothers school, where he developed a lifelong passion for Gaelic games. He cut his journalistic teeth as a cub reporter on the *Waterford Star* and soon developed a national reputation as a Gaelic games journalist, under the pen name 'Vigilant'. A close friend of Arthur Griffith, Upton played an important role in organizing Sinn Féin, both in Waterford and nationally, providing copy for the *Sinn Féin* newspaper until its suppression in 1914. While Upton's Sinn Féin activity eventually forced him to resign from his post at the *Waterford Star*, he quickly gained employment as editor of the *Kilkenny Journal*, a moderate nationalist publication that became increasingly radical under his editorship. During Upton's editorship of the *Kilkenny Journal*, his uncompromising stance in supporting socialist and trade union causes led him into a dispute with a well-known local Sinn Féin firebrand, the editor of the *Kilkenny People*, E.T. Keane.[1] In March 1919 Upton spoke at a rally in support of workers striking to achieve union recognition at the Kilkenny-based motor company Statham & Co. During the rally, the spirit of Red Clydeside was invoked, and the red flag was waved and sung. A local trade union organizer stated that the *Kilkenny People* had refused to print handbills for the strikers as Stratham often placed advertisements in the title. Upton made a speech at the rally accusing other Kilkenny newspapers of carrying adverts for 'blackleg labour' to break the strike. Keane immediately struck back, insinuating that Upton and the *Kilkenny Journal* had received favourable treatment under the censorship ushered in with the 1914 Defence of the Realm Act (DORA), censorship under which the *Kilkenny People* had been harassed.[2] This was a clear inference that the *Kilkenny Journal* and its editor had, for some reason, found favour with the British

---

1 Marie Coleman, 'Keane, Edward Thomas ('E.T.')' in *Dictionary of Irish biography* (http://dib.cambridge. org/) – hereafter, *DIB*. 2 The Defence of the Realm Act (DORA) was passed in the United Kingdom on 8 Aug. 1914, on its entry into the First World War. This legislation gave the government wide-ranging powers during the war, not least regarding censorship. An amendment to Regulation 21 in September 1914 asserted: 'No person shall by word of mouth or in writing spread reports likely to cause disaffection or alarm among any of His Majesty's forces or among the civilian population.'

authorities – an insinuation that affronted Upton. Keane's initial assault was
followed by a second swipe at Upton's reputation when he attacked the *Journal*
for hypocrisy over running adverts to recruit Irishmen into the British military
while espousing the Sinn Féin cause. Keane argued that greed had motivated
the decision to publish the adverts, something that Keane had refused to do,
notwithstanding the lucrative incentives, in order to save young Irishmen from
slaughter in the service of the crown. These attacks clearly stung Upton, who
replied in the next edition of the *Journal*. Stating that he took sole responsibility for his speech, he assured his readers that he would always defend his class
against those who would exploit workers. Regarding Keane's charge of hypocrisy, Upton asserted that Keane had been wrong to attack him for the adverts
displayed in the newspaper as he had no control over this as an editor, arguing
it was a decision taken by the owner and not the editor.[3] Notwithstanding this
defence, the charge clearly stung Upton as in later years he became hypersensi-
tive in ensuring that adverts placed in any journal that he edited afforded no
opportunity for any such claim.

Upton, in addition to his work on the *Kilkenny Journal*, wrote weekly copy
for Joseph Stanley's Gaelic Press publication *Gaelic Athlete* and was a leading
light on several 'mosquito press' publications,[4] also produced at Stanley's print
works. He edited *Scissors and Paste, Honesty* and *The Spark*, under the pseudonyms Ed Dalton and Gilbert Galbraith, both pen names he resurrected during
Honesty's second run.[5] During March 1916, the Gaelic Press' printing presses
were seized by the British authorities, but Stanley and Upton continued their
work using a borrowed printing press in the basement of Liberty Hall, under
an armed guard provided by the Irish Citizen Army.[6] Subsequently, Upton
and Stanley were attached to the General Post Office garrison, the epicentre
of the Easter Rising. Under orders from Pádraig Pearse and James Connolly,
they commandeered a small printing works in Halston Street, from where
they printed Pearse's bulletins to the citizens of Dublin.[7] Indeed, what was
due to be the last issue of *Honesty*'s initial run (October 1915 to April 1916)
was produced under the title *Irish War News*, the only publication known to
have been printed during the Rising in the area of central Dublin controlled
by the rebels.[8] Following the Rising, Upton avoided arrest, slipping back to
Kilkenny to continue his editorial role and republican agitation, notably using
the *Kilkenny Journal*'s presses to publish the short-lived yet influential republican

3 *Kilkenny Journal*, 5 Apr. 1919.   4 A term used to describe revolutionary publications, usually short lived,
that published below the 'radar' of the governments that they opposed.   5 Ben Novick, *Conceiving revolution: Irish nationalist propaganda during the First World War* (Dublin, 2001), p. 34.   6 James W. Upton, 'History
of the GAA' [unpublished] (Dublin, 1934).   7 Tom Reilly, *Joe Stanley: printer to the Rising* (Dublin, 2005), p.
33.   8 *Honesty*, 10 Aug. 1929.

journal *The Phoenix*.[9] Upton resigned as editor of the *Kilkenny Journal* in 1922. His journalistic contribution to the republican cause was acknowledged in 1936 by Joseph J. Bouch of the National Library, who, writing in the *Irish Press*, described Upton as 'next to Griffith the most trenchant of republican journalists'.[10] Upton's career under British rule had been punctuated by a fiercely independent, uncompromising voice, a feature of his journalism that would continue in the Irish Free State, irrespective of which party was in power. His republican credentials and his close friendships with many leading republicans may go some considerable way to explaining why Upton was able to say the things he did about the realities of life in the Free State, in the uncompromising way he did, for so long. Upton's republican campaigning credentials, combined with the fact that he had worked with Joseph Stanley to produce and distribute *Irish War News* during the 1916 Rising, afforded him a significant store of social and political capital that he was to deploy in the service of the marginalized, or rather those marginalized sections of society Upton had sympathy for and found common cause with, though these conspicuously did not include homosexuals, or Ireland's Jewish population. Upton's stance on exposing the realities of life in the Free State was tolerated until the strategic direction of Fianna Fáil's political manoeuvring ensured that his nuisance value was to eventually trump his political capital.

HONESTY

On 28 February 1925, the journal *Honesty: A Weekly Journal of Independent Criticism* commenced publication. Upton had chosen this name as he viewed its mission as to continue the radical editorial policy that he had pursued in the editions of *Honesty* he edited between October 1915 and April 1916. *Honesty's* second incarnation was forthright and uncompromising, and by far and away the most socially radical journal published in the Free State, exposing what it viewed as Ireland's sordid underbelly and the cant of its political and journalistic classes. Upton, from the very beginning, made it clear that *Honesty* would publish without fear or favour, asserting, 'our pages will have at times to express many hard and unpalatable facts on different men and matters and on many phases of social and national life'.[11] The journal combined in-house reporting and comment with opinion pieces that were frequently printed under pseudonyms.[12] From the very beginning Upton pursued a policy of inviting

9 *Kilkenny Journal*, 4 Feb. 1922.   10 *Irish Press*, 15 Apr. 1936.   11 *Honesty*, 28 Feb. 1925.   12 Names including 'Mia-Eow', 'Red Light', 'Investigator' and 'Progress'.

controversial contributors with whose views he did not necessarily concur. Indeed, this policy ultimately played a significant part in *Honesty*'s demise. It is difficult to ascertain how much of the copy that appeared in *Honesty* under the guise of being written by staff writers was penned directly by Upton, but much of its content, stylistically, indicates this possibility, as does the deployment of pen names associated with Upton's earlier journalism. Whatever the reality of its in-house authorship, *Honesty*'s formula quickly established a healthy nationwide readership and attracted high-profile contributors that included W.T. Cosgrave, president of the Executive Council, and Éamon de Valera, the leader of Sinn Féin and later Fianna Fáil. Notwithstanding the fact that documentary evidence regarding *Honesty*'s print runs, sales and distribution is virtually non-existent, when secondary evidence is considered, *Honesty*'s first three years of publication indicates that it was a successful and growing publication. One indicator of this is the willingness of high-profile figures to pen articles for its pages. Additionally, the number of its pages increased from sixteen to twenty-eight in its first three years of publication before falling back to sixteen pages in the wake of a debacle with Fianna Fáil (explored below). Additionally, its readers' letters indicate a wide geographical spread of readers within Ireland and the UK. A further indication of the paper's success was its steadily improving advertising content, which, over its first three years of production, saw a rise in the number of adverts carried, as well as a move from exclusively local Dublin advertisers to include some regional advertising and national advertisers, such as Irish BP and Hutchinson's Tyres.

Written for a literate, engaged readership, *Honesty* commanded attention because of the reality it portrayed and the socio-political analysis it offered, exploring issues usually viewed in the Free State as the product of personal depravity and/or spiritual and social inadequacy.[13] Domestic issues covered included political corruption, poor educational opportunities, poverty driving women into prostitution, poor health and housing, unemployment, the maltreatment of children in the care of the state and the plight of unmarried mothers and their children.[14] *Honesty*'s international coverage included critiques of Britain's wider colonial policy, which, in common with its domestic coverage, was viewed through an anti-capitalist, anti-civilizing-mission, anti-imperial lens that anticipated the work of later post-colonial theorists.[15] In

---

13 Harry Ferguson, 'Abused and looked after children as "moral dirt": child abuse and institutional care in historical perspective', *Journal of Social Policy*, 36:1 (2007), 123–39; Una Crowley & Rob Kitchin, 'Producing "decent" girls: governmentality and the moral geographies of sexual conduct in Ireland (1922–37)', *Gender, Place and Culture*, 15:4 (2008), 355–72. 14 Anthony Keating, '*Honesty*: the stinging fly on the rump of Free State respectability', *Estudios Irlandeses*, 12 (2017), 60–72. 15 For examples see *Honesty*, 7 Mar. 1925, 7 May 1925, 27 July 1929, and 21 Sept. 1929.

this regard, *Honesty* was part of a rich vein of republican journalism offered in a range of mosquito press publications produced in Ireland in the 1920s and 1930s.[16] However, unlike many of these publications, *Honesty* published openly and while dissatisfied with partition, was not a revolutionary anti-statist publication. Upton, though conceiving *Honesty* as a serious journalistic irritant to the political settlement that created the Free State, believed that it should operate within that political settlement to advocate for the poor and to challenge partition. There were, however, less progressive and, from a contemporary perspective, contradictory aspects to the journalism of *Honesty*, not least its anti-Semitism, a feature that found some traction in Irish republican circles of the period.[17] Additionally, homosexuality, dance halls, jazz, cabaret and contraception were castigated in its pages, and, despite its editor's adherence to freedom of journalistic speech and expression, *Honesty* was largely supportive of literary and advertising censorship of what it viewed as salacious material that was likely to harm public morality.

It regularly deployed cartoons to very good effect to drive home its written journalistic narrative and this usage is no better illustrated than in support of its anti-Semitic content. 'Your Money or Your Life', published 31 October 1925, was supported by two cartoons, one of a caricatured Jewish man counting coins with the legend 'A Vampire' and the other of an Irish woman, babe in arms, sitting dejectedly before an empty hearth with the legend, 'A Victim'. These cartoons would not have seemed out of place in European ultra-right-wing publications of the day and this kind of anti-Semitic cartoon had been a feature in earlier Irish publications.[18] However, Upton, even in articles that attacked certain Jews for seducing young Christian women and for immorality in trade, both mainstream and moneylending, would go to the effort of saying that he was not 'anti-Hebrew', that he welcomed the fact that Ireland had a Jewish population and that he acknowledged the positivity they brought to Irish society.[19] Additionally, Upton regularly asserted that sectarianism of any sort was at odds with republicanism. An example of his views on this subject were published in *Publicity*, on 23 May 1931:

> The Editor of Publicity has now, as in previous journals with which he was connected preached the nationalism of Wolfe Tone, Davis and

---

16 Caoilfhionn Ní Bheacháin, 'The mosquito press: anti-imperialist rhetoric in republican journalism, 1926–39', *Éire-Ireland*, 42:1–2 (2007), 256–89. 17 Dermot Keogh, *Jews in twentieth-century Ireland* (Cork, 1998); Bryan Fanning, *Racism and social change in the Republic of Ireland* (Manchester, 2012). 18 One example being in Thomas Fitzpatrick's, *The Lepracaun Cartoon Monthly*, a favourite of Dublin society published 1905–15. See James Curry & Ciaran Wallace, *Thomas Fitzpatrick and* The Lepracaun Cartoon Monthly (Dublin, 2015). 19 *Honesty*, 7 Mar. 1925.

Rooney – namely, the Nationalism that embraces every Irishman as a citizen of the Irish nation irrespective of his creed.

The anti-Semitism in *Honesty*, in spite of these caveats, was a variant, albeit less vicious in application, of the same religio-ideological strand that was a widespread phenomenon in Ireland.[20] Notwithstanding his anti-Semitic pronouncements, Upton – like his friend and mentor Arthur Griffith – retained the leading Irish-Jewish republican solicitor Michael Noyk, and both men numbered him as a close personal friend.[21] Indeed, in the article 'Young Jews and Fair Gentiles', Upton acknowledges the debt that republicans owed to several Jews and in a clear reference to Noyk, he asserted: 'I know, in particular, one of these gentleman whose character and ability reflect credit on his race and the land of his adoption and whose unselfish service will never be forgotten by the old prisoners of the Sinn Fein movement.'[22]

Both Griffith and Upton wrote similarly contradictory comments in regard to Ireland's Jews. This duality of narrative regarding Irish Jews has led Colum Kenny to suggest that Griffith was far from an anti-Semite; indeed, he has argued that Griffith was more of a Zionist.[23] However, no similar proposition regarding Upton's views is offered here. Whatever the ideological underpinning of this form of wavering narrative, the anti-Semitism, no matter how hedged, in the articles and cartoons carried in *Honesty* in 1925, 1926 and to a lesser extent into 1927, is irrefutable.

Outside of *Honesty*'s anti-Semitic and homophobic content, the journal demonstrated an incredible level of compassion in its analysis of contentious social issues such as women working in prostitution, unmarried mothers and their children, the unemployed, alcoholics and those moralized against and demonized by 'respectable' Free State society. This coverage set it apart from its contemporary publications. *Honesty*'s compassion was matched by an uncompromising assault on those who claimed the moral high ground yet abused their status and privilege. One example is found in a piece penned by 'Our Reporter' that castigates the lauding of a deceased businessman in a national newspaper because he was thought to have left a small legacy to

20 Natalie Wynn, 'Jews, antisemitism and Irish politics: a tale of two narratives', *PaRDeS: Zeitschrift der-Vereinigung für Jüdische Studien*, 5:18 (2012), 51–66.   21 Michael Noyk (12 Aug. 1884–22 Oct. 1966) was a solicitor and Irish republican politician. Born in Lithuania, his family emigrated to Ireland when he was twelve months old. He was educated at The High School, Dublin and entered Trinity College Dublin, graduating in classics in 1907, prior to training as a solicitor. As a result of Noyk's friendship with Arthur Griffith, he became sympathetic to the cause of Irish republicanism, eventually joining Sinn Féin shortly after the Easter Rising. Noyk was responsible for defending a number of Irish Republican Army prisoners. He was Griffith's personal solicitor until his death in 1922.   22 *Honesty*, 7 Mar. 1925.   23 Colum Kenny, 'Arthur Griffith: more Zionist than anti-Semite', *History Ireland*, 24:3 (2016), 38–41.

'Magdalene Asylums or a Society for saving fallen women'. The article argues that the businessman may well have made his fortune on the back of slave wages paid to Irish women and thereby driving them towards these institutions.[24] *Honesty* confronted the reader with the uncomfortable assertion that these 'evils' were not simply the result of personal failings, but rather the result of failings of the religio-political entity that was the Free State.

Honesty's brand of compassionate, cerebral, unflinching exposure of the political and social underbelly of the Free State certainly seemed to provide a solid readership and advertising base. During its first three years of publication, *Honesty* was contradictory, vibrant and iconoclastic and said what other openly published journals did not dare to say in an age of increasing censorship and intolerance of those who were perceived as betraying the nation by simply offering a counter-hegemonic analysis of life in the Free State.[25] *Honesty's* mission was to challenge hypocrisy and injustice, a mission which it declared in September 1925 by informing its readers that it was against the duplicity it viewed as being endemic in the Free State.[26] It was not only the issues that *Honesty* addressed that made it stand out. It avoided victim blaming. Within *Honesty's* pages the usual assaults on the morality of those women engaged in prostitution, or the 'few degenerates' who availed themselves of their services, would not be found. *Honesty's* focus was on the economic conditions that left women with no choice but to prostitute themselves and on the 'respectable', pious middle classes who preyed upon and condemned them in equal measure. *Honesty* was forthright in its coverage of the sexual and physical abuse of children, the poor treatment and stigmatization of unmarried mothers and their children, women's rights and the maltreatment and deaths of children in state-funded foster care. In addition, corruption and profiteering in Irish charitable organizations, youth offenders and their care, the reporting of political corruption, appalling housing conditions, 'slave wages' and the social problem of alcoholism were all explored through a systemic lens, rather than the victim-blaming one deployed in the mainstream and religious press. *Honesty's* ability to stay in business while doing this was itself a testament to Upton and Stanley's standing, as it did so in an era of postcolonial uncertainty when both government and opposition were highly sensitive to any criticism and protective of the Free State's image to a domestic and international audience.

Upton viewed *Honesty* as separate and distinct from mainstream Irish journalism, which he viewed as 'reptilian', 'pro-imperialist' and in the pay of the

---

24 *Honesty*, 13 June 1925.   **25** Maurice Curtis, *A challenge to democracy: militant Catholicism in modern Ireland* (Dublin, 2010).   **26** *Honesty*, 19 Sept. 1925.

Free State government, which dispensed its patronage to compliant news-papers through lucrative government advertising and showed its displeasure through withholding or withdrawing advertising from newspapers that did not conform.[27] Irrespective of Upton's view of mainstream Irish journalism, what is irrefutable is that *Honesty*'s journalism was far grittier, socially foren-sic and hard-hitting on these issues than any other journal in the Free State and Upton was unwilling to compromise upon freedom of expression. Where *Honesty* deployed a sociological lens, others sought to blame and patholo-gize individual weakness or wickedness rather than addressing the underlying causes.[28] The mainstream journalistic approach was on the atomization of problems and behaviours that could be ascribed to moral degradation, and, or, individual pathology – an approach that suited the stance of church and state and which was to be reinforced under law with the passage of the Censorship of Publications Act 1929, a piece of legislation that was supported by gov-ernment, opposition and, inexplicably, Irish journalism, both those from the mainstream press, who felt that it could gain financially and be largely untouched from what was seen as legislation that would restrict the sales of British newspapers in the Free State and those like Upton who simply failed to see that it could be used, as it was, to silence indigenous journalism.[29]

The forensic social realism of *Honesty*'s first three years of publication had, by 1929, morphed into a more cerebral engagement with the mainstream political and economic debates of the day. This editorial move deprived the publication of much of its journalistic immediacy and colour. Consequently, this change in editorial focus, the cause of which has eluded identification to date, narrowed the paper's appeal and circulation to those who moved in anti-Treaty republican circles, the largest constituency of which were members of, or sympathetic to, the Fianna Fáil party. This reliance would leave Upton in a vulnerable position. Upton had warned the Fianna Fáil party that he would not fear to focus on their activities with the same forensic eye that he had on the Cumann na nGaedheal government.[30] This was a promise he fulfilled, but at great cost. *Honesty*'s demise was all but guaranteed when Upton's insistence on editorial freedom and a plurality of expression clashed with the ambitions of the leadership of Fianna Fáil, who subsequently used the party machinery to deprive *Honesty* of a viable readership.[31] This row with Fianna Fáil and its impact on the sales of *Honesty* undermined Upton's position with the new owners of the Gaelic Press, a group of Cork-based businessmen who had

27 Ibid., 1 Oct. 1927. 28 Louise Ryan, *Gender, identity and the Irish press, 1922–1937* (Lewiston, NY, 2002), p. 42. 29 Anthony Keating, 'Censorship: the cornerstone of Catholic Ireland', *Journal of Church and State*, 57:2 (2015), 289–309. 30 *Honesty*, 20 Oct. 1928. 31 Anthony Keating, 'Killing off the competition: Fianna Fáil's "Dublin Junta's" attack on *Honesty*', *Media History*, 22:1 (2016), 85–100.

taken over the company in March 1929, when Upton's long-time friend and collaborator, Joseph Stanley, decided to sell his interest. This sale not only undermined Upton's position from within, it also deprived him of the patronage of a man who upheld *Honesty*'s critical independence and enjoyed equal, if not greater, political capital in republican circles as Upton himself. Ultimately, Upton concluded that *Honesty*'s new owners sought profit over journalistic integrity and that he was unable to continue as editor. He resigned in January 1931, resolving to establish his own journal so that he would never again be compromised journalistically because of commercial expediency.

PUBLICITY

On the 16 May 1931 the *Leitrim Observer* announced that it had received a copy of *Publicity*, which 'possesses all the force and pungency which we expected' and for which Upton had 'attracted a virile band of writers, who put the issues clear and straight from the shoulder'. It welcomed this addition to Irish journalism, for which it predicted 'a big future'. It noted that 'those who are fortunate enough to secure the first number are certain to become regular subscribers in future'. Upton made it clear on the front page of *Publicity*'s first edition that he had embarked on this new venture to continue the work of *Honesty* under a different name because the 'honesty had been taken out of *Honesty*'. He used the first edition of *Publicity* to print an explicit manifesto of his journalistic creed, stating that he would publish the 'best Irish thought, irrespective of creed, class or party'. Of particular concern was the growing tide of sectarianism, which Upton viewed as an anathema:

> During the whole of our life we have resolutely opposed the narrow sectarian bigotry that divides Irish people on religious lines. Undoubtedly, most of these small-minded people are of the despicable sort, and use religion to further their own material ends – mean minded men who would like to convey the idea that they are more Catholic than his Holiness the Pope, or on the other hand more Orange than King Billy 'of pious and immortal memory'.[32]

In the same issue Upton expanded on his decision to leave *Honesty*, citing the 'commercialization' of the title that had led him to have to 'choose between remaining as nominal Editor, or sort of catspaw editor, under a "censoring

32 *Publicity*, 9 May 1931.

authority" or walk out'. Upton asserted that he chose to set up a new journal rather than seek work elsewhere as he knew that there was room for
'honest journalism and that there was an honest public to support us'. While
Publicity was launched with gusto and commitment, it never quite found
the right tone in order to attract a viable readership. Its mix of well written, intelligent and earnest discussions regarding race, cultural, economic and
physical imperialism, trade, banking and finance never captured the dynamism
of *Honesty* in the mid-to-late 1920s. *Publicity* pursued three central themes:
(1) Britain's economic domination of the Free State; (2) Britain's cultural domination of the Free State; and (3) the resultant deleterious impacts on 'native'
employment, culture and morality – menaces that Upton viewed as being
ignored by mainstream politics and the national press. In one editorial, he
stated that poverty and unemployment in the Free State could be accounted
for by British imports,

> but our imperialist newspapers feel sure that such a condition of affairs
> is all in the natural fitness of things, and so it will be as long as the peo-
> ple permit the country to remain in the menial position of serving the
> servile purpose of Britain's economic complement in accordance with
> the plans of William Pitt and his successors and native Irish abettors.[33]

Always an economic protectionist, Upton attempted to right what he viewed
as a hegemonic wall of complacency. He attempted to persuade his readers to buy Irish shirts, shoes and matches. The sale of foreign matches in
Dublin made the front page of *Publicity's* launch edition, a scourge that by its
second number *Publicity* was claiming to have driven off.[34] While these efforts
were heartfelt, they did not come close to the powerful and meaningful campaigning that typified *Honesty's* output between 1925 and 1928. On its launch,
Honesty's opening campaign focused on the economic causation and reality of
prostitution in the Free State. *Publicity's* opening edition simply did not carry
that sort of punch, and with its ongoing focus on economic protectionism
and the 'buy Irish' campaign, it never achieved it. Echoing the types of campaign that had led to *Honesty* becoming rather more worthy than exciting and
dynamic, in *Publicity* Upton homed in on what he viewed as the root cause
of poverty rather than engaging in the way *Honesty* had with the human damage caused by poverty, hunger, family dysfunction, crime and prostitution.
However, Upton was convinced of the necessity of this approach, reminding
his readers in 1931 that 'we have been continually emphasising the importance

33 Ibid., 23 May 1931.   34 Ibid., 16 May, 1931.

of concentrating on the economic question as the one important inch before the saw just now and for a considerable time to come'.[35] It was not that in its later stages of publication *Honesty* had forgotten the detailed human-interest aspects of reporting, or that *Publicity* also failed to do so, but rather that the economic analysis too heavily outweighed the more human coverage, losing the successful balance between the two that had enlivened *Honesty*'s earlier editions. There are few examples in *Publicity* of the human-interest side of the story and when these did appear, the economic lesson was sure to follow. For example, in December 1931, in the penultimate edition, a piece entitled 'Remember the Poor' begins in a narrative rather Dickensian in tone – 'The coming of Christmas is casting its pleasant shadow before it. The principal thoroughfares of our cities and towns are radiant with the colour and light of brightly emblazoned shop fronts' – before Upton exalts readers to remember that the 'poor are always with us' and that the joyous nature of the festivities makes them feel their want even more keenly. However, the piece quickly moves on to the style of economic analysis more usual on the pages of *Publicity*, with Upton asserting that 'the poverty of our workless people reminds us of the causes of this poverty – want of work – that should and could be procurable here at home if we had a really sane and economic system in operation'.

However, it should not be assumed that Upton was only interested in the plight of the poor and oppressed in Ireland in the pages of *Publicity*. He was unequivocal in asserting that capitalism and imperialism were one and the same entity and therefore all struggles of oppressed people should be the concern of all freedom movements. Commenting on the Indian struggle against the British Empire, Upton asserted:

> British Imperialism has left its track of blood and tears and suffering deeply in India, just as it has done in Ireland. To-day the West Britons and the petty capitalist with their interest in the Indian Jute Market and other 'stocks and shares' want nothing to be said about Indian oppression in this country. But Irish Nationalism now as ever is on the side of every oppressed nation rightly struggling to be free.[36]

Notwithstanding Upton's initial optimism, *Publicity* only managed to run as a weekly journal for four months, before running for a further five months as a monthly publication and finally closing with no notice, following its January 1932 edition. It had only been in existence for nine months. Upton, in the

35 Ibid., 10 Nov. 1931. 36 Ibid., 6 June, 1931.

penultimate edition, attempted to rally support for what was then a failing publication, asserting:

> Amid so much that is depressing and disheartening in our partitioned country to date, it is cheering to know from personal experience that there is still a big number of people who stand fast in support of honesty in Irish journalism [and] that are prepared to support it in the most practical way. Without that support *Publicity* could not exist. We do not doubt that the support will not only last, but that it will increase.[37]

This was a piece written more in hope than expectation. Upton, the committed rebel journalist who had courted unemployment and insolvency for much of his career, had married a young woman and become a father for the first time at 60 and faced different priorities. Notwithstanding his passion to produce a journal unfettered by financially concerned owners, Upton now had to make a choice between continuing to produce *Publicity* and providing for his family. He chose the latter. In an interview with Seamus Upton, James W. Upton's son, the present author was informed that it was Upton's wife who convinced him to immediately cease publication of *Publicity*. Its launch had coincided with the birth of Seamus and the venture had haemorrhaged money from the start. Upton was never to edit a journal or newspaper again. In the early 1930s he was commissioned to write a history of the Gaelic Athletic Association (GAA) to mark its silver jubilee in 1934, though this was never published.[38] Thereafter he worked as a freelance journalist before taking up employment with Waterford City Library as a reference librarian in 1945. While he continued to provide occasional copy for the *Waterford Star*, the *Waterford Standard* and a scattering of other publications, his long and distinguished career as a journalist was over. James W. Upton died in Waterford in 1956.

---

37 Ibid., Dec. 1931.   38 A dispute over content resulted in the GAA refusing to publish the work. Proof copies can be found in the GAA Archives. See Anthony Keating, 'A politically inconvenient aspect of history: the unpublished official history of the Gaelic Athletic Association of 1934', *Sport in History*, 37:4 (2017), 448–68.

7 / The *Church of Ireland Gazette* and the twentieth century: 'a Church paper for Church People'?

IAN D'ALTON

The churches of the Anglican Communion – of which the Church of Ireland is the second oldest – are noted for lively and contentious debate within and between them.[1] In their myriad services it is indeed surprising that there isn't one for 'Schism Sunday'. That liveliness has since the nineteenth century been energized and underpinned by a periodical church literature. The *Church of Ireland Gazette* is a venerable survivor.[2] Founded in 1856 in Dublin as the *Irish Ecclesiastical Gazette; or, Monthly Repertory of Miscellaneous Church News*, it has chronicled church disestablishment, war, revolution, political upheaval, civil violence and theological argument. It has withstood financial crisis.[3] Editorially independent of the church, it became a weekly paper in 1880. In 1963 its locus shifted to Northern Ireland. It reverted to a monthly paper in 2019.

A rival – the *Irish Churchman*, based in the North – criticized the paper's 'narrow, lanky columns' and its world view: 'A Church paper should only deal in Church news.' In riposte, the *Gazette* went for satire – 'Good fat columns and only Church of Ireland news from the proverbial angle of Portadown – a Herculean editorial feat.'[4] The paper rested on a bedrock of diocesan and institutional news, but it was more than a 'mere glorified parish magazine'.[5] It ranged widely through the spiritual and secular – serving as 'a forum of discussion on subjects of interest and importance for our common life', as Primate Gregg put it.[6] That diversity – and its openness to debate – made the *Gazette* an object of almost pathological interest to those outside the fold eager to take the pulse of the opposition, demonstrated in correspondence from members of other Protestant denominations as well as from the occasional

1 See P.E. More & F.L. Cross (eds), *Anglicanism* (London, 1935; 2nd ed., Cambridge, 2008), *passim*. 2 My gratitude is especially due to Dr Alan Ford for guidance on writing this chapter. I also thank Revd Peter Hanna, Dr Susan Hood, Revd Robert Marshall, Dr Ida Milne, Dr Kenneth Milne, Mr David Nolan, Dr Suzanne Pegley, Revd Earl Storey and Professor Brian Walker for valuable suggestions and comments on drafts. 3 See Ian d'Alton, 'The *Irish Ecclesiastical Gazette*, 1858–1900' in David Finkelstein (ed.), *The Edinburgh history of the British and Irish press*, ii: *Expansion and evolution, 1800–1900* (Edinburgh, 2020), pp 395–9. 4 *Church of Ireland Gazette* (hereafter *CoIG*), 8 Dec. 1922. 5 Leigh-Ann Coffey, 'The price of loyalty: southern Irish loyalists and the work of the Irish Grants Committee' (PhD, Queen's University, Kingston, Canada, 2014), p. 53. 6 *CoIG*, 28 Jan. 1955.

reader who claimed to be Roman Catholic or to hold nationalist or republican sympathies.[7]

MANAGEMENT

A newspaper may have high-level objectives – in this case, the dissemination of intelligence about a religious denomination – but it has to rest upon a sound business and managerial base. On the face of it, the *Gazette* should have had a massive advantage over the generality of publications in this volume – a captive and loyal audience. But it was never able to garner more than a fraction of its potential market.[8] The Anglican population of the island declined from 579,000 in 1901 to 393,000 in 2001. Even assuming a readership larger than sales, the *Gazette's* circulation was always a tiny fraction of that – averaging about 4,000, and fluctuating between 2,500 and 9,700. It was, accordingly, always financially precarious.

From 1896 to 1963, the paper was published by the independent Church of Ireland Printing and Publishing Company Limited (CoIPPC).[9] From mid-century, the paper struggled. In 1946, the proprietors had discussions with the General Synod's Standing Committee (the church's 'government') about widening the appeal of the paper to the laity. In January 1947 a 'popular supplement' was added to the paper, and the title was changed to the *Church of Ireland Gazette and Family Newspaper.*[10] The hope was that the new arrangements might be the beginning of a revival.[11] That did not materialize. In 1954, the church was again concerned about the *Gazette* and encouraged the appointment of a lay professional, Norman Clark, as editor. The paper was given a stylistic makeover. References in its masthead to the former 'Irish Ecclesiastical Gazette' and to 'Family Newspaper' were dropped, and henceforth it was titled 'The Church of Ireland Gazette'.[12] But by the early 1960s circulation had slumped to about 2,500. It was losing about £100 per month.[13] The directors resolved to close it.

7 Coffey, 'The price of loyalty', p. 53; see, for example, *CoIG*, 17 July 1936, letter from 'Cilothac', a Roman Catholic; *CoIG*, 6 Mar. 1992, letter from Msgr Daniel S. Hamilton, a Catholic priest in Lindenhurst, NY. 8 See comments by Archbishop Barton of Dublin in *CoIG*, 28 Jan. 1955. 9 *Irish Ecclesiastical Gazette* (hereafter *IEG*), 28 Feb., 6 Mar. 1896. 10 General Synod (hereafter GS) Standing Committee (hereafter SC), Report of Proceedings, 1947 – *Journal of the General Synod of the Church of Ireland, 1947* (Dublin, 1947), 159. 11 GS, SC, Report of Proceedings, 1947, pp 159–60. 12 See *CoIG*, 21, 28 Jan. 1955. 13 'Memorandum for the SC of the General Synod', drawn up by the APCK, n.d., but probably early 1963 – *CoIG* Advisory Committee minutes and papers, 1963, Representative Church Body Library (hereafter RCBL), GS/2/40.10.

This alarmed the church. In early 1963 action was taken by the Standing Committee. An attempt to involve the Association for Promoting Christian Knowledge (APCK) – active in Ireland since 1792 as a publisher of religious material – in a rescue was unsuccessful.[14] The unionist newspaper *Belfast News Letter* was brought in as contractor and advisor.[15] The *News Letter's* suggestions included fortnightly, rather than weekly, publication and that circulation would be boosted by effectively suppressing existing parish and diocesan magazines. In a relatively decentralized and territorially sensitive church, that was never going to be acceptable.[16]

To gauge the church's temperature, the General Synod – in private session because of the sensitivity of the matter – discussed the *Gazette* in May 1963.[17] Among the points raised in a sharp debate were that there should be a 'complete break' with the existing journal, since its existing goodwill was 'negligible'; the church should control the paper; there should be no 'sensationalism'; it was to be non-political and non-party; and professional staff was a necessity. In 1955 Archbishop Gregg of Armagh had commended the decision to leave the *Gazette* in private hands;[18] by 1963 there was now a tacit recognition that it would have to be effectively controlled by the church and that it would require subsidy – 'commercial interests should not be allowed to cloud this issue'.[19] A new company under the church's aegis – Church of Ireland Press Ltd, registered in Northern Ireland rather than the Republic and limited by guarantee – was established. The existing title was transferred free of charge by the CoIPPC.[20] The paper was now 'our very own'.[21] The existing editor (Canon Andy Willis) remained in post, albeit with a co-editor based in the North, Revd Gilbert Wilson. A free paper got the ball rolling on 25 October 1963.[22]

One week earlier the old *Gazette's* valedictory comment had been headed 'With Reservations' and while it wished its successor well, the tone was more sour grapes than celebratory. In the last issue, its long-time columnist 'Cromlyn' – although not attracted to the idea of seeing parochial news 'prefaced with the latest on the search for Miss Choir Girl, 1963' – looked

---

14 *CoIG* Advisory Committee minutes, 22 Apr. 1963 – RCBL, GS/2/40.10; APCK, 'CoIG, Memorandum for the SC of the General Synod' (n.d., but early 1963) – RCBL, GS/2/40.10. **15** *CoIG* Advisory Committee minutes, 22 Apr. 1963; Report of the Advisory Committee to the SC, 22 Apr. 1963 – RCBL, GS/2/40.10. **16** *CoIG* Advisory Committee minutes, 22 Apr. 1963, 1 May 1963 – RCBL, GS/2/40.10. **17** Minutes of SC meetings, 12 Mar., 23 Apr. 1963 – RCBL, SC papers, 1963, GS/2/12/1/8, pp 41, 46. **18** *CoIG*, 28 Jan. 1955. **19** *CoIG* Advisory Committee minutes, 15 May 1963 – RCBL, GS/2/40.10. **20** Minutes of SC meetings, approval of reports of the *CoIG* Advisory Committee, 18 June, 16 July 1963 – RCBL, SC papers, 1963, GS/2/12/1/8, pp 49, 52. **21** *CoIG*, 25 Oct., 1, 8 Nov. 1963. **22** Memorandum and Articles of Association of Church of Ireland Press, at https://tinyurl.com/yxdv3jr8; minutes of SC meeting, 16 July 1963 – RCBL, SC papers, 1963, GS/2/12/1/8, p. 52.

for change in the new publication.[23] Primate James McCann saw it as 'a paper with a youthful appeal to the new generation – not to the squares'.[24] The main change was in its style – a broadsheet with snappy headlines and shorter articles. It still contained its staples of Irish, international and diocesan news, the occasional theological piece and book review, but featuring more photographs and enhanced features for children and on cookery, fashion and records. A crossword and (for a while) a section on sporting activities in the church, differentiated it from its predecessor.

How did the venture fare? By May 1964 circulation had increased from 2,500 to about 9,700 per week. Of that, some 4,000 came in from a 'supplement scheme', whereby the *Gazette* was inserted into individual parish notes newsletters as a supplement. While 140 parishes were participating by January 1964, that arrangement only lasted until the end of 1965 and the circulation fell back again.[25] Changes in printing arrangements saw a relocation to Lurgan in 1966,[26] with the benefit of a new web offset printing process and business management by the printers.[27] But a dedicated office, with a small professional staff, including a circulation and advertising manager, cost money, with an annual salary bill of some £2,635. Even with voluntary help and a doubled cover price, the new *Gazette* was still losing between £75 and £100 per week.[28]

In 1963, the church had pledged a single allocation of £5,000 towards the cost of the first year's publication under the new arrangements.[29] It was obvious, however, that the paper was unviable without external support; the church's Representative Church Body (RCB, the church's financial arm) Finance Committee in 1964 saw 'no prospect of the *Gazette* ever being able to pay its way'.[30] If the church wanted to see the *Gazette* continue without 'commercial interests' dominant, it would have to pay up. Which it did, with annual subsidies of between £3,000 and £3,500, and occasionally more (from 1973 to 1979 it was £5,000 per annum, and in 1980 £6,000). Another crisis was averted in March 1975 as there were 'strong indications' that the paper would cease as a weekly in July; the paper was revamped and the church of Ireland Press took back the management of the business side of the *Gazette* from the printers.

23 *CoIG*, 18 Oct. 1963. 24 *CoIG*, 25 Oct. 1963. 25 *CoIG*, 30 Oct. 1964; SC papers, 16 Nov. 1965 – RCBL, GS/2/12/1/9, p. 25. 26 Letter of 3 Feb. 1966 from Morton Newspapers (Lurgan and Portadown) to the Church of Ireland Press, enclosed in the minutes of the SC, 19 Apr. 1966 – RCBL, GS/2/12/1/19. 27 *CoIG*, 27 May 1966. 28 Copy of a letter, deputy chief officer, RCB, to assistant secretary, GS, 8 May 1964, enclosing a letter and report from John H. Armstrong and John H. Lamb, hon. treasurer and hon. secretary, Church of Ireland Press – RCBL, SC papers, 1963, GS/2/12/1/8; APCK, '*CoIG*, Memorandum for the SC of the General Synod' (n.d., but early 1963), RCBL, GS/2/40.10. 29 GS, SC, *CoIG*, Advisory Committee, interim report, 11 Mar. 1963 – RCBL, GS/2/40.10. 30 SC minutes – RCBL, GS/2/12/1/8.

Not much was expected – 'Should the paper by some chance of fortune, make a profit, this would go to the RCB'.[31] In 1983, a proposal by the Church's Commission on Communications to turn the *Gazette* into a monthly journal was rejected.[32] In 1987, proposals for a takeover were considered together with reports from the directors of the Church of Ireland Press and the Central Communications Board of the church. Both reports advocated that the *Gazette* should remain under the control of the Press.[33] From 1963 to the end of the millennium, the church's subsidy amounted to some £125,000.[34] In later years this expenditure went principally to subvent the cost of distribution in the Republic, for promotion and for setting up an online presence.

The paper always priced itself to sell – 1*d*. from 1900 to 1918, when war-time paper shortages forced a 50 per cent price increase to 1½*d*. That remained until January 1945, when it was increased to 2*d*. By 1955, it was 3*d*.; and from October 1963, 6*d*.[35] Yet as the price increased, the number of pages fell from twenty-eight to twenty-four per issue in the 1900s; by 1925 that had decreased to twenty; by 1949 to twelve; and during its last year under the CoIPPC, to between eight and twelve pages. There was a brief resurgence to sixteen pages in the first two issues of the new publication, but then it shrank to a more or less constant twelve pages from the late 1960s to 1976, when a resize increased the number of (smaller) pages to sixteen per issue.[36] The design remained the same until January 1945, when advertisements finally moved off the first page and some new features – a serialized story, kitchen hints, gardening – were added.[37] Redesigns took place in 1955 and in late 1976. Two-colour printing came in the 1970s; full colour was adopted in October 2002.[38] In the later twentieth century the *Gazette*'s circulation was about 4,300 weekly.[39] The current (2020) monthly journal's is about 5,000 copies.

MARKET AND AUDIENCE

The *Irish Ecclesiastical Gazette* had been founded in 1856 as primarily a paper for the clergy, filling 'the want of some Paper devoted to the communication of Ecclesiastical Intelligence'.[40] But with disestablishment and the rise of the

31 *CoIG*, 21 Mar. 1975. 32 https://www.ireland.anglican.org/news/10167/the-church-of-ireland-gazette. 33 *Journal of the General Synod of the Church of Ireland, 1987* (Dublin, 1987), 88. 34 This figure is derived from the annual grant figures in the *Journal of the General Synod*, 1964–2000: 1964–81 between pp 38 and 49; 1992–2000, between pp 86 and 141. The amount in 1967 was £3,000 – *Journal of the General Synod of the Church of Ireland, 1967* (Dublin, 1967), 30; *Journal of the General Synod of the Church of Ireland, 1975* (Dublin, 1975), 74. 35 *CoIG*, 28 Jan. 1955. 36 *CoIG*, 26 Nov., 3 Dec. 1976; 24 Dec. 1999. 37 *CoIG*, 15 Dec. 1944; 5 Jan. 1945. 38 *CoIG*, 4 Oct. 2002. 39 *CoIG*, 21 Mar. 1975. 40 *IEG*, 1 Mar. 1856.

voluntarist church came a sea change. The clergy now had clerical societies
and synods to foster a sense of caste and to network (these were reported on
extensively in the paper). The *Gazette's* new sub-title from 1880 – 'A Church
paper for Church people' – reflected its transformation from an intelligence
sheet for the clergy towards a newspaper for the laity.

Where lay the *Gazette's* market? Clues emerge from representative issues
at the beginning, middle and end of the century.[41] In 1900, of twenty-four
pages, nine were comprised of advertisements. In 1949, about two pages out
of twelve were advertisements.[42] Protestant-owned firms (mostly from the
South) made up the majority of advertisements in 1900 and 1949 – McBirney's
and Switzers department stores in Dublin, Cash & Co. and McKechnies Dry
Cleaners in Cork, the Condensed Milk Company of Limerick, makers of
Cleeve's Toffee.[43] In truth, these advertisements were another form of subsidy
to the paper – Protestant businesses advertising to tribal Anglicans was probably somewhat unnecessary.

In December 1949 the advertisements had a wider geographical spread than
fifty years before, with firms in Dublin, Cork, Kilkenny, Nenagh, Waterford,
Drogheda, Limerick and Carlow. A few Northern companies advertised –
from Belfast, Enniskillen and Londonderry – but they were few compared to
those from the Republic. That may be a significant indicator of the paper's
relatively limited attractiveness in the areas of greatest church population. The
last issue of the old *Gazette* in 1963, published in Dublin, still had a preponder-
ance of advertisements from the Republic. One week later, most were from
Northern Ireland, mainly from Belfast firms. The correspondence and contributor columns were probably carefully balanced by editorial intervention,
but the advertisements were a better indicator of the market at which the
Gazette was then aimed.

The volume of advertisements declined sharply during the second half
of the century. By the end of 1999, advertisements from businesses had all
but vanished; those few (about two pages out of sixteen) that remained were
almost all church-related – events, positions vacant, church renovation and
construction businesses and so on. This probably reflected changes in the
communications and advertising world generally, with advertisements becoming increasingly targeted at very particular groups, and on multiple media
platforms.[44]

41 *CoIG*, 5 Jan. 1900; 9 Dec. 1949; 26 Nov. 1999.   42 *CoIG*, 28 Oct. 1949.   43 See Frank Barry, 'The life
and death of Protestant businesses in independent Ireland' in Ian d'Alton & Ida Milne (eds), *Protestant and
Irish: the minority's search for place in independent Ireland* (Cork, 2019), pp 158–62.   44 The example consulted
is *CoIG*, 26 Nov. 1999.

EDITORS AND CONTRIBUTORS

The *Gazette* had eleven editors during the twentieth century, excluding a series of unknown 'temporary' editors between 1930 and 1934.[45] One problem for the paper was that most of these were part-time, leading to unevenness of presentation and content. Of the eleven, three – Warre B. Wells, Norman Clark and Robert Beattie – were laymen. The most influential and hands-on editors during the century were probably Wells (1914–18), Revd Ernest Greening (1934–54) and Revd Cecil Cooper (1982–2001). Wells, marooned in the *Gazette*'s premises in Middle Abbey Street, was an on-the-spot chronicler of the Rising in 1916.[46] Greening's long editorship spanned the first de Valera government, the Second World War and the declaration of the Republic. After the retirement of Canon Andy Willis in 1975, all later editors were based in the North.

Prominent contributors included – from 1910 to 1916 – 'Shebna the Scribe', unionist in outlook and a proponent of the idea of St Patrick as a sort of proto-Protestant. He was Revd W.S. Kerr, later dean of Belfast and bishop of Down and Dromore.[47] His political outlook was not in tune with that of the editor, Wells, and he left the paper rather abruptly at the end of 1916.[48] In the immediate aftermath of the Rising, he endeavoured to educate the *Gazette*'s readership into understanding it in more transcendental terms. He blamed the 'literary cult of the Rebels of the past' for firing the enthusiasms of the 'sentimental dreamers, visionary enthusiasts, of romantic young men living in a fanciful realm'.[49] Between 1918 and 1920, he contributed to the *Gazette*'s rival the *Irish Churchman*, under the same nom de plume. In 1922, he was briefly back in the *Gazette*, under the name 'Boreas'.[50]

The longest-running columnist was 'Cromlyn', Canon John Barry, rector of Hillsborough, Co. Down. He wrote for nearly half a century.[51] 'A legend in his own lifetime',[52] he brought a distinct North-centric perspective to the *Gazette*

---

45 https://www.ireland.anglican.org/cmsfiles/pdf/AboutUs/library/Archive/Aug13/Editors.
pdf. **46** *CoIG*, 28 Apr.–5 May 1916. **47** Confirmed by the *Gazette* as Shebna – *CoIG*, 15 Dec.
1944. **48** W.B. Wells to W.S. Kerr, 9 Dec. 1916 – Kerr papers, RCBL, MS 813/2/1, no. 8. **49** *CoIG*, 19
May 1916. **50** Kerr papers, RCBL, MS 813/4; also Revd Dr Wagner to the editor of the *Gazette*, 26 July
1922 (copy) – Kerr papers, RCBL, MS 813/2/3. See also Alan Ford, 'Fishing for controversy: W.S. Kerr and
the demise of Church of Ireland anti-Catholicism' in Claire Gheeraert-Graffeuille & Geraldine Vaughan
(eds), *Anti-Catholicism in Britain and Ireland, 1600–2000* (London, 2020), pp 237–54. **51** See https://
www.ireland.anglican.org/news/651/death-of-the-revd-canon, 22 Sept. 2006; also obituary in *Irish Times*,
30 Sept. 2006; a northern obituary is at http://lisburn.com/history/memories/memories-2006/canon-
john-barry.html **52** *CoIG*, 29 Sept. 2006.

[He] more than anyone else opened a window on the core mentality of the Northern Protestant. It was a window through which southern politicians in particular seldom seemed to look, and, if they did, it was quickly closed because they didn't like what was revealed.[53]

In 1976 Barry's review of Dean Victor Griffin's book *Anglican and Irish* disputed Griffin's contention that an Anglican could be Irish – 'He is Irish', wrote Barry, 'but only in a sort of a way'[54] – although by 1983 he maintained that 'I, and the like of me, are every whit as Irish as any of those who keep talking about it in terms of Nationalism'.[55] Barry's oft-articulated conviction that Southern Protestants were an alienated, dispossessed and discriminated against minority was persistently met with dismissive letters published in the *Gazette* from Southern Protestants. 'Cromlyn' both encouraged and provoked debate – in 1968, a correspondent, in reply to one piece, suggested that 'young rectors should confine the expression of controversial opinions to suitable occasions of mutual admiration ... [when] it might not matter if they are both impertinent and flatulent'.[56] There was always genuine debate between laity and clergy in the opinion columns and letter pages.

'JBS' was Canon J.B. Shea of Tuam. His columns, running from the 1930s to the 1950s – an age of religious disputation – often featured polemical diatribes against the papacy and Roman Catholicism. In July 1936, writing of Catholic teaching on freemasonry, he excoriated 'the old trite pathetic fallacy that a Roman Catholic can obey the Pope up to a certain point, and is then free'.[57] Other columnists included Frances Condell, a prominent Limerick civic personality and politician – her contributions were a potpourri of gossip, agony aunt, and tips for women. In the 1970s, 1980s and 1990s the *Gazette* carried columns entitled *Gazebo* (Canon Andy Willis), *Crannog* (a sort of cerebral version of the 'Cromlyn' columns) and *Touchline*.[58]

NORTH AND SOUTH

If the paper was always teetering on the edge, it was in relatively good company in twentieth-century Ireland, littered as it was with the corpses of fine journals, from *Shan Van Vocht* through the *Irish Statesman* and *The Bell* to *Hibernia* and *Dublin Opinion*. All these had to chart difficult courses through sometimes contradictory constituencies and fashions. The *Gazette* was no different. In its

53 Bishop Roy Warke, letter in *CoIG*, 27 Oct. 2006.　54 *CoIG*, 19 Mar. 1976.　55 *CoIG*, 7 Oct. 1983.　56 *CoIG*, 9 Feb. 1968.　57 *CoIG*, 10 July 1936.　58 See, for example, *CoIG*, 8 Nov. 1963; 21 Apr. 1972; 14 Dec. 1990; 12 Sept. 1997.

case, the paper had to accommodate the church's Northern and Southern memberships, which despite a public face of unity and harmony, were often fissured and fractured, politically and theologically.[59] Columns ostentatiously titled 'Belfast Notes' and 'Notes from the North' emphasized a divide,[60] which was not helped by the *Gazette's* being 'based in Dublin and edited from the depths of the country'.[61] Even after the 1963 reorganization that saw the appointment of a Northern co-editor, the Southern editor was still the final arbiter.[62]

When an entire diocese in Connacht could have less church members than a single Belfast parish, a perceived unfairness in the allocation of church assets was a constant theme (and still is). Reports in the paper show an undercurrent of resentment from stretched Northern parishes. For example, in November 1965 a Cavan correspondent condemned the expenditure of £8,000 on a new rectory at Portarlington, Co. Laois as 'extravagant'.[63] But alongside that there were also instances of generosity and solidarity – in the late 1920s, for example, Southern members rallied to an appeal for funds for the 'mission' parish of Ballymacarrett in Belfast.[64]

The church's North-South controversy and conflict was often distilled through politics. This was particularly evident during the editorship of Wells – 'imparted of Nationalist sympathies' – between 1914 and 1918.[65] Comments like 'the Church cannot effectively seek to promote an Imperial Irish outlook until she has identified herself with "Irish national ideals"'[66] did not go unnoticed by the Northern die-hards. The *Irish Churchman* disparaged the *Gazette* for being 'anti-partitionist, and that does not suit our Northern palate'. The bishop of Clogher, Maurice Day, who was on the *Gazette's* editorial committee, was equally critical of the journal's line. In a letter to Northern ultra-unionist Hugh de Fellenberg Montgomery he wrote that

> As regards the recent articles in the *Ch. of I. Gazette* I quite agree that they are of a kind which are disapproved of by most members of our Church,

59 See an editorial, *CoIG*, 12 Jan. 1975. 60 See *CoIG*, 21 June 1910, 3 Apr. 1914. 61 'Cromlyn', *CoIG*, 18 Oct. 1963. 62 *CoIG*, Advisory Committee minutes, 9 July 1963, RCBL, GS/2/40.10; see also SC report, *Journal of the General Synod of the Church of Ireland*, 1963, 13 (Dublin, 1963), 70–1. 63 *CoIG*, 24 Nov. 1965, letter from E. McElderry. See also a letter from E.K. Hamilton, designated curate-in-charge of the new parish of Stormont, seeking prayer books, hymnals and hassocks from underused Southern parishes – *CoIG*, 1 Jan. 1960. 64 B. Walker, 'Outreach in the midst of conflict: the Revd John Redmond in 1920s Belfast', RCBL, Archive of the Month, Aug. 2020, www.ireland.anglican.org/library/archive. 65 W.B. Wells to W.S. Kerr, 9 Dec. 1916 – Kerr papers, RCBL, MS 813/2/1, no. 8; also John Horgan, 'The press in 1917: wars and rumours of wars 1917' (Aftermath of Rebellion – a Public Symposium, St Patrick's College, DCU, 28 Jan. 2017), http://doras.dcu.ie/21701/1/1917_-_Symposium_paper.pdf, pp 9–10. 66 *CoIG* 16 Feb. 1917, editorial titled 'Church and nation'.

especially in the N. of Ireland – and I include myself among the number – tho' others, I regret to say, seem quite to approve of them.[67]

Attempts to police the editorial slant – 'I recently had a Cmmtt. appointed (of whom I am one) to supervise the policy of the Paper', wrote Day – do not seem to have been particularly successful. In 1917, Primate Crozier took 'strong steps in the matter' in relation to Wells:

> I got the Directors to meet and take advice and they unanimously decided (so they told me) on a concise policy which has altered completely, as any one can see, the tone of the *Gazette* for some weeks past. Wiser men than I see in the future the awful danger of divided aims and interests in one small Church of Ireland.[68]

The next year Wells resigned.

The establishment of two jurisdictions in 1922 had the potential to cause serious problems for an all-island church, a situation not unique to the Church of Ireland. There was, however, a determined attempt in church circles to avoid the partitionist mentality so prevalent in Protestant politics, especially in Ulster.[69] When it was reported in December 1922 that Irish Free State Governor-General Tim Healy had claimed that an attempt to separate the Northern church had been defeated in General Synod, Primate d'Arcy issued an immediate denial that such had ever been discussed and asserted that 'political divisions cannot break the unity of the Church'.[70]

The *Gazette* had to cater for differences within the church's belief communities. While these did not always coincide with geopolitical boundaries, the North-South divide was broadly mirrored in theological and doctrinal strands. The North tended towards emphasising its 'Reformed' nature, exhibited in a strong evangelical streak. The South identified more with a low-church 'catholic' outlook (although strongly anti-ritualist), with a few high-church redoubts in Dublin's leafier suburbs.[71] And while controversial issues – sexual morality, ritualism, ecumenism, women priests, missionary activity – were often framed through differing North-South lenses, it helped that they could be moderated and contained within an international, Anglican Communion context in the columns of the *Gazette*.[72]

67 M. Day to H. de F. Montgomery, 1 June 1918 – PRONI, D627/434/35.   68 J.B. Crozier to W.S. Kerr, 16 Jan. 1917 – Kerr papers, RCBL, MS 813/2/1, no. 9.   69 See a strongly anti-partitionist editorial in *CoIG*, 9 Dec. 1921.   70 *CoIG*, 8 Dec. 1922.   71 Letter from M. McCaughan, Down – *CoIG*, 3 Jan. 1992; also Alan Ford, 'The cost of democracy: the Church of Ireland and its ritual canons, 1871–1974', pp 6–19, unpublished paper, by kind permission of the author.   72 A column on 'Censorship', *CoIG*, 23 Oct. 1983, compared the regimes on the island.

From the 1960s, just as Protestants were experiencing 'a new sense of ease and satisfaction with conditions in the Republic',[73] Northern Ireland was about to erupt into a long, vicious and bloody sectarian conflict that dwarfed what had happened in the early 1920s. This raised questions of identity and belonging for Northern Protestants that had been sublimated during the period of Stormont rule. The Church of Ireland in Northern Ireland attempted to be a calming voice, despite many of its clerics and prominent laymen being involved in the Orange Order. The *Gazette* mirrored that moderation. When in February 1967 the bishop of Ripon was barred from preaching in Belfast, largely through Orange Order-led protests against his high-church 'Roman' views, the *Gazette* prominently printed a sermon heavily critical of the Order's 'competitive denominationalism'.[74] The church's overt support for 'moderate' unionism, in the forms of Captain Terence O'Neill and Major James Chichester-Clark, was frequently highlighted in the paper.[75] The paper, however, often went against the government. During the 1930s and 1940s it took on the Northern government's education policy. In 1936 it aroused the ire of its former columnist Dean W.S. Kerr for an editorial fearful of the sectarian nature of the Twelfth of July Orange celebrations.[76] In 1964, 'Cromlyn' castigated Belfast Corporation for closing children's playgrounds on Sundays – 'Ulster Stands Firm. No Swings on Sundays.'[77] In 1968, it gave front-page prominence to the bishop of Derry's call that 'bigotry must be challenged'.[78] Equally forthright on Southern matters, the *Gazette* strongly opposed the imposition of compulsory Irish in the Free State.[79] On the destruction of Nelson's Pillar in Dublin in 1966, it took the Southern government to task for what it claimed were intelligence failures in preventing it.[80]

If one word encapsulates the *Gazette*'s view of the Troubles for the thirty years from 1968, it is 'bewilderment'.[81] All it could say on the introduction of internment (without actually using the word) in August 1971 was that 'the situation in Northern Ireland almost defies comment from sources whose outlook must be based on the Christian gospel'.[82] One week later, its report on a sermon by Bishop Butler of Connor was headed 'What Can We Do?', juxtaposed with a photograph of the bishop at the Requiem Mass for a Catholic priest

73 Eugenio F. Biagini, 'A challenge to partition: Methodist open-air work in independent Ireland, 1922–1962', *Bulletin of the Methodist Historical Society of Ireland*, 19 (2014), 5–44 at 41. 74 *CoIG*, 10 Feb. 1967. 75 *CoIG*, 13 Dec. 1968; 7 Feb. 1969. 76 *CoIG*, 3 July 1936; Kerr papers, RCBL, MS 813/5/4, draft letter of 10 July 1936. It does not seem to have been printed in the *Gazette*. 77 *CoIG*, 13 Nov. 1964. 78 *CoIG*, 15 Nov. 1968. 79 *CoIG*, 20 June 1924, editorial. 80 *CoIG*, 18 Mar. 1966. 81 For details of reporting the Troubles see https://www.ireland.anglican.org/news/10134/charting-a-course-through-the. 82 *CoIG*, 13 Aug. 1971.

shot by the British Army.[83] By 1972 it was full of angst, asserting that those who insisted that religion had made 'no contribution' to the situation were 'breathtakingly unrealistic'.[84] In 1988 'Cromlyn' jettisoned his jauntiness as he wrote hauntingly of the IRA murders of the Hanna family of Hillsborough (whom he knew well), ending his column: 'Ah, my friends, can nothing be done to dry the tears? These endless, endless tears?'[85]

It took a fortnight for the *Gazette* to marshal its thoughts on the 1998 Good Friday Agreement. It wrote of the 'moral penury of community relations', but its line was politically moderate and strongly supportive of the settlement, and it urged the passage of the approving referendums in both jurisdictions. It was uneasy about 'pirates' retaining guns and amnesties for murderers, but it noted that while nationalists had not participated in or recognized Northern Ireland between 1922 and 1972, the 'greater responsibility' lay on the unionists to move.[86]

IDENTITY AND ETHOS

Running through the journal over the century were questions of identity — theological, denominational, historical. It was always interrogating the idea of the Church of Ireland. What *was* it, exactly? Ecclesiastically, was it a Patrician church, a Lutheran one or an invention of Tudor monarchs? Historically, how did it fit into an Irish narrative? And how did that suggest its trajectory, especially in the Free State? As one clerical correspondent wrote in 1929, 'there exists within our fold two distinct visions of the future of our Communion,' one that advocated 'controversy' and the other 'accommodation'.[87] 'Controversy', though, was never a sensible option. More likely was withdrawal into self-imposed comfortable ghettos.[88] The impetus for that principally came from class considerations and the relentless dilution of the tribe occasioned by Catholic insistence on the children of mixed marriages being brought up as Catholics. The *Gazette* was concerned when the results of the 1926 Free State census showed a decrease of a third in the Protestant population since 1911 — from 313,000 to about 208,000.[89] (In contrast, in what

---

83 *CoIG*, 20 Aug. 1971; https://www.irishnews.com/lifestyle/faithmatters/2019/05/23/news/the-fearless-love-of-fr-hugh-mullan-and-fr-noel-fitzpatrick-ballymurphy-s-martyred-priests-1624354/.
84 *CoIG*, 16 Apr. 1972. 85 *CoIG*, 5 Aug. 1988. 86 *CoIG*, 24 Apr. 1998, editorial; also columns by 'Cromlyn' and 'Durrow'. 87 *CoIG*, 20 Sept. 1929, letter from Revd W. Lindsell Shade (Limerick). 88 In such as the *Irish Statesman*, 1919–20 and 1923–30 – see Nicholas Allen, *George Russell (Æ) and the new Ireland, 1905–30* (Dublin, 2003), pp 141–232. 89 *Saorstat Eireann, Census of Population, 1926*, vol. 3, table 1A, p. 1; *CoIG*, 1 Mar. 1929, editorial.

was to become Northern Ireland the Protestant population *increased* by some 2 per cent in the same period.) The effect in the South was to circle the wagons, to embed an already-existing Lilliputian *civitas* based around the church and its associated bodies – sporting organizations, schools, hospitals, charities.[90] The structure was economically underpinned by Protestant firms and farms. The *Gazette*'s reportage faithfully reflected and chronicled that ghettoized reality right up to the 1960s, as it did its gradual breakdown.

'Accommodation' brought its own problems. To work, it had to be reciprocated – for the state and its Catholic inhabitants to see value in its Protestant population. The state was not always in listening mode, though. The *Gazette*'s call in late December 1921 for Southern loyalists to be brought into the provisional government – on the grounds that they were patriotic and the administration could do with their business and financial experience – was not taken up.[91] That did not deter the paper. Under a new clerical editor, Revd G.A. Chamberlain, in December 1921 it was surprisingly upbeat about the prospects for the 'loyalists of the South and West', claiming them 'as good Irishmen as any'.[92] An editorial entitled 'At the Cross-Roads' in January 1922 urged Protestants to look forward, not back; and for them to realize 'no less than by the majority, that they are an integral part of the State'.[93] In October 1923, commenting on a service in St Patrick's Cathedral to mark the meeting of the Oireachtas, the *Gazette* stated: 'we can now enter the main streams of Irish public life … the Reformed Church of Ireland is anxious and willing to take her share in the task before the Reformed State'. On the 'render to Caesar' principle, its all-Ireland loyalism before 1921 morphed into acceptance of both states – 'Loyalty to lawfully constituted authority is our principle'.[94] Thus the *Gazette* could legitimately espouse the church as having a moderating influence on the perceived religious and political excesses of the Free State (although noticeably not so much in regard to Northern Ireland).[95]

Citizenship was elevated to a virtue that Southern Protestants could proclaim with pride. 'Peace, order, and righteousness' were the watchwords.[96] Civic participation through the ballot box was frequently urged: 'the person who refuses to use his franchise is a rotten citizen', wrote the *Gazette* in 1932.[97] A

90 Martin Maguire, 'The organisation and activism of Dublin's Protestant working class, 1883–1935', *Irish Historical Studies*, 29:113 (1994), 65–87. See also the dean of Christ Church's talk on 'Social Service' at the Patrician Conference, where he lists the organizations – William Bell & N.D. Emerson (eds), *The Church of Ireland A.D. 432–1932*. See further *The Report of the Church of Ireland Conference held in Dublin, 11–14 October, 1932, to which is appended an account of the Commemoration by the Church of Ireland of the 1500th Anniversary of the Landing of St Patrick in Ireland* (Dublin, 1932), pp 186–90.   91 *CoIG*, 30 Dec. 1921.   92 *CoIG*, 9 Dec. 1921.   93 *CoIG*, 6 Jan. 1922.   94 *CoIG*, 5 Oct. 1923.   95 Coffey, 'The price of loyalty', p. 66.   96 Primate Charles d'Arcy, quoted in *CoIG*, 5 Jan. 1923.   97 *CoIG*, 5 Feb. 1932.

leading article in 1965 on Michael Viney's 'The Five Per Cent' reckoned that the Protestant voting record in the Republic was 'not unworthy of their traditions'.[98] In 1968 the *Gazette* highlighted the prominence of Anglicans on the committee of Rathvilly's (Co. Carlow) award-winning Tidy Towns campaign – 'the Protestants mustn't let the side down'.[99] Eventually, of course, the religious divide in the Republic ceased to have much meaning or relevance; today, the denominational make-up of societies, professional bodies, committees and voluntary organizations would seldom be a matter of public comment or private concern. In not being irredentist, the paper legitimized its often critical commentary on the Free State's role in regard to such as literary (though not film) censorship and compulsory Irish.[100]

But the *Gazette* also reflected and accommodated Southern Protestants' strong residual sense of attachment to and affinity with cultural Britishness and loyalty to empire, which only gradually tailed off during the century. King George VI's death in 1952 was marked by memorial activity in wholly Southern dioceses – there were services in Cashel Cathedral and St Finn Barre's in Cork, while Limerick Mothers' Union said prayers.[101] As Nora Robertson put it in 1960, 'In respecting new loyalties, it had not seemed incumbent upon us to throw our old ones overboard.'[102] It was wholly typical of the *Gazette* that, on the coming into force of the Republic of Ireland Act in 1949, editorially it contented itself with a rather sour reference to Bishop Kerr's polemical *The independence of the Celtic church in Ireland*, noting the papal bulls that had 'energetically ceded Ireland to King Henry II'. Otherwise, it simply reproduced the message from George VI, in which he highlighted the participation of Irish in 'the recent war'.[103]

The prominence of Anglicanism in the civic and political life of the North contrasted with its post-partition peripherality in the South. This was the Church of Ireland acting as if it were still established – 'In its relations with the Government of Northern Ireland, the Church of Ireland had stepped easily into the position a State Church would have occupied.'[104] That existed from the first – on 7 June 1921 Primate d'Arcy said prayers at the first session of the Northern Ireland Parliament, and again at its state opening by King George V later in the month.[105] In 1932 d'Arcy was involved in the Northern celebrations for the 1,500th anniversary of the arrival of St Patrick in Ireland.

98 *CoIG*, 2 Apr. 1965.   **99** *CoIG*, 15 Nov. 1968.   **100** For censorship, see editorials in *CoIG*, 8 Mar., 19 July 1929; for compulsory Irish, *CoIG*, 20 June 1924. A column in Irish, 'Litir on life', is in the issue of 9 Dec. 1949.   **101** *CoIG*, 14 May 1937, 22 Feb. 1952.   **102** Nora Robertson, *Crowned harp* (Dublin, 1960), p. 9.   **103** *CoIG*, 22 Apr. 1949.   **104** David Hume, 'Empire Day in Ireland, 1896–1962' in Keith Jeffery (ed.), *An Irish empire* (Manchester, 1996), pp 149–67 at p. 153.   **105** Charles d'Arcy, *The adventures of a bishop: a phase of Irish life: a personal and historical narrative* (London, 1934), p. 239.

In contrast to the Church of Ireland celebratory events in Dublin, in which there was no official or governmental representation, it had many elements of a state occasion, including the attendance of the Northern Ireland governor, the duke of Abercorn.[106]

JOURNEYS AND DESTINATIONS

Through its editorials and successive columns 'Notes by the Way', 'Notes of the Week', 'The Week', 'Here, There and Everywhere' and 'Newsdesk', the *Gazette* kept the minority well-informed about itself and the wider world. In its reprints of sermons, theological lectures, reports of missionary and youth societies and articles on controversial issues like the ordination of women and the 1983 abortion referendum in the Republic, it exhibited the extensive range of Anglican thinking and activity over the period. The cultural empire remained a sort of reality in the wider Anglican Communion, extensively covered in the *Gazette*. The distinguishing feature of the paper, especially during the first half of the twentieth century, was not only its breadth but also its depth, giving a real flavour of the debates in the church, helping its readers 'to see their Church life in its true perspective'.[107] These – such as the church's Patrician lineage; pacifism; the moral difficulties of divorce and remarriage and later abortion and same-sex marriage; whether prayers for the dead were allowable; ritualism and the position of the cross on the altar; the role of the Divinity School in Trinity College in shaping the clergy; the baptismal service and the extent to which it allowed for baptismal regeneration – crop up time and again, both in the letters columns and in editorial/opinion pieces.

The paper went easy on the other Protestant denominations on the island. A shared political outlook before 1921 in the face of an aggressive Catholic nationalism overrode any theological unease – in October 1910, for instance, the paper had a special supplement on the Church of Ireland Conference in Belfast, in which it highlighted the attendance of a Presbyterian delegation led by the moderator. Relations between Anglicans and Methodists were always more cordial, especially in the missionary sphere,[108] and between the 1930s and 1950s, regular reports and correspondence commented on moves to unify the two denominations. There were limits – from the mid-1960s, in an ecumenical

---

106 D'Arcy, *Adventures of a bishop*, p. 289; *The Church of Ireland, AD 432–1932*, pp 257–8; *CoIG*, 17 June 1932. 107 Archbishop Gregg, *CoIG*, 28 Jan. 1955. 108 See, for instance, *CoIG*, 8 Feb. 1924.

age, Ian Paisley's anti-Catholic antics and his Free Presbyterian Church feature in critical comment pieces.[109]

That marked a change for the *Gazette*. Up to the end of the 1950s, it had not been shy when it came to publishing anti-Catholic points of view. Paisley would have had little difficulty in endorsing the many articles and pieces of correspondence on the Mass as sacrifice, papal infallibility, priestly authoritarianism and political interference, idolatry and image worship, and salvation by works. Mariology was a particular target. A flavour was seen in 1950 (it may have been a Holy Year, but unholy spats seemed to characterize it) on the occasion of Pope Pius XII's promulgation of the dogma of the Assumption. The paper's usual column 'In Quietness and Confidence' belied its title with a vitriolic attack, proclaiming that 'there are no grounds for the extravagant honours which the Roman Church pays to the Blessed Virgin, endangering as they do the doctrine of the Holy Trinity'; and 'the Assumption is a complete fiction without a shred of historical evidence'.[110] The *Gazette* wrote about all these issues because they were those about which laity as well as clergy felt passionately.

That laity was always alert to possible discrimination against the minority, and the *Gazette* did not shirk from speaking its mind about what it saw as the machinations and manipulations of Roman Catholicism, most especially by non-state actors. The Mayo librarian imbroglio in 1930[111] (when the appointment of a Protestant woman TCD graduate as county librarian was opposed by local interests and the Catholic Church) and the Tilson mixed-marriage child custody case in 1950 were highlighted by the paper. In the latter episode, the paper reflected the sensitivities of Irish Protestants to the proscriptions of the *Ne Temere* decree. Somewhat uncharacteristically, it lent its entire front page to Revd William Giff of the evangelical Irish Church Missions, backer of Tilson, to argue against a high court judgment that, on the surface, appeared to give credence to the 'special position' of the Roman Catholic Church as articulated in Article 44 of the 1937 Irish constitution.[112]

In 1956, the *Gazette* lambasted those who advocated that Southern Protestants 'should keep ourselves to ourselves and, if we speak, confine our remarks to platitudinous exhortations on non-controversial subjects ...

---

109 See *CoIG*, 25 Feb. 1969 ('Cross channel commentary'); 7 Mar. 1969 ('Cromlyn'); 6 June 1969 ('Gazetteer'); 13 Oct. 1969 ('Markus'). **110** *CoIG*, 3 Nov. 1950. **111** Pat Walsh, *The curious case of the Mayo librarian* (Cork, 2009), pp 24, 136; *CoIG*, 5 Dec. 1930. **112** *CoIG*, 11 Aug. 1950; Heather Crawford, *Outside the glow* (Dublin, 2010), pp 113–14; John V. Kelleher, 'Can Ireland unite?', *Atlantic Monthly* (April 1954) – http://www.theatlantic.com/past/docs/unbound/flashbks/ireland/kelle.htm; Finola Kennedy, *Family, economy, and government in Ireland* (Dublin, 1989), pp 70–1; Gerard Hogan, 'A fresh look at Tilson's case', *Irish Jurist*, 33:1 (1998), 311–32 at 311.

lest such attention should result in material or social disadvantages'.[113] The Fethard-on-Sea boycott of Protestant businesses the following year showed just how such attention could be injurious to Protestant interests. The boycott was covered extensively in the paper.[114] From the Northern station, 'Cromlyn''s perspective was predictable: the boycott represented 'the contemporary application of Article 44 of the Éire Constitution, which is at present being applied in Fethard'.[115]

The point about these controversies, though, is that they were notable because they were generally exceptional. The Church of Ireland was never as out of tune with independent Ireland as often assumed. Archbishop Gregg and Eamon de Valera not only looked alike but exhibited similar mindsets. The church's membership was socially and economically conservative. This sometimes led to a 'holy alliance', as in 1951 when – condemnatory of socialism and suspicious of statism – the *Gazette*'s characterization of the Republic's Mother and Child Scheme as 'communist interference in the family'[116] put it firmly in the Catholic hierarchy's camp. That, though, was not the case in 1983, when church and *Gazette* came out hard against the Eighth Amendment to the Constitution, on abortion. The primate, Dr Armstrong, called it 'a deeply regrettable episode'. The *Gazette* opined that 'nothing has been solved by the exercise … some of the ecumenic tide has flowed back',[117] seeing it as sectarian, with adverse implications for 'this history-torn country of ours'.[118] As it turned out, primate and paper were right.

The 1983 referendum reawakened echoes of an earlier, disputatious age, which had seemed to be on the wane since the 1960s. At the beginning of that decade, the *Gazette* had expressed wariness of John F. Kennedy's Roman Catholicism.[119] Yet by the time of his assassination it praised him 'in proving that men of goodwill of many faiths could work together for the common good'.[120] Ecumenism was the single biggest subject covered in the *Gazette* in the decade, especially after the Vatican Council's influence began to permeate even traditional and devout Ireland. Correspondence and articles wrestled with the question of how, in a more tolerant age, to interpret the anti-Catholic elements of the church's foundational Thirty-Nine Articles – although the

---

113 *CoIG*, 30 Nov. 1956.   114 A major editorial on 14 June 1957; others on 28 June, 12, 19 July, 2, 9 Aug., 25 Oct. 1957. See also Tim Fanning, *The Fethard-on-Sea boycott* (Cork, 2010) and Eugene Broderick, *The boycott at Fethard-on-Sea, 1957: a study in Catholic-Protestant relations in modern Ireland* (Newcastle-Upon-Tyne, 2011).   115 *CoIG*, 21 June 1957.   116 *Irish Times*, 18 Nov. 2014, http://www.irishtimes.com/news/social-affairs/religion-and-beliefs/previous-generations-would-be-astounded-at-attitudes-to-churches-in-ireland-today-1.2004480.   117 *CoIG*, 16 Sept. 1983.   118 *CoIG*, 25 Feb. 1983. The paper gave prominent space on 11 Mar. 1983 for a pro-amendment article by Revd Cecil Kerr, Rostrevor, Co. Down.   119 *CoIG*, 18 Nov. 1960.   120 *CoIG*, 29 Nov. 1963.

Gazette was at pains to point out that it had never cast the pope as 'The Man of Sin', unlike more polemical Protestant publications. A monthly column, 'Ecumenical Record', was in the paper in 1966 and early 1967. A typical example of thoughtful coverage was Bishop Henry McAdoo's five interrogatory articles, 'Unity in Truth – What Are the Chances?', in June and July 1968.[121] Improving interdenominational relations on the ground were evidenced in the *Gazette* by such events as the opening of the aforementioned new rectory at Portarlington, attracting the (possibly slightly envious?) good wishes of the local Catholic priest.[122] In April 1966 the *Gazette* reported a visit by Catholic pupils to an Anglican church in Belfast.[123] Photos like that in July 1968 showing the local Catholic priest attending the opening of a new Church of Ireland primary school at Bagenalstown, Co. Carlow, were becoming commonplace.[124] In December 1969, the paper noted an ordination in Westport, Co. Mayo, in which several Catholic clergy played prominent roles.[125] In 1970, the *Ne Temere* decree was replaced by the (slightly) more flexible *Matramonia Fixta*. Even if later, in the 1990s, the *Gazette* was chronicling the effective breakdown of Roman Catholic-Anglican unity discussions and lamenting the lack of progress, the charismatic movement saw a unity in joyful faith rather than legalistic theology.[126]

'A RECORD OF CHURCH HISTORY'

Apart from the big issues, the paper was a mirror to the myriad trials and tribulations of the century. In December 1918, for example, it informed its readers that the Spanish flu had 'carried off one of our expert operators and seriously reduced our printing staff'.[127] The classified advertisements featured throughout the period – situations vacant and wanted, clerical positions and seeking homes for indigent Protestants – reflected changing economic conditions, the social environment and cultural mores. It was useful in establishing what Irish Anglicanism seemed to be, both for those inside the church and those outside it. In the absence of a church press bureau, it was often mined for stories about the church by other media.[128] Entertaining and provocative, it could (and did) scandalize thin-lipped bishops and crusty old colonels. It received the Hibernia Press Award for the best religious publication in 1972. During the formative years of independent Ireland, the *Gazette* pushed a line

121 *CoIG*, 5 Oct. 1990; 13 Sept., 22 Nov. 1991; 17 Jan. 1992, article by 'Cromlyn'. 122 *CoIG*, 17 Sept. 1965. 123 *CoIG*, 8 Apr. 1966. 124 *CoIG*, 19 July 1968. 125 *CoIG*, 2 Jan. 1970. 126 See a letter from Revd Gordon Pamment, *CoIG*, 7 Aug. 1992, detailing progress at grassroots level. 127 *CoIG*, 13 Dec. 1918. 128 *CoIG*, 5 Oct. 1923.

of 'loyal opposition' for those who saw themselves as beached on the wrong side of a revolution. In the North, it attempted to leaven and moderate the often blind and aggressive sectarianism that eventually provided an excuse for the violence of the '70s, '80s and '90s. It sat on the hyphen between that North-South divide for a hundred years so that it could 'do what we can to preserve and strengthen the links between church people in both parts of this island'.[129] In that, it exhibited a classic Anglicanism. 'Middling through' might have been its text for the century.

The *Gazette*'s reach was limited. While up to 1963 it had also been sold through newsagents, the paper was overwhelmingly sold by subscription and distributed directly to subscribers through parishes.[130] In 1900, the journal complained that while 'almost all' the clergy and a large proportion of 'our leading and influential laity' were subscribers, it had failed to achieve a mass following.[131] That did not really change over the century, despite the numerous reconfigurations, revamps and relaunches. A central problem was that it never appealed to the generality and majority of those who identified as 'Church of Ireland' – occasional Protestants, recipients of a simple theology, beneficiaries of the comforts of religion at important life moments. If the paper saw itself as 'an arena for informed encounter in the discussions of those issues which affect the Church in the proclamation of its message and fulfilment of its ministry',[132] that encounter was, in essence, primarily with insiders – the professional learned clerics and the committed laity that went to church every Sunday and served on vestries, ran Sunday schools and organized church fetes. The news, articles, opinion pieces, letters and columns rarely represented much more than a small church elite talking to itself. It is perhaps revealing that the magisterial correspondence in 1931–2 between Archbishop Gregg and Cardinal MacRory on the Patrician antecedents of the Church of Ireland was carried out in the columns of the *Irish Times* rather than the *Gazette*.[133]

So: given the journal's tiny readership, why was the church so determined to keep the *Gazette* alive? One answer to that question is the acute sensitivity of Irish Anglicanism (and, indeed, a wider Protestantism) to its identity and history. That was a constant background hum to virtually everything that appeared in the journal. It applied as much to the North as the South. Irish Anglicanism was on a march to marginalization in the twenty-six counties over the century – not until the 1960s did it start to properly reclaim a place

129 *CoIG*, 12 Jan. 1975. 130 Brian M. Walker, 'A Northern Ireland perspective on the *Gazette*'s coverage of the 1960s', https://www.ireland.anglican.org/news/10018/a-northern-ireland-perspective-on, 2 Oct. 2020. 131 *CoIG*, 5 Jan. 1900. 132 *CoIG*, 21 Mar. 1975. 133 Ian d'Alton. 'Religion as identity: the Church of Ireland's 1932 Patrician celebrations' in Jacqueline Hill & Mary Ann Lyons (eds), *Representing Irish religious histories: historiography, ideology and practice* (Cham, Switzerland, 2017), pp 197–210 at p. 200.

in the polity. In the North, as the ruling unionist oligarchy (which had been overwhelmingly Anglican) disintegrated in the face of more evangelical and extremist groups, its gentlemanly demeanour had less purchase.

The *Gazette* was an expensive indulgence for the church after 1963, and to let it go would have seemed a rational decision. Yet there was more than money at stake. Despite protestations of independence from both sides – the paper pronouncing that 'This paper holds no brief for the RCB',[134] and the church denying for a long time 'any assumption or suggestion that the paper is an official organ of the Church of Ireland'[135] – it was ultimately a symbiotic relationship. To survive, the journal depended upon the church. But the church also needed the *Gazette*. As an institution that tended to be rather obsessed with and sensitive about its temporal history and spiritual place on the island, it was important to have, in Archbishop Gregg's words, 'a record of Church history as it is being made'.[136] Maybe that is really why a historicist church could not afford to let the *Gazette* go under: who would then chronicle Irish Anglicanism from a (mostly) sympathetic viewpoint? In being 'a Church paper for Church people', the *Gazette* was equally – if not more so – 'a Church paper for the Church'.

134 *CoIG*, 21 July 1939.   135 *CoIG*, 3 Jan. 1947. In the 1870s the *Gazette*'s subtitle had been 'The Organ of the Church of Ireland', which the Church forced it to disavow in 1880; *Irish Ecclesiastical Gazette*, 3 Jan. 1880.   136 *CoIG*, 28 Jan. 1955.

8 / Political capital: *In Dublin*, advocacy and opinion, 1976–83

MARTINA MADDEN

In Dublin made its debut as a fortnightly 'what's on' listings guide in April 1976. Within three years it had evolved to become a features-led magazine that included a significant quantity of social affairs and political content focusing on issues of local politics, planning and development, and social issues including the gay rights movement and feminist activism. This chapter explores this evolution in terms of periodicals acting not only as barometers of social change, but also as 'a catalyst, shaping the social reality of their sociocultural moment'.[1] Despite their relative neglect within media research, magazines have 'a cultural importance that is far greater than their appearance (ephemeral, disposable) and image (lightweight, stopgap) suggests'.[2] As noted by David Abrahamson, 'in many instances the editorial content of magazines is specifically designed by its editors and looked to by its readers as something that will lead to action. It is not information for information's sake.'[3]

The introduction of free second-level education in 1967 had changed Ireland's economic, social and cultural landscape, and *In Dublin*'s appearance coincided with the coming-of-age of the first generation to benefit from this radical development in education policy. This better-educated generation had grown up in a more 'outward-looking and globally connected state' and was, perhaps, more willing than preceding generations to challenge the status quo.[4] In addition, a referendum in 1972 had lowered the voting age from 21 to 18, providing this cohort with a means of engaging in politics much earlier than previous generations. Socially, while Ireland remained a conservative country, the authority of the Catholic Church and its influence on the state and the media was beginning to wane. A parallel referendum on the day the voting age was lowered had removed the 'special position' of the Catholic Church in the Irish Constitution. But in 1976, contraception, divorce, homosexuality and abortion all remained illegal and were considered unacceptable by many. In addition, amid the economic crisis of the late 1970s/early 1980s

1 David Abrahamson, 'Magazine exceptionalism', *Journalism Studies*, 8:4 (2007), 667–70 at 667. 2 Tim Holmes, 'Mapping the magazine', *Journalism Studies*, 8:4 (2007), 510–21 at 510. 3 Abrahamson, 'Magazine exceptionalism', p. 670. 4 Mark O'Brien, *The fourth estate: journalism in twentieth-century Ireland* (Manchester, 2017), p. 228.

unemployment and emigration rates soared. All of these issues would become political battlegrounds on which *In Dublin* would campaign as the voice of a new generation.

INCEPTION AND EARLY YEARS

The person most closely associated with the founding of *In Dublin* is John Doyle, a Dublin man and University College Dublin arts graduate and law student who had lived in Paris after university, where he had formed the initial idea for a listings magazine for Dublin. The magazine he envisioned was inspired by *Pariscope* – that city's listings and entertainment magazine; the 'Goings on about Town' section of the *New Yorker*; and the London events guide *Time Out*. The idea took off when Doyle met Ciaran McGinley from Ballinasloe, Co. Galway, who had previously been responsible for the production and dissemination of a magazine for squat dwellers in London. The meeting occurred by chance: Doyle was driving a van from Galway to Dublin and picked up McGinley and his girlfriend, who were hitchhiking. The conversation that took place among the three on the journey led to a meeting with visual artist Ted Turton the following week. Turton, from Warrington, England, was working in Dublin using his artistic skills to create designs for vintage mirrors. He had studied illustration at art college in Leicester, but what was more pertinent to the production of *In Dublin* were the graphic-design skills he had acquired later at Wolverhampton Art College. His knowledge base – which included lithography, typography, photography, screen printing and sketching – was instrumental in getting the magazine off the ground.

The first issue of *In Dublin* appeared, six weeks after the three met, on Good Friday, 16 April 1976. The cover bore an illustration featuring a man carrying a ladder and brush, in front of a poster on a wall advertising 'exhibitions, drama, sports, cinema, music, and theatre'. Its masthead, a three-arched bridge, would become the magazine's trademark image. It was hand-drawn by Turton, whose creativity established the visual style of the magazine, and was based on 'a mishmash' of several of Dublin's River Liffey bridges. An A5, twelve-page publication, it cost 10p and carried a contents list of 'Beaches, Children, Cinema, Drama, Exhibitions, Food, Lectures, Libraries, Music, On The Air, Parks, and Sport'. Listings were free to place, though paid advertisements were sought from the same venues that listed their events. The note 'Small ads will be taken now for inclusion in future issues, 20p a line' reveals the model of business the magazine was following at the start. Under the heading 'Note for the Reader', it set out its intent to be a fortnightly publication and to be 'a useful community notice-board for information of all kinds'. The first issue contains a hint of the sense of fun and irreverence that would become a feature of *In Dublin*. The humorous quip – 'many thanks for the indispensable help of many kinds from many people and to the brothers for the use of the hall' – evokes what Doyle referred to as 'a sort of attitude in the magazine and also a good deal of cheek, I think, and it was probably very annoying to lots of other people who weren't feeling the same way'.[5]

In Dublin's first office was John Doyle's parental home in Dublin 6. It would move premises several times over the course of its first decade – to Henrietta Street, the *Trinity News* office on Pearse Street, Westmoreland Street (above Bewley's Café), Bachelor's Walk and Lower Ormond Quay. Having a city centre office was crucial 'for people to drop in, to hand in listings for publication, to pass on news, to offer ideas for articles, to show illustrations and photographs, as well as to put in small ads and collect copies for street-selling'.[6] Despite the perception that *In Dublin* was a youth-oriented magazine, Doyle disliked the term:

> That notion of youth culture, which was a marketing thing anyway, was just getting going at that time, but really *In Dublin* ... myself and the rest of them involved at the start had lots of people who were our own age, friends our own age, older friends, friends of our parents' generation, you know, there was a great mix, we would never have felt 'this is going to be for us'. There was an egalitarian air.[7]

For its first year, *In Dublin* continued as a straight-up listings magazine, which gradually introduced contributors to review theatre, books and music. By November 1976 its stated circulation was 17,000 copies. On its first anniversary, Doyle described himself as being full of 'irritating caution' in taking care to build its circulation base. This caution had been missing in Irish magazines that had previously launched, and in their first issue had attacked 'the Church, the Establishment, and Conor Cruise O'Brien' to the detriment of their future, as they could not survive without advertising.[8] When, Doyle concluded, *In Dublin* 'becomes the sort of magazine that advertisers can't afford to ignore, then we can break out and be more adventurous'.[9]

Despite this cautiousness, Doyle was deeply concerned about the development of Dublin and the lack of coverage the destruction of the city was

---

5 Interview with John Doyle, 2018. 6 Ibid. 7 Ibid. 8 Doyle, quoted in *Irish Times*, 9 July 1977. 9 Ibid. By the magazine's first anniversary McGinley had departed for Galway, where he launched the short-lived *In the West* magazine; Turton later joined him in the venture.

receiving from the mainstream press. He felt *In Dublin* had a role to play in this issue, and observed that while the broadsheets devoted a lot of space to national politics, few publications gave much coverage to local Dublin affairs:

> Dublin Corporation's laissez-faire approach to planning allowed the demolition of large parts of the city's Victorian and Georgian fabric and its replacement with poor-quality speculative development. We felt very strongly about this and about the rezoning of green fields on the edge of the city to make vast, badly-planned housing estates.[10]

In Dublin's activism in the campaign to stop the destruction of Wood Quay by Dublin Corporation began in November 1977. A three-page article by Lindie Naughton, 'Wood Quay, Now or Never', criticized the corporation's approach to the development of the Viking site to make way for civic offices and appealed to readers to sign a petition, organized by the group Friends of Medieval Dublin, to oppose the development. Signing petitions in the 1970s was a more arduous affair than it is in the online era: the magazine listed a telephone number that people could call to receive a form in the post. A column adjoining the article carried a strongly worded call to action by Naughton and Doyle, who told readers, 'But now it's up to YOU. It's your city and YOUR heritage that they're destroying. ACT!' While the development ultimately went ahead, *In Dublin's* collection of an additional 12,000 signatures for the petition was a remarkable feat for a small magazine. In a similar vein, in 1979 *In Dublin* opposed the city council's plan to run a motorway-style road (the Inner Tangent) through the heart of Dublin, which would have rendered the city centre unrecognizable – a plan that was ultimately shelved.

Among other significant content from its early years was a rebuke of Dublin City Council, which froze funding to the Project Arts Centre after it hosted a gay theatre group from England. Having invited readers to contribute to a fund, in May 1977 *In Dublin* reported that it had raised £1,000 for the theatre. It also addressed itself to feminist issues: in February 1977 it criticized the decision by the Censorship of Publications Board to ban the British feminist magazine *Spare Rib* on grounds of indecency. In a January 1978 issue, it welcomed the opening of Dublin's new sexual health and contraceptive advisory centre, the Well Woman Clinic.

In March 1979, just before its third anniversary, *In Dublin* underwent a redesign, doubling in size from A5 to A4 and announcing an expansion in its editorial content. The revenue from advertising had increased steadily each year,

---

10 Interview with John Doyle, 2018.

due to the efforts of advertising manager Roger Cole, who had joined the magazine in 1977. Cole sold ads not by showcasing circulation figures but by using the argument that the people who bought it had disposable income.[11] In terms of circulation, John Doyle estimated that at its peak the magazine sold over 12,000 copies, which compared well to national magazines considering that its circulation was limited to the capital.[12] Joint National Media Research (JNMR) surveys at the time, Doyle and Cole have asserted, showed that due to the listings each copy of *In Dublin* was read by up to ten people, and that those readers were the type of people that cigarette and alcohol advertisers sought. JNMR survey data from 1984–5 which was reproduced in an advertising rate card for the magazine stated that it had 95,000 readers per issue, with 69 per cent of these in the 15–34 age group and 58 per cent of readers coming from the higher socio-economic categories.[13] Although in its new iteration it would attract many new writers and develop into a features-led publication that carried political and social affairs content, this did not emerge from any strategic intent to disrupt or challenge 'the establishment'. As stated by Doyle, 'none of the people who started *In Dublin*, or who came to it in the first few years, considered themselves to be journalists, or had thought of that as a career. They were people who, in their different ways, wanted to write, and one of the strengths of the magazine was that it attracted so many of them.'[14]

In its tenth anniversary issue it observed that 'from the old left to the new right, the only discernible theme was diversity through adversity, or, never let them know what you're up to'. Noting that it had been described by commentators as 'alternative', it concluded that 'for many of those involved the only alternative was the terrible anonymity of the unemployable scribbler'.[15] But as it moved from being a listings magazine to a current affairs-led listings and review magazine — with striking covers by Robert Armstrong, Syd Bluett and others, cartoons by such regular contributors as Tom Mathews, Aongus Collins and Arja Kajermo and the photography of Tony O'Shea, Tony Murray and Tom Grace — the increased workload that curating and developing this additional content entailed required someone who could give it their full attention.

DAVID MCKENNA AS FEATURES EDITOR, 1979–81

In April 1979 David McKenna was appointed features editor. With a background in theatre, McKenna is first listed in the magazine as drama critic

11 Interview with Roger Cole, 2018.   12 Interview with John Doyle, 2018.   13 National Library of Ireland, MS 45,993/1 (*In Dublin* advertising rate card).   14 Interview with John Doyle, 2018.   15 *In Dublin*, issue 252.

in November 1976. The dynamic between Doyle and McKenna worked well: while Doyle oversaw the style and quality of the content and would offer an opinion, he was known for letting the editors edit.[16] As Colm Tóibín, by then a contributor to the magazine, put it, 'sometimes it was hard to see how the roles worked. David was features editor, John was editor. But, in fact, David was editor, John was publisher. That *really* was how it worked.'[17] For his part, McKenna viewed William Shawn, legendary editor of the *New Yorker*, as a role model and 'really wanted good writers … I wanted writers who had a voice.'[18]

He also took the technical aspect of the role of editor seriously and focused on making every piece of writing the best it could be. Tóibín recalled that 'he would make you rewrite pieces. Fintan [O'Toole] would come in with something, and he would sit with Fintan for hours talking about the beginning of it and how it needed one more thing. A lot of us were trained by David in this way.' Tóibín also recalled that McKenna 'had a very particular vision' for *In Dublin* that was 'really extraordinarily far-seeing' in terms of how he wanted to develop the magazine.[19] On the magazine's tenth anniversary, Fintan O'Toole described this period of transition as having 'a great atmosphere of something new, and a sense of something being broken'.[20] McKenna put together and carefully managed a coterie of writers that included Fintan O'Toole, Colm Tóibín, Mairéad Byrne, Simon Devilly and Mary Raftery. Also writing for *In Dublin* in the 1980s were Eamonn McCann, Derek Dunne, Kevin Dawson, Brian Trench, Mark Brennock, Colm Keena, Sam Smyth, Declan Lynch, Jonathan Philbin Bowman, Kate Holmquist, Padraig Yeates, Helen Shaw and Ann-Marie Hourihane. Of particular note in this era was McKenna's fostering of three arts reviewers who developed a following because of the calibre of their criticism. Michael Dervan (classical music), Aidan Dunne (art) and Michael Dwyer (film) were (with Fintan O'Toole on drama) 'the best critics working anywhere in Ireland', according to Colm Tóibín.[21] They all went on to become arts critics in the *Irish Times*. McKenna also invited Nell McCafferty to write for *In Dublin*, having previously been an admirer of her 'In the Eyes of the Law' column in the *Irish Times*.

McKenna was interested not only in the topic being covered, but in looking for different angles and perspectives. He commissioned playwright Tom MacIntyre to attend and write about the Fianna Fáil ard fheis because, 'as somebody who was himself from the Fianna Fáil heartland he would understand the people. I wasn't really interested in another Dublin point of view

16 Interview with Roger Cole, 2018. 17 Interview with Colm Tóibín, 2018. 18 Interview with David McKenna, 2018. 19 Interview with Colm Tóibín, 2018. 20 *Morning Ireland*, 17 Apr. 1986, available at https://www.rte.ie/archives/2016/0415/782034-10-years-of-in-dublin-magazine/. 21 Interview with Colm Tóibín, 2018.

on the culchie party, you know? But also I thought that as a playwright, as somebody used to performance, he would bring that kind of perspective to it as well.'[22] In a similar vein, he commissioned Anthony Cronin to interview Francis Stuart, a writer who had spent time in Berlin and who had made political radio broadcasts from Nazi Germany to neutral Ireland. The interview extends to four and a half pages, at the outset of which Cronin states that he may disagree with some of the content but is 'neither shocked nor horrified' and indeed 'with some part of my mind have full empathy with every part of what he says'. In the course of the interview, Stuart expresses his hatred for morality and convention and holds the view that high-brow writers should use their own lives as inspiration. He rails against what he refers to as 'phoney moral values' of state and church, declaring that 'the people you're up against – the authority, the law of the land – are no less ready to wreak violence and of a more horrible kind, actually. I saw it first in Hitler.'[23] McKenna's goal was that *In Dublin*, above all, should produce compelling journalism by writers who had something to say, rather than focus on furthering a liberal agenda, with the result that 'it wasn't a left-wing magazine, although it probably found itself taking positions more on the left than on the right'.[24]

Editorially, McKenna recalled that he was not really interested in covering mainstream politics – with one exception: 'Dublin Corporation and in the city, and planning'.[25] In one of his first issues as features editor, McKenna declared that '*In Dublin* will in future consistently report on the activities of the three Councils … and compare the councillors' decisions with their promises at election time'.[26] Under his guidance, coverage of Dublin Corporation's activities and other urban planning issues in the city became a core focus. Gary O'Callaghan wrote on planning matters, and he and McKenna attended council meetings assiduously. They singled out those they felt were responsible for the city's demise, referring to them in the publication as 'bête noires'. This monitoring of Dublin's development culminated in *Irish Times* journalist Frank McDonald's piece in May 1981. In his article, McDonald criticized a political elite who cared nothing for the problems plaguing Dublin – unemployment, public transport, air pollution and urban decay – and saw in that caste 'precious little idealism and a great deal of cynical opportunism [with the] objective to achieve power at any cost'.[27]

Issues of sexuality and morality also loomed large. The government's response to the McGee judgment (which struck down the ban on contraception) – the Health (Family Planning) Act 1979 – was tackled in one of the

22 Interview with David McKenna, 2018.   23 *In Dublin*, issue 92.   24 Interview with David McKenna, 2018.   25 Ibid.   26 *In Dublin*, issue 77.   27 *In Dublin*, issue 129.

few pieces written by McKenna, in which he criticized the limited access to contraception to married couples, and described it as 'depressing for people to whom easy access to contraception is vital'.[28] The need to visit a GP to obtain a prescription for condoms was explored by Colm Tóibín, who visited six Dublin doctors to test the limits and implementation of the legislation, in a piece that illustrated the risible nature of the concept.[29] The constitutional challenge on gay rights undertaken by David Norris also received much coverage. An article in 'Under the Bridge' – a section at the front of the magazine of short, unsigned contributions on matters relating to the city – was headlined 'Who Fears to Speak?' It declared that 'all right-thinking people' would support Norris and called for donations to be sent to Norris to fund the case.[30] An increase in the number of female writers during McKenna's tenure is also evident. He described himself as 'getting to grips with feminism' during the 1970s.[31] One such voice was that of Nell McCafferty, who covered topics that touched on many aspects of feminism with writing that was often empathic, insightful and humorous. In one column, McCafferty observed how a reading by US feminist Kate Millett at Liberty Hall drew questions from Irish women as speaker after speaker came to the microphone with a shopping list of minimum demands – for contraception, divorce, abortion, support for rape victims.[32] In another, she remarked that 'the bulk of organized female labour is working for rates well below those paid to men and those who work alongside men are not receiving either equal pay or equal opportunity'.[33]

Another comparable writer, Mairéad Byrne, explored an alternative aspect of women's lives and sexuality in a sympathetic and respectful interview with a Dublin woman who worked as a prostitute. In 'A Woman Among the Pharisees', the woman discussed the travails of a life spent loitering on street corners and the behaviour of her clients, who were highly regarded members of society, before wryly concluding that she had 'earned more than the Taoiseach over the years'.[34] There were, however, limits to how far the magazine would be allowed to deviate from the status quo. To mark the September 1979 visit to Ireland by Pope John Paul II, *In Dublin*'s cover, which was designed by Robert Armstrong, featured an image of the pope, with the face cut out and the tagline 'Guess Who?'[35] John Doyle recalled that it was a fairly innocuous cover, but in the heightened reverence brought on by the papal visit a lot of people were offended.[36] The cover caused a furore among newsagents, many of whom refused to stock the issue. Another commotion erupted when

28 *In Dublin*, issue 109. 29 *In Dublin*, issue 110. 30 *In Dublin*, issue 104. 31 Interview with David McKenna, 2018. 32 *In Dublin*, issue 114. 33 *In Dublin*, issue 111. 34 *In Dublin*, issue 128. 35 *In Dublin*, issue 86. 36 Interview with John Doyle, 2018

McKenna assigned Fintan O'Toole to examine the anti-nuclear protest at Carnsore Point, Co. Wexford, the site of a mooted nuclear power plant to be built by the Irish government. O'Toole's three-page article was scathing about the protestors, maintaining that 'the movement of which they are part is a schizophrenic beast … part political pressure group, part commune, part children's crusade':

> The young people who form the real alternative society of this decade are not crusaders. They do not need to wear flowers in their hair or erect barricades in the street … to differentiate themselves from the establishment. They are already on the other side of the invisible barricade of unemployment … [They] have no power, no dream.[37]

Recalling the article, McKenna said that 'it was a critique of alternative politics in a way, what you could broadly call "hippydom", and it caused a bit of a fuss because it was a sacred cow'.[38] By this time, those writing for *In Dublin* had, encouraged by Mary Raftery, begun to join the National Union of Journalists (NUJ). Colm Tóibín was not a natural advocate of the union and joined unwillingly: his entry in the Dublin Freelance Branch directory listed his specialization as 'State of the Nation Rants'. He recalled the change in mood at *In Dublin* – 'suddenly people were professionalising in different ways. I started writing for *Magill*. I started putting my eggs in a few different baskets and loving going around the different offices. But the only office I was comfortable in was the *In Dublin* one.'[39] In July 1981 Tóibín succeeded David McKenna as features editor.

COLM TÓIBÍN AS FEATURES EDITOR, 1981–2

Tóibín, who, like McKenna, John Doyle had met at UCD, first wrote for *In Dublin* in the autumn of 1978, having returned to Ireland after three years in Spain. He called in regularly to the city-centre office recalling that 'it would be a place to go if you were around town for the afternoon, just drop by the *In Dublin* office to see if anything was going on' and eventually (perhaps inevitably) he began to write for the magazine. Soon he became one of its most ambitious contributors, and in July 1981 he filled the vacancy left by David McKenna's departure. His editorial style was very different from that of his predecessor, and at the interview for the job, he presented Doyle and

---

37 *In Dublin,* issue 83. 38 Interview with David McKenna, 2018. 39 Interview with Colm Tóibín, 2018.

McKenna with a twenty-page manifesto on the direction he felt *In Dublin* should take.

Tóibín's vision was largely concerned with developing the magazine's arts coverage. It also included a proposal that *In Dublin* should have its own correspondent to report on local elections and urban planning. He also argued that going beyond local city politics was vital to *In Dublin*'s development, perceiving that 'the only way to broaden out, was into the political realm'.[40] Unlike McKenna, Tóibín was interested in the machinations of national government and in the words and actions of national politicians. He was also a different personality type. More impulsive than Doyle or McKenna, Tóibín was not merely unafraid of causing controversy, but actively revelled in being a provocateur. An example of his instinct for trouble was the March 1982 cover, which had a colour drawing of a controversial property developer and the inflammatory caption 'Patrick Gallagher: Property Speculator and Brat'.[41] The progress that McKenna had made in developing *In Dublin* into a platform for serious long-form, colour journalism was something that Tóibín could take advantage of when he stepped into the features editor role. He retained the people McKenna had brought to the magazine, including Fintan O'Toole, Mairéad Byrne and Mary Raftery, who were now highly accomplished writers. Tóibín was also able to build on the reputation for quality journalism that *In Dublin* had attained during McKenna's time, rather than having to start from scratch – but he also had the steadying hand of John Doyle to rein in his more outlandish ideas. As he recalled, 'I would have bursts of enthusiasm, things I wanted to do, but John would stop me if he thought it wasn't stylish or the writer wouldn't fit into the tone of the magazine.'[42]

In contrast to David McKenna and John Doyle, Tóibín loved to write as an editor and was keen to express his disillusionment with the entire political establishment. As he noted many years later, 'I thought it was our job to set up a world apart from politics, to write from a position of total opposition to how power was held and wielded.'[43] Tóibín was features editor for the period of political instability during which three general elections were held in the space of just eighteen months (June 1981; February 1982; and November 1982). Having not commented on the short-lived Fine Gael-Labour Party coalition that was in government between June 1981 and January 1982, *In Dublin*'s first foray into mainstream politics was in the weeks preceding the general election of February 1982. Tóibín decided to cover it 'on a whim', saying 'fuck it, actually we're going to do this'.[44] What he meant by 'this' was not purely the

40 Ibid.   41 *In Dublin*, issue 149.   42 Interview with Colm Tóibín, 2018.   43 Colm Tóibín, 'A brush with the law', *Dublin Review*, Autumn 2007.   44 Interview with Colm Tóibín, 2018.

inclusion of electoral coverage, but a challenge to an impending victory by
Fianna Fáil, and more pointedly, an objection to its leader Charles Haughey
becoming taoiseach. This followed a meeting at the magazine that discussed
the likelihood of Haughey being successful. As recalled by John Doyle, 'it was
more a sense of cheek and a sort of restlessness that led to us writing about
politics. I don't think it ever really intended to be a political magazine. We certainly would never have thought we must defend a certain line or something
like that. It didn't really develop like that.'[45] In the issue before the general election of February 1982, the cover of *In Dublin* was emblazoned with the words
'Anything Is Better than Charlie Haughey' in large black typeface on a white
background accompanied by a photograph of Haughey.[46] For his part, John
Doyle felt the cover was reflective of the public mood at the time:

> It was a bit disgraceful really to have a magazine cover that was like a
> political poster but it was one way of expressing a point of view which
> an awful lot of people would have felt. Because it was like … for a lot
> of people the idea of Charlie Haughey as Taoiseach was unthinkable …
> since the arms trial and all of that.[47]

Similarly, Tóibín thought the cover mirrored public sentiment:

> It was a big fucking thing to do. And it was quite a big graphic, and it
> was what everybody felt at that time, you know? Charlie's fucking con-
> traceptive, Charlie's arms deal, the whole business of Charlie's hypocrisy.
> This was a creep! He's a fucking creep![48]

The controversial cover proved to be, inadvertently, a good sales move by *In
Dublin*. John Doyle remembers that the issue sold particularly well, because
'Fianna Fáil were buying them up trying to get them out of the shops, and
Fine Gael were buying them up trying to get their supporters to stick them
to their windows.'[49] Inside this issue, profiles of the two men most likely to
be taoiseach – Haughey and Fine Gael leader, Garret FitzGerald – were less
than complimentary. Under the heading 'The Man Who Would Be King',
written by Tóibín and Doyle, Haughey was described as a 'dogged little man'
who survived a car crash, a fall from his horse and the arms trial, and wanted
power to use it for his own ends rather than the betterment of the country. It
concluded that 'it would be better for both the country and the Fianna Fáil

---

45 Interview with John Doyle, 2018. 46 *In Dublin,* issue 146. 47 Interview with John Doyle,
2018. 48 Interview with Colm Tóibín, 2018. 49 Interview with John Doyle, 2018.

party if he does not win this election'. An adjoining article, 'The Wizard of Oz', authored by Tóibín, was equally disparaging about FitzGerald's short term as taoiseach and concluded that while 'his only advantage is the general feeling that anything is better than Charlie Haughey, this does not seem a good enough reason for anyone to vote for FitzGerald'. But not everyone at *In Dublin* was supportive of the controversial cover – advertising manager Roger Cole was 'horrified' and objected to it on the grounds that Haughey was not only a political actor, but 'a human being'.[50] This difference in opinion led to 'a blazing row' with Tóibín, an experience repeated when Tóibín next met Haughey's public relations guru, P.J. Mara. Mara's quibble with the cover was the use of the word 'anything'. According to him, saying 'any*body*' would have been excusable, but using the word 'thing' was intolerable.

The uncertain electoral outcome was reflected in an article the following month by Colm Tóibín about Dublin independent TD Tony Gregory, and a cover image of him, captioned 'Not for Sale'.[51] The focus on Gregory is unsurprising given *In Dublin*'s only consistent political theme – the planning and development of Dublin city. The 'Gregory Deal', in which the independent TD agreed to support Haughey as taoiseach in return for a £50 million development fund for his inner-city constituency, which was plagued by poverty, unemployment and drug problems, was covered in an article by Fintan O'Toole. Entitled 'Kiss of Life for Dublin?' it charted the progress of the negotiations.[52] However, the Haughey administration was short-lived and despite the ruckus that had followed the 'Anything Is Better than Charlie Haughey' cover eight months later, just before the November 1982 election, *In Dublin* ran an identical cover, with a photograph of Haughey and bearing the words 'Nothing Could Be Worse Than Charlie Haughey'. In 'Doom, Bloom, Gloom & Boom: The Political Parties & the Economy: A Catechism', O'Toole asked, 'How bad are things?' before referencing the high rates of unemployment, and answering, 'Bloody awful'. Another article, 'Charlie's Last Stroke', by Mary Holland, outlined how Haughey was promising a referendum on a constitutional ban on abortion in a bid to attract votes.[53]

Despite the best attempts to plan each issue, the inclusion and exclusion of topics was as unpredictable as ever, in part due to the hectic production schedule of the magazine. In addition, *In Dublin*'s cover and colour pages were printed a week in advance, resulting in a sometimes odd juxtaposition between visual themes and content. Looking back on this process, Tóibín recalled that

---

50 Interview with Roger Cole, 2018.   51 *In Dublin*, issue 148.   52 *In Dublin*, issue 158.   53 *In Dublin*, issue 166.

There was never time to stand back and say what are we covering, not covering? Everything was done on a spirit of sheer enthusiasm. Someone would come with an idea. We'd say okay, we'll put that there and that there. It was never thought out. In a way because it was never thought out there was a sort of excitement to it in that people would never know what the lead piece was going to be.[54]

Nonetheless, Tóibín tried to steer the magazine's writers to make the best use of their talents. He steered Fintan O'Toole towards writing about mainstream politics. He also encouraged Mary Raftery to progress from being a sub-editor to becoming a writer. She evolved from straightforward reporting, as in her coverage of the Stardust Tribunal in October 1981, to long-form investigative journalism with a bracing five-page exposition of Dublin's heroin epidemic in May of the following year.[55] Tóibín also commissioned the controversial Francis Stuart to write a regular column for *In Dublin* during this time. While Stuart had previously written about horse-racing for the magazine, he now wrote columns that were 'short and sharp in their blanket attacks on the establishment – Church, State, consumers all. They proposed a sort of anarchism and mysticism. The interesting thing, of course, was that the writer was an elderly man whose name carried with it an 'uncertain stigma'.[56] The success of *In Dublin's* new direction became apparent when Vincent Browne recruited Tóibín to edit *Magill* in late 1982.

A REFERENDUM AND A SUCCESSION OF EDITORS

Tóibín's departure resulted in the return of David McKenna, who had spent his time away from *In Dublin* producing and directing a play, *The golden hair*, scripted by Mairéad Byrne, at the Project Arts Centre, and as production editor of *Magill*. McKenna returned to *In Dublin* as editor, with John Doyle now listed as publisher. But it was not the same magazine he had left. He found that the new crop of writers that had arrived in his absence was quite different from those he had tended to hire:

By the time I came back to the magazine in 1983, journalism courses were up and running. And people were coming from journalism courses to me with propositions, and they'd been taught how to analyse publications,

---

54 Interview with Colm Tóibín, 2018.   55 *In Dublin*, issues 138 & 153.   56 Colm Tóibín, 'Issues of truth and invention', *London Review of Books*, 23:1 (2001), 3–11.

you know, very practically in terms of earning a living, and they'd come to me with suggestions for *In Dublin*.[57]

This brought a very different culture to the magazine. As McKenna saw it, this new crop of writers was ambitious, looking ahead to a journalism career and a staff job in the national press, with the result that with some exceptions, they were less willing to take risks with their writing and were not committed to *In Dublin* itself, seeing it merely as the bottom rung of the career ladder from which they had to move up. McKenna recalls that a piece he commissioned from a writer in this period which had the potential of having all the hallmarks of the style he had previously fostered within *In Dublin* was sanitized by the author into a flat, third-person account which, although technically proficient, was uninteresting. Unfortunately for McKenna and *In Dublin*, the original cohort of writers, whom he had trained to have a distinctive voice, were moving on – following Tóibín to *Magill* or to Vincent Browne's newest acquisition, the *Sunday Tribune*, both of which paid more than *In Dublin*.[58] Looking back, Tóibín believes that re-orienting *In Dublin* towards increased coverage of national politics and politicians was probably a mistake, given the environment in which it operated:

> I was probably wrong, in that we just couldn't compete with *Magill*. We couldn't compete with Vincent Browne's contacts. We could do it as a sort of sport, but Vincent was doing it as dead serious, and he had a team of people. He had a staff writer like Gene Kerrigan he could use, Mary Holland … he could use any number of people. But they were adults; we were adolescents, except in relation to the arts. Michael Dervan knew as much then as he knows now and wrote as seriously then as he does now. I think Aidan Dunne was the same, and so was Fintan O'Toole.[59]

Despite all this, however, McKenna took hold of the biggest political issue of 1983 with a force that had not been seen in the magazine before. When the referendum on the Eighth Amendment to the Constitution was announced early that year, he immediately commissioned Nell McCafferty to write a column that stood out as a conspicuous exception to the changed tone of *In Dublin*. In it her authorial voice is unmistakeable, her opinions strongly held

57 Interview with David McKenna, 2018. 58 For a review of the *Sunday Tribune* see Pat Brennan & Brian Trench, 'The *Tribune*'s turbulent times' in Joe Breen & Mark O'Brien (eds), *The Sunday papers: a history of Ireland's weekly press* (Dublin, 2018), pp 161–81; for a review of *Magill* see Kevin Rafter, 'The passion of particularity: *Magill*, 1977–90' in Mark O'Brien & Felix M. Larkin (eds), *Periodicals and journalism in twentieth-century Ireland: writing against the grain* (Dublin, 2014), pp 210–34. 59 Interview with Colm Tóibín, 2018.

and her opposition to the amendment unwavering. The second of her thirteen 'Countdown to Referendum' columns, in February 1983, set the tone by object-ing to the lack of women's voices in the debate, asserting that 'readers will have noticed by now the exclusive concentration in this count-down article on male names and male "leaders" and the virtual lack of reference to women, who, exclusively, are the people who become pregnant'.[60] In the months before poll-ing day, political and public unease with government as to the amendment's wording increased, McCafferty considered the positions of TDs who were for and against the proposed amendment; the position of the taoiseach, Garret FitzGerald; the positions adopted by the regional press; and, with the insight of doctors and lawyers, the ambiguous legal situation in which maternal healthcare was provided.[61] An examination of the mainstream national news-papers in the months leading up to the referendum (held in September 1983) uncovers nothing in this vein. McCafferty's columns are exceptional for their angle of analysis and in their often angry, darkly humorous tone. They disre-gard objectivity, speaking from a perspective informed by the writer's ardent feminism. Recalling her time writing for *In Dublin*, McCafferty said:

> I can say things in *In Dublin* that would not be allowed in what are called family newspapers in this country. I remember, for example, that during the terrible amendment campaign in 1983 … they gave me a fortnightly column for nearly a year and a half to say exactly what I thought of it, at a time, for example, when I wrote only one article, a fairly moderate article, in the *Irish Press* and it wasn't published. At that time I think they were the only untrammelled voice in the country.[62]

With such an approach, *In Dublin* provided an alternative view to the mainstream press, although not necessarily to its readership, as observed by McKenna:

> I think the word bravery is sometimes flung around a bit too much. Actors get called brave for playing a part with a limp. Or some journalist gets called brave for writing a thing that fundamentally the demographic of the publication wants to hear. There were a lot of people in Dublin and in Ireland who were definitely in sympathy and a lot of them in complete agreement; it gave voice to that. It wasn't out there on its own. It might have been unusual in publishing terms but that's a tiny group. What's really important is the people it spoke for and along with.[63]

60 *In Dublin*, issue 172. 61 *In Dublin*, issues 173, 174, 178 & 179. 62 *Morning Ireland*, 17 Apr. 1986. 63 Interview with David McKenna, 2018.

In comparison to the mainstream press, *In Dublin* made no claim to balance. It did not include the views of both sides of the argument, which the mainstream press had at least attempted to do. More significantly, and in keeping with its mooted alternative or countercultural attitude and style, was the way in which the topic of abortion was written about. The tone of the writing was heavily emotive, often combative and definitely provocative, but it did not lack intellectual rigour. The mainstream press was very much focused on the amendment's wording and interested in the political factions that had developed in the government because of the referendum. *In Dublin* was focused on what it meant for women; how society viewed them and the effect the amendment would have on their lives. It is the singular example of a campaign at this time that was in keeping with the previous iteration of *In Dublin*.

Significantly, David McKenna found his voice in the editorial for *In Dublin's* referendum issue. In contrast to his time as features editor, when he preferred to enhance and guide the writing of contributors, on this topic he expressed his own view. He recalled working on the referendum edition of the magazine and 'being determined that whatever impact it could have, it would have as much impact as we could make it have'.[64] McKenna's editorial derided the claim of the pro-amendment contingent 'that they speak for all decent women and men who care about life [while they] hand out manipulative, misleading and inaccurate leaflets which are designed to frighten us into agreeing with their wishes'. Noting that the amendment was 'vaguely worded', the editorial called on readers to 'vote no'. Contributors to this issue included Mairéad Byrne, Nell McCafferty, Monica Barnes TD, Frances Haines, Senator Catherine McGuinness, Molly O'Duffy, Lisa Pereira, Mary Raftery and Helen Shaw. It was no coincidence that they were all women. According to McKenna:

> By the time it came to 1983 I was very clear that this was primarily an issue for women. A decision women had to take. I don't think this is hindsight. I think I saw it then as I do now, as a decision that every woman who gets pregnant takes. It might be taken in a microsecond, but it's a decision because the option is there and it always has been, so there was that. I don't know whether we commissioned any male writers for that particular issue but certainly the emphasis was on female writers.[65]

Strikingly, Mary Raftery's article detailed the intimidation endured by politicians – such as Alan Shatter, Nuala Fennell, Monica Barnes, Maurice

64 Ibid.   65 Ibid.   66 *In Dublin*, issue 186.

Manning, Catherine McGuinness and Ruairí Quinn – who advocated a 'no' vote.[66] The cover of this referendum issue featured a colour illustration by Arja Kajermo of women in a lidded box, shouting 'No!, No!, No!, No!' as the lid hangs perilously over their heads. It is an arresting image and evocative of the magazine's view that the amendment was constraining and silencing women. Despite the fillip that such campaigning journalism gave to the magazine and to McKenna, he quickly decided that things had changed too much for him to stay on as editor:

> The second time I went back to *In Dublin* partly informed why I left. It was to my mind becoming far more difficult to find the kind of person that we'd identified the first time around as features editor, who wanted to write, really wanted to write and was looking, whether they knew it or not, for somewhere that would encourage them to do that as well as they could and would support them and would criticise them and wouldn't necessarily accept the first draft. The second time around there were plenty of young professional journalists starting out in their career, some of them became very well-known and ... it was difficult in many cases – including some of the most talented and certainly the ones who became very successful – to get them to bring that ... the personal voice.[67]

In McKenna's view, *In Dublin* was losing, or had lost, what had made it unique. To him it was no longer a publication that people happened upon and started to write for because of a need to say something, or for the joy of writing. As a result of the pragmatic, long-term goals of writers formally educated in the journalism profession, a more self-conscious editorial style had crept in. The contributors were no longer amateurs; they were journalists on a career path. As such they had reputations to protect that hindered what they could and would write, for fear it would impede future opportunities in the mainstream press. McKenna left *In Dublin* in early 1984 and later joined RTÉ as a producer. He was succeeded as editor by Ferdia MacAnna (1984) who in turn was followed by John Waters (1985–7), before John Doyle again returned as editor.

In 1988 Doyle sold *In Dublin* to Vincent Browne's Tribune Group and Fiona Looney was appointed editor. A little over a year later, amid declining circulation, Browne withdrew support and most of its writers migrated to the group's other titles – *Magill* and the *Sunday Tribune.* Subsequently, *In Dublin*

67 Interview with David McKenna, 2018.

continued on in various forms under a multitude of owners and editors and breaks in publication before finally ceasing publication in 2010.[68] But it never again captured the zeitgeist of a changing Ireland as it had in those early years.

68 *In Dublin* was banned for six months by the Censorship of Publications Board in August 1999 following complaints about its advertising. See *Irish Times*, 12 Aug. 1999.

9 / Writing from the margins: *In Touch, Identity, Out* and *GCN*

MARK O'BRIEN

In the run-up to the 2015 marriage equality referendum several commentators declared that gay people had suffered no legal descrimination in Irish society because homosexuality, as opposed to homosexual acts, was never a crime in Ireland – an argument that focused solely on the legal status of the individual and ignored their life experiences under repressive legislation.[1] A more realistic assessment had been offered forty years earlier, when, in 1975, the former minister for health Noel Browne had observed that 'the Irish homosexual was compelled to suppress his natural sexuality or face imprisonment'.[2] A search of any newspaper's online archives uncovers the abundant court cases involving consenting adults found guilty of 'gross indecency'.[3] One author has calculated that between 1940 and 1978 the state secured an average of thirteen convictions per annum, and between 1979 and 1986 it initiated an average of thirty prosecutions per annum.[4] Homosexual acts were finally decriminalized, following a lengthy legal battle, in 1993, and in 2018 the Irish state apologized to all those affected by the criminalization of consensual same-sex acts in Ireland prior to 1993.[5]

The legislation in question dated from the late nineteenth century, though in the research for his long but ultimately successful legal challenge, David Norris traced the policy of criminalization to Henry VIII's break from Rome in the early 1500s when the monarch 'assumed to the government most of the prerogative of the ecclesiastical courts'. Thus homosexuality moved 'from sin to crime and an essentially religious prohibition was arbitrarily absorbed into the common law'.[6] In 1861 the Offences Against the Person Act criminalized male homosexual acts, with punishment of penal servitude for

---

1 See, for example, RTÉ Radio 1 (*Morning Ireland*), 20 May 2015. 2 *Irish Times*, 28 Nov. 1975. Browne spoke of 'professional colleagues whose lives have been damaged irrevocably, because, through blackmail and the threat of exposure, they had been forced to leave Ireland and the intolerant inhuman attitudes to the homosexual'. 3 See, for example, *Irish Independent*, 30 Jan. 1931. 4 Chrystel Hug, *The politics of sexual morality in Ireland* (London, 1999), pp 207–8. 5 *Irish Times*, 20 June 2018. 6 David Norris, 'Homosexual people and the Christian churches in Ireland', National Library of Ireland (hereafter NLI), *Identity*, 2 (1982), 21–5 at 23. The relevant legislation was, for England, the Buggery Act 1533 and for Ireland, An Act for the Punishment for the Vice of Buggery 1634.

life.[7] Amid the campaign for home rule, *United Ireland*, the newspaper of the Irish Party, published, in 1884, articles alleging homosexual activity among high-ranking government officials in Dublin Castle, seat of British rule in Ireland. This activity, described by *United Ireland* as 'depravity unsurpassed in the history of human crime', was highlighted as a symptom of foreign rule. In a similar vein, the *Evening Telegraph* accused the government officials concerned of 'contaminating the running stream of Irish moral purity'.[8] Homosexuality, it seemed, was a British import that only further strengthened the case for home rule.

The following year, the Criminal Law Amendment Act 1885 criminalized all intimate acts, whether public or private, between males, with a penalty of up to two years' imprisonment. Referred to as 'the blackmailer's charter', this amendment to the legislation is the provision under which Oscar Wilde was prosecuted and imprisoned in 1895.[9] Thus stood the legislative situation when the Irish Free State was established in 1922 and all existing laws migrated to the Irish statute books. It would be another seventy-one years before this law was repealed. For over fifty of those seventy-one years the only mention of homosexuality in the mainstream press was in reports of court cases where a variety of euphemisms were used to describe offences. It was only in the 1970s that the Irish gay community began 'the process of self-identification and developed any consciousness of themselves as a minority community'.[10] As a campaign to repeal the 1861 and 1885 acts developed, the Irish media, and in particular, the *Irish Times*, covered it. This involved the paper's reporter Elgy Gillespie interviewing Denis Lennon, editor of the London *Gay News*, which Lennon described as a focal point for the many campaign groups then seeking change. With a staff of ten and a readership of 18,000, it carried articles on gay-related history, literature and current affairs, as well as a medical column and night club information. Gillespie concluded her article by noting that in Ireland 'the loneliness of gaydom and the still-timid colours of the gay scene so often mean enforced emigration'.[11] Gillespie also interviewed Rose Robertson, a London parent who established Parent Enquiry, an organization that offered advice and support to parents of gay teenagers. In Dublin to give a talk to Trinity College Dublin's Philosophical Society, Robertson noted that while British society had become more tolerant since it had decriminalized homosexuality in 1967, parents still found it upsetting when their children

7 This act replaced the Offences Against the Person (Ireland) Act 1829, which had reaffirmed the death penalty from earlier legislation for such offences.   8 T.C. Breen, 'Loathsome, impure and revolting crimes: the Dublin scandals of 1884', NLI, *Identity*, 2 (1982), 4–9.   9 This amendment is often referred to as the 'Labouchere Amendment' after its proponent Henry Labouchere.   10 Norris, 'Homosexual people', 22.   11 *Irish Times*, 20 July 1974.

informed them of their orientation. She also noted that she received 'lots of letters from Ireland' and while she did not find Irish parents 'any more censorious in their reaction', she found it 'hard to get to grips with the religious problems' that the parents articulated. Gillespie's article also gave contact details for the new Irish Gay Rights Movement (IGRM) and gave subscription details for the London *Gay News*.[12]

But, as so often happened with British publications, in March 1976 a complaint that several issues of the imported *Gay News* had been indecent or obscene was made to the Censorship of Publications Board, which promptly banned it.[13] In response, David Norris noted that *Gay News* had been privately imported by the IGRM as 'a service for its members' and that copies of the publication had been 'abstracted without their authority from the mail and sent to the Censorship Board'. He denied that *Gay News* was 'an obscene paper' and noted that it 'helped relieve the misery of isolation of homosexual people and keep them in contact with efforts to improve their lot'.[14] Trouble was also brewing for the magazine in Britain. In November 1976 the secretary of the National Viewers' and Listeners' Association, Mary Whitehouse, was given permission by the London high court to sue *Gay News*. Whitehouse alleged that the magazine had published a blasphemous libel, 'namely an obscene poem and illustration vilifying Christ in his life and crucifixion'. The poem in question, 'The love that dares to speak its name' by James Kirkup, centred on the thoughts of a Roman centurion present at the Crucifixion.[15] In July 1977 the case was taken over by the Crown Prosecution Service, with the noted journalist Bernard Levin appearing as defence witness for the magazine.[16] After a six-day trial, both Lennon and the magazine were found guilty of 'unlawfully and wickedly publishing a blasphemous libel concerning the Christian religion, namely an obscene poem and illustration vilifying Christ in His life and Crucifixion'. Describing the poem as 'the most scurrilous profanity', Judge Alan King-Hamilton imposed nine months' imprisonment (suspended for eighteen months) on Lennon, and imposed fines of £500 on Lennon and £1,000 on the magazine.[17]

This judgment was not lost on those in Ireland who opposed the 'normalisation' of the gay community. In a letter to the *Irish Times*, Mary Kennedy, secretary of the Irish Family League, accused the gay movement of 'seeking social acceptance and the right to propagate their ideas'.[18] In another letter, Kennedy accused the Irish Christian Student Movement of producing

---

12 Ibid., 20 Nov. 1974.   13 Ibid., 3 Apr. 1976.   14 Ibid., 3 May 1976.   15 Ibid., 30 Nov. 1976.   16 Ibid., 8 July 1977.   17 Ibid., 13 July 1977. Lennon's custodial sentence was later quashed by the court of appeal.   18 Ibid., 27 July 1977.

'blasphemous literature'.[19] In response, Rob Mitchell, secretary of that organization, noted that while Kennedy did not specify which publication she thought blasphemous, it was most likely the recently published pamphlet 'Towards a Theology of Gay Liberation', which examined the historical roots to Christianity's aversion to homosexuality. Blasphemy, Mitchell, concluded, 'was in the eye of the beholder'. Kennedy's views were also rebuffed by Cathal O'Flanagan OFM, who observed that the activities of her organization 'seem designed to delay the arrival of any such acceptance and integration', while many of its members spoke 'from a lofty tower of pure theory which has never been tested through human contact'.[20] By this time, calls for law reform in Ireland had begun in earnest. In a 1975 Seanad debate on the creation of the law reform commission, Noel Browne called on the attorney general to reform laws that were 'the cause of an enormous amount of distress for a great number of people'.[21] The following year, David Norris, chair of the IGRM, called on the government to establish a commission 'to investigate the position of homosexuals under Irish law, and in Irish society'. He also noted that 'it was a measure of the extent to which human rights were denied and liberty suppressed that so substantial a group – more than twice the size of the entire Protestant community – should be so repressed that many people were ignorant of their existence'.[22]

THE ROAD TO DECRIMINALIZATION

The publications that sought to give voice to the gay community cannot be separated from the various movements that emerged in the 1970s, the personalities involved, the priorities that different individuals felt should be pursued and the legal challenge to the law that lasted over twenty years. Recalling the origins of the gay-rights movement in Ireland, David Norris noted that it emerged following a human sexuality conference held at the University of Ulster in Coleraine in October 1973. From this conference sprang the Union for Sexual Freedom in Ireland, which in turn produced the Sexual Liberation Movement, which had branches in several universities, including Trinity College Dublin. Following a public symposium on homosexuality at Trinity in February 1974, the IGRM was established in June of that year. But there followed a split in the movement that became public in mid-1977.[23] The basis of the split – whether the movement should concentrate its energy

19 Ibid., 5 Aug. 1977. 20 Ibid., 10 Aug. 1977. 21 *Irish Times*, 11 Apr. 1975. 22 Ibid., 3 May 1976. 23 NLI, MS 45,963/7, *In Touch*, 2:7, Aug. & Sept. 1980, pp 8–10.

and resources on providing social outlets for the gay community and avoid drawing attention to itself or, alternatively, on launching a legal challenge to the 1861 and 1885 acts – was long-simmering and culminated in the establishment of a plethora of organizations and publications. Ultimately, on one side stood the IGRM, which emphasized providing social spaces for the gay community, and on the other stood the Campaign for Homosexual Law Reform (CHLR), which was established in August 1977. In 1979 the IGRM split again, with some members coalescing with the CHLR to establish the National Gay Federation (NGF) and other members remaining under the ever-fading banner of the IGRM.[24]

While such differences were being played out, for the public at large the most visible aspect of the emergent gay movement was the constitutional challenge to the 1861 and 1885 acts taken by David Norris. He lodged his challenge in November 1977, and the case was finally heard in June 1980.[25] Norris' argument rested on the principles that he was not being treated equally before the law in contravention of Article 40 of the constitution and that the legislation breached his right to privacy as established by the McGee case of 1975, which had established the constitutional right to privacy.[26] In response, the state argued that the McGee judgment had established that sexual privacy existed within marriage only; it did not extend to sexual relations outside marriage. The state also argued that the importance of religion to the life of the people was important; that morality was linked with the concept of public order in qualifying the rights granted by Article 40; and that the state had a duty to 'intervene by its laws to curb the grosser breaches of morality'. Changing the laws, the state contended, would constitute an offence against religion, public order and morality, a danger to public health and welfare, and an attack on institutions of marriage and family.[27] In October 1980 the high court granted judgment in favour of the state, but the carefully considered judgment enumerated for the first time the factors impacting on the gay community. In his findings, Justice Herbert McWilliam accepted that there existed a large gay

---

24 For a detailed outline of the various splits see NLI, MS 45,963/9, *In Touch*, 3:1, Dec. & Jan. 1980/1, 7–9. See also Paul Ryan, 'Coming out of the dark: a decade of gay mobilisation in Ireland, 1970–80' in Linda Connolly & Niamh Hourigan (eds), *Social movements and Ireland* (Manchester, 2016), pp 86–105. For outlines of the wider gay movement see Patrick James McDonagh, 'Homosexuals are revolting: gay and lesbian activism in the Republic of Ireland, 1970s–1990s', *Studi Irlandesi: A Journal of Irish Studies*, 7 (2017), 65–91 and Maurice J. Casey, 'Radical politics and gay activism in the Republic of Ireland, 1974–1990', *Irish Studies Review*, 26:2 (2018), 217–36. 25 For an outline of the case see David Norris, *A kick against the pricks* (Dublin, 2012), pp 113–28. 26 Mary McGee took this case after the Revenue Commissioners seized contraception (which was then banned) that had been posted to her from Britain. For more see Brian Girvan, 'Contraception, moral panic and social change in Ireland, 1969–79', *Irish Political Studies*, 23:4 (2008), 555–76 27 *Irish Times*, 2 July 1980.

community in Ireland, that homosexuality was not a lifestyle choice, that prejudice existed and that the law as it stood encouraged such prejudice. However,
Justice McWilliam found that the case must fail because, as an unmarried
man, Norris could not rely on the previously established principle of marital
privacy to establish his case. He also found that while 'the traditional attitudes
of the Churches and of the general body of citizens towards homosexuality
are being challenged', Christian churches still defined sexual intercourse as
existing for procreation (within marriage) only. Since the state was required to
defend marriage, it was entitled to criminalize homosexual acts. Therefore the
law as it stood was not unconstitutional.[28]

There followed an appeal to the supreme court that was heard in November
1982, a year in which the gay community came under scrutiny following several
killings. In January 1982 the murder of Charles Self prompted the gay-rights
movement to call for cooperation with the Garda Síochána's investigation
team. This was followed by allegations of profiling by the force as over 1,500
men were questioned, finger printed and photographed. In August, Declan
Flynn was killed by a gang of four youths in Dublin's Fairview Park. Having
been charged with manslaughter, the killers received suspended sentences
– which prompted a protest march of over 800 people who walked from
Dublin city centre to Fairview Park. That month also saw the Censorship of
Publications Board again ban the London *Gay News* on the grounds of indecency and obscenity. In response the NGF declared that the board's attitude
'implied that discussions of laws whose reform was the subject of public
debate was not to be allowed'. Thus, the ban, it concluded, was a 'restriction
to the freedom of speech' and an attempt 'to smother debate on controversial
issues'.[29] One of the few members of the public to protest against the ban
was Phil Moore, a Dublin mother who would later play a crucial role in the
decriminalization campaign. As the mother of a gay teenager, Moore declared
that to be gay in Ireland was 'a very lonely business with widespread prejudice and ignorance'. Publications such as *Gay News* alleviated 'this sense of
isolation' and were necessary in what she termed 'the climate of moral righteousness that is in Ireland today'.[30] In April 1983 the supreme court upheld
the high court judgment against Norris' challenge to the 1861 and 1885 acts.
Significantly, however, it was not a unanimous but a majority verdict that
upheld the high court ruling. Two dissenting judgments held that the high
court had given undue emphasis to the Christian nature of the state and had
underplayed a significant constitutional right – that of privacy – with one
dissenting justice declaring that the law was 'doomed to extinction' and would

28 Ibid., 11 Oct. 1980.   29 Ibid., 16 Aug. 1982.   30 Ibid., 14 Sept. 1982.

need to be replaced with appropriate statutory provisions.[31] In another positive move, all costs were awarded to Norris as a result of the case having raised issues of public importance.[32]

An appeal to the European courts followed, on the grounds that the supreme court had not taken into consideration a European court of human rights (ECHR) ruling in relation to the same legislation (the 1861 and 1885 acts) in a landmark case that had been taken against the British state by Jeffrey Dudgeon. In 1967 Britain had repealed the laws, but had allowed Northern Ireland to opt out of decriminalization. Taking his case under Article 8 of the European Convention on Human Rights (the right to respect for private and family life), Dudgeon had secured judgment in his favour, with the British government extending its repeal legislation to Northern Ireland in October 1982 – a month before Norris' appeal was heard in the Irish supreme court. In May 1985 the European Commission of Human Rights found Norris' Article 8 case to be admissible and at the hearing proper in April 1986, the Irish state argued that Norris had not proven that he had suffered injury under the law complained of, and that there existed no case on file relating to acts conducted in private.[33] In March 1987 the commission found in favour of Norris and referred the issue back to the Irish state for resolution: when no response was forthcoming, in May 1987 the commission referred the case to the ECHR for final judgment.[34] The following year, in April 1988, the state argued at the ECHR that the law complained of had fallen into disuse and was 'unprosecutable' [*sic*]. However, Norris' legal representative, Mary Robinson, pointed out that the state had no policy in relation to the non-enforcement of the law, which could be enforced with gusto at any time.[35] In October 1988 the ECHR ruled that the laws contravened Article 8 and instructed the state, under penalty of suspension or expulsion from the Council of Europe, to change the law.[36] The state was now obliged to act, though it showed no hurry in so doing.

IN TOUCH, IDENTITY AND OUT

Throughout all this time the various factions of the gay movement published many magazines, with, confusingly, both sides of the divide simultaneously publishing a magazine with the same title. Following the split within the

---

31 Ibid., 23 Apr. 1983. The appeal was rejected by Chief Justice Tom O'Higgins, Justice Thomas Finlay, and Justice Frank Griffin; it was allowed by Justice Seamus Henchy and Justice Niall McCarthy. 32 Ibid., 11 June 1983. 33 Ibid., 18 Apr. 1986. 34 Ibid., 25 May 1987. 35 Ibid., 26 Apr. 1988. 36 Ibid., 27 Oct. 1988.

IGRM in 1977, those who wanted the movement to concentrate its efforts and resources on providing social spaces continued to publish the IGRM magazine *In Touch*, which, by the early 1980s, was a twenty-four page A4 publication with a colour masthead.[37] Its contents consisted primarily of international news, news from its regional branches (especially Cork and Limerick), reviews and personal adverts.[38] Its April 1980 issue reproduced a letter to IGRM general secretary John Ryan from an aide to San Francisco Board of Supervisors member Carol Ruth Silver, informing Ryan that Harvey Milk's killer, Dan White, planned to move to Ireland after his release to enjoy 'the possibility of living in peace after causing havoc and distress' in San Francisco.[39] To counter this, Silver wished 'to lay the plans to cause him [White] to be as miserable as possible and to make it impossible for him to escape the results and consequences of his actions'. Suggested actions included holding a protest at his arrival in Ireland.[40] Those who emphasized the provision of social spaces also created a new magazine, *Hermes*, in 1978. It comprised twelve pages and in its first issue it referred to the Norris legal case by noting that 'by changing the law, a reaction will set in as experienced in England and Wales after 1967, and that it might be more politically sound to let sleeping dogs lie'. Declaring itself independent from both the IGRM and CHLR, it expressed the hope that its arrival represented 'one more step in breaking the padlocks on closed minds'.[41] Content-wise, it carried an advert for the 'Tel-A-Friend' advice helpline, news of the imprisonment of the Leningrad poet Gennady Trifonov, a review of Gore Vidal's *The city and the pillar*, news on developments within the IGRM, and diary listings for events in Galway, Cork and Dundalk, student society meetings, and a fundraiser for the Norris legal action. It placed particular emphasis on the non-recognition by universities of gay-friendly student societies, noting that University College Dublin had only recently vetoed recognition of such a society. Clearly operating on a shoestring budget, *Hermes* lasted for five issues, its later issues emphasizing the invisibility of the gay community within mainstream media. It noted that 'there seems to be an invisible barrier between Irish journalists and the public, making it impossible for them to discuss the subject, and the only source of news is the occasional hysterical letter from

37 This version of *In Touch* (1977) was preceded by *IGRM Newsletter* (1976).   38 NLI, *In Touch*, 3:10, Feb. 1981.   39 Harvey Milk (1930–78), the first openly gay politician in California, was shot dead by fellow politician Dan White in 1978.   40 NLI, *In Touch*, no bibliographical details, but most likely Apr. 1981. Interestingly, the *Irish Times* of 7 Jan. 1984 noted that White was a second generation Irish-American with 'a strong devotion to Ireland' and that there were rumours his relatives wanted him to purchase a farm in Co. Mayo. In October 1985 White took his own life in San Francisco, having served five years in prison.   41 NLI, *Hermes*, 1:1, Dec. 1978, 1. Decriminalization in Britain had been followed by an increase in police interest in, and prosecutions related to, public sex-related offences.

the League of Decency'. While it acknowledged 'good coverage' by the *Irish Times* and occasional coverage by the *Irish Press*, it noted hostile coverage from the *Irish Independent*. Generally, however, among the national and regional press it noted 'a stony silence or a scandalous story type article by the less reputable section of the press'.[42]

A more substantial publication was the version of *In Touch* produced as the monthly journal of the NGF between September 1979 and July 1981. A twenty-page A4 magazine, it was distributed free to NGF members and cost 30p for non-members. Its editorial board consisted of David Norris, Edmund Lynch and Tom McClean. While it carried no advertising, typical contents included health features, youth group notes, international news, pen-pal notices, theatre pages, book reviews, album reviews and numerous community notices for events and various interest groups. Its April 1980 issue carried a detailed report on the previous month's 'Open Forum on Religion and the Homosexual Person', which had been attended by official representatives of both archbishops of Dublin (Revd Dr Donal Murray had represented Dublin's Catholic archbishop, Dermot Ryan, and Revd Roy Warke had represented Dublin's Church of Ireland archbishop, Henry McAdoo). While it noted 'immediate and lively reaction from the audience' to Dr Murray's contribution, it felt that what was of most importance was that engagement was finally taking place. It also expressed disappointment that of the four national media organizations invited, only the *Irish Times* had sent a reporter.[43] The following issue carried a front-page appeal for funds to pay for Norris' constitutional challenge; inside it noted that no free legal aid was available in constitutional cases and declared that 'what is on trial is not just the constitutionality of anti-gay laws, but the will of the gay community to stand up and claim the human dignity that is its right'.[44] Later that year, the high court's rejection of Norris' action was described as 'not a total defeat' – a reference to Justice McWilliam's outline of the prejudices faced by the gay community.[45] Reflecting on the judgment, Norris noted that McWilliam 'had started off so well, conceding all our points, then suddenly seemed to change direction and came down against us'. He also revealed that he had received telephone calls from around the country informing him that clergy had used the judgment 'as a text to preach against the lack of charity and understanding in our Irish society'.[46]

42 NLI, *Hermes*, 1:3, no date or page numbers. The last issue on file is 1:5, Oct. 1979.   43 NLI, MS 45,963/4, *In Touch*, 2:4, Apr. 1980, 5–6.   44 NLI, MS 45,963/6, *In Touch*, 2:5, May 1980, 2.   45 NLI, MS 45,963/8, *In Touch*, 2:8, Oct./Nov. 1980, 9.   46 NLI, MS 45,963/8, *In Touch*, 2:8, 10 Oct. 1980 (special issue), 3.

This version of *In Touch* was succeeded by *Identity*, a more professionally, though irregularly produced, thirty-page colour magazine that described itself as 'a new quarterly review for gay women and men'. Produced by the NGF, with an editorial board consisting of T.C. Breen, Cissey Caffrey, Tom McClean and Patrick O'Byrne, its first issue announced its determination to tackle the invisibility imposed on the gay community, thereby 'bringing to our society a social diversity that should be welcomed and not feared'. Noting that the magazine would be 'an outlet for fiction, reviews, poetry, humour, cartoons and analysis of the politics of gay liberation and oppression', it asserted its belief that as 'a minority in society, with our own specific insights into the working of social relationships in that society, what we have to say is of value'.[47] Consisting principally of reviews of books, plays, restaurants and pubs, it also provided a comprehensive listing of groups in Dublin and major urban centres around the country. Significantly however, it carried advertising, with *In Dublin* magazine and USIT Travel being among the most regular advertisers. Later issues followed a similar format, with a regular contributor being Fr Joe O'Leary and a less regular contributor being Frank McGuinness.[48] Lasting for seven issues produced over two years, *Identity* co-existed for a time with *NGF News* before the latter was succeeded by *Out*.

With an editorial board consisting of Maurice Cafferkey, Jean Fitzsimmons, Carol Laing, Edmund Lynch, Tom McClean and David Twohig, *Out* was a thirty-six page, A4 magazine published between December 1984 and February 1988. Appearing every two months, *Out* was printed by *The Kerryman* with a full-colour cover and was distributed by Eason's. Its first issue carried an exclusive interview with British band Bronski Beat and singer Tom Robinson. Contentwise, it carried home news, international news, student society news, NGF news, reviews, classified adverts, listings, short stories and interviews, with the first person interviewed being future president of Ireland, Mary McAleese.[49] Its second issue carried a column by Fr Joe O'Leary in which he criticized the appointment of the conservative Dr Kevin McNamara as Catholic archbishop of Dublin. It also carried the first edition of a regular column by David Norris in which he dissected press coverage of issues relating to the gay community.[50] Significantly, *Out* carried a wider range of advertising, with Budget Travel, the Employment Equality Agency, Inter-Culture Ireland and *In Dublin* magazine being among the most regular advertisers. Political acceptance, however, was in short supply. In mid-1985 it recorded the fact that although Ireland, through the NGF, had been selected to host

47 NLI, *Identity*, 1 (1981), 3.   48 O'Leary went on to become an eminent theologian.   49 NLI, *Out*, Dec. 1984/Jan. 1985.   50 NLI, *Out*, Feb./Mar. 1985.

the annual International Gay Youth Congress, 'not a single public representative or youth work official turned up at the opening reception' despite the
Congress being funded by the European Youth Foundation.[51] Nonetheless,
Out made a conscious effort to engage with politicians: for example, it interviewed Mary Harney and Tony Gregory, both of whom expressed support for
decriminalization.[52]

Engagement with mainstream media was difficult. When, in June 1985, *Out*
was featured on an RTÉ television show aimed at young people, condemnation
was swift. The *Waterford News & Star* criticized the appearance of David Norris
'trumpeting the cause of the homosexual' and described the programme as
'undermining the values held by the majority of young people', while a letter
writer to the *Irish Times* criticized the 'subtle anti-Christ propaganda' and condemned how 'the programme gave a 10-minute or so free advertising boost to a
magazine produced by a group of homosexuals'. How much, the writer asked,
'would that much time cost the producers of a worthwhile journal?' And, he
asked in conclusion, why should 'the rank-and-file licence-paying public have
to pay for this atrocious muck, which is just adding insult to robbery?'[53] In
response, Edmund Lynch, of *Out*'s editorial board, pointed out that 'gay men
and women are taxpayers too, and have for years helped finance media coverage
which is profoundly homophobic and insulting'. He also pointedly asked 'how
many of these outraged self-appointed representatives of the plain people of
Ireland have actually read *Out*, or attempted to inform themselves of the realities of gay people's lives?'[54] More controversy followed when, in early 1986, *Out*
reported on how it had been prevented from advertising – after the 8.00 p.m.
watershed – on RTÉ Radio 2 on the basis that the first iteration of the advert
mentioned the word 'gay'. However, when this objection was overcome by the
removal of that word, RTÉ rejected the second iteration of the advert on the
basis that 'advertising a gay magazine without saying that it was gay would be
misleading to listeners'.[55] This rejection was picked up by the Gay Byrne Show
on RTÉ's Radio 1, and national newspapers subsequently covered the story.[56]
One media-spend estimate prepared for the magazine suggested that it had
received £1,000 worth of free advertising courtesy of the ban.[57]

The growing professionalism of the publication produced by the NGF is
evidenced by the market research undertaken in early 1986 into the magazine's
sale and advertising prospects. This indicated that *Out* had a circulation of

---

51 NLI, *Out*, Aug./Sept. 1985, 4.   52 NLI, *Out*, Dec. 1985/Jan. 1986, 14–15 & Oct./Nov. 1986,
16–17.   53 *Waterford News & Star*, 28 June 1985; *Irish Times*, 10 July 1985. The television programme was *TV
Ga Ga*, a music/magazine programme aimed at young people.   54 *Irish Times*, 19 July 1985.   55 NLI, *Out*,
Mar./Apr. 1986, 20.   56 See, for example, *Irish Times*, 25 Mar. 1986.   57 NLI, MS 45,989/2, Feasibility
study for *Out*, p. 8.

3,500, with a readership of 7,000 people. A canvass of Dublin newsagents involved visits to 185 shops, with the response from newsagents being 'positive'. While many were 'nervous about stocking a gay magazine, the high production values of *Out* was a good selling point. Equally, Eason's decision to both stock and distribute the magazine was a positive feature for many newsagents'. However, despite the 'major advantage of … the high spending profile of its readership', a canvass of advertising agencies was 'disappointing', finding 'a great deal of resistance by advertising agencies to placing ads in *Out*'. The research found that the agencies 'felt that placing ads in a gay magazine could involve their clients in controversy or damage their clients' sales in other market segments'.[58] *Out* thus remained 'undercapitalised', with the production of each issue delayed until 'all the proceeds of the previous issue, from sales, advertising, etc. were collected'.[59] It was succeeded in 1988 by *Gay Community News*.

THE IMPACT OF *IN TOUCH, IDENTITY* AND *OUT*

The development of magazines such as *In Touch, Identity* and *Out* was designed to achieve the same media-related objectives for the gay rights movement as other publications did for other social or political movements: to provide a platform for the dissemination of information to widely dispersed, disparate and often isolated community members; to reduce isolation; to raise consciousness via historical articles and engagement in contemporary culture; to engage in identity and community building; to provide a mechanism for affiliation to that identity and community; to provide solidarity to those engaged in such activities; and to act as an outlet for the expression of support from those outside the community. In essence, they sought to give a voice to the formerly voiceless and to disrupt the idealized image of Irishness that then prevailed and that was based on the long-term symbiotic relationship between nationalism, heteronormativity and religiosity. The three publications represented a deliberate attempt to alter this relationship, particularly 'the success of religious interests in controlling debate on the question of human sexuality by the astute method of limiting and directing the language system through which the debate is conducted'.[60] The magazines thus provided 'new spaces for alternative voices that provide the focus both for specific community interests as well as for the contrary and the subversive'.[61]

58 Ibid., pp 2–8.　59 NLI, MS 45,992/5, letter outlining the reasons for the demise of *Out* magazine.　60 David Norris, 'Homosexual people', 21.　61 Roger Silverstone, *Why study the media?* (London, 1999), p. 103.

In his work on alternative media, Michael Treber describes the contributors to such publications as 'native-reporters', whose legitimacy was grounded
in their membership of the community at which the publication is aimed.[62]
Their journalistic work thus enables the community to identify and come
together to 'analyse one's historical situation, which transforms consciousness,
and leads to the will to change a situation'. As alternative media, *In Touch,*
Identity and *Out* offered contrary political, cultural and social viewpoints to the
mainstream media's construction of society. Their clear focus was on countercultural, counter-heteronormative readings of Irish society, with a focus on
the politics of liberation through providing content not available elsewhere
and covering issues that were not reported on elsewhere. The recurring themes
present in all three magazines – presenting the lesser-known or acknowledged
'gay' history of Irish society and personalities (such as Oscar Wilde, Hilton
Edwards and Micheál Mac Liammóir), outlining the origins and impact of
the discriminatory legislation, reporting on the long-running constitutional
challenge, international news, reviewing gay-related plays, books and music,
venue listings, community groups and events, and classified adverts – played a
key role in the education and consciousness-raising of the gay community and
in breaking the stigma and social isolation that was then the norm.

For the first time gay activists recorded their own lived reality, and were
empowered as participants in the construction of alternative versions of Irish
history, making visible the repressed and advocating for change. Presenting the
perspectives of the up-to-then invisible gay community gave political legitimacy to the movement's leaders and countered the mainstream media's routine
dependence on traditional figures of authority as the only source of legitimate viewpoints. Such legitimacy was amplified by the magazines' inclusion
of 'mobilization' information – not just on campaigns to build the movement,
but also groups that offered support, advice and solidarity to community
members. Through the development of alternative news values, alternative
news-gathering techniques and alternative sites of news, the magazines made,
in the words of John Fiske, the 'repression of events explicitly political'.[63]
Thus marginalized groups 'make their own news, whether by appearing in it
as significant actors or by creating news relevant to their situation', thereby
providing 'information and interpretations of the world which we might not
otherwise see'.[64] Indeed, in relation to the AIDS crisis of the 1980s, Páraic
Kerrigan noted that 'alternative media in Ireland were pivotal in generating

62 Michael Treber, *Alternative journalism, alternative media* (London, 1985), p. 3.   63 John Fiske, 'Popularity
and the politics of information' in Peter Dahlgren & Colin Sparks (eds), *Journalism and popular culture*
(London, 1992), pp 45–63 at p. 47.   64 Chris Atton, *Alternative media* (London, 2002), pp 11–12.

public health information for the gay community, particularly when the mainstream press and Irish government were not providing the necessary resources'.[65] Thus, while many academics refer to the small print runs, limited circulation, marginality and virtual invisibility of alternative publications such as *In Touch*, *Identity* and *Out* in the wider media marketplace, it is arguable that the impact of alternative publications goes far beyond such criteria.[66] In any event, the publication of *In Touch*, *Identity* and *Out* publications goes far beyond such criteria.[67] In any event, the publication of *In Touch*, *Identity* and *Out* allowed the NGF to gradually develop its voluntary publication experience so that there existed the capacity for it to engage in the politics of persuasion that was necessary in the aftermath of Norris' victory. That politics of persuasion was played out in the NGF's longest-running publication, *Gay Community News*.

GAY COMMUNITY NEWS (GCN)

Launched in February 1988 with the support of the NGF, *GCN* was a monthly, eight-page, tabloid-format newspaper, printed by the *Meath Chronicle* and costing 20p per issue. Its initial editorial board consisted of Bill Collins, Frank Fitzgerald and Tonie Walsh, and it would have several such boards until Frank Thackaberry was appointed editor in August 1990.[68] As remembered by Tonie Walsh, *GCN*'s objective was to be 'a platform for our own stories and a mechanism to promote positive images at a time when none existed in Irish popular culture of the media'.[69] Its first-issue front-page story related to a Clause 28 protest to be held outside the British embassy to coincide with a British nationwide protest.[70] Along with community notes and an advice column, the issue featured a look back at the major events of 1987 – the year in which the European Commission of Human Rights had found in favour of David Norris. It also outlined the provisions of the 1861 and 1885 acts and advised its readers to join political parties to change their policies from within, to campaign through trade unions, to write letters to newspapers and to join the political action group of the NGF.[71] By its second issue, *GCN*'s cover price had increased to 40p and it carried a far more comprehensive listings section on

65 Páraic Kerrigan, 'Out-ing AIDS: the Irish civil gay rights movement's response to the AIDS crisis (1984–88)', *Media History*, 25:2 (2019), 244–58 at 244.   66 Fiske, 'Popularity and the politics of information', p. 47; Atton, *Alternative media*, p. 12.   67 Fiske, 'Popularity and the politics of information', p. 47; Atton, *Alternative media*, p. 12.   68 Thackaberry was succeeded as editor in May 1992 by Richard Prenderville.   69 *GCN*, Apr. 2018, p. 12.   70 Section 28 of the British Local Government Act 1988 impacted negatively on local authority support for gay organizations, with such support being viewed as promoting a 'deviant lifestyle'. It was repealed in 2003.   71 *GCN*, 10 Feb. 1988, 4–5.

relevant organizations. Later issues saw the inclusion of book and film reviews, personal adverts, a column – 'Fadó' – that commemorated key events in gay history, and a column ('Mediawatch') that reviewed mainstream media coverage of gay-related issues. Significantly, adverts were very sparse: there was very little beyond the occasional nightclub advert. This helps explain a four-month break in publication between November 1988 and February 1989. Returning to publication in March 1989, it noted its absence was due to 'a range of disasters, ranging from money to emigration'.[72] The returned *GCN* had a clearer layout of home news, international news, health news, 'Mediawatch', along with book, film, theatre reviews and listings.[73]

While its predecessor publications had covered David Norris' legal battle over the course of twenty years, such coverage was, like the hearings themselves, spread out over a long period of time. However, Norris' victory at the ECHR in October 1988 and the creation of a new lobby group, the Gay and Lesbian Equality Network (GLEN), meant that it fell to *GCN* to foreground for its readers the implications of the legal victory and the efforts needed to ensure that it was not ignored by the body politic. In its November 1989 issue, a front-page article by GLEN co-chairperson Kieran Rose demanded 'equality in the criminal law and anti-discrimination legislation'. He also called on the government to resist any action that might 'involve reinforcing our second-class status', called on the gay community to 'popularise the idea that our society should cherish diversity, not enforce conformity' and noted that there existed 'a stereotype of Ireland as hopelessly reactionary and repressive', but that it was also 'a progressive country where ideals of social justice have a strong resonance'.[74] This issue also reported that *GCN* had contacted all political parties seeking clarity on where they stood on decriminalization. While the Labour Party, the Progressive Democrats, the Green Party and Sinn Féin supported decriminalization, Fine Gael was non-committal and no reply was received from Fianna Fáil.[75] The following month, *GCN* welcomed the fact that the Prohibition of Incitement to Hatred Act 1989 included sexual orientation (along with race, colour, nationality, religion, ethnic or national origins and membership of the Travelling community) as one of the grounds on which hate speech was punishable by law. Now a free newspaper distributed at shops, cafes, venues, theatres, pubs and clubs, it also reported on a frank debate that had occurred on RTÉ television's *The Late Late Show* between Kieran Rose of GLEN, Máire Kirrane of Family Solidarity and Paddy Monaghan, a lay Catholic preacher. While no consensus emerged on what government

---

72 *GCN*, Mar. 1989, 1.   73 *GCN* would in 1990 secure support from the FÁS social-employment scheme which allowed for the recruitment of paid staff.   74 *GCN*, Nov. 1989, 1.   75 *GCN*, 3.

action should flow from the ECHR judgment, the fact that such a debate was occurring on prime time national television was an indicator of how society was changing – and an indicator of the battle for support that was ongoing as opinion polls gauged the public mood.[76]

In its issue of February 1990, *GCN* noted that a listeners' opinion poll on RTÉ radio's *Gay Byrne Show* had indicated that 65.5 per cent of listeners supported decriminalization compared to 34.5 per cent against.[77] The following month, however, it reported that a more representative survey of 1,269 adults conducted for the *Sunday Independent* found that only 30 per cent were in favour of decriminalization, with 48 per cent against and 21 per cent stating no opinion. This poll also found an urban bias in favour of change (53 per cent in Dublin as opposed to 36 per cent in Leinster, 29 per cent in Munster and 30.5 per cent in Connaught/Ulster) and an age bias in favour of change, with majorities in the 18–24 and 25–34 age groups favouring change. Comparing the two polls, *GCN* noted that the radio poll had taken place 'among people who were well informed through hearing the arguments on both sides expressed in detail'. The lesson appeared to be that advocacy worked, and *GCN* concluded that 'the more people are informed of the injustice and hypocrisy of the present situation, the more they will favour a change in our homophobic laws'.[78] As well as supporting those who campaigned for change, *GCN* also reported on the activities of those campaigning against any change. In September 1990 it dedicated its front page to political reaction to a booklet, 'The Homosexual Challenge: Analysis and Response', which had been distributed to politicians by Family Solidarity and which had been described by one politician as 'one of the most provocative documents he had ever read'.[79] It also revealed how the Council for Social Concern had written to businesses that advertised on Bray's Horizon radio station, objecting to its weekly half-hour *Outwaves* programme, which catered for the gay community. Accusing the station of 'actively supporting the very politicised homosexual lobby' and of submitting 'listeners of all ages, especially teenagers, to homosexual propaganda which is one-sided and unbalanced', the letter described the programme as 'most unhealthy and abnormal' and claimed that 'advertisers have a right, and duty, to determine [the station's] ethos and influence'. Ominously it concluded by asking business owners 'to consider whether it is in your company's best interests to be associated with a programme that is so offensive and potentially damaging'.[80]

But it covered positive developments also, including, in October 1990, the Law Reform Commission's report that called for decriminalization. That

76 *GCN*, Dec. 1989, 1 & 6.   77 *GCN*, Feb. 1990, 1.   78 *GCN*, Mar. 1990, 1.   79 *GCN*, Sept. 1990, 1.   80 *GCN*, Nov. 1990, 1 & 3.   81 *GCN*, Oct. 1990, 1 & 10.

month it also published a profile of long-term advocate Mary Robinson headlined 'Our Next President?'[81] The following month it welcomed Robinson's
election as president of Ireland 'as heralding in a tolerant inclusive Ireland'.[82]
It also reported shifts in public opinion such as a survey of 1,273 adults carried
out for the *Sunday Press* that indicated that 39 per cent favoured decriminalization with 42 per cent against and 19 per cent stating no opinion. The poll also
found large increases in both urban and rural constituencies favouring change,
and *GCN* concluded that 'opinion for and against is now almost equally
divided' with the result being 'a major blow to the intolerant groups which
used to claim to speak for the "moral majority"'. It called on the government
'to bring forward realistic proposals in the near future'.[83] By the summer of
1993, when decriminalization was finally enacted, *GCN* had evolved into a
free twenty-page, tabloid-sized newspaper with significant advertising, and a
circulation of around 8,000 copies per month.[84] Its brief 180-word, page-three
story on the Criminal Law (Sexual Offences) Act 1993, which repealed the
relevant sections of the 1861 and 1885 acts, was a sign of how life had moved
on long before the law was changed.[85]

82 *GCN*, Nov. 1990, 3. 83 *GCN*, May 1991, 1. 84 Lance Pettit, 'Ireland's alternative press: writing from
the margins', *Irish Communication Review*, 7:1 (1998), article 2 (no page numbers) reports that in 1996 *GCN*
had a circulation of 9,000 copies per month and a readership of 20,700 per issue. 85 *GCN*, Aug. 1993,
3. Post-decriminalization, other publications – *Innuendo* (1997), *GI* (2001–3) and *Free!* (2002–6), which was
edited by long-time activist Eddie McGuinness – briefly existed.

10 / *Status*: a feminist news magazine, 1981

PAT BRENNAN

On 20 February 1981 about 1,000 women and several men gathered for a conference in Liberty Hall, Dublin, that launched *Status*, a news magazine for women. It was an extraordinary event, with women attending from across the country. Opened by *Status* editor Marian Finucane, better known as the groundbreaking presenter of RTE's *Women Today*, the conference was chaired by Inez McCormack from the Irish Congress of Trade Unions. Speakers included political journalist Olivia O'Leary, social-justice activist Sr Stanislaus Kennedy, academic Dr Margaret MacCurtain, family law expert Maire Bates, barrister and later supreme court Justice Catherine McGuinness and Monica Barnes from the Council for the Status of Women. From the floor, dozens queued to add their own points of view, among them Senator Mary Robinson. In the days before the conference, Finucane had remarked that 'normally magazines are launched with a big booze-up, so we wanted our launching to be a chance for our future readers to talk about the changes we want to see. We're also going to point out that we've seen ten years of talk and now is the time for action.'[1] The event, as reported by Elgy Gillespie in the *Irish Times*, was vibrant with what she called 'a certain 1970s flavour': 'but if there have been advances for women on many fronts in ten years, there have also been ten years of talk and not enough action, as many (at the conference) were pointing out'.[2] A total of 31,500 copies of the first issue of *Status* were printed and the edition sold out quickly. Uplifted by the sales and the success of the conference, the editorial team had every confidence that they were on the right track and that the magazine would succeed. However, ten months later *Status* closed, having lost more money than its parent company could bear.

The decision to launch a magazine squarely focused on women's rights had come from the editor and publisher of *Magill* magazine, Vincent Browne, who sought a suitable sister publication to share the resources and overheads of the monthly *Magill*.[3] It too would be a monthly magazine. Convincing Marian Finucane to head up the project was an extraordinary coup. She left her

---

1 *Irish Times*, 19 Feb. 1981. 2 Ibid., 23 Feb. 1981. 3 For a review of *Magill* see Kevin Rafter, 'The passion of particularity: *Magill*, 1977–90' in Mark O'Brien & Felix M. Larkin (eds), *Periodicals and journalism in twentieth-century Ireland: writing against the grain* (Dublin, 2014), pp 210–34.

high-profile position in RTÉ for what was always going to be a risky venture. At the time she thought it was an opportunity she could not ignore:

> It must be a unique form of lunacy to leave something that you love for something that you know absolutely nothing about. But in the long term what influenced me was the unique feeling of having the chance to start something that you will never get again in your life.[4]

Magill had announced the imminent arrival of *Status* in its issue of December 1980:

> *Status* will report on news events of interest to women, it will include sections of health, consumer affairs, clothes, sport, finance, design, food and the arts ... Women's issues must be made the central issue of Election '81/'82. Otherwise women will have to wait another four years before any real progress is made.[5]

The title of the magazine was a nod to the Commission for the Status of Women, which was formed in 1970 to investigate discrimination and blocks to equality experienced by women in Ireland. The commission's report was published in 1973, sparking more than a decade of debate and some progress for women. Barriers to equality were stark. Until the so-called 'marriage bar' was lifted in 1973, women working in the civil service and semi-state bodies simply lost their jobs when they got married. Until 1976 most women had no rights to the family home. Contraception was illegal until 1979 and then available for married couples only. A married man – even one separated and living outside the family home – was legally entitled to rape his wife. Women were routinely and openly paid less than men. The aspirations of the next generation were limited by the subject choices available at girls' schools. *Status* was launched amid an atmosphere of heady debate and change. Finucane set out her stall in the first issue:

> News coverage and investigative journalism from a woman's perspective is what we're aiming for, taking into account the kind of status that a woman has, has not, wants, does not want, whether she be in the home or outside, married or single, widowed, separated, deserted and/or blissfully happy. We welcome the opportunity of presenting a fuller image of women and their lives and hope to cover the kind of stories and issues that are important to you the reader.

4 *Irish Independent*, 12 Feb. 1981.   5 *Magill*, Dec. 1980, 5.

In the first issue an investigation by Annette Blackwell focused on farming women and the failure of the Irish Farmers' Association to represent them; a news analysis piece examined the fallout from a funding crisis in the Council for the Status of Women; reporter Barbara Fitzgerald weighed up the health benefits and risks of the contraceptive pill; and Helen Quinn wrote about the humiliating situation for women in Connemara who routinely had to wait at a designated spot on the roadside to plead for financial help from a drive-by community welfare officer.[6] The usual fare of women's magazines was not totally ignored, with Finucane telling a reporter that 'we'll also have stuff on interiors, clothes and all that too'.[7] There was a new short story from Maeve Kelly, a food column from Deirdre Purcell, a feature on a converted school-house, an article titled 'Clothes' – rather than the more usual 'Fashion' – about a designer of clothing for tall women. But most of the focus was on hard-hitting news features.

Status was a sixty-four-page, glossy colour magazine, but otherwise unlike any other women's magazines on the newsstands. The contrast with *Image* and *Woman's Way*, the two most popular Irish women's magazines at the time, could hardly have been greater. A typical *Woman's Way* in 1980 featured a model on the cover, fashion, food, knitting patterns, romantic fiction, household tips, celebrity gossip and a sprinkling of gentle features on social issues. For instance, feminist activist and later TD Nuala Fennell wrote a practical guide to services available to those in troubled marriages.[8] *Woman's Way* attracted a healthy volume of advertising, much of it in colour. *Image* was similarly successful. Focused on fashion, beauty and lifestyle features, in 1980 it had certified monthly sales of 25,112, and substantial advertising.[9] The colour advertisements brought in revenue, of course, but also allowed for more colour on the editorial pages, making both magazines lively and attractive.

Marian Finucane's experience on RTÉ's *Women Today* had convinced her that there was room for another kind of women's magazine: 'I certainly became much more aware of the fact that there were gross inequities which hadn't really hit me so forcibly until I started working on the programme.'[10] As the creator and first producer of *Women Today*, Clare Duignan later recalled that 'it was a time of great social change, with women demanding equality in the eyes of the law, work and equal pay, family rights and inheritance and so on'.[11] More generally, it was a time of heightened political awareness nationally. Charles Haughey had succeeded Jack Lynch as leader of Fianna Fáil and taoiseach. Garret FitzGerald and a band of socially progressive Fine

6 *Status*, Mar. 1981.　7 *Irish Times*, 19 Feb. 1981.　8 *Woman's Way*, 1 Aug. 1980.　9 *Image*, Feb. 1981.　10 *Irish Independent*, 12 Feb. 1981.　11 *Irish Times*, 3 Jan. 2020.

Gael politicians were reshaping that party's image and eagerly anticipating the next election. Women's issues, and the votes they might attract, were in the mix of public debate. Europe provided the driving force for much reform, with EEC directives requiring the government to bring in equal pay and anti-discrimination legislation. In July 1980 the United Nations hosted the World Conference on Women in Copenhagen. As well as the official event with delegates sent by their respective governments, hundreds of women attended an adjacent forum that Marian Finucane described to her radio audience as a 'marketplace for ideas'. The point of the conference was to assess midway through the UN's Decade of Women what progress had been made on women's rights. The Irish delegation was headed by Clare TD Brendan Daly, minister of state at the department of labour. With him were Sylvia Meehan and Hilda Tweedy from the Employment Equality Agency and Monica Barnes, Audrey Conlon and Ann Kavanagh from the Council for the Status of Women.[12] Journalist Nell McCafferty was at the forum, speaking about republican women who were protesting conditions in Armagh prison. Through *Women Today* and a longer radio documentary, Marian Finucane brought the energy of the event and the voices of women from across the globe to an Irish audience.[13] Like others who were in Copenhagen, Monica Barnes came back passionate and energized about getting the UN's National Plan of Action implemented in Ireland.[14]

Status thus began life hoping to be a force for change, holding government to account on women's issues. Women at the Liberty Hall conference agreed to a charter of seven demands: equality in social welfare; comprehensive family planning services; removal of the constitutional ban on divorce; more legal protections for women in the home; employment rights for part-time workers; recognition of the contribution of women to the agricultural economy; and the introduction of women's studies in second- and third-level education. It was hoped that these relatively modest demands could form the core of a campaign to push politicians into action. As *Status* editor, Marian Finucane wrote that the magazine

> is committed to reporting the progress of this campaign. We would like you to let us know how the politicians in your area respond to the charter ... As the General Election draws closer, information on positive, negative or waffling response at constituency meetings, at public

12 Ibid., 11 July 1980. 13 'World of Women', broadcast Aug. 1980, https://www.rte.ie/radio1/doconone/2010/1215/646595-radio-documentary-world-of-women-un-conference/. 14 *Status*, Mar. 1981, 19.

meetings or even on the doorstep will all be reported. So if you keep hassling we'll keep publishing.[15]

In the weeks before the general election of 11 June 1981, *Status* was heavily involved in both supporting and reporting on those campaigning on women's issues. The May issue took a hard look at the policies of the main political parties under the headline 'Are Women Being Conned?' The sub-headline asked: 'Do recent statements on women's issues mean anything, or are the politicians just dishing up pre-election lip service?' Journalist Nell McCafferty reported on the difficulties women faced securing party nominations. She mapped out the obstacles faced by Nuala Fennell and Mary Flaherty, both of whom were subsequently elected to the Dáil.[16] In June 1981 *Status* devoted thirteen pages to election news and analysis. Regional conferences were held in Galway, Wexford and Limerick where local candidates were invited to face questions from the audience about women's issues. Many declined to attend, but some were brave. Independent candidate Jimmy Hayes told his astonished Wexford audience: 'I'm very old fashioned and frankly I believe that a woman's place is in the home.' At the Limerick meeting TD Brendan Daly, exasperated by repeated questions from the floor asking what he would do for women in the home, said: 'Sure, don't I know? Haven't I got a wife at home?' Representatives of Fianna Fáil, Fine Gael, the Labour Party and the Socialist Party were grilled by the audience well past 11.00 p.m. *Status* reported that 'the politicians went home looking older and if not exactly wiser, at least somewhat enlightened about the potential of the women's vote'.[17] In an election where there were more women candidates than ever before, *Status* included short profiles of all of them and Nell McCafferty followed ten on the campaign trail. *Status* also sent a detailed questionnaire to the main parties and to all declared or likely candidates, asking their opinion on thirty specific proposals under eight headings. For instance, under 'Violence against Women' politicians were asked for their views on whether the legal definition of rape should be extended to include violent sexual assault and rape within marriage. Fine Gael, Labour, Sinn Féin the Workers' Party and the Socialist Labour Party replied 'yes', that they agreed with this policy. Fianna Fáil said 'no'. Just fifty-nine individual candidates replied to the questionnaire, among them Fine Gael leader Garret FitzGerald who answered personally and on behalf of the party. He made several commitments, including to repeal the existing Family Planning Act and make contraceptives more widely available.[18]

15 Ibid., Apr. 1981, 4.   16 Ibid., May 1981, 26–7.   17 Ibid., June 1981, 21–3.   18 Ibid., 18.

From the start, the magazine gave over several pages each month to a 'Readers' Forum', encouraging an interactive approach which broadened the range of opinions covered. The forum was lively, often offering objections or alternative points of view to articles published the previous month. This was part of Marian Finucane's 'broad church' approach, aimed at touching the lives of as many women as possible. One woman, Catherine Kinsella, wondered why the women's movement did not sufficiently address the needs of women who chose to stay home to care for their children. *Status* subsequently published an article from her on that subject.[19] Nell McCafferty reported from inside one of the mother and baby homes where single, pregnant women effectively went into hiding until their babies were born. They told her their strategies for keeping their pregnancies secret. At that time in Ireland an increasing number of women were opting to keep their babies rather than have them adopted, but it was not an easy path. McCafferty took a scathing look at the supports available to them, arguing that

> having encouraged them to avoid termination of pregnancy, the support of society is withdrawn to the punitive point that such women must then terminate motherhood and give their babies away for adoption or raise their children in daunting conditions of abject material and emotional poverty. Lest such mothers consider themselves as natural as any other mother, their children are officially categorized as bastards.[20]

In the following month's issue, one 'unmarried mother of three year old twins' took exception to this generalization, writing that she and her children were doing fine and that McCafferty had negated 'the help and encouragement given by both individuals and organisations to unmarried mothers'.[21] McCafferty's article was typical of *Status* journalism. She came at the subject matter from an unapologetically feminist point of view and focused on those directly affected. The decision to report from inside a mother and baby home was unusual for Irish journalism. Access for photographer Derek Speirs was even more so. Similarly, reporter Barbara Fitzgerald's investigation into the conditions and pay of contract cleaners went behind the scenes. Fitzgerald got herself hired by a well-known office cleaning firm and reported that 'before I started work, I asked was it necessary to pay tax and insurance. "Not unless you want to – if you do we can arrange that later," was their reply'. Fitzgerald did two days on the 6.30–8.30 morning shift at British Home Stores in Dublin's O'Connell Street to find out first-hand what the job entailed. It was hard work for little

19 Ibid., Mar. 1981, 60–1.   20 Ibid., May 1981, 18.   21 Ibid., June, 1981, 60.

pay – £1.37½p an hour. Her fellow workers 'aged from 17 to 50 plus' were sympathetic when the heavy work defeated her inexperienced muscles, but the watching security men were disdainful: 'having watched me wash the floor, they would then walk over it'. When her shift ended, Fitzgerald 'walked along O'Connell Street reeking of bleach and Deep Clean, hot and tired. Everyone else was on their way to work in shining offices, unaware of the workers who made them spic and span.'[22]

After Garret FitzGerald's coalition government was formed in June 1981, *Status* took a closer look at his most novel and controversial election promise – the transfer of a tax credit of £9.60 a week to women working in the home. The cover of the October 1981 issue was a posed photograph of a harassed woman at the kitchen sink with a crying toddler in a high chair. The woman is wearing a tee shirt with '£9.60' emblazed across the front. The headline was 'How Much Is a Housewife Worth?' *Status* reporter Anne Byrne concluded that the true economic value of a typical mother and housewife was £10,000 a year, vastly more than the proposed tax credit.[23] *Status* also gave generous space to individual women who were having an impact or breaking new ground. Dolly Newman, a veterinarian with a farm practice in Mullingar, was one of the 3 per cent of vets who were female. Copywriter Catherine Donnelly was a rising star in a male world. Mary Finan had taken the helm as managing director in Wilson Hartnell Public Relations Company. The cover of the July 1981 issue, reporting on the newly formed government, put new TD Mary Flaherty on the cover and looked at the strides made by women politicians. More broadly, sports journalist Paddy Agnew, a *Magill* reporter, wrote in most issues of *Status* about women who were achieving in sport. Anne Leonard was making her mark on the European stage in table tennis. Athlete Deirdre Nagle was looking forward to the World Cross Country Championships. Caroline Beasley – who in 1983 became the first female jockey to win at Cheltenham – was featured in June 1981. Team sports such as cricket and squash received serious coverage. Agnew also wrote about the narrowing fitness and achievement gap in sport between men and women. As in other women's magazines, fiction was a regular feature in *Status*. Writer Anne Haverty came aboard as a fiction consultant. Maeve Kelly, Emma Cooke, Eithne Strong, K Arnold Price, Helen Lucy Burke and Mary Arrigan were among those who had stories published in *Status*. Nuala O'Faolain was a regular columnist, focusing on themes found in literature and the arts. Features on artists were also in the mix.

But despite its editorial successes, the alarm bells about the financial health of *Status* began ringing loud and clear early on. Because of the modest size

22 Ibid., Sept. 1981, 20–1.   23 Ibid., Oct. 1981, 8–14.

of the Irish market and the high cost of colour printing, it is not possible for glossy, colour magazines to break even on sales alone. Advertising revenue is essential. For *Status*, the timely support of advertisers was crucial and, perhaps naively, assumed. After all, *Magill* had espoused radical views on social equality and women's rights and attracted advertising at the same time. *Status*, it was hoped, would follow that example and also attract additional advertising targeted specifically at women. For instance, the February 1981 issue of *Image* magazine had eighteen and a half pages of colour advertisements and six black-and-white pages. In April of that year *Image* had enough advertising to increase the size of the magazine to 100 pages, with 35 pages of colour ads. By comparison, *Status* in April had five full-page colour ads. In 1981 *Image* was transformed when Clare Boylan, a well-respected print journalist and later novelist, took over as editor. Her advertising manager was Barbara Nugent, later managing director of the *Sunday Tribune* and then chief executive of the *Sunday Business Post*.[24] It was a formidable combination. Boylan infused the magazine with a gentle feminism. Her editorial comment of March 1981 introduced a feature on the changing face of marriage thus:

> When I got married ten years ago, everyone offered me congratulations and wished my husband luck, solemnly shaking his hand as if he was headed for the trenches. Nobody congratulates young brides anymore. Catching a man before your teeth and hair fall out is no longer looked on as life's prime accomplishment.[25]

Boylan's *Image* raised all sorts of feminist issues, but in a non-threatening way. She published fiction from talented women writers such as Beryl Bainbridge, Antonia White and Margaret Drabble and a range of features from women such as Dervla Murphy, Elgy Gillespie, Rosita Sweetman and June Levine. The lifestyle presented by *Image* was witty, gracious, elegant and intelligent.

Status, in contrast, was a campaigning magazine. Ireland's advertising agencies did not support it and *Magill* did not have the finances to sufficiently underwrite the loss-making venture while it established itself. The first sign of real trouble came with Marian Finucane stepping down in May 1981. She stayed on as consultant editor until August, and attended the regional conferences that were held in the weeks before the general election. However, she

---

24 For an examination of the *Sunday Tribune*, see Pat Brennan & Brian Trench, 'The *Tribune*'s turbulent times' in Joe Breen & Mark O'Brien (eds), *The Sunday papers: a history of Ireland's weekly press* (Dublin, 2018), pp 161–82. For an examination of the *Sunday Business Post*, see Ed Mulhall, 'The business start-up: the *Sunday Business Post*, 1989–2001' in Breen & O'Brien (eds), *The Sunday papers*, pp 199–222. 25 *Image*, Mar. 1981.

was back on RTÉ's airwaves in July.[26] Also in May, *Magill* announced four redundancies, including one journalist.[27] In November the cover price of *Status* was raised from 60p to 80p and a lengthy editorial addressed the problem with advertisers. The wider economy was experiencing tough times and that was reflected in advertising budgets. But that did not fully explain the lack of advertising support. As *Status* itself noted:

> There has also been a feeling among our potential clients that the medium is not right for their products. They feel that a magazine that concentrates on women's issues appeals to only a tiny minority of Irish women, a minority that would not be within their 'target market' in the first place … Potential clients and their advertising agencies [believe] that the kind of women who would be interested in women's issues would not be the kind who would be interested in their products: drinks, cigarettes, cars, cosmetics, clothes, furniture etc. In this, *Status* is a victim to a certain extent of the time lag between the reality of the new consciousness of women about their role, their potential and their ambition, and the perception of the male dominated world of advertising and marketing.[28]

Sales of *Status* would have been enough to secure its future had it been successful in attracting more advertising. The first issue sold more than 30,000. The next issue had a bigger print run and that sold well also. Sales settled around the 18,000–20,000 mark, which was respectable enough for a magazine in its infancy. But without advertising it was doomed. Jim Nolan, then president of the Advertising Practitioners of Ireland, told *Irish Press* reporter Carol Coulter: 'Advertisers do not have an obligation to support publications, but to advertise their clients' wares in the best outlets.' There was no doubt that *Status* made mistakes when dealing with advertisers. Just what these mistakes were became a matter of dispute and some acrimony after the magazine closed in January 1982. Publisher Vincent Browne felt that from the start the magazine was 'gratuitously offensive to advertisers … if you're going to take on a large and powerful body, you have to do it properly. There was too much sniping which antagonises people to no purpose.' Jim Rowe, then managing director of Dove Public Relations, accepted that advertisers did have some hostility toward *Status*. He noted that 'marketing managers are male dominated and – dare I say it – some of them, maybe, a little frightened'. *Status* was, he felt, a 'bit too aggressively women's lib'.[29]

26 *Irish Times*, 21 July 1981.   27 *Irish Press*, 20 May 1981.   28 *Status*, Nov. 1981, 4.   29 *Irish Press*, 13 Jan. 1982.

The hostility of advertising agencies came as a bewildering surprise to *Status* staff. After all, the readers of the magazine were likely to be relatively affluent, well-educated women. Amid the enthusiasm of early editorial meetings there was naivety about commercial realities. It was assumed that there would be advertising revenue. Indeed, there was lively discussion about the ethics of accepting advertisements that might work against the feminist message. As it happened, there was never any opportunity to put this to the test. Month by month, despite enormous efforts by sales staff, advertising revenue dwindled. In a fairly desperate attempt to turn the tide, editorial staff (including this writer) donned their most respectable attire, put on smiles and went along to meetings hoping to woo potential advertisers. Not surprisingly, this strategy failed. The usual rules simply did not apply. Those controlling these decisions did not want to see their advertisements in *Status* no matter how many educated women were buying the magazine. Perhaps this attitude would have softened in time, but time required money that simply was not available.

One regular feature that scared advertisers was a page headed 'No Comment', which reproduced snippets of sexist nonsense sent in by readers. For instance, a particular computer system declared that it would 'render it immaterial as to whether the modern secretary puts her shapely little bottom on a chair in Stephen's Green, Sandyford or Santry'. An advertisement for a Dublin car dealership offered a range of vehicles, 'From a Mini for the secretary or a Metro for the wife through an Ital for the sales staff to a Jaguar for the chairman'. The Gestetner company advertised the reach of its brand with the slogan 'See how good a copier can be' above a photo of eleven identical young women in swimsuits, each wearing a sash displaying the name of a different country. Under the heading, 'It's a Giveaway', the photograph of a young woman in a revealing bikini was used to advertise subscriptions to *Checkout* magazine. But for the most part, readers sent in newspaper clippings of editorial material which was gratuitously or thoughtlessly sexist. For example, from a political column in the *Irish Times*, 'Their sitting TDs, Mr Eddie Collins and Mr Austin Deasy, are regarded as "Garret men", though not fanatically so: the young and pretty Mrs Bulbulia is taken for a dedicated "Garret woman"'. Or, from the *Sunday Independent*: 'Congratulations to Fianna Fáil General Secretary Frank Wall. His wife gave birth to their first child – a girl – this week.' In hindsight, *Status* clearly needed either an innovative advertising sales policy or more money than *Magill* could ever provide. Speaking in January 1982, Marian Finucane said:

> We were very cautious … we should have just gone to the advertisers and explained what the magazine was, that it had a highly committed

and intelligent readership … I remember one conversation I had with two advertisers. They both said 'my wife wouldn't like it [*Status*]', and I asked one of them 'did you ask her?' to which he replied 'no'. So I asked him was his wife just interested in fashion and things like that or in politics and he replied indignantly that, of course, she was interested in politics, she was a very rounded person. But they both assumed they knew what their wives would read.[30]

In its final months, *Status* was a magazine starved of both advertising and editorial resources. The lack of advertising meant that more pages had to be filled with editorial content. More of the magazine was written either by this writer or by willing *Magill* staff or friends, not all of them journalists. Some found themselves writing about areas – such as fashion – way outside their area of expertise. It was a struggle, but the hope was that readers would remain loyal and advertisers would come around.

The final issue of *Status* was published in December 1981. The cover illustration, by Arja Kajermo, the talented Finnish cartoonist and frequent contributor, showed one lone woman amid a rake of men on a platform looming above ordinary people going about their daily business. The cover story was a forensic examination of the number of women in positions of power in Ireland. The cover also promised a lively mix of lighter stories inside: 'Sex: Does Love Make It Better?; Cosmo's Agony Aunt; Christmas Guide to Gifts, Clothes, Food, Restaurants'. It was a well-balanced offering with features on singer Maura O'Connell, broadcaster Doireann Ní Bhriain, and a problem page written by veteran journalist and feminist June Levine. Reporter Liz Ryan spent the day with a delegation of women from both communities in Northern Ireland who came to Dublin as part of a cross-border initiative. There was a report on the president of the European parliament, Simone Veil, who was the main speaker at a conference organized by the Women's Political Association. A lengthy extract from TD Nuala Fennell's first speech in the Dáil was also published. And there was a report on a high court case being taken against the department of social welfare for one of many discriminatory rules that ensured women received less money than men.

The main story investigated the number of women decision-makers in Irish society across sixty-three categories. There were no women in senior positions in the department of finance; no women directors of the Central Bank; no women directors of the four main banks; one on the executive of

30 Ibid.

the Irish Congress of Trade Unions; one woman in cabinet; none in top civil service jobs; none on the supreme court; one high court judge; none in a top position in the Garda Síochána; none as editors of national newspapers; and none as specialist or regional correspondents in RTÉ. The list was a telling measure of the influence of women in Irish society in 1981. And perhaps that, in part, explains why there was such a disproportionately hostile reaction to *Status* from the conservative world of advertising. In terms of women's rights, the move for change was not something naturally evolving within Irish culture. It was largely imposed, externally from Europe and domestically from the courts. From Europe came equal pay, equal social welfare payments and the right to free legal aid in civil cases. From the courts came the right to sit on juries, the right to import contraceptives for personal use, and the right for married women to be taxed on the same basis as everyone else. Women journalists – leading lights in the original Irish Women's Liberation Movement of 1970 – accelerated the pace by ensuring that the push for change was played out in public.[31]

The final issue of *Status* had almost no advertisements at all, and some of those published were virtually given away. By then, even those stalwarts of magazine advertising – cigarette companies – had abandoned the magazine. The closure of *Status* was announced on 6 January 1982, just over ten months after its heady launch before an audience of 1,000 women in Liberty Hall. A lack of advertising revenue was cited as the cause. When asked how much money *Magill* had lost on the venture, Vincent Browne simply said: 'A lot.'[32] Writing in the January 1982 issue of *Magill*, Browne expressed the hope that *Status* might resume publication in better financial times. He noted that 'the magazine failed to generate the advertising support that was necessary and there was no immediate prospect of it doing so ... we hope that when the financial and advertising climate improves it will be possible to recommence publication'.[33] This never happened, although *Magill* continued to cover women's issues. Quite apart from the lack of advertising support, it is arguable that the glossy magazine format was never right for a feminist periodical in the small Irish market. *Status* hoped to emulate the success of *Ms*, the American glossy magazine. But in the large American market, *Ms* never relied on commercial advertising revenue, but on sales, sponsorship and donations. Although *Ms* was not without financial struggles, it has been a continuing success since it began publication in 1972. It is currently owned by the Feminist Majority Foundation, a women's rights advocacy group.

31 See Anne Stopper, *Mondays at Gaj's: the story of the Irish Women's Liberation Movement* (Dublin, 2006).   32 *Irish Press*, 13 Jan. 1982.   33 *Magill*, Jan. 1982, 4.

Closer to home, *Spare Rib* was published in the United Kingdom from 1972 to 1993.[34] More radical than *Status*, it was a more modest production. Run as a cooperative of equals, paying staff nominal wages, it never tried to be a commercial success. With lots of goodwill, enthusiasm and low costs, however, it managed to survive for more than twenty years. This might have been a more feasible model for *Status*, although not practicable within the structure of Magill Publications.

34 *Spare Rib* was banned in the Republic of Ireland in 1977 for being 'indecent or obscene'. See *Irish Times*, 4 Feb. 1977.

11 / 'The mouthpiece of the ordinary woman': empowering women through the *Irish Housewife* magazine

SONJA TIERNAN

In 1939, as Europe descended into the hostilities of the Second World War, Ireland, although neutral, was placed in a state of emergency – what the Irish government termed 'the Emergency'. The Economic War had just ended, and Ireland was in a financial crisis. In October 1939, *Marrowbone Lane*, a three-act play by Dublin paediatrician Dr Robert Collis, first opened at the Gate Theatre in Dublin, causing indignation.[1] The play had been refused by the national theatre, the Abbey, but was accepted by Edwards and Mac Liammoir Productions. *Marrowbone Lane* focused on a real-life slum in one of the poorest inner-city areas of Dublin's Liberties. The drama exposed the shocking realities of tenement life in which entire families were forced to live in single rooms with no electricity, gas, water or inside toilet facilities.

The play was revived in 1941 and this time it caught the attention of a young woman, Hilda Tweedy, who resolved to help improve such deplorable living conditions. In February of that year, Tweedy set about mobilizing as many like-minded women as possible to action.[2] She wrote to friends asking:

> What is your dream of Ireland? What does the story of *Marrowbone Lane* mean to you? Are you satisfied that you are doing all in your power to build the kind of world you wish your children to live in? I am having a few friends to discuss these and other vital questions. Do come and help us, alone we can do little, together we can rouse public opinion to remove some of the blots on our civilisation.[3]

1 W.R. Collis, *Marrowbone Lane: a play in three acts* (Dublin, 1943). 2 Hilda Tweedy, *A link in the chain: the story of the Irish Housewives' Association* (Dublin, 1992), p. 13. 3 National Archives of Ireland (hereafter NAI), 'Irish Housewives' Association Correspondence, Submissions and Campaigns', Hilda Tweedy papers, 98/17/5/1/1.

THE HOUSEWIVES' PETITION

After meeting with a number of concerned women, it was decided by four members of the group to draw up a petition to government, securing as many signatures as possible before budget day on 5 May 1941. The 'Memorandum on the Food and Fuel Emergency' was submitted by Hilda Tweedy; Andreé Sheehy Skeffington; Marguerite Skelton; a member of the Quaker Jacobs family of Waterford; and Nancye Simmons, a graduate from the prestigious Dublin girls school, Alexandra College. The petition, originally signed by 51 women, was sent to the government, the opposition parties and the press.[4] A second list of 335 signatures was later sent on 30 May. The women drew up an economic plan urging the government to ration all essential foodstuff, control prices and suppress black-market sales. The memorandum included numerous proposals such as encouraging increased tillage with government financial support (such as lower-rate credit facilities for farmers); an increase of unemployment allowances proportional to the cost of living; the introduction of a mid-day meal for schoolchildren; the introduction of a comprehensive scheme to salvage waste on a national basis; and a recommendation for the government to control transport.

The memorandum was a well-considered financial plan compiled by educated women. Tweedy herself had studied mathematics at the University of London and later went on to teach the subject at Alexandra College in Dublin from 1952 to 1966. Yet it was denigrated by journalists, who described it in condescending terms as a 'housewives' petition'.[5] However, this submission marks a significant shift in women's lobbying of government in Ireland. The memorandum launched what has now become an accepted annual practice for feminist groups, including the National Women's Council of Ireland (NWCI), to make a pre-budget submission to government. For example, in 2019 the NWCI published *Equality now, invest in women*, which outlined its recommendations for the 2020 budget in 'relation to women's economic independence, health, violence against women, housing and care'.[6]

One year after the housewives' petition was submitted, some of the aims of the proposal were adopted by government. In May 1942 all of the women who had signed the petition were contacted with a view to formally establishing a committee to oversee related economic issues, including consumer rights. The Irish Housewives' Committee was co-founded on this basis, with Tweedy and Andrée Sheehy Skeffington nominated as joint honorary secretaries,

---

4 Ibid.   5 *Irish Times*, 6 May 1941.   6 NWCI, *Equality now, invest in women: pre-budget submission 2020*, https://www.nwci.ie/learn/publications/category/pre_budget_submissions.

along with the support of the president of the Irish Women Workers' Union (IWWU), Louie Bennett, and her sister, the feminist trade unionist Susan Manning, who was nominated as chair of the Irish Housewives' Committee. The aim of the committee was clearly laid out:

> To investigate living conditions amongst all sections of the community and to be the mouthpiece of the ordinary woman, that through us she may voice her opinions on her daily problems, report her grievances and offer suggestions. Our Committee welcomes the help and support of all women, irrespective of class, religion or politics.[7]

By June 1943 the group had seventy-seven members and within two years the committee rented office premises at 58a Harcourt Street. The group reconstituted as the Irish Housewives' Association (IHA) in 1946.[8] The joint secretaries were particularly effective. While Tweedy was a natural leader of the IHA, Sheehy Skeffington was already an adept political activist, and as a member of the Council of Action, formed to alleviate conditions in Ireland during the Emergency, she offered 'advice and support to tenement tenants'.[9]

ORIGINS OF THE MAGAZINE

As well as her own political background, Andrée Sheehy Skeffington had married into a prominent politically active Irish family. Her husband, Owen, was a champion of human rights and served as a senator. He was the only child of Francis and Hanna Sheehy Skeffington, themselves an intrinsic part of the first-wave suffrage movement in Ireland.[10] Hanna had co-founded the Irish Women's Franchise League in 1908, and in 1913 her husband established the *Irish Citizen*, a newspaper which Francis edited until his murder during the hostilities of the Easter Rising in Dublin, and which Hanna later edited.[11] The *Irish Citizen* became the official organ of the Irish suffragette campaign and helped disseminate vital information about the cause as well as helping fund activities. Not surprisingly, once the Irish Housewives' Association was formed, Andrée Sheehy Skeffington instantly set about establishing a journal

7 NAI, Irish Housewives' Association Constitution, Hilda Tweedy papers, NAI 98/17/1/1. **8** L.W. White, 'Skeffington, Andrée Sheehy' in *Dictionary of Irish biography* (http://dib.cambridge.org/) – hereafter *DIB*. **9** Ibid. **10** C.E.J. Caldicott, 'Skeffington, Owen Lancelot Sheehy', *DIB*. **11** For an account of the *Irish Citizen*, see Sonja Tiernan, '"Challenging the headship of man": militant suffragism and the *Irish Citizen*' in Mark O'Brien & Felix M. Larkin (eds), *Periodicals and journalism in twentieth-century Ireland: writing against the grain* (Dublin, 2014), pp 61–74.

as the group's official organ. On her initiative, an annual journal simply entitled the *Irish Housewife* was established in 1946. It continued until 1967 but
was later, in 1972, reconstituted as the *Housewife's Voice*. Sheehy Skeffington and
Tweedy took prominent positions on the editorial board. Other members of
the IHA joined the board over the years, most notably the consumer-rights
activist Maude Rooney. Rooney joined the IHA in 1949 and volunteered
on the editorial board right up until the magazine was reconstituted as the
Housewife's Voice.

The journal was established at a significant time for women in Ireland.
By 1946 there was a real concern that women had been actively forced out of
political engagement, and out of public life more generally. Women in Ireland
had not been granted the equality promised them by the provisional government of 1916 or the Free State Constitution of 1922. After the establishment
of the Free State, the position of women in Ireland deteriorated. The marriage bar was enacted in 1924, forcing female civil servants to resign upon
marriage. Furthermore, as Jennifer Redmond observes, 'the subsequent Civil
Service Amendment Act banned women from taking exams for certain civil
service positions'.[12] The bar to married women working was extended across
many other public services and even private industry over the coming years
and in December 1932 'the Department of Education announced that from 1
October, 1933 all women national teachers who commenced service after that
date would be obliged to retire on marriage'.[13] As Linde Lunney points out,
this was something that Hilda Tweedy would be personally affected by: when
she 'applied for a teaching job in a Protestant girls' school, she was told that
as a married woman she was unsuitable; the headmistress said it would not be
nice for the girls if their teacher became pregnant'.[14]

The Irish Free State continued to section women into a preferred role
for them as wife and mother when in 1934, the Criminal Law (Amendment)
Act included a prohibition on the import and sale of birth-control devices.
As Caitriona Beaumont aptly observes, 'this meant that not only literature
advocating birth control was banned in the Irish Free State, but the avail-
ability of contraceptives was also proscribed'.[15] In 1937, the redrafted Irish
Constitution declared a woman's ultimate place to be in the domestic sphere.
Article 41, which in 2021 remains unchanged, includes a section stating that

12 Jennifer Redmond, *Moving histories: Irish women's emigration to Britain from independence to republic* (Liverpool,
2019), p. 166, n. 19. For more on inequality, see Maryann Gialanella Valiulis, *The making of inequality: women,
power and gender ideology in the Irish Free State, 1922–1937* (Dublin, 2019).   13 Eoin O'Leary, 'The Irish National
Teachers' Organisation and the marriage bar for women national teachers, 1933–1958', *Saothar*, 12 (1987),
47–52 at 47.   14 Linde Lunney, 'Tweedy, (Muriel) Hilda', *DIB*.   15 Caitriona Beaumont, 'Women, citizenship and Catholicism in the Irish Free State, 1922–1948', *Women's History Review*, 6:4 (1997), 563–85 at 571.

'the State recognizes that by her life within the home, woman gives to the State a support without which the common good cannot be achieved'.[16] The release of the draft version inspired Hanna Sheehy Skeffington to write to the *Irish Independent* asserting that the Constitution is 'a Fascist Model, in which women would be relegated to permanent inferiority, their avocations and choice of callings limited because of an implied invalidism as the weaker sex'.[17] When the *Irish Housewife* was first published in 1946, there were no female cabinet ministers in Dáil Éireann and less than 3 per cent of TDs (only 4 out of 138) were female. It was time to mobilize the housewives of Ireland.

The title of the organization, and therefore of the journal, was contentious because of its use of the term 'housewife'. A member of the ad hoc committee of the IHA, Rosaleen Mills, described how

> the word housewife … conjured up a vision of a female body in an apron, bustling about with a sweeping brush, absorbed by the cookpot and the darning, whose interest in outside affairs was languid compared to her desire to be assured that we had wiped our feet on the mat, or to be informed who had left the bathroom 'in that condition'.[18]

Indeed, the Irish housewife of 1940s Ireland was viewed by many as a passive character whose chief responsibilities lay within the domestic sphere and certainly did not have any significant involvement in the public or political realm. During this era, women in Ireland, upon marriage, lost any small amount of independence they had. Diarmaid Ferriter pinpoints the IHA as 'the first organisation to present housewives as consumers and not just passive breeders and feeders'.[19] This is clearly presented in the pages of the *Irish Housewife* magazine.

Like the organization, the magazine used the term 'housewife' in the title in order to politicize housewives and portray these women as powerful consumers who could in turn become significant political lobbyists. This is made clear from the onset of the publication. Hanna Sheehy Skeffington penned a frank article entitled 'Random Reflections on Housewives; Their Ways and Works', which appeared in the first edition in 1946. In it she was scathing of the position of the housewife in Irish society and of the position that

16 'The Family, Article 41', *Bunreacht na hÉireann: Constitution of Ireland* (Dublin, 1937; 2012), p. 162.   17 *Irish Independent*, 11 May 1937 as cited in Beaumont, 'Women, citizenship', p. 563.   18 Rosaleen Mills, *Irish Housewife*, 1949, as cited in Angela Bourke et al. (eds), *The Field Day anthology of Irish writing*, v: *Irish women's writings and traditions* (Cork, 2012), p. 169.   19 Diarmaid Ferriter, 'Afterword' in Alan Hayes (ed.), *Hilda Tweedy and the Irish Housewives' Association: links in the chain* (Dublin, 2012), p. 153.

women allowed themselves to be relegated to. She called on women to take action, asking:

> what of the large mass of indifferent women who even now fail to realize that Politics control our lives, who shrug and say with coy femininity, 'I don't take any part in Politics, I leave all that to men'. The example of the Housewives has shown that women too must organize, must educate themselves in citizenship, must become vocal, if need be clamorous.[20]

This was the final article written by Hanna Sheehy Skeffington; she died on 20 April that same year. The fact that she penned an article in the first edition of the *Irish Housewife*, a magazine that reflected growing feminist activity and would lead to the establishment of a second wave of the feminist movement, highlights how the IHA formed a vital bridge between these two waves of feminism. This was a fact of which Tweedy was most aware; when she wrote the history of the IHA, she entitled it *A link in the chain* to reflect this. The IHA had actually incorporated a group that stemmed from the original Irish Women's Suffrage Association, founded in 1874 to secure votes for women.

CONTENTS OF THE MAGAZINE

The production and contents of the *Irish Housewife* were remarkable in many respects. The contents show that this publication was different to other magazines targeted at female readers in Ireland. Possibly the nearest rival was *Model Housekeeping* founded in 1927 and produced until 1966. However, as Caitríona Clear points out, its contents 'rarely carried news items from women's or community organisations'. Instead, articles mainly covered 'cookery, gardening, medical matters, "mother and baby" and quite a lot of fashion'.[21] In contrast, Tweedy highlighted how the *Irish Housewife* functioned to 'distribute information about the Association and recruit members'.[22] This was, however, only part of its function; the editors also employed a clever tactic to fund the production of the magazine while ensuring that the objectives of the IHA were achieved. Inside the front cover of most issues a statement was printed assuring readers that the association fully endorsed any company that advertised in the *Irish Housewife*. The statement confirmed

20 Hanna Sheehy Skeffington, 'Random reflections on housewives; their ways and works', *Irish Housewife*, 1 (1946), 20. 21 Caitriona Clear, *Women's voices in Ireland: women's magazines in the 1950s and 60s* (London, 2016), p. 141. 22 Tweedy, *A link in the chain*, p. 89.

that 'we believe their trading standards to be high, and we ask our readers to support them'. In this way companies strived to reach the standards set by the IHA so that they could advertise in its magazine and therefore have the endorsement of this, by now, powerful consumer group. Through the use of this tactic, readers were not only kept up-to-date about IHA matters and campaigns, but housewives could also be assured that any company appearing in the *Irish Housewife* was reputable, which made their own shopping decisions politically acceptable. The IHA did not, in fact, receive any of the advertising revenue. The association had made a rather astute business deal with an advertising agency. The agency printed and distributed the magazine and in return they kept all of the advertising income. This, of course, meant that the IHA never compromised the association's finances by producing the magazine.

However, the IHA did receive the income from sales, and when the *Irish Housewife* was first produced it sold for 1s. 6d.. This did not increase until 1960 when the charge was raised to 2s. While the cost of the magazine was kept at an affordable price, the fact that articles were contributed free to the magazine meant that the IHA had no costs of production and more profit. Articles presented in the magazine covered a wide array of subjects, including reports of ongoing campaigns such as the call for distribution of clean and pasteurized milk for schoolchildren, the improvement of the condition in women's prisons and the establishment of more children's nurseries. Other articles provided housewives with advice on running their household. An advertisement for the magazine in the *Irish Times* stressed that the *Irish Housewife* itself was good value for money, boasting that it included over thirty articles 'and is well worth 1s. 6d.'.[23]

Many feminist campaigns and campaigners can be traced through the articles published in the *Irish Housewife*. Hilda Tweedy was a regular contributor, as was her husband, Robert, who often wrote pieces offering practical information, including assessments of electricity in the home. Hilda's articles provided consumer information on matters such as 'Hire Purchase' or announced news of IHA campaigns. However, her writing was not always of such a serious nature and often displayed her appealing sense of humour. In one such piece Tweedy describes purchasing a new cooker. She declares to her readers that 'I could not wait to order my new cooker! The day after the explosion I dashed into town determined to realize my dreams – The explosion? Oh yes, the old one ended with a bang one Sunday evening while the soup was simmering for supper.'[24]

23 *Irish Times*, 20 May 1953.   24 Hilda Tweedy, 'My new cooker', *Irish Housewife*, 1965, 75.

shock this entails for the adopted child and the blow to their own affections.'[30] The 'writer and republican activist' Dorothy Macardle took up the cause and campaigned for the introduction of legal adoption in Ireland.[31] Macardle became vice president of the Irish Association of Civil Liberty when it was founded in 1949 and later became president of the organization, which was a precursor to the current Irish Council for Civil Liberties. Macardle wrote an article for the *Irish Housewife* entitled 'Chosen Child', asserting that 'everywhere experts on child welfare have concluded that institutional life is deleterious to children, retarding them in their powers of expression, emotional response, self-confidence and capacity for adaptation to normal social life. Adoption into suitable homes is recognised as much the happiest solution of the friendless child.'[32]

The year after these articles were printed, the IHA became embroiled in controversy while advocating to protect children. In 1951, when the minister for health, Dr Noel Browne, proposed the Mother and Child Scheme to improve awareness and access to medical care, the IHA instantly showed its support. The proposed bill came at a time when Ireland had the highest infant death rate in Europe. Free medical services to mothers and children would certainly have reduced this. However, the Catholic archbishop of Dublin, John Charles McQuaid, strongly objected. In his statement on the issue, he maintained that 'the public authority, without qualification, is entirely and directly contrary to Catholic teaching on the rights of the family, the rights of the Church in education, the rights of the medical profession and of voluntary institutions'.[33] While the government withdrew the scheme and Browne resigned in protest, the IHA stood firm in its support, sending Taoiseach John A. Costello a telegram:

> We, the Committee of the IHA, affirm our belief that the principle of equal opportunities, enshrined in our Constitution, should be applied in the sphere of health to those least able to fend for themselves: the mothers and children of Ireland. We consequently reaffirm our support of the Mother and Child Scheme as proposed by the Minister for Health.[34]

Tweedy and members of the IHA maintained their support by taking to the streets on the back of a truck that circled College Green in Dublin city

30 A Social Worker, 'Nobody's child', *Irish Housewife*, 1950, 58.   31 As described by Patrick Maume, 'Macardle, Dorothy Margaret', *DIB*.   32 Dorothy Macardle, 'Chosen child', *Irish Housewife*, 1950, 34.   33 As cited in Sylvia Walby, *Globalization and inequalities: complexity and contested modernities* (London, 2009), p. 391.   34 Telegram from IHA to An Taoiseach Mr Costello and the minister for health, Dr Browne, 11 Apr. 1951, NAI 98/17/5/2/2.

centre. But when they attempted to address the crowds from the back of the truck, they were drowned out by people singing a Catholic hymn 'Faith of our fathers'. Not surprisingly, such a demonstration of perceived anti-Catholic behaviour drew media attention. On Saturday, 12 April 1952, an article entitled 'Dangerous Trends in Ireland' appeared in the *Roscommon Herald*. The article noted that the Irish Housewives' Association 'had always been used as a medium of expression' by Marxists, Communists or fellow travellers.[35] This was, in fact, the second time that the organization was accused of having communist sympathies, a damning accusation during the 1950s. Previously the weekly Catholic paper, *The Standard*, had printed similar accusations. This time the IHA took legal action and won its case in August 1953. The *Roscommon Herald* printed an apology stating that there was no foundation for the allegations against the IHA. However, the damage was already done. Many members resigned over the controversy and some branches closed down entirely.

The pages of the *Irish Housewife* provide solid evidence of other feminist campaigns during a time – after the votes for women campaign and before the women's liberation movement – often considered void of such activity. During this supposed void, another key topic of feminist concern appeared in the pages of the magazine. In 1956 an article addressed the need for women in the Irish police force. The honorary secretary of the Joint Committee of Women's Societies and Social Workers (JCWSSW), Mrs W.R. O'Hegarty, asked readers of the *Irish Housewife*, 'Why have we no women's police force?' O'Hegarty had, in fact, been a constant driving force behind the campaign to introduce women to policing in Ireland. As early as 1939 she wrote to Taoiseach Éamon de Valera, maintaining that 'in the administration of justice there are certain duties which it is difficult, or impossible for men police to carry out, and which could be performed appropriately and efficiently by a force of women police'.[36] Understandably, after over twenty years of campaigning on this issue, O'Hegarty was becoming despondent and wrote an account about the lack of progress for female policing in the *Irish Housewife*. O'Hegarty wrote that

> Since 1935 a constant campaign has been waged by the JCWSSW, on which no less than 16 women's societies are represented; many other societies working on social problems have called for it; large numbers of county councils and public bodies have repeatedly asked for it; members

---

35 *Roscommon Herald*, 15 Aug. 1953, as cited in Tweedy, *Links in the chain*, pp 70–1.   36 Letter from W.R. O'Hegarty to de Valera, 25 May 1939, as cited in Christopher Shepard, 'A liberalisation of Irish social policy? Women's organisations and the campaign for women police in Ireland, 1915–57', *Irish Historical Studies*, 36:144 (2009), 564–80 at 569.

of the Oireachtas and the judiciary have supported the demand; constant questions as to the cause of the delay have been addressed to the minister for justice in the Dáil, and his answer to all questions, letters and resolutions is that the matter is under consideration. It has been under active consideration for two years and still we wait.[37]

This article could not have been better timed. The previous year, department of justice officials had accepted that the introduction of female members to the Garda Síochána was 'both necessary and inevitable'.[38] However, the issue did not clear the Dáil until 1958 and, during the debate on the issue, the independent TD for Dublin North-Central, Frank Sherwin, highlighted just how misogynistic politics in Ireland was at that point by suggesting to the minister that 'while recruits should not be actually horsefaced, they should not be too good-looking; they should be just plain women and not targets for marriage'.[39] It was eventually agreed to hire a grand total of twelve female gardaí who would be confined to the Dublin Metropolitan area. This move was seen as an experiment before consideration could be given to introducing female police into the ranks across the country. On 9 July 1959, the twelve selected female recruits were accepted as members of the Irish police force.

CULTURAL ASPECTS IN THE MAGAZINE

Articles of political interest, calls for social reform and feminist campaigns sat alongside articles on art, literature and culture written by esteemed commentators, authors and painters. In the same edition that O'Hegarty made her plea for women to be accepted into policing in Ireland, the artist Stella Frost wrote a tribute to her friend and mentor, the stained-glass artist Evie Hone, who had died the previous year. Hone was a highly respected artist in her day. She had received the great honour of being commissioned by the Irish government to design stained-glass windows for the Irish pavilion at the New York World's Fair in 1939. Frost's article includes a significant list of places in Ireland where Hone's stained-glass windows can be seen. Frost concluded that

> we are too close to Evie Hone's life, and too much shaken by her death, to be able to appreciate herself and her work in their true and lasting

37 W.R. O'Hegarty, 'The need for women police', *Irish Housewife*, 1956, 55–8.   38 Department of justice memorandum, Nov. 1955, cited in Shepard, 'A liberalization', 576.   39 Dáil Éireann, vol. 168 (5), Garda Síochána Bill 1958, 22 May 1958.

colours. We stand like the little figures in a crowd in one of her windows, hushed by a miracle that we barely understand. For her life, and the work she has left to the world and to us, are as near a miracle as we are likely to meet.[40]

Possibly one of the most important aspects of this article is not what it tells us about the work of Evie Hone but rather the insight it provides into the author of the piece, Stella Frost, who, in fact, we know very little about. The year after this article was published, Frost edited a book in tribute to two of her friends and artistic inspirations: *A tribute to Evie Hone and Mainie Jellett*.[41]

In addition to giving space to established Irish art and artists the *Irish Housewife* found room to encourage the next generation to be artistic. In 1950 Anne Butler Yeats, a successful painter and daughter of W.B and George Yeats, published an article titled 'Can Your Child Draw?', in which she warned: 'don't be too cautious! Beware of all that restricts a child's boldness of hand and of imagination. More is at stake than his future as an artist.'[42] The IHA employed the *Irish Housewife* to inspire future generations of artists through art competitions. Such competition clearly also encouraged men to read and contribute to the magazine. In 1960, it was a Mr J. Cogan, a student at the National College of Art, who won the competition to design a front cover for the magazine. The entrants were restricted to ages 16–25 and the prize was the decent sum of £10.

It is testimony to the high regard in which the *Irish Housewife* was held that articles by notable Irish personalities often appeared in its pages. In the 1948 issue, the children's author Patricia Lynch published poetry, while later in the same issue of the magazine a short story by the writer, nationalist and suffragist Rosamond Jacob could be read. In 1952 the celebrated Irish author and editor Seán O'Faoláin contributed an extract from his forthcoming travel book *An autumn in Italy*.[43] Also, the novelist Kate O'Brien, who had had two novels banned in Ireland – *Mary Lavelle* (1936) and *The land of spices* (1941) – wrote a personal account of her birthplace, 'Limerick', for the magazine.[44] This appeared in the magazine in the same year that her novel *As music and splendour* was published. That novel depicts, as Lorna Reynolds and Bridget Hourican describe, 'the only full, consummated lesbian relationship in her fiction'.[45] While this could have been viewed as scandalous, and O'Brien's work

40 Stella Frost, 'Evie Hone', *Irish Housewife*, 1956, 57.   41 Stella Frost (ed.), *A tribute to Evie Hone and Mainie Jellett* (Dublin, 1957).   42 Anne Butler Yeats, 'Can your child draw?', *Irish Housewife*, 1950, 68. The article was illustrated by Gillian O'Donovan, aged 6.   43 Seán O'Faoláin, 'An autumn in Italy', *Irish Housewife*, 1952, 53–5.   44 Kate O'Brien, 'Limerick', *Irish Housewife*, 1958, 56.   45 Lorna Reynolds & Bridget Hourican, 'O'Brien, Kate', *DIB*.

was already seen by many in this light, this certainly did not dismay the editorial board of the *Irish Housewife*, which was more than happy to include her
work in their pages. In the article, readers are given an insight into O'Brien's
disillusionment with life in a small country town, describing how 'when we are
young I think that no matter how true our affection for the place of our birth,
a strong desire in most of us, many of us, is to travel away from it. Especially
if it be a small or smallish place.'

The renowned columnist Brian O'Nolan also appeared in the pages of
the *Irish Housewife*.[46] His articles are aptly described by his biographer, Anne
Clune, as

> a vast amalgamation of satire, parody, odd inventions, linguistic games,
> and fantastic biographies, which allowed its author to comment on every
> aspect of contemporary Ireland and its culture and to create charac-
> ters and concerns that became established features of everyday Irish life,
> repeated and retold all over the country.[47]

O'Nolan often reprinted articles from his *Irish Times* 'Cruiskeen Lawn' column
in the *Irish Housewife*. It is noteworthy that such articles found their way into
the pages of this magazine, showing that the editors appreciated the place
of satirical commentary. O'Nolan also penned an article exclusively for the
magazine under his alter ego Myles na gCopaleen entitled 'Pots and Pains'. In
it, he concludes that 'married life and cookery are almost undistinguishable.
If the heart be the seat of love, the stomach next door is its spare room. A
husband may patiently endure tantrums, temper, a dirty and damp bed. But
cold, wretchedly cooked food? The fat will be in the fire then, and no cookery
transaction will be in question!'[48]

TOWARDS A NEW ERA

In 1961 the IHA deemed it necessary to promote the sale of the *Irish Housewife*
and rented a stand at the largest agricultural event of the year, the RDS Spring
Show. Tweedy and other volunteers commanded stand number 105 in the
Dublin event centre. As well as selling more than £55 worth of copies of the
magazine, they attracted many new members to the IHA and resolved to take

46 Brian O'Nolan wrote novels under the pseudonym Flann O'Brien and a satirical column, 'Cruiskeen
Lawn' (little brimming jug), in the *Irish Times* under the name Myles na gCopaleen (Myles of the little
horses.)   47 Anne Clune, 'O'Nolan, Brian (Flann O'Brien)', *DIB*.   48 Myles na Gopaleen, 'Pots and
pains', *Irish Housewife*, 1963, 69–70.

a stand at the Horse Show, also in the RDS. However, the advertising market began to slow down in the 1960s and by 1966 it was no longer viable for the advertising agency to print the magazine. In what would be the final edition, the twentieth volume, of the *Irish Housewife* in 1966, the IHA celebrated the 'golden jubilee' of the 1916 Easter Rising. The cover of the magazine, specially designed by Michael Troughton-Smith, boasts a black and white image of the GPO on O'Connell Street taken in 1966 and a comparison picture taken during Easter Week 1916 after the rebellion had devastated the area. The two photographs are flanked by the colours of the republic: green, white and orange. In the foreword, the chair of the IHA at the time, Maude Rooney, announced:

> We salute the women who took part in this struggle, either actively or by inspiring others. We fear, however, that the women of to-day are so inclined to take independence for granted, that they have become apathetic in their outlook, even to the extent of failing to exercise the franchise properly. We wonder why intelligent women of Ireland are so reluctant to go forward into public life, or to support those few women who do so ... Have the women of 1916 pointed the way all in vain?[49]

The first article in the volume is simply entitled 'Women of 1916'. Written by Lucy Kingston, it pays homage to the women who played roles in the Easter Rising, noting that it was not simply men who rebelled but also 'several outstanding and courageous women, whom it is fitting that we should remember, now fifty years later, when there has been time for many changes in the point of view regarding those exciting days'.[50] She recalls the work of Countess Markievicz, Eva Gore-Booth, Maud Gonne, Grace Plunkett, Helena Molony and Hanna Sheehy Skeffington. A short extract from the conclusion identifies how remarkably hard-hitting the content of this magazine for housewives could actually be:

> Ah, but how are the women treated now in the Republic? What has gone wrong in the vision of this generation? Who is to blame? If we had such dedicated fire-brands in our midst to-day – devoted to the *women's* cause, not only the nation's – we might have a better position than the cold reality of the present, where the Republic – whatever its virtues and achievements – is definitely, confessedly and regrettably 'a man's country!'[51]

---

49 Maude Rooney, 'Foreword', *Irish Housewife*, 1966, 9. **50** Lucy Kingston, 'Women of 1916', *Irish Housewife*, 1966, 15. **51** Ibid., 18.

After twenty years the *Irish Housewife* ceased publication in 1967, though the editorial board did not disband. Tweedy continued to seek alternative methods for the IHA to spread word of its campaigns and to provide vital consumer information. She contacted mainstream women's magazines requesting a page to be given over for IHA news. She suggested a joint endeavour with other women's organizations to produce a communal newsletter or magazine. All of these efforts were to no avail.

In 1972 the IHA established a new editorial board chaired by Nora Browne. An estate agent and businesswoman, Browne served as chair of the IHA from 1968 to 1972. It was during her time that a new magazine, *Housewife's Voice*, was launched. It was felt that a new magazine empowering women as consumers and spreading details of feminist campaigns was much needed. By the end of that year, journalist Mary Maher summed up the position of women in Ireland with her headline 'Women in 1972: Not Much to Be Triumphant About'.[52] The IHA stepped up their production and the *Housewives Voice* was published three times a year: spring, summer and winter editions were produced, rather than the previous annual magazine. Additionally, the editorial board chose to distribute the magazine for free to members and to the public at recruiting drives; it was also exchanged with magazines from women's organizations in other EEC countries, providing an international exchange of ideas. The *Housewife's Voice* ran for eight years, finally ceasing publication in 1980.[53]

CONCLUSION

Since the 1940s consecutive government ministers had recognized the importance of the IHA, or at least were wary of them as formidable lobbyists. Politicians including Seán Lemass, John Costello, Charlie Haughey and Jack Lynch all took heed of the IHA, or at least faced pressure from it as an organized group. Such lobbying brought many successes for gender equality in Ireland, not least by demanding that the government answer the United Nations directive to establish the National Commission on the Status of Women in Ireland.[54] This action alone has left us a legacy that continues to shape and influence us today. By the time the Irish Housewives' Association

---

52 *Irish Times*, 30 Dec. 1962.   53 A complete collection of these magazines was deposited in the National Archives of Ireland by Hilda Tweedy in 2005, providing a wonderful source that will hopefully be utilised by future researchers.   54 The Commission on the Status of Women – to 'make recommendation on the steps necessary to ensure the participation of women on equal terms and conditions with men in the political, social, cultural and economic life of the country' – was established by the government in 1970 and reported in 1973.

disbanded in 1992 the group had seen fifty years of activity and had success-
fully published two magazines over a period of four decades. During this time
Ireland witnessed immense moves towards gender equality. During the early
years of the IHA, Tweedy had been refused a teaching job at a girls' school
because she was a married woman. By the time the association dissolved, a
married woman was president of Ireland, causing Tweedy to reflect: 'Who
would have thought in 1942 that women would move from the kitchen to Áras
an Uachtaráin.'[55]

---

55 *Irish Times*, 9 July 2005.

12 / Irish-produced women's magazines in the 1950s and '60s

CAITRIONA CLEAR

'Think pink, on the long and lonely road ahead!' booms Kay Thompson as Maggie Prescott, editor of *Quality* magazine, in Stanley Donen's 1957 film *Funny Face*.[1] Challenging personal journeys, her song suggests, can be helped by a simple colour wash. This is a caricature, and not a particularly extreme one, of women's magazine content, where earnest and sane counsel on body and soul was supplied literally alongside whimsical directives about fashion.[2] Magazines have been criticized for this apparent frothiness and triviality, and for appearing to stereotype women.[3] However, a range of scholarly works on magazines in twentieth-century Britain, Australia, New Zealand, Canada, the USA, the Netherlands and Ireland have demonstrated convincingly that these publications supported women by taking their preoccupations seriously in a world that belittled domestic and emotional labour. They also argue that women appreciated magazines in many different ways, as relaxation and fantasy (fiction, fashion and beauty) as well as for practical information (the so-called 'service content' – cookery, household and health). Far from being passive consumers, readers often 'resisted' magazines' prescriptive and advertising content.[4] They even derived economic benefits from these publications; the knitting and sewing patterns that were an essential component of all magazines up to the late 1960s enabled women not only to dress themselves and

---

1 Paramount Pictures 1957; also starring Fred Astaire and Audrey Hepburn. 2 As this is a historical article, the past tense is used throughout, even though much of what is said could apply to women's magazines today. 3 The classic criticism is in Betty Friedan, *The feminine mystique* (New York, 1963). 4 Cynthia White, *Women's magazines, 1693–1968* (London, 1970); Irene Dancyger, *A world of women: an illustrated history of women's magazines* (Dublin, 1978); Marjorie Ferguson, *Forever feminine: women's magazines and the cult of femininity* (London, 1983); Janice Winship, *Inside women's magazines* (London, 1987); Roz Ballaster et al. (eds), *Women's worlds: ideology, femininity and the woman's magazine* (London, 1991); Jennifer Scanlan, *Inarticulate longings: the* Ladies' Home Journal, *gender and the promises of consumer culture* (London, 1995); Joke Hermes, *Reading women's magazines: an analysis of everyday media use* (Oxford, 1995); Brian Braithwaite, *Women's magazines: the first 300 Years* (London, 1995); Linda Korinek, *Roughing it in the suburbs: reading* Chatelaine *magazine in the 1950s and 60s* (Toronto, 2000); Linda Walker, *Shaping our mothers' world: American women's magazines* (Jackson, 2000); Lesley Johnson & Justine Lloyd, *Sentenced to everyday life: feminism and the housewife* (New York, 2004); Noliwe Rooks, *Ladies' pages: African-American women's magazines and the culture that made them* (Newark, 2005); and Caitriona Clear, *Women's voices Ireland: women's magazines in the 1950s and 60s* (London, 2016).

their children cheaply, but often to earn extra money.[5] Women's magazines
have been almost completely ignored by historians of Irish media.[6] Yet Irish
women's magazines in the 1950s and 1960s were both witnesses to, and agents
of, the slow transformation of women's lives.

WOMEN IN IRELAND IN THE 1950s AND '60s

The 1950s is usually seen as an era of stasis in Irish history, followed by the
rapid change of the 1960s.[7] High levels of emigration for women and men
in the earlier decade have obscured the fact that life for those who stayed in
Ireland changed permanently too. For women in particular, the slow changes
of the 1950s broke ground for the more visible changes of the 1960s. There
were over 31,000 more girls and women in office work, shop work, factory
work, hotel service, teaching, nursing and other professions in Ireland in 1961
than there had been in 1946, and a rise of over 10,000 in female trade union
membership in the same period.[8] From the late 1940s, growing numbers of
women took enthusiastic part in organizations, urban and rural, social and
cultural, religious and secular – Muintir na Tire, Macra na Feirme, the Irish
Countrywomen's Association, the Legion of Mary, Conradh na Gaeilge.
Amateur drama (in which female participation was essential) flourished to
such an extent that an annual festival was inaugurated in Athlone in 1953.
Oral history and popular autobiography tell of regular carnivals, concerts,
plays, cinemas, marquees and dances.[9] More women than ever before were
leaving home for work and for entertainment, and spending money on their

5 Fiona Hackney, 'Making modern women stitch by stitch: dressmaking and women's magazines in
Britain, 1919–39' in Barbara Burman (ed.), *The culture of sewing: gender, consumption and home dressmaking* (Oxford,
1999), pp 73–95. 6 John Horgan, *Irish media: a critical history since 1922* (London, 2001) mentions *Woman's
Way* once, p. 147, in the context of the 1980s. Women's magazines are not mentioned at all in Chris
Morash, *A history of the media in Ireland* (Cambridge, 2010); Paul Lindsay (ed.), *The media and modern society
in Ireland* (Celbridge, 1993); Mary J. Kelly & Barbara O'Connor (eds), *Media audiences in Ireland* (Dublin,
1997); Damien Kiberd (ed.), *Media in Ireland: the search for diversity* (Dublin, 1997); or John Horgan, Barbara
O'Connor & Helena Sheehan (eds), *Mapping Irish media: critical explorations* (Dublin, 2007). 7 J.J. Lee,
Ireland: politics & society, 1912–1985 (Cambridge, 1989), pp 271–410; Dermot Keogh, *Twentieth-century Ireland:
nation and state* (Dublin, 1994), pp 214–94. 8 Caitriona Clear, *Women of the house: women's household work in
Ireland, 1922–1961* (Dublin, 2000), pp 13–26. Regarding trade union membership see Marianne Heron,
Sheila Conroy: fighting spirit (Dublin, 1993). 9 Stephen Rynne, *Father John Hayes: founder of Muintir na Tire*
(Dublin, 1960) and *Rural Ireland* (Muintir na Tire annual periodical) 1948–65; *Macra: a way of life* (Dublin,
2005); Aileen Heverin, *ICA: the Irish Countrywomen's Association: a history* (Dublin, 2000); Finola Kennedy, *Frank
Duff: a life story* (London, 2011); Eleanor O'Leary, *Youth and popular culture in 1950s Ireland* (London, 2018);
Síle de Cléir, *Popular Catholicism in twentieth-century Ireland: locality, identity, culture* (London, 2017); interviews
about rural Galway in the 1940s and 1950s by Pauline Bermingham Scully, in *Two cigarettes coming down the
boreen* (Galway, 2015). See also extensive evidence from *Woman's Life* magazine in the 1950s, referenced below.

appearance. In 1946 there was one female hairdresser to every 768 females; twenty years later, the rate was 1 to 308.[10] The 1960s accelerated these changes, bringing more and varied employment, improved housing, broader educational access, better transport and vastly expanded media engagement with everyday life. Right into the middle of this decade, women in Ireland were marrying later than the European average, usually after they had been earning for several years, and sometimes for up to a decade. They had, therefore, acquired experience in handling and spending money, even if marriage, as women often lamented, redirected spending from the self to the family and the house.[11]

The house envisaged by magazines everywhere, even in Ireland, was invariably a dedicated domestic space. Homes that incorporated businesses – farms, shops, on-site workshops, smithies or garages – were ignored. However, by the 1950s in Ireland, the farmhouse was beginning to modernize, with the slow onward march of rural electrification and aquafication, and the gap between it and the modern urban home, as far as services, facilities and even layout was concerned, was narrowing.[12] Magazine discourse, therefore, began to be more meaningful to women all over the country, if only in an aspirational way. Women running houses, however, were not magazines' only intended audience; women in the paid workforce with disposable income (however little) were the other and perhaps the greater part of magazines' 'target demographic'. White sees the improvement in British women's economic position in the post-war years as crucial to the development of a strong women's magazine sector,[13] and in Ireland, where only 5 per cent of all married women were in the paid workforce in 1961 and 7.5 per cent in 1971,[14] female earners were overwhelmingly single. Irish-produced magazines, therefore, addressed themselves to public as well as to private life, to the workplace as well as the home, to friendship and working relationships as well as marriage and parenthood.

MAGAZINES' CIRCULATION AND READERSHIP

Not all women read magazines, of course, and certainly not all Irish women did so, especially in the 1950s. There is little reliable information on newspaper or periodical circulation in Ireland before the 1950s, but a response to a Dáil question about spending on government advertising in periodical

---

10 Clear, *Women of the house*, p. 204.   11 Ibid., pp 171–215.   12 Michael Sheils, *The quiet revolution: the electrification of rural Ireland* (Dublin, 1979). See also Clear, *Women of the house, passim.*   13 White, *Women's magazines*, pp 155–215.   14 Clear, *Women's voices*, p. 146. Comparable figures for percentages of married women who were in the paid workforce in the UK are 35% in 1961 and 40% in 1971.

publications in 1955 gives some indication of it. The only women's magazine to supply numbers, the monthly *Model Housekeeping*, claimed a circulation
of 27,000 to 28,000. (To put this into context, the popular weekly *Ireland's
Own* boasted a circulation of 37,958, the *Sunday Press* 383,716 and the *Sunday
Independent* 380,995).[15] Going on this (slight) evidence, Ireland had a much
lower rate of women's magazine readership per head of the population than
Britain in the middle of the 1950s – although the cheaper titles *Woman's Life*
and *Woman's Mirror*, discussed below, did not supply any numbers.[16] Readership
of Irish-produced women's magazines increased in the 1960s, and one source
puts the circulation of *Woman's Way* in 1966 at 240,000 – still a lower rate per
head of the population than the UK, but a huge increase on the previous
decade.[17] Irish women, of course, read British magazines, which were on sale
in Ireland, though subject to occasional censorship.[18] Letters to the editor
from women with Irish addresses appeared occasionally in British magazines,
and Irish women who returned from Britain might have built up loyalties to
particular magazines.[19] This chapter is concerned with Irish-produced magazines in these crucial decades, but magazines produced in Britain and sold in
Ireland offered keen competition, and will be referred to from time to time.
There were no mastheads giving names of editors and other contributors on
Irish magazines until *Woman's Way* appeared in 1963, but there were addresses
for correspondence and occasional clues in the magazines themselves about
publishers, contributors and managing directors.

THE IRISH TATLER & SKETCH: IRELAND'S PREMIER
AND SPORTING MONTHLY

This publication began as a women's magazine, *The Lady of the House*, when
founded by Henry Wilson Hartnell in 1890. It became the *Irish Tatler & Sketch*
in the 1920s, and has since become a women's magazine again as the *Irish
Tatler*.[20] In the 1950s and '60s, with its columns on 'rugger', motoring, tennis, golf, hunting and the 'turf' (horse-racing), it was aimed at men as well

---

15 Dáil Éireann, vol. 149 (5), 24 Mar. 1955.   16 White, *Women's magazines*, appendices IV and V.   17 This
claim is made in a letter to *Woman's Way* (hereafter *WW*) 23 Sept. 1966 by Jane Nolan, Dublin 4. *Woman's
Way*, which did not keep records, could not verify it.   18 Peggy Makins, *The Evelyn Home story* (London,
1975), pp 143, 174.   19 See Clear, *Women's voices*, pp 1–2; and, just a sample, Irish letters to *Woman's Realm*,
Mrs J.D., Westmeath, 9 Aug. 1958; Mrs M.W., Sutton, Dublin, 11 Apr. 1959; Mrs C.N., Tralee, Co. Kerry,
12 July 1959; and to *Woman's Own*, Mrs M. Doyle, Waterford, 29 Jan. 1966; Mrs K. Gallagher, Co. Donegal,
12 Feb. 1966; Mrs M. Norris, Dublin, 9 July 1966; Mrs A. Baldwin, Waterford, 3 Dec. 1966.   20 Thanks
to Norah Casey, Harmonia Publications, for this information.

as women; there were also health, fashion and beauty articles, and items of interest on people in the arts. Appearing monthly, it was expensive, at 1s. 6d.; on one of its typical front pages, Heidsieck Champagne, Courvoisier Cognac, Elverys' Sports Equipment, Bradmola Nylons and Redgauntlet Gloves shared advertising space. Announcements, and sometimes photographs, of engagements and weddings, comings of age, hunt balls and equine events, cardinal investitures and presidential events were staples. The arts featured regularly; for example, in the magazine's reporting of the president's reception for PEN in July 1953, attended by Stephen Rynne, Alice Curtayne, Patricia Lynch and Teresa Deevy among others.[21] But there were no knitting and sewing patterns, readers' letters pages, problem pages, competitions or buy-and-sell clubs. Above all, the *Irish Tatler & Sketch* lacked the intimate, friendly tone that characterized all other women's magazines (in Ireland, Britain and everywhere) in these decades.

MODEL HOUSEKEEPING

This colourful, attractive magazine began in 1927 and ran until 1966. Although its name changed to *Woman's View & Model Housekeeping* from 1962, the words '*Model Housekeeping*' were always larger. In the 1950s it cost 6d., rising to 9d. in the early 1960s, and it appeared monthly. By the 1950s it carried the usual service articles – cookery, 'mother and baby', fashion and beauty. There were two short stories in each issue, for which the default location was usually either Britain or the USA, though there were sometimes stories with an Irish setting by Patricia Kennedy, Moira Scanlon, Mary E.M. O'Donovan, Charlotte M. Kelly and others.[22] The arts section was extensive, with about ten books reviewed in every issue, from Rebecca West's *The fountain overflows* (London, 1956) in February 1957, to Prionsias Mac an Bheatha's *Tart na córa: Seamus Ó Conghaile, a shaol agus a shaothar* (Baile Átha Cliath, 1962) in May 1963. Plays, operas and other metropolitan theatrical events were also reviewed. Zanzibar was recommended as a holiday location in August 1957, and *One woman's Morocco*, by Martine Howe, was Book Choice of the Month in April 1956. Women's magazines are, of course, aspirational, but aspirations must be within the realm of possibility for readers. Not until the mid-1960s did any of the other

21 *Irish Tatler & Sketch* (hereafter *ITS*), 1950–66, *passim*; advertisements, *ITS*, Jan. 1953; new cardinal, Jan. 1953; president's reception for PEN, July 1953; Kildare Hunt Ball, Dec. 1958; Goff Bloodstock Sales, Nov. 1959; marriage of marquis of Dufferin and Ava to Lindy Guinness, Oct. 1964.   22 *Model Housekeeping* (hereafter *MH*), July 1956, Oct. 1956, June 1957, Apr. 1963, June 1963. It is not clear whether these were pseudonyms or not. More research is needed.

Irish-produced magazines mention foreign holidays. This provides a clue to the social class of *Model Housekeeping* readers.

This magazine's diary pages featured Irish women prominent in business, public life and the arts. The February 1956 issue, for example, carried an exclusive on Irish dress designer Irene Gilbert. Clonmel author Una Troy, whose novel *We are seven* (London, 1955) was widely translated and made into a film, featured in May 1958. Betty Morrissey of the Irish Housewives' Association was profiled in September 1962, and Mrs J.M. Doyle, of the Radio Éireann Symphony Orchestra was interviewed in June 1963. Also featured in January 1963 was Miss Hamilton-Reid, Ireland's only female chairman of a department store (Switzers in Dublin).[23]

Reader engagement with *Model Housekeeping* was almost non-existent. There was no problem page and no readers' letters page; and there were no competitions, beauty or health queries, or buy-and-sell club. Clues about readers' geographical location or marital or employment status can only be inferred from the magazine's content. The British magazine most comparable to it was *Woman's Illustrated*; although this had a readers' letters page (which mainly consisted of philosophical musings and local history observations), it had no problem page, and it had plenty of the same kind of thoughtful articles that characterized *Model Housekeeping*. For example, an issue of *Woman's Illustrated* in 1956 has a column by Lady Violet Bonham Carter on her favourite books and on the importance of self-denial during Lent, the reminiscences of Lady Isobel Barnett on her time as one of Scotland's earliest female medical students, an article on the life of Jesus, and the usual service content.[24]

WOMAN'S MIRROR

Woman's Mirror commenced publication in 1933 and ceased in 1956. It was published at 270 North Circular Road, Dublin (the same address as *Model Housekeeping*), cost 3d. and appeared monthly. By the 1950s much of its content was taken up with syndicated film news – Jeanne Crain, Doris Day, Gene Tierney, Glynis Johns, Joan Crawford and Barbara Bel Geddes were among those featured. The magazine noted that Maureen O'Hara was shooting a film in Mayo in 1951, but *The quiet man*, directed by John Ford, with two leading Hollywood stars in main roles, many celebrated Irish actors in minor roles and

23 All *Model Housekeeping* references as for months specified in main text.   24 *Woman's Illustrated* was published by Amalgamated Press and folded in 1961; at its most popular its sales were about a quarter of those of *Woman* (White, *Women's magazines*, p. 97 and Appendix IV). *Woman's Illustrated*, 18 Feb. 1956.

a sizeable number of Galway and Mayo people drafted in as extras, was never mentioned at all subsequently in the magazine.[25]

The diary pages were entitled 'Mirror of the Month', or 'We Halt the Passing Pageant'. Sometimes Irish women and their achievements were featured; in 1951–3, folklorist Bríd Mahon, playwright Louise Murphy, actor Maureen Cusack and comedienne Paddy Dunlea all featured, and a piece on the inauguration of President Seán T. O'Kelly for his second term in 1952 mentioned that the mauve suit worn by his wife Phyllis had been designed by her niece. However, it was not mentioned that Phyllis was a veteran of the War of Independence (she was one of the revolutionary Ryan sisters from Wexford), and the designer-niece's name, Neilí Mulcahy, was not given. A similar insouciance about detail surfaced in March 1955 when 'Mirror of the Month' claimed that 'our own capital city has become quite a centre of world fashion with amazing rapidity', but did not mention the world-famous Sybil Connolly, Irene Gilbert, the up-and-coming Mulcahy or any of the other designers mentioned by *Woman's Life* (see below), instead mentioning Digby Morton, a London-based male designer who had set up a branch in Dublin, and John Cavanaugh. Perhaps Morton and some of the actors mentioned above sent out press releases, but it is difficult to imagine President Seán T. O'Kelly, or folklorist Bríd Mahon doing so. Or indeed, Clare County Council; the diary mentioned that the distinctive new local authority houses in Ennis, Co. Clare (actually Clarecastle) were designed by a 'lady'; her name was not given. Interest in current affairs and a sense of Irish identity blinked on and off like a defective light bulb: reference was made to John A. O'Brien's celebrated book about Irish population decline, *The vanishing Irish* (New York, 1953), readers' opinions on the low marriage rate were solicited and there was mention in the succeeding issue of a 'big pile of letters' received, but these were never referred to in the magazine again.[26]

Reader engagement, slight though it was, suggests a mainly single and earning readership. Six finalists in a competition for household hints (the prize was nylon stockings) came from Tipperary, Kildare, Offaly, Cork and Wexford, four from numbered urban addresses, and all were titled 'Miss'. A beauty advice column advised 'Silly Sue' not to smoke so much, and a 'stout' bride-to-be was advised to avoid white in favour of a floor-length blue.

25 See *Woman's Mirror* (hereafter *WM*): film stars, Apr. 1953, Apr. 1951, Aug. 1951, Oct. 1951, June 1954, July 1955, *passim*; O'Hara, *Quiet man*, Aug. 1951. 26 *WM*, Mahon, Cusack, Feb. 1951; Murphy, Nov. 1951; Dunlea, Mar. 1951 and Apr. 1952; President O'Kelly, July 1952; Clarecastle, Nov. 1951; *Vanishing Irish*, Mar. 1952, and Apr. 1952; July 1952, Oct. 1952. For information on Neilí Mulcahy, I am indebted to Dr Therese Moylan, Institute of Art, Design and Technology, Dún Laoghaire; on the Ryans, see Senia Pašeta, *Irish nationalist women, 1900–1918* (Cambridge, 2013), *passim*.

(White did not become the norm for brides until the late 1950s, so this was normal advice.) The geographical origin of 'problems' was sometimes given; a woman who worried that her lipstick never looked right at a party came from Co. Louth, 'Kerry Girl' worried about the hairs on her legs, and Miss E.N.R from Leix (as Co. Laois was then known) asked how she could make her eyes appear larger.[27] Still, while the beauty and clothes advice was aimed at 'business girls' and single women generally, the service articles supplied knitting patterns for children's clothes, and the health and cookery advice was aimed mainly at mothers and women in charge of a house. It is difficult to find a comparable British magazine to *Woman's Mirror*; the strong impression given is that of a magazine on its last legs, and it ceased publication without warning in February 1956.

WOMAN'S LIFE

While not as colourful or as expensively produced as *Model Housekeeping*, *Woman's Life* was nonetheless an attractive magazine. Begun in 1936, it was based in the 1950s at Harcourt Street, Dublin, and owned by the Murray family; Mrs Lily Murray was closely identified with it. In this decade it appeared fortnightly and cost 4*d*. Irish identity was more important to this magazine than to any of the others. In 1954 it referred more than once to An Tóstal, the Irish cultural and economic festival, and its diary pages, while in no way insular — mention of Hungarian toymakers in one issue of 1953 was typical — made a point of showcasing Irish female achievement and activity.[28]

Woman's Life readers, judging by the reader engagement, were mainly in Munster and Leinster (town and country), and in towns in Connacht and Ulster. Prize-winning household hints sent in in February 1954 came from Emly, Co. Tipperary; Kilrush, Co. Clare; Athlone, Co. Westmeath; Gorey, Co. Wexford; Castlepollard, Co. Westmeath; Enniscrone, Co. Sligo; Piltown, Co. Kilkenny; Ballinalee, Co. Longford; and Kilsyth, near Glasgow. Of seventy-three advertisements in the *Woman's Life* Service Club (the buy-and-sell service hosted by the magazine) in one issue in 1952, 60 per cent (44) came from Leinster, eleven of these from Dublin but the others from Offaly and Kildare; 16.4 per cent (12) each from Munster and Connacht; and 6.8 per cent (5) from

---

27 *WM* competition, Nov. 1952; 'Silly Sue', May 1951; Louth lipstick, Jan. 1955; 'Kerry Girl', May 1955; big eyes, Oct. 1955. On brides, see Caitriona Clear, 'The minimum rights of every woman: women's changing appearance in Ireland 1940–1966', *Irish Economic & Social History*, 35 (2008), 68–80. **28** Hugh Oram, *The Advertising Book* (Dublin, 1986), p. 164, re: Mrs Murray and named as MD, *Woman's Life* (hereafter *WL*), 24 July 1954; Tóstal, 3 Apr. 1954 and 17 Apr. 1954; Hungary, 31 Oct. 1953.

Ulster (all Cavan in this instance, though other Ulster counties, including those in Northern Ireland, featured in other issues). The items sought and offered for sale indicate farming and non-farming readers; clothes and shoes were the most common, but also included were books, bikes, prams, plants, machinery (sewing and knitting machines, poultry incubators), children's toys, holiday accommodation and even poultry. One advertisement from Wicklow in 1952, for example, offered prize-bred Aylesbury drakes for 25s. each, black patent court shoes ('as new') for 17s. 6d. and black suede laced high heels for 14s. The social and occupational class of readers seems to have been mixed. Finalists in the Limerick city 'Personality Girl' contest in 1954 hailed from lower-middle-class/skilled working-class Janesboro and Fairgreen, and from upper-middle-class O'Connell Avenue. The Galway finalists were all domiciled in the city itself, except for one from Loughrea; they were teachers, shop assistants, students and 'business girls' (i.e. office workers). Some emigrants must have had the magazine sent to them; the 'bonnie babies' featured in May 1956 hailed from Cork city, Louisburgh, Co. Mayo, Sligo, Bradford and Wakefield. In one issue the following year, only five of the thirteen infants featured had addresses in Ireland.[29]

The diary pages, two or three of them, relied heavily on solicited content – 'all items of news, gossip etc. . . . will be paid for at our usual rates'[30] – although the magazine itself also seems to have sought out stories. Called 'Gossip with Finola' for most of the decade, for eight months in 1955–6 the diary was taken over by popular broadcaster Maxwell Sweeney ('Talking Things over with Maxwell Sweeney'), and then reverted to 'Finola' again. While there were occasional wedding and coming-of-age photographs, most of the diary pages concerned Irish women's organizational, occupational and artistic activities and achievements. Ireland's only female harbourmaster, Claddagh woman Kathleen Curran of Galway, was featured in 1953. Eight machinists in Cassidy's lingerie factory in Dublin were profiled individually, giving their names, ages, home circumstances and hobbies, in the same year. Female workplaces like the Stork factory in Drogheda, Co. Louth, CIÉ's office in O'Connell Street in Dublin, Reckitt's factory in Dublin and the Greenmount & Boyne Linen Company in Drogheda, were also described in greater or lesser detail. Irish actresses Valerie Hobson, Constance Smith, Annie Dalton and Siobhan McKenna, musicians Mary O'Hara and Kathleen Watkins, singers Máire Ní Scolaí and Ruby Murray, writers Kate O'Brien, Bridget Boland, Maura Laverty, Sinéad de

---

29 *WL* hints, 20 Feb. 1954; buy-and-sell, 19 Feb. 1952; Wicklow drakes, 19 Apr. 1952; holiday accommodation, 2 May 1953; Limerick personality, 12 June 1954; Galway ditto, 10 July 1954; 'bonnie babies', 26 May 1956 and 6 July 1957. 30 *WL* 8 Aug. 1953.

Valera and Mary Purcell popped up every so often.[31] Irish female dress designers were boosted; not just Connolly, Gilbert and Mulcahy, but also Madeleine
Keenan, Sheila Mullally, Gertrude Brady, Peta Swift and many more. The Irish
Countrywomen's Association, the Irish Housewives' Association, Muintir
na Tire and Macra na Feirme featured from time to time, as did amateur
dramatic societies and public speaking and debating organizations.[32] Some
of these personalities, businesses and organizations no doubt sent in press
releases, a sure sign of growing confidence on their part and an understanding
of the magazine as a valuable vehicle for publicity. There were very few Irish
women in political life in this decade, but Dáil deputies Maureen O'Carroll
and Kathleen O'Connor were mentioned, and the election of the first woman,
Sheila Williams, to the Irish Transport and General Workers' Union Council
in 1956 was greeted with satisfaction. Maxwell Sweeney, in his brief period
in charge of the diary, regularly berated women for not being more active in
public life. Seán O'Sullivan, when he edited *Woman's Way* 1963–5, did the same,
and this was also a favourite practice of male editors and columnists in British
and Australian women's magazines. 'Finola' preferred to accentuate the positive – for instance, with the pleased observation that four times as many 'girls'
as 'boys' were getting work in junior grades in the civil service.[33]

Woman's Life carried the usual service articles, with slightly more content and
advertising on fashion and beauty than on motherhood, health and childcare.
A predominantly single readership was likely enough in this decade of late
marriage, although we must remember that many married and single women
– mothers and adult daughters, single and married sisters – lived under one
roof and might have shared reading material. There were, in any case, at least
two knitting or sewing patterns in each issue, and the cookery articles were
mainly aimed at family catering. A serial and at least one short story appeared
in every issue and these were often written by well-established British authors
like Monica Dickens and Norah Lofts, while journalist, cookery expert,

---

31 *WL* Curran, 10 Feb. 1953, Cassidy's, 25 July 1953; Stork, 21 Mar. 1953; CIÉ, 12 Dec. 1953; Reckitt's, 11
Dec. 1954; Greenmount, 14 Apr. 1956. Actresses (just a selection), *WL* 10 Mar. 1951, 19 May 1951, 4 Sept.
1954; musicians and singers (selection), *WL* 31 Mar. 1956, 17 Mar. 1956, 2 Mar. 1957; writers (selection),
WL 19 Mar. 1955, 25 June 1955, 25 Oct. 1955, 14 May 1955. 32 Connolly, Gilbert and Mulcahy featured so
often that only a sample of references is given: *WL* 6 Mar. 1954, 18 Sept. 1954, 19 Feb. 1955, 17 Aug. 1957, 2
Sept. 1958; other designers, *WL* 24 Mar. 1956, 26 Apr. 1958, 27 Sept. 1958 and many more. ICA, IHA and
other activities (just a sample): *WL* 8 Aug. 1953, 9 Jan. 1954, 6 Feb. 1954, 20 Feb. 1954, 11 June 1955, 22 June
1957. 33 *WL* TDs, 25 June 1955, 21 Mar. 1956; trade union, 23 July 1955, 21 July 1956. Sweeney berating
(just a sample): *WL* 21 Jan. 1956, 30 Apr. 1956, 26 May 1956. Similar themes in O'Sullivan-edited *Woman's
Way (WW)*, 15 Mar. 1963, 31 Jan. 1964. On British and Australian magazines, Makins, *Evelyn home*, p. 174, and
Johnson & Lloyd, *Sentenced*, pp 23–54. Finola's positivity, *WL* 28 Apr. 1956.

playwright, novelist and broadcaster Maura Laverty contributed several characteristically well-written stories set in Ireland. In one of the issues celebrating
An Tóstal, there were three mini-short stories by Laverty that would later
appear in her most famous cookery book, *Full & plenty*, in 1960.[34]

Unlike the other magazines, *Woman's Life* had always had a problem page.
The agony column was already a feature of most (though not all) British
women's magazines.[35] *Woman's Life's* agony aunt was Mrs Wyse — who was, at
some stage, Maura Laverty.[36] Problem pages in women's magazines, while they
cannot be seen as 'straight' evidence of difficulties women may have had at
any time, tell us about the problems of people who are motivated and articulate enough to write to a magazine, and the problems that the magazine can
publish. There are, for example, several possible reasons why, in this decade
of haemorrhaging female emigration, having to leave Ireland never featured
in this problem page as a problem.[37] Courtship was the largest single category
of problem between 1951 and 1959, and seeking information on work and
education was more common than asking for advice on marital problems. In
the 1950s in Ireland, single life could change; married life could not. Girls and
women who resented giving up the prospect or the reality of independence to
act as carers for younger siblings or elderly parents were sternly reminded of
their duties by Mrs Wyse, but it is significant that the correspondents in this
decade framed as a problem a destiny that would have been seen by previous
generations as inevitable.[38]

Woman's Life gave readers some indications of its struggles over the 1950s,[39]
but it maintained its price of 4*d.* even after a glossy makeover in August 1958.
In February 1959, however, it announced that it had 'great news' for readers;
the magazine thenceforth would be known as *Woman's Realm & Woman's Life*. The
Woman's Realm masthead, complete with editor and contributing journalists, was

---

34 Dickens, *WL* 13 Jan. 1951; Lofts, 7 Apr. 1951; Laverty, 12 Jan. 1952, 4 Apr. 1953, 22 Jan. 1955, 25 May 1957
and *passim*. The Tóstal 'short-short' stories, 17 Apr. 1954, can be found (slightly altered) in Maura Laverty,
Full & plenty: a complete guide to good cooking (Dublin, 1960), pp 94–6, 346–7, 368–71.   35 Problem pages have
a history going back to the eighteenth century, see Robin Kent, *Aunt agony advises: problem pages through the ages*
(London, 1979).   36 Interview with the late Barry Castle (1935–2008), daughter of Maura Laverty, 25
July 2001. See also Seamus Kelly, *The Maura Laverty story* (Kildare, 2018).   37 Interpreting problem pages
historically needs more discussion than can be given here. See Clear, *Women's voices*, pp 27–9 and *passim*, and
also memoirs of two British and two Irish agony aunts; Peggy Makins, *Evelyn Home*; Claire Rayner, *How
did I get here from there?* (London, 2003); Linda James (Valerie McGrath), *Dear Linda: a selection of letters to the
problem pages of the* Sunday World (Cork, 1974), Angela Macnamara, *Yours sincerely* (Dublin, 2003).   38 All
problems in *WL* from Jan. 1951 to Feb. 1958 were looked at: for lengthier discussion and full statistical
breakdown of categories of problem in both magazines see Clear, *Women's voices*, chapter 2.   39 For example, an editorial reminder of the magazine's quality and the duty of everybody to buy Irish, 31 May 1952,
and again on occasion of its 21st birthday, 6 July 1957.

reproduced for readers' benefit. This magazine was at this stage the brightest and newest women's magazine in Britain, begun in 1958 by Odhams.[40] No such magazine as *Woman's Realm & Woman's Life* can be found either in the British Library or in the National Library of Ireland. In February 1959 Irish readers were not welcomed to *Woman's Realm* in any way, and there was no mention of *Woman's Life* then or in any issue thereafter.

WOMAN'S WAY, 1963–9

Woman's Way was more successful than any other magazine had been, due to improved transport and distribution and people's increased spending power. Its appearance at the dawn of a new Irish media age also helped. Charles Mitchel, Frank Hall, the aforementioned Maura Laverty and Al Byrne (whose fame would later be eclipsed by his brother Gay) contributed some articles or wrote regular columns, as did cookery media star Monica Sheridan and many others. Even the readers' letters page came to be titled 'Over to You' in a clear echo of broadcasting handovers.

While *Woman's Way* modelled itself faithfully on the successful British women's magazine format, it was self-consciously and proudly Irish. It was also self-consciously feminist, though it might not have used that term. One of its founding columnists was the former first female mayor of Limerick, Mrs Frances Condell, whose gently insistent tone urged readers towards civic responsibility. Founding editor Seán O'Sullivan, as mentioned earlier, insisted on women's duty to speak up, but from 1965 Caroline Mitchell insisted more on women's right to be heard. *Woman's Way* certainly gave them this opportunity.

A wide range of well-written and lengthy feature articles on social issues sparked a lot of reader reaction. Journalists such as Monica McEnroy, Mary Leland, Veronica Kelly, Heather Lukes and Sheelagh Lewis tackled women in politics, prostitution, children in institutions, women's legal rights within marriage, bedsitter life, interracial marriage, women in the Salvation Army, the female religious life, education, married women working, women in unpensionable jobs, birth control and many, many other topics. On the fiftieth anniversary of the 1916 Rising, veteran republican Maire Comerford

40 *WL* 14 Feb. 1959; White, *Women's magazines*, pp 170–2, and David Kynaston, *Modernity Britain: opening the box 1957–59* (London, 2013), pp 113–14.   41 *WW* politics (Mary Leland, hereafter ML), 15 Oct. 1965; wives' legal rights (ML), 15 Mar. 1966; prostitution (Veronica Kelly, hereafter VK), 15 Apr. 1966; bedsitter life (Heather Lukes), 10 Feb. 1967; interracial marriage (VK), 14 Oct. 1966; female religious life (Monica McEnroy, hereafter MMcE), 13 Jan. 1967; Salvation Army, 1 July 1965; working wives, 21 Oct. 1966; education (VK), 1 Mar. 1966; (Sheelagh Lewis, SL), 21 Oct. 1966; women unpensionable (ML), 1 Feb. 1966; birth

contributed a four-page article on the women who fought in Easter Week.[41] Women from all over the country wrote in letters to the editor (the 'Over to You' page) in response to these articles and also commented on current affairs. These letters are the only concentrated source we have on the opinions of Irish women who were neither in public life nor, most of them, in the paid workforce in the 1960s. Many topics were debated and discussed, a small sample of which were: decentralization of civil servants; Travellers (then known as 'Itinerants'); home versus hospital birth; education and work for young people and the Kennedy-Onassis marriage. Contraception was vigorously discussed from 1966 onwards, with many cogent and articulate letters on both sides of the debate. However, commentary on marital relationships was invariably light-hearted, divorce was rarely mentioned and never recommended, and when contraception was supported, it was always within the context of family life. Even though *Woman's Way*, like all magazines, assumed its readers were urban, girls and women either from farming backgrounds, or working on farms, used its letters page to talk to one another about rural living and working conditions, ignoring the derision of some urban readers.[42]

The magazine's service content was eye-catching and well-designed, with cookery columns by Audrey O'Farrell and Una Lehane, fashion, beauty and knitting patterns, and plenty on house decoration in this decade of domestic modernization. For a short period from October 1966 to March 1967, every second issue of the magazine was edited in Belfast ('Hello Ulster and Welcome') and the problems were responded to by Sylvia Grace.[43]

Woman's Way's four most commonly featured advice columns give a clue to its intended universality: a regular 'Guide to Careers' for schoolgirls; 'Young Motherhood Bureau' for expectant mothers and mothers of young babies; 'Patients' Postbox' for health problems across the age-spectrum, including post-menopause; and Angela Macnamara's problem page, which dealt mainly with emotional and personal queries from all age-groups. Macnamara's tone was invariably kindly and sympathetic, although her implacable opposition to birth control placed her at odds with some of *Woman's Way*'s own contributors

---

control, the first article (MMcE), 23 Sept. 1966, and others *passim*. Máire Comerford, 1 Apr. 1966, 'Carve their names in pride: the women of 1916'.   42 All letters to the editor from Apr. 1963 to Dec. 1969 were looked at. Full statistical breakdown and references are provided in Clear, *Women's voices*, chapters 3 & 4. For *small* sample of letters on the new educational reforms, *WW* 7 Dec. 1967, 5 July 1968; on 'itinerants', *WW* 14 Mar. 1964, 27 Jan. 1967; on contraception, *WW* 14 Oct. 1966 and many other contributions up to and including *WW* 27 Sept. 1968 and 16 May 1969; decentralization, *WW* 15 Mar. 1968, 8 June 1969; home-hospital birth, 11 Nov. 1966, 2 May 1969; Kennedy-Onassis, 15 Nov. 1968, 3 Feb. 1969; women of rural origin talking about country life, *WW* 1 May 1965, 15 May 1966, 7 Apr. 1967, two letters deriding, 1 Mar. 1966.   43 I have been unable to find any information about why this step was taken and subsequently abandoned, or any information about Sylvia Grace.

and correspondents. However, she insisted on the need for sex education, strongly condemning parents who did not provide it. Never refusing a request for information, she told anxious readers, for example, what VD (venereal, i.e. sexually transmitted, disease) was and what 'French letters' (condoms) were; and while she abhorred and discouraged 'necking and petting' (non-penetrative sexual experimentation), she assured readers that pregnancy could result only from full sexual intercourse. Nearly a third (31.5 per cent) of all the problems published in her column between 1963 and 1969 were requests for basic information about sex, pregnancy and childbirth, and her provision of that information no doubt enabled many readers to make up their own minds about their behaviour. Other problems were about courtship, extended family including parent-child/adult child relationships, and queries about work and education. Girls and young women were strongly urged to acquire education and training for jobs they would enjoy and to relish their financial independence for as long as they could. Macnamara (in contrast to the 1950s Mrs Wyse) was so opposed to young adult daughters staying at home to care for younger siblings or elders, that she even recommended early marriage (which she usually discouraged) as a preferable alternative.[44]

MISS AND YOUNG WOMAN

Miss came out monthly from May 1965, changing its title to *Young Woman* and coming out fortnightly from 31 May 1967. Its last issue came out in August 1968. The magazine(s) cost 1s., rising to 1s. 3d. before it vanished. Some of *Model Housekeeping*'s correspondents turned up in *Miss*; but *Miss* and *Young Woman* were published by Creation magazines, which also brought out *Woman's Way*. Norman Barry edited *Miss*, and Clare Boylan edited *Young Woman*.

These magazines had very few knitting or sewing patterns and only novelty cookery (cakes for Halloween for example). Music featured a lot: Irish, British, American, showband, 'beat' and folk, from Brendan Bowyer, the Dubliners and the Johnstons to the Troggs, the Yardbirds, the Rolling Stones, Jim Reeves and Johnny Cash – with B.P. Fallon as the main journalist here. A great variety of books and films were reviewed in every issue. These magazines were jam-packed with cultural content and controversial commentary.

44 It is impossible to reference all problems, see Clear, *Women's voices*, chapters 5 & 6 for a fuller discussion and statistical breakdown. Angela Macnamara wrote about her own life in *Yours sincerely* (Dublin, 2003); for a discussion of her problem-page responses in the *Sunday Press*, see Paul Ryan, *Asking Angela Macnamara: an intimate history of Irish lives* (Dublin, 2011).

In one of the opening issues there was an extensive interview with Susan Maughan, 'Traveller Girl on the Go!', about her hopes and dreams – her favourite band, after the Beatles, was the Dave Clark Five. (Use of the term 'Traveller' – preferred by Travellers themselves, rather than the official 'Itinerant' – demonstrates an unusual respect for this section of the population.) Other features over the magazines' existence included a panel on education chaired by Teilifís Éireann continuity announcer Thelma Mansfield, in which Biddy White-Lennon ('Maggie' in the popular Teilifís Éireann drama, *The Riordans*) participated; Sheila Russell's 'I Worked with Mary Quant'; 'Sex, Religion and the Younger Set' by Clare Boylan and 'The Torture of our Children in Schools' by Tanis O'Callaghan. Dolores Rockett wrote the diary pages and even answered problems for a brief period. Cliff Richard, David Jensen and Terence Stamp were interviewed in December 1966. Eileen Murphy told 'The Heartbreak Stories of Two Unmarried Mothers' in 1967, and Terry Wogan came out against bikinis for Irishwomen in the same year. The prevalence of television personalities can be noted; there was also a regular column by Bunny Carr, quizmaster on TV programme *Quicksilver*.[45]

In September 1965 the winner and runners-up of the Bristow Hair Spray Lovely Hair Contest all had addresses in the greater Dublin area – the winner was Sabina Coyne, from Dublin 6.[46] This, and Berenice Russell's assumption of metropolitanism in an article about whether 'we' want country girls in Dublin or not in October 1967, give the impression of a readership confined to the capital. However, letters to the editor in both *Miss* and *Young Woman* show a national readership, with letters from Galway, Cavan, Cork, Sligo, Offaly, Tipperary, Waterford and Wexford. Eileen Quinn from Westport, Co. Mayo, and Patricia Burke from Portlaoise, Co. Laois, both of whom had letters published in *Woman's Way*, also wrote to *Miss/Young Woman*.[47]

A wide variety of opinions was expressed in these letters pages and in the features. A suggestion in 1966 that Irish rural people knew nothing about sex provoked quite a storm, with rural people writing in, some agreeing, some disagreeing. Mrs J.K, from Co. Waterford, who had seventeen grandchildren, believed dancehalls and clubs were 'safer' than lonely country roads for courting couples. One brave letter from Mrs B, in Dublin, recommended

45 Maughan, *Miss* (hereafter *M*), June 1965; education, *M*, Sept. 1965; Cliff, et al., *M* Dec. 1966; Quant, *M* Oct. 1966; sex, religion, *M* Oct. 1966; torture, *Young Woman* (hereafter *YW*), 15 July 1967; working wives, *YW* 15 Aug. 1967; unmarried mothers, *YW* 15 July 1967; Wogan, *YW* 15 July 1967.   **46** *M* Sept. 1965. Sabina Coyne would later marry Michael D. Higgins, president of Ireland since 2011.   **47** Country girls article, *YW* 27 Oct. 1967; letters, *M* and *YW*, *passim*, but Eileen Quinn see *YW* 1 Sept. 1967 and 24 Nov. 1967, and *WW* 27 Sept. 1968; Patricia Burke, *M* Sept. 1965, and *WW* 1 Mar. 1966.   **48** Reactions to sex article *M* Nov. 1966; letter from grandmother, *M* Dec. 1966; sex before marriage, *YW* 31 May 1967.

pre-marital sex as a way of stopping young couples from getting married just because of sexual desire.[48]

Although there was a frankness about 'sex' in the abstract like this, there was no explicit content in the magazine. Neither was there criticism of any of the churches or their personnel. The nuns who ran St Patrick's mother and baby home in Cabra, Dublin were praised unreservedly, and the advice given on sexual matters in the problem pages reflected religious teaching without exception. Close hugging and prolonged kissing were discouraged, going steady in late teens was discouraged, unmarried couples being alone together was discouraged, going away on holidays as an unmarried couple was discouraged. This conservatism might offer a clue as to why the magazine(s) went out of business. By 1968, young Irish women were probably turning to British magazines like *Honey* and *Petticoat*, which, now that censorship was relaxed, were on sale in Ireland.[49]

CONCLUSION

A correspondent who wrote to the *Young Woman* problem page wondered if the fact that she had had a baby outside marriage two years before (she had given him up for adoption) would be 'held against' her when she applied to emigrate. A woman who had been married four years without conceiving wrote to Angela Macnamara worried that she had been preventing conception by taking part in sporting activities and driving on bumpy roads: 'My confessor does not seem to understand my difficulty.' Macnamara hastened to reassure this woman that she was committing no sin.[50] The 1960s saw far more public commentary on controversial topics than ever before, and more physical and financial independence for young, single people in general, but there was still ignorance, guilt and fear.

So was the new freedom Irish magazines had been promising women since the early 1950s, 'all talk'? Up to a point, it was; but talk is where change begins, and magazines in these two decades contributed to Irishwomen's emancipation by enabling them to publicize their doings, communicate with each other, trade with each other and confide their worries. The 1960s magazines, in addition, gave women space to express their opinions, which sometimes were at variance with the culture of the magazine. The new integrated media world did not

---

49 St Patrick's, *YW* 15 July 1967; problem pages, *passim.* White, *Women's magazines*, pp 172–3, 185–6. This writer can remember *Honey* and *Petticoat* being read by friends' older sisters in late 1960s Limerick.   **50** *YW* baby and emigration, 1 Sept. 1967; confessor, *WW* 1 Aug. 1966.   **51** 'Maureen', *M* Sept. 1965; holidays, *WW* 1 Aug. 1966 and 30 July 1967.

please everybody, and 'Maureen' wrote to *Miss* in 1965 to complain about TV personalities who wrote magazine columns being 'pushed down our necks'. Two correspondents, Mrs N.O'B. from Sligo and E.N, from Clondalkin, Co. Dublin, wrote to *Woman's Way* to take issue with the magazine's assumption that all its readers went on holidays. Most did not, E.N. insisted; Mrs N. O'B said that for her, the summer meant 'more light to mend children's clothes by'.[51] The magazine's urban bias and assumption of the evening-homecoming spouse as normative were challenged in comic verse by 'Weary-worn', Mallow, Co. Cork, in the *Woman's Way* letters page. Responding to a fatuous article in which Al Byrne and his 'panel of experts' insisted that it was possible for a woman to do a day's housework and then make herself glamorous for her man coming in from work, 'Weary-worn's' poem pointed out that a farm woman's husband, first of all, had to see her in her working clothes all day, and secondly, had more on his mind during that day than his wife's appearance ('Her hubby's been up all night with a pig/So he won't notice her curlers or wig'). Patricia Burke, from Portlaoise, gave a sharper response to this article, turning Byrne's complaints on their head to complain about how men let themselves go after marriage: 'then marriage, honeymoon, a complete metamorphosis. Hair barely combed, shoes unpolished, any old suit'. And 'Irish Mother', writing to *Young Woman* in 1967 in response to an article about marriage, went further than any other correspondent: 'Women's magazines without exception make me positively sick. They appear to be written for women, yes, BUT with men in mind. This is to keep men and their egos fed … Where are the articles which tell women to make sure their husbands treat them well?' Women's magazines, however, were the only publications that had any interest in the opinions of 'Irish Mother' on this or any other topic relating to domestic life or personal relationships.[52]

---

52 'Weary-worn's verse', *WW* 14 May 1966; Burke's letter, 1 May 1966. The article by Byrne was 'Home For Tea', *WW* 15 Mar. 1966. 'Irish Mother', *YW* 24 Nov. 1967.

13 / *Comhar*, a post-revival case study of Irish-language publishing: 'inné, inniu agus amárach'[1]

REGINA UÍ CHOLLATÁIN & AOIFE WHELAN

Pioneering thinking and the promotion of modern Irish literature were to the fore in the approach adopted by the Irish-language journal *Comhar*.[2] In the mid-1930s, some university students came together under the initiative of Máirtín Ó Flaitheartaigh and the group Comhchaidreamh emerged. 'Comhchaidreamh' translates as 'association' or 'partnership' in English, with the wider understanding of a collaborative group coming together with a common purpose. This group welcomed any class of religious, political and other school of thought with the only requirement being a common interest in promoting and developing the Irish language. It was from this university background that the periodical *Comhar* was founded in May 1942, at the outset of the post-revival period.[3]

Ten years later a review of the periodical by one of the most renowned Irish-language writers of the twentieth century, Máirtín Ó Cadhain, indicates that *Comhar* was well on track in achieving its aims. Ó Cadhain's review was

1 This subtitle, 'inné, inniu agus amárach' [yesterday, today and tomorrow], is taken from the title of the editorial of a special edition of *Comhar*, April 1980, entitled *Foilsitheoireacht na Gaeilge*. This edition considered the state of play of Irish-language publishing in all forums. The title included the names of two other twentieth-century Irish-language newspapers, *Inniu* and *Amárach*. 2 Significant analysis and collections of *Comhar* have been published in Irish-language forums including two commemorative volumes. We would like to thank Dr Aisling Ní Dhonnchadha for her kind permission to use some of the work in Aisling Ní Dhonnchadha & Regina Uí Chollatáin (eds), *Cnuasach Comhar, 1982–2012: Aistí. Ailt. Agallaimh* (Baile Átha Cliath, 2012). The other commemorative volume is Caoilfhionn Nic Pháidín (ed.), *Comhar, 1942–1982* (Baile Átha Cliath, 1982). All quotes have been translated by the authors. Bilingual versions of all titles of the Irish-language articles quoted in this chapter are provided and the full text of the original Irish-language articles is available in the referenced issues of *Comhar*. These can be found in hard copy or on JSTOR, and some issues are online at comhar.ie. 3 The revival period refers to the Irish-language and cultural revival in Ireland which spanned *c*.1880–1940. During this period, the Irish-language revival was a very prominent aspect of the new vision for Irish-Ireland. Journals and periodicals were among the tools used to revive the language, with a flourishing of Irish-language material in journals from 1880 onwards. With the founding of the Gaelic League in 1893, the revival movement developed further – prominent Gaelic League members were involved in political milestones, including the foundation of the new state in 1922. The language revival continued in the context of language and literature, and many journals and newspapers played significant roles. The cultural and language revival movement was very active during this period and 1940 is considered the cut-off point for that flurry of activity as Irish language and culture was acknowledged as a central part of Irish society by then.

quoted approvingly by Dónall Ó Móráin in the preface of a commemorative collection of *Comhar* published in 1982: 'On this occasion I must say how much modern writing owes *Comhar* … *Comhar* cut a new path and other periodicals followed its course.'[4] As director of the periodical, Seán Sáirséal Ó hÉigeartaigh pioneered the venture in the early years. This was not an easy task due to timing, as its launch coincided with the Emergency of the Second World War. It was not only difficult to find writers and contributors, but also to source paper. Ó Móráin and Ó hÉigeartaigh were both on the governing authority of Comhdháil Náisiúnta na Gaeilge [National Irish Language Congress] through which they had significant input into the government's decision to support the patronage of Irish-language journal publications in 1948.

Many editors of repute have overseen the publication of *Comhar* and in May 1982, under the editorship of Caoilfhionn Nic Pháidín, *Comhar* published a commemorative edition with a selection of the most prominent literature and articles from the previous forty years.[5] In another special commemorative issue in early 2012, then editor Ian Ó Caoimh wrote that the issue offered only a small insight into the wealth of material in *Comhar* if one were to fully investigate the fountain of its archive.[6]

Setting the scene for the aspirations of this periodical, the inaugural issue in May 1942 was launched with an opening statement from Douglas Hyde, president of Ireland:

> I know well the amount that Comhchaidreamh Cumann Gaedhealach na n-Ollsgol has done and is doing for the Irish language, and I ask God to bless this work which they are now undertaking as they launch 'Comhar'.
> Dubhghlas de h-Íde
> Uachtarán na h-Éireann.[7]

However, in May 1942 the world was in turmoil. While the president endorsed *Comhar*'s work and endeavour, its editorial acknowledged the current turbulent times:

> Comhar, a Ghaedheala! [Come together, Gaels]
> With the world as volatile as it is, it could be said that this is not a very suitable time to begin publishing a periodical like this. It is true that the war is putting us all in a difficult situation in many ways; but it must be

---

4 *Comhar*, June 1952. 5 Nic Pháidín (ed.), *Comhar, 1942–1982*. 6 *Comhar*, Jan.–Feb. 2012. 7 *Comhar*, May 1942.

said that it is gradually directing the public mind towards the nation and in that context there isn't a more suitable time to publish a new periodical ... There is a special significance, however, in the word 'Comhar' as the title of this Comhchaidreamh periodical, because it represents the idea behind the foundation and growth of our organisation. It is now our aim to issue a monthly periodical ... It is our aim that *Comhar*, insofar as a periodical like this can, will give interesting reading material to Irish speakers; guidance to the nation on current questions; a resource for the university community to relate to and to inspire each other to utilise their study and their substance for the good of the nation; and provide a literary platform for all, especially for young writers ... If we have collaboration among our own people, the university community and the Irish community, *Comhar* will be a permanent guiding flame and light of learning.[8]

In a very ambitious and perhaps above average remit for a periodical at that time, *Comhar's* focus was literary and scholarly while also addressing public discourse. It was, however, rooted in university principles to begin with. The editorial clearly outlines the aims of the periodical and the roots from which *Comhar* emerged as a collaborative venture between the universities of Ireland and the Irish-speaking public. Its foundation is explained at length and defined as the product of a group of students who came together to create a network to link all Irish-language societies in every university and third-level college. As a university-based Irish-language organization with a scholarly focus, the association also acknowledged the wealth and roots of the Irish language in the twentieth century with an annual week-long summer conference in each of the Gaeltacht areas, with an attendance of over 350 delegates at the gathering in An Spidéal, Galway, the summer prior to the periodical's launch. The editorial cites the universities as the nation's leaders with responsibility for providing a national education to develop both the economy and the intellect of the nation. It qualifies the role of *Comhar* by saying that even if its only function were to assess the work of the universities, it would be doing a good job.

The editorial continues by stating that it is a godsend that they managed to get the issue out, but that there is uncertainty about further issues. The editor explains this further in the context of the implications of a government directive that after 4 May 1942 any periodical which had not been published during 1940 could not be published without the minister's permission. This was to ensure that the most productive use would be made of the paper available

---

8 Eagarfhocal [Editorial], *Comhar*, May 1942.

during wartime. It was not a good start, but the journal survived. The editor
gives several examples of what he would classify as bad uses of paper and fin-
ishes with a description of what *Comhar* will be publishing, which, according
to him, classifies it among the higher quality journals:

> Furthermore, Irish language periodicals have a special importance in cul-
> tural and national affairs, especially this inter-university one ... There
> was never a need for them until now, when the public's mind must be
> directed on all that is related to their country and their own heritage so
> that they will be ready to defend that if they are called to do so.[9]

For almost eighty years *Comhar* has provided a platform for Irish writing and
discourse. *Comhar* remains a monthly journal in which literature, debate, analysis, current affairs and other themes are discussed and it has had a wide
circulation to Irish speakers in Ireland and all over the world, with increased
online accessibility now. There were many challenging times with three main
Irish-language periodicals, *Feasta*, *Comhar* and *An tUltach*, focusing on niche
journalistic material. While the aim is not to fully capture eighty years of
Irish-language journalism in the context of *Comhar*'s role in supporting the
Irish language and literature, the remainder of this chapter will highlight some
of the more important articles, some of which may not have reached general
journalistic discourse despite *Comhar* and other Irish-language periodicals taking a leading role in the mediascape of the events outlined in each case.

Pól Ó Muirí, former Irish-language editor of the *Irish Times*, became editor of *Comhar* in December 2008. His first editorial provided a retrospective
view of the ideology on which *Comhar* was founded, which highlights the
independence and standing of the periodical. He also contexualized the partnership approach adopted by *Comhar* by comparing it to Obama's vision for
his upcoming presidency as being one of collaboration and 'partnership':

> Pioneering you say? Maybe it is bold of us to use that word in the
> context of a periodical which is in print for 60 years. However *Comhar*
> started out as a pioneering venture and it will always remain so. This
> periodical does not belong to one ideological wing; it belongs to the
> intellect and to sharpness of mind. We don't stand under one party or
> one politician or one narrow school of thought ... *Comhar* lasted this
> long because the founders of the journal ignited a spark which could not
> be extinguished. However a spark is not enough for us; we need a fire,

9 Ibid.

an enormous hungry literary fire which will be seen from one end of the country to the other … It won't be long until Barack Obama will be the new president of the United States of America … The Irish language public will recognise what he has in mind. It is a partnership.[10]

CONTROVERSY AND COMMENT

In its early years, the column under the pen name 'Bricriú' is insightful in the context of *Comhar*'s stand on Ireland's economic situation. Séan Mac Réamoinn referred to Bricriú, or Séamus Ó Néill (1910–81), as

one of the most prolific writers in Ireland. Neither is he a one type provider: he has written long and short dramas, light and heavy poetry, short stories and essays and – *mirabile dictu* – two novels. Furthermore he is one of the few truly professional writers we have in Irish.[11]

Ó Néill, from Co. Down, was a well-educated writer-journalist having graduated with an MA from Queen's University Belfast and having spent a further year studying under Eoin Mac Néill at University College Dublin. Ó Néill travelled to Frankfurt am Main on a scholarship and, although he was a teacher, he served as a sub-editor and writer of editorials in the *Dundalk Examiner*. He was also editor of the periodical *An tUltach*. He was involved in journalism at some level throughout his life. Tomás Ó Floinn has referred to Ó Néill also as one of the people who did the most work for *Comhar*.[12] Ó Néill contributed regularly to the Irish-language newspaper *Inniu* [*Today*], as well as *An Iris* [*The Periodical*] and *Scéala Éireann* [*Irish Press*]. He also contributed to a radio journal, *An Tréimhseachán Teann* [*The Strong Periodical*], with Ciarán Ó Nualláin, brother of Brian O'Nolan, aka Flann O'Brien.[13]

Perhaps one of the most telling insights into life in the early 1940s in Ireland is Bricriú's 'Cúrsaí Reatha' ['Current Affairs'] column. In February 1944, Bricriú criticizes the *Irish Independent* for supporting what he calls 'naimhde na tíre' [the country's enemies]. The tone indicates the broader discourse, demonstrating *Comhar*'s engagement with social issues of various eras in what was primarily a literary and language journal:

It is difficult to understand the mindset of these papers. They have never changed their stance. But we never thought that people would have so

10 Eagarfhocal [Editorial], *Comhar*, Dec. 2008.　11 *Comhar*, July 1960.　12 *Comhar*, July 1981.　13 www.ainm.ie (Séamus Ó Néill).

little regard for value and honesty that they would pretend that things should be now as they would be in peaceful times. People in Cork were asking the government to make pre-war flour available. Are they completely out of their mind? They should be thankful to God that they have any kind of flour ... Those in the *Sunday Independent* are trying to say that the Gaelic League and the Irish language are responsible for the decline of the country. They almost blamed the Gaelic League for the Great Famine a few Sundays ago.[14]

Ó Néill's article also demonstrates the animosity towards the Irish language at the time, especially in the *Irish Independent*, which by the 1940s was no longer considered a strong supporter of the Irish-language movement.[15] However, politics are never far away from language and social issues and Bricriú is pulled up for his opinions in a letter in April 1944 stating that he only supports anything that favours Fianna Fáil.

Comhar did not generally hide from controversy even when the controversy stemmed from the institutions it was representing. Towards the end of its first decade in print, when it was felt that journalistic principles and values of freedom of cultural expression and thought were being threatened, *Comhar* asserted its role as an inter-university publication in December 1949.[16] The article alleged that the sale of *Comhar* was prohibited in UCD. This article included a letter from Cláir Ní Dhuigneáin on behalf of *Comhar* outlining the three reasons why Dr Michael Tierney, president of UCD, prohibited the sale of the periodical. Dr Tierney believed, firstly, that an inter-university organization should not be allowed to circulate a periodical that reviewed the activities of that university in an unfair manner; secondly, that *Comhar* had an ongoing policy of criticizing the National University of Ireland, and especially UCD, for not doing anything to expand teaching through the medium of Irish; and thirdly, that Dr Tierney believed that academic subjects could not be taught through the medium of Irish. Although the ban was to take effect upon publication of the November edition, *Comhar's* representatives had a meeting with Dr Tierney on Wednesday, 3 November at noon. The account of the meeting opens by noting that other students not involved in the controversy were gathering sociably outside the Main Hall as the *Comhar* representatives were going in and commenting that these students did not realize the effort that was in hand to secure

14 'Cáineadh ar son cáinte' ['Criticism for the sake of criticism'], *Comhar*, Feb. 1944.   15 Aoife Whelan, '"Irish-Ireland" and the *Irish Independent*, 1905–1922' in Mark O'Brien & Kevin Rafter (eds), *Independent Newspapers: a history* (Dublin, 2012), pp 67–80.   16 '*Comhar* fé Chosc i gColáiste Ollscoile' [*Comhar* banned in University College], *Comhar*, Dec. 1949.

their freedom of speech. When the delegates met with Dr Tierney it was a friendly gathering at first:

> We greeted Dr Tierney in Irish and then we reverted to English as he had requested when the delegation from *Comhar* was arranged. He put us at our ease and offered us cigarettes. He lit one up himself.[17]

Reports indicate that it was a lively meeting but it concluded without a resolution. Dr Tierney continually reverted to the fact that Irish was a dead language and that the main issue was the fact that *Comhar* was supporting teaching third-level academic subjects through Irish. Quoting Professor Séamus Ó Duilearga, Professor Gearóid Ó Murchú, Professor Bergin, Professor Micheál Ó Briain, Professor Maolmhuire Diolún and Professor Binchy, who he said had much more knowledge about education and the revival than anyone else in the country and opposed teaching through Irish, Dr Tierney refuted the students' claims forcefully. He concluded the meeting by stating that, although people publicly supported the revival of Irish, this was not always indicated when talking privately:

> Anyhow no one can point anywhere to a single example of a dead language being revived ... there are only a few cranks who believe in the revival and within 15 years a government will come in which will get rid of Irish in the schools ... when that day comes, a day for which I do not wish, University College Dublin will be an island where Irish will still be studied by those interested in it.[18]

At this time UCD was not opposed to Irish as a subject but its leadership did not believe in the possibility of reviving the language, which was the very essence of what *Comhar* represented as a journal promoting modern literature, continuing one of the founding aims of the Gaelic League set out in 1893. These debates and the stand taken by the group of students demonstrate the centrality of *Comhar* as a public Irish-language organ rooted in the principles of the Comhchaidreamh organization. The access afforded the students to the president of UCD at the time was premised first and foremost on the quality of the periodical and the stand it adopted on these principles. The Irish language was clearly a worthy subject of public and university focus at that time. This controversy was one of the benchmarks for a robust tradition in UCD Irish-language student journals such as *Nua-Aois*

17 Ibid. 18 'Tuairim an Uachtaráin' ['The president's opinion'], *Comhar*, Dec. 1949.

and the Irish-language columns in university newspapers.[19] *Comhar* remains a very central publication for students and scholars of Irish, on which the UCD Irish-language community and its scholarship remains dependent. This tradition is currently documented in the fifty-year commemoration of UCD's Belfield campus.[20]

Some of the more interesting articles in *Comhar* over the next decade included the coverage of the resignation of Dr Noel Browne in 1951 due to the controversy surrounding the Mother and Child Scheme.[21] *Comhar* was criticized for the anti-clerical stand it took in these articles. Allowing that Browne was the only government minister to attend the 1949 Church of Ireland funeral of former Gaelic League president, Douglas Hyde, it is not difficult to understand why the Irish-language inter-university periodical would fall on the side of Browne as opposed to that of the Catholic Church. While the article acknowledged the role of the bishops with regard to the 'social teaching of the church', it also stated that the government had no obligation to adhere to the church's teaching. The article focuses on the Irish Constitution and the taoiseach, John A. Costello, is accused of failing the public due to the fact that he sided with the Catholic Church when he should have made his decision based on the interests of the people of Ireland, regardless of creed, profession or class. The article ends with recognition of Browne's commitment to the Irish language, stating that his resignation would be a great loss to the Irish-language community. Browne's support for the language is evidenced in his article 'Dualgas Orainn Tionscail Mhóra a bhunú sa Ghaeltacht' ['Our Duty to Found Important Industries in the Gaeltacht'] in 1952.[22]

Political comment in *Comhar* is not limited to Ireland. After spending two months in the United States in 1954, Deasún Ó Fionnaile wrote about the work of Senator Joseph McCarthy there. Ó Fionnaile's article concludes with a focus on the US as the land of opportunity regardless of nations or borders:

> That is one of the things which most impressed me in America, the faith, the love and the hope with which the general public (whose fathers and mothers were poor immigrants) would say to me: This is the land of opportunity. There's no country like America. Here every man has the

19 *Nua-Aois* digital editions dating back to 1971 can be accessed through Issuu (https://issuu.com/nua-aois). See also UCD's *College Tribune* (https://collegetribune.ie/) and *University Observer* (https://universityobserver.ie/), both of which continue to publish Irish-language columns.   20 Regina Uí Chollatáin, 'Spás don Ghaeilge' in Finola O'Kane & Ellen Rowley, *Making Belfield* (Dublin, 2020), pp 242–50; Críostóir Mac Cárthaigh, 'The National Folklore Collection' in O'Kane & Rowley, *Making Belfield*, pp 250–5.   21 Eagarfhocal [Editorial], *Comhar*, May 1951.   22 *Comhar*, Sept. 1952.

same chance, certainly in the context of worldly wealth, but America's power was founded on this faith, love and hope.[23]

De Valera's death in September 1975 was another important milestone marked by *Comhar*, acknowledging his prominent role in Irish society by stating that it went far beyond that of a public figure, bestowing on him the role of an icon of the twentieth century. The article states that de Valera was essentially part of the formation of Ireland, whether this was in regard to the politics of the day or the politics of the past:

> A part of the life of everyone on this island has gone with the death of Éamon de Valera … whether they are Republican or Unionist. The name 'Dev' was on everyone's lips until he died. For young people he was a living part of the history of the country and in another way everything good and bad about us as a nation was to be seen in that dignified old man.[24]

From the 1970s onward, the focus on European affairs, and especially Ireland's membership of the European Economic Community (EEC, now the EU), increased. This was incorporated into many contributions from senior figures of the era, including articles from Charles Haughey, Garret FitzGerald, Jack Lynch and Alan Dukes. The supplement *Eorascáil* attests to the fact that *Comhar* was acknowledged as a platform for debate on these European and global issues. Special editions on the importance of Ireland's membership of the EEC added to the publication of two special supplements in June and July 1987. These and the special edition in June 1989, 'Cultúr agus Comhphobal' ['Culture and Community'], reported on new insights and a global perspective on the Irish-language discourse on the role of Ireland in Europe.

Towards the new millennium there was a significant increase in debates on economic, political and social affairs with the series 'Ar Thairseach na Mílaoise' ['On the Threshold of the Millennium'] in January 1999. In his article in 2008, almost ten years later, Fionnbarra Ó Brolcháin makes a substantial case for the assessment of the country's economy in a revival context. This article was meticulously executed and, in keeping with the pioneering theme, focused on the character of the pioneers of the revival movement as a source of inspiration for a vision of Ireland. Ó Brolcháin argues that this is the vision that needs to be revived to repossess financial, cultural and entrepreneurial

23 'Bhfuil an tSaoirse i mbaol i Meiriceá?' ['Is freedom in danger in America?'], *Comhar*, Dec. 1954. 24 'De Valera', *Comhar*, Sept. 1975.

values. It is interesting in the context of Ireland in Europe and it reflects some of T.K. Whitaker's earlier musings in the 1980s in *Comhar*:

> Those who participated in the revival saw natural, cultural and human resources as very important aspects of self-dependence and innovation ... The revival organisations – the Gaelic League, the Co-ops, the GAA and the Abbey Theatre – stood as a broad self-help alliance which helped to change the social, economic and political life in Ireland from top to bottom – Irish has unbelievable possibilities as a resource of self-discovery, sensitivity for difference, imagination, meaning and the nurturing of other aesthetic qualities ... The language has possibilities therefore to be a central part of the reconception of any economy – as the founders of the League once imagined.[25]

This train of thought is continued in articles by Dónall Ó Riagáin in March and April 2004, in which he acknowledges the value of Irish as a European language.[26] Similar articles on various political and economic issues by Micheál D. Ó hUiginn, Aengus Ó Snodaigh, Éamon Ó Cuív and Pat Rabbitte were published in June 2007.[27]

Unique journalistic insights include analysis into the terror and violence of the Troubles in Northern Ireland, as well as an insight into the joy of Irish people, North and South, when the peace talks resulted in a breakthrough that promised a resolution to the troublesome situation. These articles in *Comhar* provide a commentary on both discord and peace, with discussion of the Anglo-Irish Agreement in the 1986 November edition, analysis of the 75th commemoration of the 1916 Rising in May 1991, accounts of Bloody Sunday in April 1997, a series of articles on the Northern Troubles by Deirdre Ní Ghrianna in 1998, and the reporting on the Saville Enquiry in 1999. Living only 400 metres from the main street in Omagh, Anton Mac Cába was the first journalist on the scene after the Omagh bombing. His piece on this tragic event is one of the most poignant pieces of writing in the history of the periodical.[28] He opens by comparing Conrad's trip to the 'heart of darkness' with his own five-week journey as a journalist at the coroner's inquest in Omagh. Mac Cába queries the contradictory role of the journalist as a public storyteller and as a witness, and explores the internal conflict and struggle between the role of the journalist as a community witness and as a public witness.

25 'Acmhainní Cultúrtha sa tSochaí Nuálaíoch' ['Social resources in the innovative society'], *Comhar*, Dec. 2008. 26 'Cearta Teanga agus Cultúir san Eoraip Nua' ['Language rights and culture in the new Europe'], *Comhar*, Mar.–Apr. 2004. 27 *Comhar*, June 2007. 28 'Uafás na hÓmaí' ['The terror of Omagh'], *Comhar*, Nov. 2000.

In the first part of the article, he examines this conflict as a member of this community which depended on him to tell its story to a greater public, while respecting the impact of the event on families and local people:

> The relatives come from the same community as me. They think that I should have a better understanding of them than that of a stranger ... It is difficult to do two things at once, to explain to those on the outside without upsetting the local community ... An in-depth account of the evidence of the Inquest could be sort of pornographic. Unfortunately, there are those who like that sort of terror. The relatives were not in agreement about the issue. Some proposed that everything should be told, that the videos of the horror that were shown to the Inquest should be shown in their entirety on television. Of course, the terror of Omagh should be explained. It was a crime against the human race, the very same as Bloody Sunday or America's attacks on Iraq. Without journalism the whole world would be unaware of these things.[29]

Bridging his role as a member of the community with his role as a journalist, Mac Cába does not minimize the horror of this event in this article. This very powerful piece of Irish journalism remains in the annals of *Comhar* as an Irish-language publication written by a journalist talking to a certain public where the language really is only the medium. Mac Cába's concluding statement demonstrates the conflict for those involved in an event that not only changes their individual lives but the lives of an entire community where all are committed to finding the truth while preserving their values, regardless of class or creed:

> The most notable thing about the relatives was that they were the very same as the poor creatures who died. They all had country faces and forms. They were Catholics and Protestants, Republicans, Nationalists, Unionists and Loyalists, yes and one Mormon. The same as those who were killed, they belonged to the class that would never be in the news, except that people who were related to them were on the street in Omagh.[30]

A significant element of *Comhar* at the time, and throughout its history, has been its series of multi-faceted, multi-coloured covers. These commissioned pieces of artwork deserve further study and would merit an exhibition. The

29 Ibid. 30 Ibid.

individual approach of each editor created an added dimension while maintaining the continuous central aspects rooted in the founding principles of
journalism and literature. Many articles also trace the history of *Comhar*, hon-
ouring its writers and writing, resulting in commemorative issues such as the
fifty-year celebratory issue in 1992. In his last editorial, Vivian Uíbh Eachach,
editor between February 1995 and 1997, describes comprehensively the challenges for the editor and the periodical, acknowledging the need for Ó Muirí's
'comhar' [partnership] referred to at the start of this chapter:

> It is a particular art to produce a monthly periodical, and there are many
> difficulties and problems with doing this. It takes special people to do
> that work – especially when these people are functioning voluntarily or
> part-time. One of the most important resources, particularly in an area
> in which people are voluntarily contributing, is the vision. Without that
> vision, the blade that cuts through the challenges of the day is missing.
> Those who founded *Comhar* had a vision and today's publishers of the
> periodical have that vision. The vision is to provide a periodical of the
> highest standard which deals with a varied discourse and which provides
> modern Irish language readers with information. They are not taken up
> with the 'golden days which were'. It was our privilege to assist in helping
> them to realise that vision.[31]

LANGUAGE AND LITERATURE

The main content of *Comhar* comprises Irish language writing ranging from
early texts to modern literature. Over the years it was a noted journal for the
publication of proceedings of prestigious annual Irish-language gatherings
and lectures, such as the annual UCD Ó Cadhain lecture and the Merriman
winter and summer schools. Topics that arise include the role of the writer,
the medium, the forum and writing itself. A central element of the partnership ethos of the periodical was the forum it provided for writers and
artists at all stages. Examples of this include features such as Caoilfhionn Nic
Pháidín's call for writers and artists in August 1982 and the special editions
in the early years of the twenty-first century for 'Scríbhneoirí Úra' ['New
Writers'].[32] The forum that *Comhar* and similar journals provided for renowned

31 'Iris le hAisling í *Comhar*' ['*Comhar* is a periodical with a vision'], *Comhar*, Apr. 1997.   32 'Scríbhneoirí
agus ealaíontóirí óga ag teastáil ó *Comhar*' ['*Comhar* needs young writers and artists'], *Comhar*, Aug. 1982;
Eagrán na Scríbhneoirí Úra [New Writers Issue], *Comhar*, Oct. 2009; *Eagrán na Scríbhneoirí Úra*, *Comhar*, Sept.
2010.

writers, journalists and politicians who wrote about language and literature issues in both Irish and English allowed for dual-language debate and analysis, providing access for the general public to this kind of reading material. In the absence of cultural and literary periodicals like this in the pre-revival and revival period, this discourse was often limited to an academic readership. The access provided by *Comhar* opened alternative avenues for dual-language writers and journalists. For example, the achievement of one of the most prolific editors of *Comhar*, Breandán Ó hEithir, as a dual-language writer and journalist in many genres, is acknowledged by Póilín Ní Chiaráin in her Ó hEithir documentary *Faoileán Árann* [*A Seagull of Aran*]. She writes:

> The experts thought that his journalism was the most important part of his work and that that was what would remain. They thought that he was a great loss to journalism and creative writing and that the learned institutions should do comprehensive study on his legacy.[33]

Ó hEithir often used the journalistic forum to bring attention to minority language issues, lamenting the state of the Irish language in the Gaeltacht and the lack of government support for industrial and public schemes to enhance the language and the Gaeltacht community.[34] Minority languages are also dealt with in the broader European context. In an interview for *Comhar* in 1979, John Hume examines minority cultures in Europe in the context of securing diversity within the European Union. When asked if he believes this cultural aim can be achieved through political legislation, Hume's reply reflects his approach to many issues in which he played a subsequent prominent role, not least the Good Friday Agreement:

> That kind of thing is not related to legislation. What is needed, I think, is to put the good will of the community into action to begin with, and to have collaborative talks with the minority language communities themselves to see what educational, cultural and economic aspects need to be focused on.[35]

The function of various writing forums is also examined in *Comhar*, with the role and importance of the book, as opposed to the periodical, in the promotion of Irish literature highlighted in February 1961 in Máirtín Ó Direáin's

---

33 'Focail ag rince' ['Words dancing'], *Comhar*, Nov. 2000.   34 'Idir Údarás agus Ghaeltacht' ['Between authority and Gaeltacht'], *Comhar*, Nov. 1979.   35 'Agallamh John Hume' ['John Hume's interview'], *Comhar*, Feb. 1979.

lecture to the Cumann Liteartha [Literary Society] in UCD. In this piece Ó Direáin acknowledges the importance of the periodical as a platform for bringing new writers and poets to public attention, but he also defends the need to compile anthologies of poetry if the genre is to develop. Using examples of poets such as Pearse Hutchinson and Tomás Tóibín, he states that they need to create books, not just periodicals for random poems.[36] Another example of the variation on media form and style for modern literature is Antain Mag Shamhráin's interview with Breandan Ó Doibhlin in April 1985. Ó Doibhlin asserts that he strongly believes in the repossession of heritage through language and literature, stating that:

> There is a basic difference between looking at images – whether it is a film, television or whatever – and reading … [thus] reconnecting with Irish literature in the first instance, that is, the mental equipment which a cultural man or learned person or wise person in this country would have if we had a natural history.[37]

In September 2010 Ríona Nic Congáil's interview with three emerging Irish poets examines the choice of medium and the use of translation in a contemporary context. Ailbhe Ní Ghearbhuigh and Caitríona Ní Chléirchín's view is that translation is a necessary part of the artist's work as it is difficult for an Irish-language poet to maintain momentum if they are talking in a vacuum. They refer to the advantages of YouTube as a contemporary tool to demonstrate poetic expression where the image as a form of expression takes precedence over the language as the main and possibly supplementary focus. However, Proinsias Mac a'Bhaird draws on literary criticism on the issue of the ownership of the translated poem: 'With the artistic translation, something new is done to the poem. If that is the kind of translation you mean, the poem no longer belongs to the poet; it belongs to the translator.'[38] Translation was a significant tool in the creation of modern literature in Irish in the revival period but these interviews demonstrate the evolution of Irish-language writing through the twentieth- and into the twenty-first century. Clearly using translation to make Irish-language literature available to a wider audience of learners has been replaced with a new focus on translation as a medium of

36 '"Cuireann Máirtín Ó Direáin síos ar an Nuafhilíocht": léacht a thug sé don chumann liteartha i gColáiste na hOllscoile ag a mór-chruinniú' ['"Máirtín Ó Direáin describes modern literature": a lecture he delivered to the general meeting of the UCD Literary Society'], *Comhar*, Feb. 1961.   37 'Agallamh na míosa: Antain Mag Shamhráin ag caint le Breandán Ó Doibhlin' ['Interview of the month: Antain Mag Shamhráin talking to Breandán Ó Doibhlin'], *Comhar*, Apr. 1985.   38 'An Lucht Fileata' ['The poets'], *Comhar*, Sept. 2010.

literary expression and criticism. Marking almost one hundred years of the creation of a modern Irish literature, Siobhán Ní Fhoghlú explores the coming of age of Irish writing and language in the early 1990s:

> We get to know many of this century's writers through the medium of Irish and that is progress. Many Irish people get to know writers in Irish through the medium of English, which means that much knowledge of Irish writing is lacking. It is not clear that that is generally understood in the country, even amidst scholars. We have Irish language writers who are not acknowledged even though knowledge of their work would greatly benefit those who work in the cultivation of literature in Ireland at this time. In the nineteenth century it was understood that Irish was a language which would be worth studying by linguists. It is necessary to understand at the end of the twentieth century that Irish language literature should be experienced by the youth in the language in which it is being created in order to fully understand the life and story of Ireland, today and yesterday.[39]

In the foreword for the commemorative volume *Cnuasach Comhar, 1982–2012*, literary scholar and critic Aisling Ní Dhonnchadha emphasizes that one of the most central philosophical, cultural and aesthetic questions that came to the fore in the context of shaping, practising and reviewing Irish creative writing was the stand that the writer took in the context of 'tradition'. This reflects Ní Fhoghlú's need 'to fully understand the life and story of Ireland'.[40] Prior to this, in the commemorative issue of *Comhar, 1942–2012*, the acclaimed Irish-language writer and journalist Alan Titley acknowledged *Comhar* as an essential source for the study of literary works and criticism, emphasizing its importance in 'practising and reviewing Irish creative writing' and noting that '*Comhar* is speckled with flashes of criticism and anyone who wants to embark on current Irish-language literature should have it as his regular source.'[41] Ní Dhonnchadha's comprehensive treatise on the literary aspects of *Comhar* in the aforementioned essay creates a framework to review almost eighty years of literary writing and criticism as a central element of Irish periodicals.

Live performance is also given its own stage in *Comhar*, with contributions from notable artists such as Siobhán McKenna (Siobhán Nic Cionnaith),

---

39 *Comhar*, May 1992. 40 Aisling Ní Dhonnchadha & Regina Uí Chollatáin (eds), 'Réamhrá', *Cnuasach Comhar, 1982–2012: Ailt. Aistí. Agallaimh* (Baile Átha Cliath, 2014), p. 29. 41 'Cruthú, Clampar agus Conspóid' ['Creation, commotion and controversy'], Forlíonadh [Supplement], *Comhar*, Oct. 2012.

who discusses the way that Irish drama is interpreted in British and American theatres.[42] McKenna offers an excellent insight into the reception of many Irish writers, claiming that Americans cannot portray Irish drama effectively as they do not fully understand the Irish psyche. Comparing her role in Ibsen's *Ghosts* in London, which was highly acclaimed by critics, she attributes its success to the diversity of style, with a mix of English, Irish, American and Hungarian actors, ensuring that no one style or language dominated. This is probably best understood in the context of a developing post-revival artistic mindset where language and cultural diversity needed to be embraced on the performing-arts global stage. She emphasizes the need for the actor to understand the mind of the author. She goes on to state that she prefers to see people emigrating to the US instead of England due to the esteem in which the Irish are held in the US and even more so if they speak Irish. McKenna recounts appearances she had made on television and at public events in Harvard and Boston, for example, where she has always been asked to recite some poetry or literature in Irish, and concludes with an anecdote about a native Irish speaker from Kerry who spent seventy-four years in the States, for whom she reignited a spark of interest in the arts through this common linguistic thread.

MEDIA AND JOURNALISM

The nature of the media in general is explored extensively in *Combar*, with a focus on some important milestones or 'media events'. Quoting material from English dailies in January 1919, in 1959 Proinsias Mac Aonghusa examines the reportage on the First Dáil. Most accounts assert that the assembly of the First Dáil was false and without a future. Phrases such as 'so-called parliament' (*Daily Mail*) and 'childishly illegal' (*Daily Telegraph*), present a dim picture of the initial expectations of the First Dáil. The statement in the *Daily Express* regarding the use of the Irish language by the First Dáil questions the very existence of the language for any meaningful purpose:

> It is difficult to believe that the public will continue to take an absorbing interest in the tame proceedings conducted in dull fashion in a language that most people do not understand and with which only a comparative handful are really expertly familiar.[43]

42 'Aniar as Nua Eabhrac' ['From New York'], *Combar*, Apr. 1959.   43 'An Chéad Dáil agus na Nuachtáin' ['The First Dáil and the newspapers'], *Combar*, Jan. 1959.

Other newspapers in Mac Aonghusa's review include the *Irish Times, Daily News, Belfast News Letter, Daily Telegraph, Irish Independent, Freeman's Journal* and *Cork Examiner.* The quote from the bishops' statement in the *Irish Catholic* on 23 January 1919, criticizing the emphasis on 1916 as a cornerstone for the Dáil proceedings, cuts to the core of the resistance to the First Dáil:

> We feel bound to say that we do not consider it of good omen that the events of Easter 1916 were solemnly made the basic fact of the proceedings. What we thought of the insurrection of 1916 was clearly stated at the time, and accorded with the express views of many of the Irish Bishops. We have seen no reason since to change our opinion of the indefensibility from the point of view of Catholic morality of the Rebellion of 1916, nor can after-events, however deplorable, be made to serve as a justification for it. Hence to us, the proceedings on Tuesday seem vitiated at the core, however loftily inspired their object.[44]

Mac Aonghusa concludes his review of the media reportage of the time by asserting that

> This shows that the newspaper coverage demonstrated to the people of Ireland and the UK that the Dáil was nonsense or at least that it was a danger to the country ... However, many of the readers of the bigger papers understood that the story they were reporting was biased and they didn't pay too much attention to them.[45]

Mac Aonghusa closes the piece with the following quote from Griffith's *Nationality*, stating that while many in Ireland would not have had access to this paper, Griffith's conjecture is indicative of what most would have believed at the time:

> The Irish nation was defeated at the Battle of Kinsale 300 years ago and on the 21st January 1919 it lifted its head again. On that day the Irish delegates announced to the world that Ireland is a free state and that message went out to the greater world in the language of the Gael. This first assembly of Dáil Éireann is the greatest event since O'Neill's departure to go overseas ... the Irish race and the true Irish are again in charge ... The parliament of the true Gael came together, the Irish language

44 Ibid. 45 Ibid

their language, the courage of the Irish inspiring them to action, the eternal desire of the Irish for freedom their gospel.[46]

The 1960s was a time of growth, but as *Comhar* moved towards the 1970s the decline of Irish-language newspapers was becoming clear. The piece on the government refusing to renew *Amárach's* grant in September 1974 is not very encouraging, with its forlorn suggestion that *Amárach* should be supported 'ar son na cúise' ['for the cause'] if nothing else.[47] The piece presents an in-depth case regarding the state of the Irish-language press, especially the roles of editors and publishers. Although the overriding sentiment is the concern about the lack of government support, the question is raised as to 'Why not even one of them would survive on its own?' The reason is the small readership, which does not attract quality advertising; in truth, this really was and still is a major obstacle for all Irish-language publications.

A special issue was devoted to a general review of Irish-language publications in April 1980.[48] In his overview of the tradition of Irish-language periodicals, Séamas Mac Gabhann examines their role in the promotion of a modern literature in Irish:

> As Breandán Ó hEithir, a former editor of the periodical, says: '*Comhar* was brought into the world without any grant except for the money of a few people who had a vision and enough endeavour to go into the venture. If it wasn't for *Comhar* it is unlikely that modern Irish writing would have grown as it has.' He is completely right, of course, as *Comhar* put a new slant on the fate of Irish literature.[49]

By the 1990s the discussion had progressed to the ethics of professional journalism, and 'citizen' journalism is debated in the context of the contemporary journalist's role. The role of the professional journalist is acknowledged but challenged on the basis of the need to do more than simply find the story and tell it. According to this article, the journalist must be part of the story:

> If you are to be proper journalist … It is essential that the greater public know you – the journalist as the prophet and hero. The journalist has another role … the role of a witness.[50]

46 Ibid. 47 Eagarfhocal [Editorial], *Comhar*, Oct. 1974. 48 'Foilsitheoireacht na Gaeilge' ['Irish-language publishing'], *Comhar*, Apr. 1980. 49 'Na hIrisí Gaeilge – Scoileanna Scairte na hAoise seo?' ['Irish-language periodicals – the hedge-schools of this age?'], *Comhar*, Apr. 1980. 50 'Cad é an ról don iriseoir?' ['What is the role of the journalist?'], *Comhar*, July 1998.

This is echoed in Anton Mac Cába's reporting on the Omagh bombings in 2000 as referred to earlier and reinforces the standards of journalism which were aspired to in *Comhar* and in Irish-language journalism generally. Essentially this brings us back to the founding aims of *Comhar* outlined by An Comhchaidreamh. Journal sales and circulation may depend on a niche readership but the content is worth applauding. Follow-on articles on the ethics of journalism by established journalists such as Fachtna Ó Drisceoil are especially useful in tracing the development and progression of Irish-language journalism in an environment where English language journalism mostly took precedence over Irish-language content.[51]

From the 1980s onward, many journalistic forums came and went, and Irish-language journalism flourished in its own milieu. At this time, T.K. Whitaker conducted an assessment on world change in the context of development in Japan, the US and in Europe over the previous thirty years, noting education and age issues as the greatest global challenges for the future. In this assessment published in *Comhar,* he recommends the refurbishment of the industrial system for modern technology with the aid of government macro-policies. New communication forums and technology would be essential instruments for a new era of open communication.[52]

This pre-figured a new era of telecommunications, including film and television. In his interview with Peadar Ó Flatharta, film-maker Bob Quinn asserts that cinema is a particular type of art in which language and screen interact to produce new perspectives, regardless of the controversial themes for a conservative screen audience.[53] It was a vibrant time in Irish-language media and journalism, with special articles and issues focusing on innovative developments, culminating in the special issue following the launch of Teilifís na Gaeilge (now TG4) in 1996.[54] The main article in this issue was the speech given by Micheál D. Ó hUiginn, later to be president of Ireland. Despite the seventy year gap between this and the first broadcast of 2RN in 1926 by future first president of Ireland, Douglas Hyde, there are similarities in their messages at pivotal watershed moments when Irish took a brief precedence over English as the language of the national media and a specific aspect of Irish life — even if it were only for a brief media moment:

> The question that has to be raised today is: what is the meaning of citizenship, a community of people with their differences or a group of

51 'Sciolladóireacht, Stialladóireacht agus Cáineadh Stuama' ['Abuse, backbiting, and wise criticism'], *Comhar,* Jan. 1999. 52 'Cora an tSaoil' ['The twists of life'], *Comhar,* Dec. 1982. 53 'Scannán aniar: agallamh le Bob Quinn' ['A film from the west: an interview with Bob Quinn'], *Comhar,* Apr. 1987. 54 'An Craolachán in Éirinn' ['Broadcasting in Ireland'] , *Comhar,* Apr. 1995; 'TNaG', *Comhar,* Nov. 1996.

shareholders or customers? I think that the North-South debate is the most important one in the world ... If the imagination is narrowed and if the only meaning for freedom is the permission of the customer to press the on / off button, we will have a poor image of the human being. Let democracy which is rooted in diversity be our guide.[55]

This also echoes the sentiments of John Hume regarding minority language diversity in Europe referred to earlier. Tracing these links attests to the value of media analysis of this kind. This increases our understanding of the power of media networks, especially in the context of a journal that hosted very prominent Irish leaders throughout its eighty-year history of reportage, despite the perceived role of *Comhar* as a niche Irish-language journal.

Clearly the founding of TG4 set a new benchmark for Irish-language media as we approached the millennium. A year later, in April 1997, Raidió na Gaeltachta celebrated its twentieth-fifth year on air. Radio was a constant source of debate in *Comhar* with specific series from 1986 onwards such as Gabriel Rosenstock's radio column 'Dialann Éisteora' ['A Listener's Diary']. One interesting article on the founding of Raidió na Life in the 1990s almost puts the foundation of this urban Irish-language radio station in the capital city in the east of the country on a par with the foundation of TG4 as a fully Irish-speaking national television station in the heart of the Conamara Gaeltacht. Raidió na Life was building on the strong pioneering tradition of Raidió na Gaeltachta founded in 1972, but the title of this article, 'Raidió Gaeilge don Ardchathair' ['Irish-language Radio for the Capital'] leaves no doubt as to the target audience of the new station:

> The decision of the Independent Radio and Television Commission to grant a broadcasting licence for a full Irish language radio in Dublin is a great forward step for the language as well as a valuable development in the cultural and community life of the capital city. This is a worthy result of the work of the co-operative Dublin Radio which was founded in 1988 to get an Irish radio station in Dublin. They launched Raidió na Life in Dublin last October for a fortnight ... The ultimate aim of this radio station is to bring people closer to each other by the participation of the various scattered communities which are dealing with Irish all over the area and to provide a communication service for them which will strengthen their identity and future. As well as that, this radio station will provide a very important opportunity here so that the use

---

55 'Cead cnaipe a bhrú' ['Permission to press a button'], *Comhar*, Nov. 1996.

and resource of the language can be developed in a context outside the classroom, which will benefit all our young people who are receiving Irish-medium education.[56]

To some extent it can be claimed that the inherent media 'partnership' between these platforms, which was central to the ethos of *Comhar*, goes some way to ensuring that all avenues are explored and exploited to the maximum potential for Irish-language usage and to the highest standards.

CONCLUSION

Comhar has already had commemorative volumes and collections to attempt to capture the essence of eighty years of Irish-language journalism. It has been, and remains, one of the main Irish-language literary and cultural journals of the twentieth- and twenty-first centuries. Although this chapter barely dips into the fountain of its archive referred to at the beginning, there is no doubt as to the wealth of writing, debate and literary criticism that *Comhar* has contributed over this period. It has provided a forum for many Irish-language writers to develop their craft in post-revival Ireland. Building on the initial seeds and tradition of Irish-language literature in the revival period, the inter-university focus was certainly aligned with Douglas Hyde's vision for the language as a founding father of the revival and later as the chair of Modern Irish in UCD. Journals such as *Comhar* continue to play an important role not only in the development of literature, but of writers and the media they use. Its role as an inter-university journal has changed to the point that many university presidents now would barely even be aware of *Comhar's* existence. However, the literature and general discourse in *Comhar* continue to serve the Irish-language community and the creative arts. The title and the sentiment behind it have not changed despite many challenges to its survival, including the ongoing question of government support for Irish-language publications. Despite this, it is quite possible that if Douglas Hyde were to look at the work and content achieved since his inaugural address in the first issue in 1942, he would probably surmise that it achieved and even surpassed what it set out to do from the outset, while also providing a forum for many leaders who followed in his footsteps.

56 *Comhar*, Sept. 1992.

14 / The *Catholic Bulletin*, 1911–39: battle of civilizations or long revolution?[1]

PATRICK MAUME

The monthly *Catholic Bulletin*, published by M.H. Gill & Son between 1911 and 1939, has experienced a long afterlife in Irish cultural historiography, usually as a quotable compendium of extreme expressions of Catholic Irish-Ireland ideology derived from the early twentieth-century Gaelic revival. F.S.L. Lyons in *Culture and anarchy in Ireland* encapsulated Irish cultural politics in the 1920s in the conflict between the *Catholic Bulletin* with its claims to represent Catholic Gaelic tradition and the weekly *Irish Statesman* edited by George Russell (Æ) as representing the Anglo-Irish tradition – which is how the *Catholic Bulletin* saw it.[2] This chapter first discusses the historiography of the *Catholic Bulletin*. It then provides a brief account of the *Bulletin*'s foundation and early years (1911–22) under the editorship of J.J. O'Kelly ('Sceilg') before tracing its participation in the cultural and political conflicts of the 1920s and 1930s, with particular reference to its principal contributor, Timothy Corcoran, SJ, whose vision of nationalism combined backward-looking agrarian populism with keen bureaucratic jobbery for protégés at the expense of Protestants and 'Castle Catholics'. These conflicts were shaped to a great extent by cultural formations dating back to the Land War, Young Ireland and the religious polemics surrounding the nineteenth-century Irish university question, and the *Bulletin* embodied the autarkic isolationism and nativist Anglophobia often attributed to its hero Eamon de Valera.

In the 1920s, when the aspiring novelist Francis MacManus addressed the Dublin Radical Club on Catholicism and literature, Rosamond Jacob compared him to the *Catholic Bulletin*.[3] Shortly afterwards, the Trinity student R.B. McDowell wondered what could be said for Irish nationalism and Catholicism, and after perusing the *Catholic Bulletin* and the works of Pearse, remained a Protestant unionist.[4] Paul Blanshard cites it in his well-known survey *The Irish*

1 I thank the staff of the Central Catholic Library. This paper draws on research for the *Dictionary of Irish biography* (http://dib.cambridge.org) – hereafter, *DIB*. An earlier version was given at the 2019 Belfast conference of the Newspaper and Periodical History Forum of Ireland. 2 *Catholic Bulletin* (hereafter *CB*), May 1930, 424–8. 3 Brian Trench, 'The Radical Club: a 1920s forum for progressive cultural activity', *History Ireland*, 27:5 (Sept./Oct. 2019), 44–7. 4 David Dickson, 'R.B. McDowell: a tribute', *History Ireland*, 19:6 (Nov./Dec. 2011), 36–40.

and Catholic power.[5] James Meenan's memoir of the University College Dublin (UCD) economist George O'Brien, principal academic defender of the economic policies of W.T. Cosgrave's agriculture minister Patrick Hogan (based on export-oriented agriculture with quality control to maintain Ireland's share of the British market), notes Corcoran's attacks on O'Brien as 'the Hamlet of Earlsfort Terrace … Economist in Chief to Green Grazierdom'.[6] Patrick O'Farrell's *Ireland's English question* sees the *Bulletin* representing an unrealistic primitivist nostalgia among early twentieth-century Anglophobic Irish Catholic clergy, expressing an unhealthy merger of politics and religion in its eulogies of insurgents killed in the 1916 Rising.[7] Brian P. Murphy, OSB, argues in response that the *Bulletin's* merger of religion and politics was forced by the need to evade official censorship, and that its attacks on the Anglo-Irish tradition were based on legitimate historical evidence.[8] Margaret O'Callaghan pointed out in response to Lyons that the *Statesman* was less representative of wider Anglo-Irish society than the *Irish Times* and the Trinity College of John Pentland Mahaffy, and that to take the *Bulletin* rather than the Jesuit quarterly *Studies* as exemplifying the Catholic-nationalist tradition gives an unbalanced view.[9] (The *Bulletin* attacked *Studies* for promoting the *Statesman*.)[10] Again, this needs qualification: the *Bulletin* regularly denounced the *Irish Times* and Trinity (it stated that the last fortress of the English garrison stretched from Westland Row to College Green and D'Olier Street – i.e. the Trinity campus and the *Irish Times* office),[11] with Mahaffy described as a boor, snob and clerical unbeliever who delighted in undermining students' faith and morals, Oscar Wilde being his prime victim.[12] Corcoran had been the first editor of *Studies* and his *Bulletin's* combination of Catholic apologetic antiquarianism and surveys of world affairs differed from *Studies* in tone and intellectual depth, but not in subject matter. Perhaps the journals might be seen as Dr Jekyll and Mr Hyde, or the *Bulletin* as *Studies'* evil twin. More recently, Brian Ward includes the *Bulletin* in his examination of Irish periodicals in 1912, seeing it as representing official Catholic nationalism dominant in the post-independence era.[13]

5 Paul Blanshard, *The Irish and Catholic power* (London, 1954), pp 112, 130, 197, 215.   6 James Meenan, *George O'Brien: a biographical memoir* (Dublin, 1980), pp 133–6; *CB*, July 1930, 648–53.   7 Patrick O'Farrell, *Ireland's English question: Anglo-Irish relations, 1534–1970* (London, 1971). For O'Farrell's liberal Catholicism, see Patrick Maume, 'Patrick O'Farrell reassessed – a view from Ireland', *Australian Journal of Irish Studies*, 13 (2013), 11–28.   8 Brian P. Murphy, *Patrick Pearse and the lost republican ideal* (Dublin, 1991); *idem*, *The Catholic Bulletin and Republican Ireland with special reference to J.J. O'Kelly (Sceilg)* (Belfast, 2005); *idem*, 'The canon of Irish cultural history: some questions', *Studies*, 75:305 (1988), 68–83 (lists pseudonyms used by Corcoran).   9 Margaret O'Callaghan, 'Language, nationality and cultural identity: the *Irish Statesman* and the *Catholic Bulletin* reappraised', *Irish Historical Studies*, 24:94 (1984), 226–45.   10 *CB*, Oct. 1935, 776–9.   11 See, for example, *CB*, June 1930, 519–21 & Feb. 1937, 73–4.   12 *CB*, Nov. 1935, 898; Mar. 1937, 209; Apr. 1939, 250–3; May 1939, 326–9.   13 Brian Ward, *Imagining alternative Irelands in 1912: cultural discourse in the periodical press* (Dublin, 2017).

As Ward highlights, the *Catholic Bulletin* was founded as an offshoot of the pre-war Evil Literature Crusade, intended to promote Catholic literature as a complement to suppression of indecent British newspapers by bonfires at railway stations and pressure on newsagents.[14] This, incidentally, would benefit Gill by promoting its products; the guidance was offered to priests and others stocking local libraries as well as to individuals for their private reading, and the *Bulletin*'s advertisements generally included a list of Gill publications. Other long-term advertisers included manufacturers of religious goods, Player Wills cigarettes and Kennedy's Bread. Much of its early content consisted of pious and improving literature, with some popular reading. Literary sketches by Thomas Aloysius Fitzgerald, a Franciscan from Callan, Co. Kilkenny who served for a period in Australia, featured regularly in the magazine's first decade; these were often illustrated and contained humorous references to current events (sometimes to the *Bulletin* itself). Fitzgerald's writings enjoyed contemporary popularity and several collections were published.[15] The most prominent clerical contributors to the *Bulletin* included Peter Elias Magennis, prior-general of the Calced Carmelite Order 1919–31,[16] and two successive rectors of the Irish College in Rome, John Hagan (as 'Scottus') and Michael Curran (whose brother Constantine wrote for the *Irish Statesman* and was duly denounced).[17] The Irish College priests who were the *Bulletin*'s Roman correspondents were driven by the memory of British intrigues in Rome during the 1880s against the Land War and home rule movements, and the suspicion (never explicit in the *Bulletin*) that Rome might sacrifice the interests of Irish Catholicism for Catholic influence on the British empire.[18] The monthly notes on French affairs published by the *Bulletin* throughout its existence appear to have been contributed by clerics at the Irish College in Paris.

Its first editor was 'Sceilg' (J.J. O'Kelly), a Gill employee and Gaelic Leaguer.[19] The *Bulletin*'s crucial sponsor, however, was Patrick T. Keohane, Gill's managing director, and its demise took place soon after Keohane's death in 1939. Keohane's role helps to explain how the *Bulletin*, especially in its later years, could survive as the publisher's vanity publication.[20] Although any surviving business records were destroyed when Gill and Macmillan's Dublin premises burned down in 1979, an impressionistic overview suggests that it circulated among sections of the Catholic clergy and provincial schoolteachers.

14 Maurice Curtis, *The splendid cause: the Catholic Action movement in Ireland in the twentieth century* (Dublin, 2008). **15** *CB*, Oct. 1926, 1100–2. **16** *CB*, Oct. 1937, 737–45; 760–8. **17** Tom Feeney, 'Magennis, Peter Elias', *DIB*; *CB*, Oct. 1935, 777–8n. **18** Dermot Keogh, *Ireland and the Vatican: the politics and diplomacy of church-state relations, 1922–1960* (Cork, 1995); *CB*, Apr. 1930, 289–341; Ambrose Macaulay, *The Holy See, British policy and the Plan of Campaign in Ireland, 1885–93* (Dublin, 2002). **19** Brian P. Murphy, 'O'Kelly, John Joseph (Sceilg)', *DIB*. **20** *CB*, Dec. 1939, unpaginated obituary addendum by 'Fear Faire'.

The *Bulletin* regularly published obituaries for veteran rural clergy who had won a reputation as 'patriot priests' arrested or prosecuted during the land agitations of the 1880s – some of whom were noted to have written for the *Bulletin*.[21] It emphasized its circulation among the clerical diaspora, claiming a circulation of 25,000 (5,000 outside Ireland) in 1932.[22]

The *Bulletin* developed such standard features of contemporary magazines as a students' corner with advice on how to pass examinations, a column of household hints 'for mothers and daughters', a section on Gaelic games by P.J. Devlin and a children's column with essay competitions called 'Nead na nOg' and conducted by 'Meadhbh'. Until the mid-1930s the *Bulletin* was profusely illustrated with photographs and line drawings (many of the latter signed with a shamrock and the initials 'F de S'). In the 1930s it regularly repro-duced Leo Whelan's portrait *Mary, queen of Ireland* (commissioned by Gill for the Eucharistic Congress) with Justin Keating (later a prominent atheist), son of the painter Sean Keating and the political activist May Keating, as the child Jesus.[23] The original cover showed photographs of the Rock of Cashel and the Catholic cathedral at Armagh within a Celtic framework, surmounted by the papal coat of arms. In 1930 it adopted the plain cover design (masthead and leading topic of the month in dark ink on a green parchment cover) that characterized the *Bulletin* for the remainder of its existence.

Unlike other religious magazines of the same era, such as the Dominicans' *Irish Rosary* and the Jesuits' *Messenger of the Sacred Heart*, the *Bulletin* was not published by a religious order. It was originally submitted to the Dublin archdiocesan censor, but this gesture towards official approval was dropped by mutual agreement after members of the Dublin Jewish community com-plained to Archbishop Walsh about an article by Fr Thomas H. Burbage (a semi-regular priest-contributor, subsequently a prominent Sinn Féin activist in Carlow) which asserted that Jews engaged in the ritual murder of Christians and that Mendel Beiliss, accused of ritual murder in Kiev in 1913, had been wrongly acquitted through international Jewish influence.[24] Initially the *Bulletin* supported John Redmond, and did not oppose his early support for the British war effort. From the formation of a Liberal-Conservative coalition government in May 1915 the *Bulletin* began to insert hints of political discon-tent, and after the 1916 Rising it published numerous biographical sketches of deceased rebels, emphasizing their piety and high moral character. Ignatius O'Brien (lord chancellor of Ireland 1913–18) recalled:

---

21 See, for example, Fr John Cunningham – *CB*, Jan. 1936, 70–1; Fr Joseph Pell – Mar. 1936, 204–5; Archdeacon Casey – *CB*, Apr. 1936, 301–2. **22** *CB*, Jan. 1932, 20. **23** *CB*, May 1938, 420; July 1938, 603; *Irish Times*, 16 June 2012. **24** *CB*, July 1916; Mar. 1925, 193–4.

The executions which had followed the rebellion ... were used as evidence conclusive that the Saxon was now, as evermore, the enemy, unsympathetic and relentless ... in some three or four monthly magazines which were ostensibly devoted solely to religion. They were circulated amongst religious communities, in schools, colleges, convents and monasteries ... It may have been injudicious to have taken any direct measures to prevent the sale of these publications; but ... this special brand of propaganda could have been prevented if representations had been made in the proper quarters and in the proper way [i.e. to the church hierarchy].[25]

The *Bulletin* was an outspoken supporter of Sinn Féin in the following years, publishing, for example, a celebratory account by Fr Michael O'Flanagan of his campaigning experiences at the 'Election of the Snows' (the January 1917 North Roscommon by-election, where Count Plunkett defeated the Irish Party candidate) and a denunciation of 'Colonial Home Rule' (dominion status) as insufficient, by the same author.[26] An editorial welcoming the first meeting of Dáil Éireann rejoiced that Ireland was finished with 'London of the cocaine and the drugs, nursery of hypocrisy and infamy and of corruption that knows no end'.[27] The *Bulletin* hinted that William Martin Murphy and the *Irish Independent* were committing sedition by suggesting that the electorate voted for a republic only as a negotiating position and might accept dominion status.[28]

Sceilg resigned the editorship in autumn 1922 to undertake an overseas political mission, after which the *Bulletin*'s moving spirit was Timothy Corcoran, SJ, professor of education at University College Dublin 1911–43. Corcoran's father had been a prominent Nenagh Land Leaguer, later first chairman of North Tipperary County Council;[29] a tribute to the nation-building role of the nineteenth-century nationalist story magazines, the *Shamrock* and the *Irish Fireside*, may indicate Corcoran's childhood reading.[30] Corcoran wrote much of the *Bulletin* under different pseudonyms – because much of it was devoted to personal abuse of public figures, including fellow Jesuits. Under his guidance the proportion of the *Bulletin* devoted to original writing declined, though it continued to publish flowery reminiscences and devotional essays and verse. A

25 Typescript *Reminiscences* of Ignatius O'Brien, Lord Shandon, held in King's Inns, Dublin p. 392. These *Reminiscences*, edited by Daire Hogan and Patrick Maume for the Irish Legal History Society, are due to be published by Four Courts Press in 2021 as 'The reminiscences of Ignatius O'Brien, lord chancellor of Ireland, 1913–1921: a life in Cork, Dublin and Westminster'. 26 *CB*, Mar. 1917, 146–51; *CB*, Sept. 1917, 147–50. 27 *CB*, Jan. 1919, 1. 28 *CB*, Mar. 1919, 109. 29 Patrick Maume, 'Corcoran, Timothy', *DIB*; Séamus Ó Riain, *Dunkerrin: a parish in Ely O'Carroll* (Dunkerrin, Co. Tipperary, 1988). 30 *CB*, Nov. 1936, 902ff.

particularly oddly juxtaposed – and apparently mutually oblivious – pair of contributors were Sophie Raffalovich O'Brien (widow of the prominent home rule MP William O'Brien,[31] a Catholic convert proud of her Jewish ancestry), who provided sketches and recollections,[32] and the anti-Semite Fr Denis Fahey. The anonymous 'Sacerdos', whose lucubrations about Jewish Bolsheviks and Jewish bankers were based on such malevolent Continental Catholic publications as the *International Review of Secret Societies*, may have been Fahey or Burbage.[33]

Corcoran's *Bulletin* reacted against the genteel intellectualism and lukewarm 'Whig' nationalism of such earlier Jesuits as Matthew Russell, who had made the *Irish Monthly* into a literary organ publishing poets of different standpoints (including the young W.B. Yeats) and novels by middle-class women writers such as Rosa Mulholland, who suggested (amid the Land War) that Ireland's problems could be solved by sympathetic Catholic landlords.[34] By the 1920s and 1930s, however, the *Irish Monthly* had become a major platform for Corcoran's promotion of his educational philosophy under his own name as distinct from his anonymous, and therefore formally unacknowledged, contributions to the *Catholic Bulletin*.[35] Another 'Catholic Whig' was Thomas Finlay, SJ, editor of *Studies*' precursor the *New Ireland Review*, who worked with Horace Plunkett in the cooperative movement (and was distrusted by both supporters of the mainstream Irish Parliamentary Party and hardline unionists for his closeness to Tim Healy and skill at pulling official strings to advance his own agenda and his professional protégés). Corcoran shared Finlay's interest in string-pulling and, in a considerably cruder manner, Finlay's fear that the Catholic Irish might fall prey to Jewish capitalists or international socialists.[36]

Russell and Finlay did not represent nineteenth-century Irish Catholicism as a whole. Corcoran could draw on a legacy of antiquarian controversy in which Catholic and Protestant writers argued rival claims of descent from the early Irish church, and on nineteenth-century debates over 'the University question' – the demand for a Catholic university that could rival Trinity College, the question of whether Catholics should be allowed to attend Trinity and whether Catholic or Protestant academic standards were higher. He imitated

---

31 Her presence may reflect Corcoran's personal respect for William O'Brien – cf. *CB*, Jan. 1928, 57–62; Mar. 1928, 227–30; Apr. 1928, 346.   32 See, for example, *CB*, Feb. 1930, 156–61; Mar. 1930, 245–7; Apr. 1930, 381–5; July 1930, 675–6; Aug. 1931, 818–23.   33 See, for example, *CB*, Dec. 1930, 1136–44 (favourably quotes Alfred Rosenberg); Feb. 1931, 144–54; Mar. 1931, 277–84. Compare signed Fahey articles *CB*, Jan. 1928, 25–32; Feb. 1928, 159–64; Mar. 1928, 159–64.   34 James H. Murphy, *Catholic fiction and social reality in Ireland, 1873–1922* (Westport, CT & London, 1997).   35 E. Brian Titley, *Church, state and the control of schooling in Ireland, 1900–1944* (Dublin & Kingston, Ontario, 1983), pp 94–100.   36 Thomas J. Morrissey, SJ, *Father Thomas Finlay, 1848–1940: educationalist, editor, social reformer* (Dublin, 2004). See *CB*, Oct. 1930, 907–8 on Finlay.

the vitriolic public rhetoric deployed against Protestant loyalism by Daniel O'Connell,[37] the Land War-era paper *United Ireland*,[38] Tim Healy[39] and D.P. Moran in the *Leader*, with the aim of dispelling deference by calculated disrespect. Corcoran's frequent deployment of cloacal imagery of Joycean intensity contrasted with a nineteenth-century gentility that complained that Shane Leslie's novel *Doomsland* described a woman dying in childbirth as the result of an adulterous affair as having blood on her feet.[40]

The fact that Sceilg refused to follow de Valera into Fianna Fáil led some later commentators to assume the *Bulletin* also supported the post-1927 Sinn Fein rump. In fact, Hagan, Curran and Magennis were all personal friends and admirers of de Valera, while in the *Bulletin* Corcoran treated devotional Catholicism as coextensive with support for Fianna Fáil. In 1914 Corcoran had led an attempt to secure the chair of mathematics in University College Cork for de Valera as a suitably Catholic Gael. The college president and Catholic convert Bertram Windle succeeded in appointing a better-qualified Presbyterian.[41]

One underexplored area of nineteenth- and twentieth-century Irish cultural and intellectual history is tension between Irish and English Catholicism. Irish Catholicism, especially its more literate and aspirational adherents, drew on the cultural prestige and relative intellectual sophistication of English Catholicism; English Catholic intellectuals often wrote for *Studies*, while Irish emigrants, lay and religious, provided the numerical and organizational backbone of Catholicism in much of Britain. Many English Catholics regarded Irish Catholicism as a tribal religion subservient to nationalist demagoguery and averse to inconvenient commandments. Many Irish Catholics saw English Catholics as snobs influenced by conscious and unconscious adjustment to a non-Catholic society, particularly wanting not to be Irish.[42] The *Bulletin* noted that Stonyhurst, the Jesuit school, lent pre-Reformation vestments to an exhibition marking the coronation of George VI; they were displayed near Queen Victoria's gin bottle.[43] Corcoran's contempt for John Henry Newman should be seen in this context, as should his view that the English bishops should reinstate the former prohibition on Catholics attending at Oxford and Cambridge and renew Cardinal Manning's attempt to create a Catholic university in England. This was also a riposte to questions about why Irish Catholics should not attend TCD if English Catholics attended Oxbridge.[44]

---

37 Seán Ó Faoláin, *King of the beggars* (London, 1938). **38** Myles Dungan, *Mr Parnell's Rottweiler: censorship and the* United Ireland *newspaper, 1881–1891* (Dublin, 2014). **39** Frank Callanan, *The Parnell split, 1890–1891* (Cork, 1992); *idem, T.M. Healy* (Cork, 1996). **40** *CB*, Mar. 1924, 211–17; Apr. 1925, 357–60; Apr. 1926, 355–60; May 1926, 449–51. **41** Ann & Dermot Keogh, *Bertram Windle: the Honan bequest and the modernisation of University College Cork, 1904–1919* (Cork, 2010), pp 96–105, 244. **42** *CB*, Feb. 1925, 99–100; Nov. 1926, 1125–32; Mar. 1927, 262–8. **43** *CB*, May 1937, 329. **44** *CB*, Jan. 1930, 43–7; Sept. 1937, 665–6.

When attacking criticisms of de Valera by the *Tablet*'s Dublin correspondent, Corcoran recalled that in the 1880s the *Tablet* and *Dublin Review* denounced the Land League and the home rule movement as 'Jacobin', supported by such figures as the convert poet Aubrey de Vere.[45] Eoin MacNeill's denunciation of the view of the English Catholic historian of civilization Christopher Dawson that the failure of Gaelic Ireland to develop a centralized state apparatus showed backwardness was applauded by the *Bulletin*.[46] Corcoran hinted that lectures in Ireland by English Catholics provoked trouble and should be illegal.[47] The *Bulletin* was assisted in its crusade against English Catholicism by the fact that some English Catholic intellectuals were attracted to the religion as a means of expressing a wider Bohemian nonconformity ill at ease with Catholic mainstream attitudes. When *Tablet* editor Ernest Oldmeadow attacked Evelyn Waugh's *Black mischief* for mentioning contraceptives, ridiculing old ladies concerned about cruelty to animals and portraying a female character entering the protagonist's bedroom, twelve English Catholic intellectuals signed a petition supporting Waugh. The *Bulletin* plunged into the fray in defence of Oldmeadow (noting as proof of the disinterested nature of its defence of the Sixth Commandment that Oldmeadow was a Tory diehard on Irish matters), while pointing to Waugh and his defenders as evidence that English Catholics were scarcely Catholic at all.[48]

Corcoran offered a coherent interpretation of Irish history centred on a Catholic educational system (rather than political movements and institutions) as the guiding thread of Irish history. He emphasized the early modern, Counter-Reformation period as key to identity formation. As a young Jesuit Corcoran worked with the martyrologist Denis Murphy, SJ; one of his abiding grievances against the pre-independence National Board of Education was that the Trinity physicist George Francis Fitzgerald had kept a school history of Ireland written by Murphy from being approved by the board because it idealized mediaeval Gaelic Ireland.[49] Corcoran thought the century 1580–1680 'in some respects the greatest in our history' in cultural and spiritual terms, and maintained that Irish Latin writers from that period should be added to Latin courses in Irish secondary schools.[50] (Perhaps the accessibility of early modern Latin texts to educated nineteenth- and early twentieth-century popularizers – especially clerics – has been underestimated as contributing to the formulation of Irish national identities.) His ideal was the Confederation of Kilkenny, as a Catholic body, with the division between temporizing Ormondists and

45 *CB*, June 1925, 3–9; July 1936, 543–5   46 *CB*, May 1935, 333–5; Aug. 1938, 603; May 1939, 342.   47 *CB*, Jan. 1937, 11.   48 *CB*, Jan. 1933, 90–4; Mar. 1933, 194–7; May 1936, 380–2.   49 *CB*, May 1932, 345–53; Oct. 1936, 902ff.   50 *CB*, Oct. 1936, 813–17.

uncompromising supporters of Rinuccini, the papal nuncio, presented as between Old English and Gaels. During the War of Independence the *Bulletin* serialized a translation (by Mgr John Hagan) of a memoir by Rinuccini's secretary, Monsignor Massari; editorial comment during the Civil War implicitly paralleled Ormondists and Free Staters, Nuncio's men and republicans.[51] In the late 1920s Hagan published another series, Wine from the Royal Pope, on sixteenth-century Irish history, as 'C.L. MacFaelain', which is extensively cited in Myles Ronan's book on *The Reformation in Ireland under Elizabeth*.[52] The most distinguished antiquarian writer to contribute to the *Bulletin* in its later years was the Westmeath priest Paul Walsh, whom the *Bulletin* regularly cited when asserting its intellectual credentials.[53]

Corcoran carried out extensive archival research on Irish education under the penal laws, publishing lists of schools and schoolmasters from official records. (He later co-founded the Irish Manuscripts Commission.)[54] Corcoran argued that the hedge schools had been an indigenous, popularly created denominational education system suppressed in favour of inferior state national schools designed to proselytize their inmates. Daniel Corkery's *The hidden Ireland* was incorporated into this narrative by suggesting the poets became hedge-school masters.[55] Catholic inspectors employed by the Board of Education who reported unfavourably on hedge schools were dismissed as traitors to faith and fatherland; Corcoran cited travellers who gave favourable accounts of hedge schools (silently excising their criticisms).[56] He maintained that priests and people had succeeded in defeating this conspiracy and establishing a Catholic education system in all but name, not least through the leadership of Daniel O'Connell.[57] Corcoran rejected the Young Ireland view, maintained by Arthur Griffith and other separatists, of O'Connell as opportunistic and time-serving 'Whig', presenting O'Connell's mobilization of the people in his struggle against the remnants of the Catholic gentry for leadership of the Catholic community as yet another anticipation of the Civil War.[58] Corcoran believed John Henry Newman could have established a Catholic University by similar means – providing a utilitarian education for poor scholars seeking to enter the professions, granting degrees on the strength of a papal charter and challenging the state to prosecute or recognize them – if he

51 *CB*, Mar. 1937, 197–201.   52 *CB*, May 1930, 416–20.   53 *CB*, Aug. 1935, 646–53; Jan. 1936, 27; June 1937, 415–20; Nollaig Ó Muraíle, 'Walsh, Paul', *DIB*; Nollaig Ó Muraíle (ed.), *Irish leaders and learning throughout the ages: Paul Walsh – essays* (Dublin, 2003).   54 *CB*, Feb. 1939, 93–6; Michael Kennedy & Deirdre McMahon, *Reconstructing Ireland's past: a history of the Irish Manuscripts Commission* (Dublin, 2009).   55 *CB*, Feb. 1925, 159–62; Dec. 1934, 986–92; Dec. 1938, 890–3.   56 *CB*, Apr. 1935, 299–304; Jan. 1936, 56–62; May 1938, 384–5; June 1938, 501–9; D.H. Akenson review of P.J. Dowling, *The hedge schools of Ireland* in *Irish Historical Studies*, 16:62 (1968), 226–9.   57 *CB*, Jan. 1925, 60–6.   58 *CB*, Apr. 1937, 305.

had not been 'the spearhead of British Imperialism and of English penetration into the Catholic system in Ireland', distracted by English deference to unjust authority and attachment to the snobbish Oxford model.[59]

Corcoran's version of educational history allowed flexibility; when he wished to revise the curriculum in a more 'Christian' direction, by introducing scholastic philosophy or replacing geography lessons about foreign cities and international trade with explorations of local features within the natural unit of the diocese (which he hoped might replace the alien and imposed county in administration), these could be presented as undoing colonial mutilations.[60] Conversely, he defended such features of contemporary Irish education as corporal punishment, rote learning and payment by examination results as immemorial traditions even when they were nineteenth-century innovations. Corcoran opposed pupil-centred education, maintaining that students should be taught not to think for themselves but to copy the teacher.[61] Thinking for themselves was an English and Protestant fallacy promoted by that effete snob Newman and that pseudo-Catholic denier of original sin, Maria Montessori. He offered successive Irish governments the tempting prospect that the Irish language could be restored as vernacular in one generation by using the school system for immersive assimilation on the model of American public schools, whether pupils or parents wanted it or not.[62] Corcoran implemented his philosophy of teaching answers without bothering with workings by providing his students with cribs and citing the exam results to improve his own standing.[63]

Finlay and Russell were, at least on the surface, irenic figures seeking common ground between genteel Catholics and Protestants. The *Bulletin* under Corcoran was about othering – maintaining that the Anglo-Irish and Protestant tradition represented nothing but bigotry, greed and vice, and should be eradicated. In opposition to Ireland's Counter-Reformation scholars, Corcoran placed the foundation of Trinity and its feeder schools as the core of the attempt to subjugate and seduce Catholic Ireland from the sixteenth century to his own day. Regarding the Reformation as a land-grab whose religious content was mere pretence, Corcoran declared it impossible that anything of value could have been produced by godless tyrants. He quoted many eighteenth-century sources to refute claims by nineteenth-century liberal and nationalist apologists that such figures as Swift, Berkeley and Samuel Madden (founder of the Royal Dublin Society) had been Irish nationalists or

59 *CB*, May 1925, 458–65; June 1925, 584–91; Jan. 1933, 41–5; Feb. 1933, 132–7; Mar. 1933, 232–7; Apr. 1933, 320–6; May 1933, 419–24; Michael Tierney, 'Catholic University' in Michael Tierney (ed.), *A tribute to Newman* (Dublin, 1945), pp 172–206, critiques Corcoran. 60 *CB*, Dec. 1936, 992–5; Jan. 1937, 32–6; Feb. 1937, 107–11; Oct. 1937, 781–6. 61 Titley, *Church, state and the control of schooling*, pp 94–9, 117. 62 Ibid., pp 97–8. 63 John Joseph O'Meara, *The singing-masters* (Dublin, 1990).

had not supported the penal laws with 'the savagely brutal mind of England's Dean Swift'.[64] To suggest that the Protestant tradition was of equal standing with the Catholic-Gaelic, or that an Irish identity would be formed by merging them, was denial of 'the one Irish nation'.[65] Catholics seen within the boundaries of Trinity College or Alexandra College were denounced for giving scandal; targets included the historian Mary Hayden[66] and the art critic Thomas Bodkin.[67] The Cosgrave government's giving TCD a one-off grant in the early 1920s was an abiding grievance, and Cosgrave's acceptance of an honorary Trinity doctorate was denounced as a corrupt pay-off and neo-colonial servility.[68] Corcoran saw existing endowments of Protestant educational institutions as stolen from the Catholic Irish and claimed granting them public money condoned the theft at the expense of Catholic schools and students.[69] The *Bulletin* headed a report about Church of Ireland dignitaries hoping their community might make its separate and distinct contribution to national revival, 'WHY SEPARATE? WHY DISTINCT?'[70]

Corcoran admired Somerville and Ross' 'really great novel', *The real Charlotte*, as a ruthless expose of the inner emptiness of the Ascendancy,[71] and praised Constantia Maxwell's *Dublin under the Georges* as displaying the moral nullity and parasitism of the Ascendancy, whose vaunted Georgian town houses and country mansions could only have been built and maintained by ruthless rackrenting, and even then were chronically indebted. He suggested Malton's prints of *The views of Dublin* were designed to impress English moneylenders.[72]

Corcoran noted the quasi-pornographic element in elite Trinity classicism[73] (as in post-Renaissance humanism generally) and presented contemporary 'immoral' writers as heirs to this distinctively Ascendancy and British decadence. The *Bulletin* frequently attacked the *Irish Statesman* and its opposition to literary censorship as a combination of obscenity deriving from Protestantism degenerating into paganism (W.B. Yeats' 'Sordid Swan Song', 'Leda and the Swan', was a favourite target)[74] and neo-colonial economics promoted by the Theosophist George Russell, 'the Mouthing Mahatma'.[75] Yeats was regularly described as 'Pollexfen', apparently to highlight his description of his maternal uncle's Masonic funeral in the poem 'In memory of Alfred Pollexfen'.[76] Long after the demise of the *Irish Statesman*, the *Catholic Bulletin* was still denouncing

---

64 *CB*, July 1931, 679–83; July 1933, 589–92; Dec. 1933, 1000–4; Mar. 1938, 211–16; Mar. 1926, 300–6; Mar. 1936, 256 (Swift); Apr. 1936, 315–19 (Berkeley); May 1939, 333–6.   65 *CB*, July 1937, 546–7; June 1939, 409–11.   66 *CB*, Apr. 1930, 367; June 1931, 537–9; July 1931, 641–5.   67 *CB*, Apr. 1933, 288–91.   68 *CB*, Dec. 1931, 1163; Jan. 1933, 18–19; July 1933, 573.   69 *CB*, Feb. 1936, 148–55; May 1936, 402–7; July 1938, 563–5.   70 *CB*, Aug. 1939, 429.   71 *CB*, Feb. 1937, 118–22.   72 *CB*, Aug. 1936, 667ff; Nov. 1937, 846–7.   73 *CB*, Oct. 1933, 830.   74 *CB*, Mar. 1926, 248–51.   75 *CB*, Oct. 1928, 988–92; Mar. 1938, 185–6.   76 *CB*, Sept. 1926, 937–43; Aug. 1927, 821–5; Mar. 1936, 183–4; Apr. 1939, 241–4.

its contributors as producers of smutty literature for the British market, paid for by the Teapot Dome scandal (in which the *Statesman*'s sponsor, the Irish-American oil magnate Edward Doheny, had been implicated).[77] Corcoran, who had been acquainted with Roger Casement through Gaelic League work for Connemara and recalled him as a stainless knight errant,[78] denounced Yeats for capitalizing on the publication of William Moloney's *The forged Casement diaries* with a 'bockety ballad':

> The door should have been finally and firmly shut on all such pretend-ers. They have elected to address themselves to the literary world of [John] Bull. To Bull, then, they should go, and having gone, they should be made to know that in Bulldom they should stay placed.[79]

The literati were not the only target of the *Bulletin*'s attacks; much polemic was directed against the attempts of the Cosgrave government to use art and literature to promote the Irish Free State abroad. The Abbey Theatre, which received a government subsidy, was the principal target. Desmond FitzGerald provided ammunition by praising James Joyce. (The *Bulletin* noted FitzGerald's connection with the Central Catholic Library.)[80] The *Bulletin* exacerbated the controversy over the stained-glass window showing Irish literary characters commissioned from Harry Clarke for the League of Nations headquarters in Geneva. It denounced the nature of the figures and the choice of writers (e.g., 'Augusta Persse Gregory posing as St Brigid') and suggested that the window be located in Plunkett House as the shrine of Russell's new religion.[81]

The Central Catholic Library, linked to members of the government, was regularly attacked for such offences as inviting Yeats to lecture.[82] In 1936, when the library's founder, Stephen Brown, SJ (who contributed lists of suitable Catholic reading to early issues of the *Bulletin*), suggested in *Studies* that at one time the *Bulletin* had used intemperate political language, Corcoran replied:

> We have poured out corrosive language, time and again, on the sor-did Catholic flunkeyism of Catholic societies which are largely and continuously associated with alleged Catholic families infected by the putrescence of Cromwellian Puritanism, in whose secularist effluent they souse themselves within Trinity College Dublin.[83]

77 *CB*, Sept. 1935, 702–4; Aug. 1936, 657–61; Oct. 1936, 826; Ian d'Alton, 'In a "comity of cultures": the rise and fall of the *Irish Statesman*' in Mark O'Brien & Felix M. Larkin (eds), *Periodicals and journalism in twentieth-century Ireland* (Dublin, 2014), pp 102–22. 78 *CB*, May 1936, 431–2. 79 *CB*, Mar. 1937, 171. 80 *CB*, Jan. 1933, 52–6. For Joyce see *CB*, July 1931, 690–4. 81 *CB*, Feb. 1931, 108–9; Mar. 1931, 218–20. 82 *CB*, Feb. 1930, 97–101; 107–10. 83 *CB*, Oct. 1936, 784–6.

The *Bulletin*'s attacks on alleged Catholics-in-name-only were not confined to such obvious targets as Oliver St John Gogarty, whose Senate membership provided an opportunity to denounce Cosgrave – 'Malachi Mulligan emerged from the sewer-stream of *Ulysses*, and dripped his delicate way into Leinster House'[84] – but extended to Michael Tierney, denounced for alleged feebleness on opposing divorce and for criticizing literary censorship legislation as a TD in the late 1920s.[85] When Tierney and the Celtic scholar Daniel Binchy claimed that compulsory Irish as favoured by Corcoran was damaging education and failed to convey the actual content of Gaelic culture, the *Bulletin* denounced them for opposing the will of the majority, equating Binchy with the Trinity academic Robert Atkinson (who in 1899 tried to have Irish removed from the school curriculum on the grounds that the spoken language was hopelessly corrupt). The *Bulletin* also denounced 'the peculiar quality of his published opinions on the position of the German State'.[86] Binchy, formerly a diplomat in Berlin, had criticized the Third Reich in *Studies*.[87]

Corcoran saw commercialization and pastoralization of Irish agriculture ever since the Famine as an ongoing genocide, depopulating Ireland while supplying Britain with cheap food and cheap immigrant labour to be deracinated and ground up in its industrial cities: 'For eighty years, down in fact to the fall of Cosgravism, fortune seemed to be on the side of the exterminators.'[88] The *Bulletin* responded to Royal Dublin Society bicentenary celebrations with impassioned diatribes about 'the licentious Masonic Powerhouse at Ballsbridge', in unholy alliance with the Railway Companies and the Ranchers' Association.[89] It suggested that the RDS should be taken over by the state because important national functions should not be entrusted to a body devoted to rearing horses and livestock for export.[90] Corcoran called Sir Horace Plunkett's cooperative movement a top-down state-subsidized imposition attacking the superior indigenous system of cooperation through mutual aid, which Corcoran believed was documented in Conrad Arensberg's *The Irish countryman*.[91] Where Finlay saw Plunkett's cooperativism as revitalizing a Catholic rural civilization, Corcoran regarded Plunkett as the incarnation of West British corruption, his attempts to professionalize agricultural and technical education as a scheme to provide jobs for hungry and incompetent Freemasons, and his promotion of Irish commercial agricultural exports as fostering dependence and exploitation.[92] Plunkett's elevation of Denmark (which had overtaken Irish agricultural goods in the British markets by emphasizing marketing and quality control)

84 *CB*, May 1937, 324. **85** *CB*, Feb. 1929, 97–104; Feb. 1933, 142–8. **86** *CB*, Dec. 1936, 949–57. **87** Tom Garvin, *The lives of Daniel Binchy: Irish scholar, diplomat, public intellectual* (Dublin, 2016). **88** *CB*, Apr. 1936, 347. **89** *CB*, Feb. 1931, 126–33; Jan. 1933, 20–2; 31–2. **90** *CB*, June 1936, 479. **91** *CB*, Oct. 1930, 904–11; May 1937, 381–2. **92** *CB*, Mar. 1928, 221–6; Feb. 1931, 110–16; July 1935, 518–22; 558–66.

as a model for Ireland was met by claims that praise for the Danish folk-school model undermined Catholic schools,[93] and by noting damage inflicted on Danish agriculture in the interwar years by British attempts at greater self-sufficiency in food.[94] The Cosgrave government's continuation of Plunkett's policies under Hogan was seen by Corcoran as one of the surest signs of its servility. Corcoran advocated turning away from exports and creating a nation of tillage-based self-subsisting smallholders existing outside the monetary economy altogether. (From 1915 the *Bulletin* published articles by Patrick Nolan, OSB, arguing that eighteenth-century opponents of the establishment of the Bank of Ireland were correct and banks in general were harmful.)[95] Corcoran described Dublin as an alien city only reclaimed by the Irish nation after the 1885 extension of the parliamentary franchise,[96] and wanted industry limited to the decentralized supply of necessary goods for a predominantly rural population.[97] Even J.M. Keynes' 1933 UCD lecture, a partial defence of protectionism, was denounced as 'laudation of … Pasture policy [by] a smug mouthpiece of Britain'.[98] Corcoran, who frequently declared a high birth rate desirable for its own sake (he cited statistical analysis by Roy Geary to dispute claims that the Irish birthrate was decreasing),[99] predicted that through land division, turning pasture to tillage and reclaiming waste land, Ireland could support a population of 13 million.[100] This reflected an idealized view of pre-Famine Ireland; it also reflected the 'distributism' of the English Catholic writers G.K. Chesterton (whom Corcoran admired as one of the few English patriots not to be a hater of Ireland)[101] and Hilaire Belloc, who advocated a Merrie England of small producers free from 'Jewish' international finance. The *Bulletin* noted Belloc's despair at the inability of degenerate Britain to implement this, but suggested Ireland was well placed to succeed.[102]

The term 'bureaucracy' was first used in English in the 1820s to refer to the Dublin Castle administration and during the nineteenth century nostalgic Tory-paternalists, farmers who considered themselves overtaxed, and religious spokespersons who believed social services better delivered by religiously inspired volunteers rather than secular professionals, complained that a colonial bureaucracy was denying local elites the powers of their British counterparts. Corcoran shared this distrust of bureaucratic professionalism, suggesting in the 1930s that de Valera's government should halve the salaries of all civil servants, a privileged class living in luxury.[103] At the same time Corcoran

93 *CB*, Jan. 1926, 10–13. 94 *CB*, Jan. 1933, 1–6; Aug. 1936, 631. 95 *CB*, Mar. 1929, 267–70. 96 *CB*, Mar. 1937, 207 but see June 1937, 441–5. 97 *CB*, June 1936, 471ff; July 1936, 575. 98 *CB*, May 1933, 398–9; July 1933, 529–35. 99 *CB*, Dec. 1936, 943ff. 100 *CB*, Sept. 1936, 746, 101 *CB*, July 1936, 612; Aug. 1936, 693. 102 *CB*, Mar. 1936, 232; July 1936, 611; Mar. 1937, 220. 103 *CB*, Feb. 1933, 104–6; Feb. 1935, 99–107.

was a skilled bureaucratic warrior building a clientele of graduate students and placing protégés in academic posts. Corcoran as bureaucratic warrior appears in his commentary on the appointment of the Protestant Trinity graduate Letitia Dunbar-Harrison as county librarian of Mayo in 1930–1. Where some who maintained that a librarianship was an educational post to be filled on denominational lines exempted Dunbar-Harrison from accusations of personal malice, Corcoran emphasized uncertainty surrounding her name (she was brought up by relatives and hyphenated their name with her birth name) and hinted that female Trinity students were devoid of religion and morality.[104]

Corcoran drew on claims of low academic standards in Trinity (made during long-running late nineteenth- and early twentieth-century debates over the creation of a rival academic institution acceptable to Catholics) to call Dunbar-Harrison's academic qualifications worthless; he ascribed her appointment to a conspiracy by Masonic civil service networks adjusting supposedly neutral job requirements to favour their candidates, and claimed proper Catholic administrators could only be secured by appointments at local level rather than through the Local Appointments Commission set up by the Cosgrave government.[105] The *Irish Times*' statement that the commission had cleaned out an Augean stables of local corruption was dismissed as a snobbish assault on Irish capacity for self-government.[106] Corcoran maintained that Protestants should receive civil service jobs in proportion to their share of the twenty-six county population – 7 per cent – and be excluded from any post, especially educational occupations such as librarian, which might enable them to undermine the faith and morals of the Catholic people.[107] Cosgrave and his ministers were presented as uneducated pawns, with Richard Mulcahy (who, as minister for local government, oversaw Dunbar-Harrison's installation) dismissed as a 'Politico-Military Bully' guided by 'Brass-Hat Boyos'.[108] Corcoran maintained that even if Dunbar-Harrison was the academically best-qualified candidate, she would still be unfit; even if she succeeded in learning Irish, she would be the successor of nineteenth-century Protestant proselytizers who used Irish to advance their nefarious aims.[109] A suggestion that Dunbar-Harrison might inspect local library branches (rapidly closing down through a boycott) produced a comparison with inspection tours by eighteenth-century Church of Ireland officials aimed at detecting and suppressing Catholic schools.[110] When the Dáil debated Dunbar-Harrison's appointment, Sean T. O'Kelly reiterated the *Bulletin*'s accusations:

104 *CB*, Jan. 1931, 1–7. 105 *CB*, Jan. 1931, 4–5; Feb. 1931, 102–5. 106 *CB*, Jan. 1931, 13–14. 107 *CB*, Jan. 1931, 17–18. 108 *CB*, Jan. 1931, 16; Feb. 1931, 97–8; Mar. 1931, 216. 109 *CB*, Jan. 1931, 6–7; Mar. 1931, 210–15. 110 *CB*, Mar. 1931, 235–9; Apr. 1931, 321–3.

> I happen to have read ... the *Catholic Bulletin* for January ... I was informed
> on the most reliable authority that the person who writes them is almost
> as well qualified as the Minister for Local Government to know what he
> is writing about ... I have been reading the *Catholic Bulletin* for many years
> [except during the Civil War] ... the Minister for Local Government
> would not allow good Catholic literature like the *Catholic Bulletin* into
> prisons.

The government specifically repudiated the *Bulletin*'s accusations, with W.T.
Cosgrave adding that he had not read that publication since its comments on
Michael Collins' death – 'a very serious mistake against Christianity'.[111]
   Corcoran opposed any safeguards for minorities as an unacceptable restriction on the freedom of the majority; he opposed proportional representation
and advocated unicameralism after the abolition of the Free State Senate.[112]
The *Bulletin* claimed the Cosgrave government of 1927–32 was illegitimate
because by-elections showed Fianna Fáil was supported by the majority of
Catholics and Cumann na nGaedheal was kept in power by Protestant/
unionist TDs.[113] During the Mayo Library controversy, the *Bulletin* suggested
that Dunbar-Harrison's appointment reflected a corrupt bargain by Cumann
na nGaedheal to secure Protestant votes in a Co. Dublin by-election by winning the approval of the *Irish Times*.[114] The *Bulletin* repeatedly attacked Eoin
O'Duffy and the Blueshirts for not being proper fascists. It argued that de
Valera's policies of encouraging wheat cultivation, land reclamation and rural
repopulation and his promotion of autarky were more in line with those of
Mussolini than the warmed-over Hoganism of the Blueshirts.[115] To increase
the resemblance to Mussolini, the *Catholic Bulletin* called for elections to be
suspended during the Economic War and criticism of Fianna Fail's economic
policy to be punished as treason.[116] Corcoran had doubts about protectionism, which he noted led to profiteering and favouritism. Instead, he argued,
the government should pursue a 'Reserved Home Market' – allowing imports
only when a demand could not be met by home industry, while encouraging
import replacement.[117]
   Corcoran failed to realize how far his advocacy of suppressing unCath-
olic intellectuals and artists encouraged outward conformity and inward
insincerity. Joseph O'Neill, the secretly atheist secretary of the department

111 Dáil Éireann, vol. 39 (4), 17 June 1931.   112 *CB*, Mar. 1933, 210–11; Apr. 1936, 282–8, 320ff; Oct. 1936, 867–9.   113 *CB*, May 1930, 430–3 & 441–5; Jan. 1933, 19.   114 *CB*, Jan. 1931, 13–15 & 28–9.   115 *CB*, Oct. 1933, 820–; Nov. 1933, 890–8; Dec. 1933, 979–90; Jan. 1934, 39–45; Feb. 1933, 132–40; Mar. 1934, 235–43; Apr. 1934, 315–20; May 1934, 388–406; June 1934, 476–85; Feb. 1938, 116–21.   116 *CB*, Jan. 1933, 33–4.   117 *CB*, Feb. 1928, 121; Mar. 1928, 217–20.

of education, publicly flattered Corcoran as promoter of Catholic faith and learning.[118] O'Neill also wrote fantasy fiction, including the 1935 novel *Land under England* whose narrator discovers descendants of Roman legionaries living in a vast cave system near Hadrian's Wall, with a totalitarian system worshipping the Roman state. One chapter describes a schoolroom where children are tormented and brainwashed into mindless conformity. The novel implicitly attacks O'Neill's ancestral Catholicism, as the ghost of the Roman empire, and Corcoran's vision of education. Corcoran may have suspected O'Neill was less devout than he pretended: a brief review of O'Neill's 1936 *Day of wrath*, a nihilistic novel of future world war, protests that 'this trashy, English book, empty of all trace of culture, gravity and taste goes to the world as the work of an official whose vocation it is to watch over Irish youth and to foster the culture of the Christian Gael'.[119] Another beneficiary of Corcoran's intellectual myopia was Robin Dudley Edwards. Although Corcoran expressed concern over Irish historians such as Edwards attending the Institute of Historical Research in London University (which he saw as a centre of Protestant imperialist propaganda) and wanted academics trained at Louvain and the Roman colleges,[120] he praised Edwards' *Church and state in Tudor Ireland* as a great Catholic historical work exposing the cruel and sordid imposition of the Reformation.[121] The *Bulletin* welcomed *Irish Historical Studies* while regretting 'its extreme detachment … When will some scholars learn that nationality is not a sin against enlightenment?'[122] Corcoran also admired an article by Edwards in the Franciscan magazine *Assisi* describing an attempt by elements in the Confederation to establish the duke of Lorraine as Catholic monarch of an independent Ireland; Corcoran compared its Ormondist opponents to Catholic Basques who supported the republic in the Spanish Civil War.[123]

By the late 1930s Corcoran, though still praising de Valera as a combination of Benjamin Franklin, Bertrand du Guesclin and the ancient Gaelic nobility who emigrated to Spain, was concerned that Fianna Fáil was not fully implementing land division. He was annoyed when the minister for agriculture suggested the live cattle trade had some value and the Economic War was not an unmitigated blessing.[124] Corcoran feared industrialization behind tariff barriers encouraged an influx of Jewish capitalists, whose exploitative profit-seeking would create a deracinated urban proletariat and produce Soviet-style socialism, especially if a deteriorating England repatriated Irish emigrants

118 Titley, *Church, state and the control of schooling*, 100 & 102–3; Patrick Maume, 'O'Neill, Joseph James (Seosamh Ó Néill)', *DIB*; M. Kelly Lynch, 'The smiling public man: Joseph O'Neill and his works, a literary biography', *Journal of Irish Literature*, 12 (1983), 3–72. 119 *CB*, June 1936, 516–17. 120 *CB*, June 1935, 442–3. 121 *CB*, Aug. 1935, 630–7. 122 *CB*, Apr. 1938, 323. 123 *CB*, Nov. 1936, 931. 124 *CB*, Apr. 1935, 267–8; Nov. 1936, 889–96; June 1938, 475–6.

exposed to leftist influence (he thought this likely within a decade).[125] The *Bulletin* cited J.B. Priestley's account of industrial collapse in northern England, *English journey*, as proof of the dangers of over-industrialization, adding that British unemployment was due to physical and mental degradation of a native population devoid of religion and morality.[126]

Despite Corcoran's fears of Ireland succumbing to urbanism, international developments in the 1930s provided consolation. The *Bulletin* did not share de Valera's faith in the potential of the League of Nations, which it compared to the Tower of Babel. Stephen Brown, SJ was attacked for promoting the League of Nations Society of Ireland.[127] It noted that attempts to regulate bombing aircraft failed because Britain (represented by Lord Londonderry as air minister) insisted on maintaining bomber forces outside Europe to use against colonial rebellions.[128] The *Bulletin* added that if Britain could spend huge sums on rearmament in the second half of the 1930s, 'Bull the Bilker' could have resumed payment on First World War debts to the United States.[129] The disclosure of the Hoare-Laval Pact (a surreptitious attempt by the British and French foreign ministers to end the Italo-Abyssinian War on terms reducing Abyssinia to a landlocked rump state) was greeted by mockery of the impotence of the League to restrain its strongest members, and of British hypocrisy in abandoning Haile Selassie. At the same time, the *Bulletin* attributed the failure of the Pact to Anglo-French realization that they could not challenge Italian naval power in the Mediterranean, where Mussolini was as supreme as Caesar Augustus.[130]

Hitler was a more awkward object of admiration because of conflict between Nazi neo-paganism and assertion of state control and Catholic attempts to assert independence within the state, symbolized by Pius XI's encyclical *Mit brenneder sorge*. The *Bulletin*'s Roman correspondent reported with distaste a lecture in Rome by Hitler's legal adviser Hans Frank (sentenced to death at the 1946 Nuremberg trials), who declared that papal criticism of Nazi eugenics reflected reliance of Roman law on abstract concepts, which should give way to the 'law of the blood'.[131] Nevertheless the *Bulletin* made valiant attempts to square the circle. A regular commentator on foreign affairs, 'Fear Faire' (a schoolteacher),[132] presented the Anschluss as comparable to ending partition, remarking that if a new Wolfe Tone were to arise in the North and reunify Ireland as Hitler regained Austria, Irish Catholics might overlook his failings. Invoking an idealized image of the Hapsburg empire as the

---

125 *CB*, Jan. 1937, 27–31; May 1937, 354; Sept. 1937, 686–94.   **126** *CB*, Oct. 1934, 815–22; Aug. 1935, 603–7; Sept. 1935, 672–82.   **127** *CB*, Oct. 1930, 920–2; Dec. 1935, 924–33.   **128** *CB*, July 1933, 647–9; Jan. 1938, 2–9.   **129** *CB*, Jan. 1933, 6–10; Aug. 1936, 630.   **130** *CB*, Jan. 1936, 1–20; July 1936, 535ff.   **131** *CB* May, 1936, 399–401.   **132** Pat Walsh (ed.), *The* Catholic Bulletin *on peace, war and neutrality* (Belfast, 2004).

last remnant of Catholic Christendom, 'Fear Faire' claimed that although the
Nazi leaders might be imperfect, Germany's natural Catholic traditions would
reassert themselves if Britain would cease to intrigue against German reclamation of her natural position in Europe.[133] Corcoran and 'Fear Faire' denounced
Czechoslovakia as an artificial state created by Freemasons at Versailles, a
Russian dagger into the heart of central Europe now rightly dismantled by
Hitler; Corcoran attributed the outcome of the Munich crisis to the power
of prayer defeating the intrigues of British and French warmongers.[134] He
nevertheless expected a war in the near future, as resurgent Germany and Italy
sought to share the African empires of decadent Britain and France.[135] 'Fear
Faire' described Hitler's demand for the Polish Corridor as reasonable.[136] The
Bulletin accompanied reprints of its 1916 coverage with a commentary stating
that the First World War had been 'a sordid trade war' caused by British jeal-
ousy of Germany, implying that sympathy for the Allies in the coming war
was as foolish as Redmondite acceptance of British promises and appeals for
little Belgium. Thus, in its dying years, the *Catholic Bulletin* advocated the policy
attributed to de Valera during the Second World War by overseas opponents:
self-righteous isolationism in foreign affairs; complete economic autarky,
with poverty seen almost as intrinsically desirable; and exultation over Axis
advances and coming British downfall, combined with assertions that Nazi
Germany was morally equivalent or superior to Britain.

This chapter suggests that the break between nineteenth- and twentieth-
century nationalism has been overestimated, and that the conflicts of which
the *Catholic Bulletin* was part can be traced back, in terms of the self-perception
of the participants, to the Land War and earlier struggles over the decline of
Protestant Ascendancy. In previous research on D.P. Moran and the *Leader*, I
suggested Moran's version of nationalism fitted nicely with Ernest Gellner's
modernist analysis of nationalism as driven by ethno-religious struggles for
control of education, bureaucracy and the professions in the context of the
modern requirement for universal literacy.[137] The *Catholic Bulletin*'s emphasis on
defeating Trinity College and its influence networks can be seen in Gellnerian
terms, but its self-image is more reminiscent of Anthony D. Smith's rival pri-
mordialist analysis presenting nationalism as the development of older identity
narratives, often religiously based and formed in the early modern or medieval
periods.[138] More case studies of Irish newspaper and periodical culture would
be useful in testing these and similar theories.

133 *CB*, May 1938, 362–5; Apr. 1939, 224–34.   134 *CB*, Nov. 1937, 830–1; Oct. 1938, 741–2; Nov. 1938,
797–99 & 808–15.   135 *CB*, Feb. 1936, 106–10; Apr. 1937, 243–5.   136 *CB*, June 1939, 373–5.   137 Patrick
Maume, 'Irish-Ireland and Catholic Whiggery: D.P. Moran and the *Leader*' in O'Brien & Larkin, *Periodicals
and journalism*, pp 47–60.   138 Anthony D. Smith, *National identity* (Reno, NV, 1991).

15 / Influencing the influential: Irish Jesuit periodicals

DECLAN O'KEEFFE

In 1814 the Society of Jesus was restored worldwide and returned to Ireland against a background of the relaxation of the penal laws. The Jesuits were the great educators of Europe, and Ireland in the nineteenth and twentieth centuries would provide fertile ground for their mission. Their aim was to influence the influential in society and to gradually change the system from within. They realized their vision most obviously through education and more subtly through publications. In addition to founding six schools and a theological faculty, [1] they had considerable involvement in the Catholic University. Institutions such as these were important breeding grounds for the Jesuits, who wanted to have their men in position to take on a leadership role when home rule arrived. In the absence of local political institutions in Ireland, the arts, and literature in particular, assumed greater importance and were central to the hopes and aspirations of the burgeoning Catholic middle class. In the second half of the century the Jesuits laid the foundations for several significant journals, three of which have survived to the present day. These ranged from the devotional *Irish Messenger of the Sacred Heart* and *Madonna* to the avowedly intellectual *Lyceum, New Ireland Review* and *Studies* by way of the *Irish Monthly*. In addition Thomas Finlay, SJ, who had a hand in the founding of all but one of these, founded the *Irish Homestead*, the mouthpiece of the Irish cooperative movement. Tom Finlay was accepted and respected in salon and farmstead alike and appreciated that 'the way to influence was by the printed word, lectures and informed conversation'.[2] Finlay knew the importance of the written word, and in particular periodicals, in polite society and noted in his first editorial in the *Irish Homestead* that 'Not to have a publication is to be in danger of being thought insignificant.'[3]

THE *IRISH MONTHLY*

In 1834 Matthew Russell was born in Ballybot, Newry, Co. Down into a family of high achievers and a society in search of high achievements.

---

1 Clongowes, Tullabeg, Belvedere, Crescent and Mungret Colleges and Coláiste Iognáid.   2 Thomas J. Morrissey, SJ, *Thomas A. Finlay, SJ, 1848–1940: educationalist, editor, social reformer* (Dublin, 2004), pp 56–7.   3 Ibid., p. 94.

His uncle, Dr Charles Russell, was president of Maynooth, while his elder brother Charles was attorney general under Gladstone and the first Catholic lord chief justice since the Reformation. Matthew entered the Society of Jesus in 1857 and cut his literary teeth on the English *Messenger of the Sacred Heart* while studying in Wales. When Ireland was consecrated to the Sacred Heart in 1873, he felt that the country should have a *Messenger* of her own, but trouble arose when he wrote to the English editor, William Meagher, SJ, as a courtesy to tell him of his plans, only to be told that an Irish rival would ruin the English *Messenger*. The issue was resolved when Russell agreed not to use the title *Messenger of the Sacred Heart*, and the first issue of his new journal, *Catholic Ireland*, appeared on 20 June 1873, the feast of the Sacred Heart of Jesus. Russell's colleague, the aforementioned Thomas Finlay, suggested the name *Catholic Ireland*, to which Russell mischievously added *A Monthly Memorial to the Sacred Heart of Jesus*, 'with the abortive *Messenger of the Sacred Heart* in my mind'. Although an avowedly religious magazine, Russell noted that the contributions 'soon gave the little magazine a more literary character' and in December the title *Irish Monthly: A Magazine of General Literature* was used, with a flyleaf 'to explain that we were not worthy of so high a name as *Catholic Ireland*'.[4] It would be another twelve years before an Irish *Messenger* would appear courtesy of James Cullen, SJ

From the outset the Jesuits were very supportive of the magazine and did not overburden Russell with priestly duties, as well as 'freeing him from temporal cares which he was not very well fitted to deal with'.[5] Russell's talents lay in editing, writing and persuading others to contribute to the fledgling monthly; he was less happy when dealing with the practical side of producing a magazine, and finances were a regular concern.[6] The *Irish Monthly* was 'a landmark of Irish publishing [which] published a steady trickle of creative writing of the highest order'.[7] It was remarkably successful in an era when the average life span for such publications was five years.[8] The early volumes of the monthly gave a good flavour of the sort of contributions and contributors that would be found in its pages. Articles of a religious nature featured, while religious poetry from the pen of Aubrey de Vere was scattered among works by D.F. McCarthy, J.F. O'Donnell and Lady Georgiana Fullerton. Initially, in keeping with the original title, *Catholic Ireland*, books reviewed were of a pious nature such as *Devotion to the Sacred Heart*, but poetry,

---

4 Matthew Russell, 'The origin of the *Irish Monthly*', Irish Jesuit Archives (hereafter IJA), J27/175, 2–8. 5 George O'Neill, SJ, 'In memoriam', *Irish Monthly*, 40:472 (Oct. 1912), 543. 6 Russell, 'The origin of the *Irish Monthly*', 9–12. 7 Tom Clyde, *Irish literary magazines; an outline history and descriptive bibliography* (Dublin, 2003), p. 136. 8 Lambert McKenna, SJ, 'Our golden jubilee', *Irish Monthly*, 51:595 (Jan. 1923), 1.

history and fiction soon found favour and the monthly quickly established a reputation for publishing fiction favourable to the hopes of the Catholic upper middle class.

William Delany, SJ (of Catholic University fame), his friend since student days, noted that Russell 'was to provide openings for many of the young writers who inaugurated the Anglo-Irish literary revival' and people of many different backgrounds and beliefs wrote for him, including Hilaire Belloc, Rosa Mulholland, Katherine Tynan, W.B. Yeats and Oscar Wilde.[9] Yeats called it 'a kind of college of the bards'[10] and advised one aspiring writer to 'send these poems to the *Irish Monthly* ... the only literary magazine in Ireland'.[11] Katherine Tynan, in her tribute, called Russell the 'the young writer's saint'. Echoing Yeats' 'college of the bards', she argued that not only did he provide a mouthpiece for aspirant writers, but he helped to train them. In Ireland, the nineteenth century was a fertile period for female writers, and the *Irish Monthly* 'was especially diligent in promoting writing by women, and in recording biographical information about the women published'. In its first twenty-five years, the magazine published novels by nineteen writers, of whom thirteen were women.[12] In 1886 the monthly commenced a series of 'Nutshell Biograms', condensing into a paragraph 'the chief facts in the careers of various interesting persons ... for the most part Irish',[13] and for some female writers these constitute the only biographical source.[14]

The Catholic Church was resurgent in the late nineteenth century in Ireland and, given their mission to educate the influential in society and change the system from within, it is not surprising that the Jesuits encouraged the *Irish Monthly* and Matthew Russell in his efforts to produce a periodical that 'may be the forerunner of a Catholic literature in Ireland'.[15] In 1885 Russell serialized one of the most significant novels of the Land War, Rosa Mulholland's bestselling *Marcella Grace*. The aim of such fiction was to challenge the stereotypical view of John Bull's other island that pertained in Britain and to replace it with the image that the Catholic upper middle class envisioned, 'that of being a respectable and respected centre of a peaceful society in harmonious relationship with metropolitan Britain'.[16] Russell was concerned about British perceptions and misconceptions of Ireland and was keen that the monthly be

9 Thomas J. Morrissey, *Towards a national university: William J. Delany, SJ (1835–1924)* (Dublin, 1983), p. 17. 10 Yeats to Russell, 31 Jan. 1889, IJA, J27/148. 11 Dominic Daly, *The young Douglas Hyde* (Dublin, 1974), p. 214. 12 Anne Colman, 'Far from silent: nineteenth-century Irish women writers' in Margaret Kelleher & James H. Murphy (eds), *Gender perspectives in nineteenth-century Ireland: public and private spheres* (Dublin 1997), p. 204. 13 *Irish Monthly*, 14:152 (Feb. 1886), 108. 14 Colman, 'Far from silent', p. 204. 15 Matthew Russell, 'Irish literature and our twelfth anniversary', *Irish Monthly*, 13:145 (July 1885), 335 16 James H. Murphy, *Catholic fiction and social reality in Ireland, 1873–1922* (Dublin, 1991), pp 18–22.

non-judgmental in its attitude to non-Catholics in general and non-Catholic writers in particular. In the preface to the first issue, he wrote of his intention 'to enlist the sympathy of others besides those who are attracted towards piety and religion for their own sake',[17] and he was as good as his word. For Yeats he was 'a Catholic priest of the most courteous, kindly and liberal mind',[18] and Katharine Tynan said that 'everywhere he touched ... he dispelled a prejudice. No Protestant who had ever known Father Russell could go on believing evil of Catholics and Catholicism.'[19]

The nature of the Irish literary scene was changing as the century turned, and to some extent the monthly got lost in the twilight and seemed to be losing touch with contemporary literature.[20] Change was also afoot among Jesuit publications. *Studies* was launched in 1912, the year Russell died, and the monthly began to transform from a literary journal 'to concentrate on Catholic social and educational thought' thereafter.[21] It was probably inevitable that the monthly would be squeezed between *Studies* and the devotional *Irish Messenger,* with *Studies* competing with it for both readers and advertising. Circulation had never exceeded 1,000 copies and under the editorship of Lambert McKenna, SJ it began to specialize and to give 'more attention to contemporary issues, particularly education'.[22] Writing in 1930 McKenna lauded the monthly for its 'long career of service, a period during which over a score of magazines of a somewhat similar literary character ... have been founded, and passed away'. He notes how, 'of late years the *Irish Monthly* has been somewhat less detachedly literary and somewhat more energetically interested in all the developments of modern Irish thought and feeling [with] more space and attention ... given to points of Catholic doctrine and ethics ... the rights and duties of Catholic citizenship ... and to discussions of Irish educational problems'.[23]

McKenna expanded on the last point, explaining that there was no journal in Ireland 'expressly devoted to the discussion of Irish Catholic educational affairs ... while our educational system is in a tentative and unstabilised condition'. He went on to explain that henceforth the monthly would 'devote itself mainly to educational matters' ranging from the organization and management of schools 'to those actually engaged in teaching'. The editor accepted that popular support for such a publication was unlikely to be forthcoming and hoped that sustenance might come from 'those people whose interests it

17 Russell, 'Our aims and hopes', *Irish Monthly,* 1:1 (July 1873), 3.   18 Daly, *The young Douglas Hyde,* p. 214.   19 Katharine Tynan, 'Dearest of friends', *Irish Monthly,* 45:472 (Oct. 1912), 551–4.   20 Clyde, *Irish literary magazines,* p. 136.   21 Fergus O'Donoghue, SJ, 'The *Irish Monthly*', IJA, J27/195.   22 *Idem,* 'Irish Jesuit publications', *Doctrine and Life,* 38 (1988), 324–6 at 325.   23 Lambert McKenna, 'The *Irish Monthly*' in *The Irish Jesuit Directory and Year Book* (Dublin, 1930), 168–70.

serves: Irish Catholic teachers, Primary and Secondary, Clerical, Religious and Lay' and (in a sales pitch worthy of Russell) encouraged immediate subscriptions as well touting for written contributions from such folk with 'fruitful suggestions to put forward, and reasoned judgments, whether of commendation or complaint, to pronounce'.[24] Despite talk of closure in 1929 the journal continued to appear, but by 1933 it was in financial difficulties, with a circulation of about 600.[25] A new editor, T.J. Mulcahy, SJ, tried to make it more sociological, 'less literary and less vague', but in 1937 his provincial thought that 'it was still too literary'.[26] Nonetheless, it managed to continue at eighty pages per issue for another twenty years until – in September 1954 – it begged 'to inform our subscribers, contributors and advertisers that publication of the *IRISH MONTHLY* is to be temporarily discontinued from this issue'[27] and the journal quietly departed the periodical scene following an unbroken run of 973 issues in eighty-one years.

FROM *ATLANTIS* TO *NEW IRELAND*

Many of the periodicals in nineteenth-century Ireland adhered to various 'traditions' or lines of thought such as the Fenian tradition, the Young Ireland tradition, the colonial tradition and so on. One such 'tradition' found its apogee in *Studies*. We may trace a line from Cardinal Newman's *Atlantis* through Finlay's *Lyceum* and *New Ireland Review* to *Studies*. *Atlantis: A Register of Literature and Science*, 'Conducted by Members of the Catholic University of Ireland', was founded by Newman in 1858 'in order to afford to the faculty of the Catholic University … an organ in which they could give to the public the results of their studies [and] to aid in the creation of a Catholic Literature'.[28] The journal contained long scholarly articles replete with detailed footnotes and diagrams. It was intended that it would appear twice a year, but this only occurred in 1858 and 1859. Number V appeared on schedule, but number VI made its tardy appearance two years late and contained an insert 'To the Reader' explaining that 'Henceforward the *Atlantis* will be published at irregular intervals'.[29] It quickly ran out of steam and appeared only three more times before its demise in 1870, by which time its founder had long departed these shores.

24 Ibid. 25 O'Donoghue, 'The *Irish Monthly*', IJA, J27/195. 26 *Idem*, 'Irish Jesuit publications', 325. 27 'Front matter', *Irish Monthly*, 89:973 (Sept. 1954), 2. 28 Stephen J. Brown, *The press in Ireland: a survey and a guide* (New York, 1971), p. 68. 29 *The Atlantis: a Register of Literature and Science* (conducted by members of the Catholic University of Ireland), no. VI (1862).

THE *LYCEUM*

Nonetheless, *Atlantis* provided the germ of an idea and in 1887 the *Lyceum: A Monthly Educational and Literary Magazine and Review* was founded by the 'occupational descendants of Newman ... a group of professors in University College, chief among whom were the brothers [Tom and Peter] Finlay'.[30] The 'Prefatory' was not shy about the new journal's religious provenance and echoed the aims of its spiritual predecessor: 'To promote a higher *Catholic* literature, to discuss questions of scientific and literary interest from the *Catholic* point of view, and under guidance of *Catholic* teaching, to contribute something ... to the solution in *Christian* fashion of the great problems social, scientific or religious'. Noting that the staff was 'for the most part composed of men who are engaged in the practical work of education', the 'Prefatory' hoped that they would 'be doing a work in which all parties can find their advantage' and that they 'may hope for the co-operation of all who make the general good their primary object'.[31] The *Lyceum* ran to seventy-seven monthly issues and met with much success, ranging across issues as varied as land nationalization, evolution, 'pauperism', unearned investment as a basis of taxation, Rome and communism, higher education for women and anti-clericalism. It 'endeavoured to lift Irish Catholics out of a blinkered political groove, and to develop a Catholic consciousness and a critical sense which would enrich life and extend horizons'.[32]

This did not mean that it avoided controversy. Peter Finlay, SJ was not as politically savvy as his brother and an article by him on 'The theology of land nationalisation' in the second issue appeared to support Henry George's theory that there should be no private ownership of land. Letters from Robert Whitty, SJ, the Rome-based English assistant to the general, to the Irish provincial, said the matter revealed 'a fatal and fundamental flaw in the *Lyceum* as a Jesuit Periodical. It shows that from the very beginning it has been and will continue to be (if they are allowed to direct it) not an Organ of the Society but an Organ of Fr Thos Finlay and his brother.'[33] A meeting of the provincial's consultors in February 1890 decided to suspend the Finlays from writing.[34] Tom Finlay was soon back in harness but the incident highlighted an issue for the Jesuits as the anonymity of the authors encouraged adventure, but also meant that the editors were held accountable in their place, as well

---

30 Brown, *The press in Ireland*, p. 68.   31 'Prefatory', *Lyceum* (Sept. 1887), 1.   32 Morrissey, *Thomas A. Finlay, SJ, 1848–1940*, p. 50   33 Letters: Generalate to Ireland, 9: 8 Apr. 1890. ADMN 1, IJA.   34 Jesuit consultors' minute book, 1890, IJA.   35 Letter from Fr Whitty to the assistant provincial Fr Alfred Murphy on 15 Apr. 1890. ADMN/36/72 (1–2), IJA.

as the order itself, for 'a publication which derives weight from the name of [the] Society'.[35] The lesson would not be forgotten. By 1894 Finlay felt that, given the changes in Ireland in recent years and the growth in the number of educated readers, 'there was scope for a review that appealed to all class[es] of readers'. The last issue, in February 1894, heralded the imminent arrival of a successor periodical, which would treat 'all current questions of interest, theological, historical, scientific, economic and educational, as well as the lighter and more popular social and literary topics'.[36]

NEW IRELAND REVIEW

The *New Ireland Review* appeared as promised in the following month and quickly became 'a forum for the exciting literary, artistic, political, economic and historiographical ideas of the day'.[37] The opening editorial noted the marked changes in Ireland such as the emergence of farmers as landowners and the improvements in education, and determined to provide a forum for the new thinking that would be needed.[38] By contrast with its predecessor, the preface to the *New Ireland Review* only used the word 'Catholic' once, when referring to Catholic emancipation, but the editor signed off with the 'ambition to promote enlightened discussion … within the limits which a rigorous respect for the religious faith of our countrymen imposes'.[39] The review attracted a much wider group of contributors, many of whom were friends and/or past pupils of Tom Finlay. Old hands from the *Lyceum* such as W.P. Coyne and William Magennis began to sign their articles and were joined by the likes of Arthur Clery, Douglas Hyde, Eoin MacNeill, Tom Kettle, D.P. Moran, Horace Plunkett, W.B. Yeats, J.M. Synge and George Moore. However, the most frequent and consistent contributor was the indefatigable Tom Finlay, who averaged one article in each of the thirty-four volumes, in addition to his monthly contribution 'From the Study Chair'. There were typically six or seven articles per issue, and they rarely ran to more than ten pages. Although there were no categories for the various topics covered, many of them fall easily into such groups as economic affairs, the land question and nationalism, while there was also a leavening of poetry and fiction. Education in all its guises featured regularly and it is perhaps appropriate that the last article published in the review dealt with Newman's thinking about the university.[40]

36 'Prefatory', *Lyceum*, Feb. 1894.   37 Louis McRedmond, *To the greater glory: a history of the Irish Jesuits* (Dublin, 1991), p. 234.   38 Clyde, *Irish literary magazines*, pp 124–5.   39 'New Ireland', *New Ireland Review* (Mar. 1894), 1–3.   40 Murtagh McPolin, 'Newman's university ideals', *New Ireland Review*, Feb. 1911, 354– 68.   41 'To our readers', *New Ireland Review*, Feb. 1911, 321.

In 1911 the review ceased publication after an unbroken run of 203 monthly issues. The final issue opened with a valedictory notice, observing that although 'the work has had its difficulties ... we are content to have held the field till larger and better equipped forces could occupy it. In quitting it, we make grateful acknowledgement of our obligations to all who have aided us in rendering what, we would fain believe, has been a service to Ireland.'[41] 'Perhaps it had had its say,' Stephen Brown wrote. 'Two years before, the old University College from which it had taken its rise had ceased to be: the new National University had arisen.' Perhaps the Jesuits had grander plans and felt that 'the new institution called for some publication on a larger scale and of a more academic nature'.[42] The *Lyceum* and *New Ireland Review* were two of the more significant Irish journals of their day. They were central to the Catholic nation-in-waiting at a key period of transition for Irish society and the modernization of Catholicism, and are prisms through which we may view the preparation of the Catholic upper middle class to assume control of the country with the anticipated advent of home rule.

STUDIES: AN IRISH QUARTERLY REVIEW

Studies first saw the light of day in March 1912 and has appeared without fail four times a year ever since. Inspired by one Jesuit journal (*Etudes*), modelled on another (*America*), it was the latest in the apostolic succession of publications attached to the Catholic University/UCD that had commenced with Newman's *Atlantis*. Pending approval from Rome, the preferred title for the new journal was *Lyceum*, with *Studies* as an alternative.[43] Lessons had been learned from its two predecessors, as is evidenced by the careful and structured approach that preceded its launch. The first meeting of the *coetus redactorum* (board of editors) of 'the Review' in September 1911 was chaired by the provincial, William Delany, SJ, and reference was made to 'negotiations with V. Rev. Fr General' to whom a version of the proposal to publish had been sent the previous year.[44] Delany approved the appointment of 'censors in addition to those forming the Editorial Board'. Finlay was appointed moderator, with Timothy Corcoran, SJ as editor, while Fr General in Rome was kept apprised of developments. A subsequent meeting decided that the title of the review would be *Studies: An Irish Quarterly Review of Letters, Philosophy and Science.* As noted

---

42 Brown, *The press in Ireland*, pp 71–2.   43 Minute Book, detailing the origins and early years of the publication *Studies* (IJA: J31/17). All further references in this section are to this document unless otherwise indicated.   44 De Novo Libello Periodico (IJA: ADMN 27/3[1] – [15]).

above, the *Lyceum* had not been shy about its religious provenance, whereas the preface to its successor had only used the word Catholic once. *Studies* also seemed intent on soft-pedalling its religious affiliation when the November meeting decided that the contents were to be listed on the cover without 'SJ' after the writers' names. Presumably, with home rule on the horizon, all was to play for and the board had no wish to upset any apple carts. In a similar vein, a meeting the following June decided that 'books of a strictly devotional character are not suitable for review in *Studies*'.

Continuing the lineage that had commenced with the *Lyceum* and echoing Newman's aims for *Atlantis*, the foreword to the first issue makes explicit the link with 'Higher Studies in Ireland'. The National University of Ireland had commenced business in October 1909 and the foreword suggests that 'the occasion would appear a fitting one for an effort to produce a Review which would give publicity to work of a scholarly type, extending over many important branches of study, and appealing to a wider circle of cultured readers than strictly specialist journals could be expected to reach'. It laments that 'Irish scholarship has for centuries suffered under many disabilities, [including] the limited provision of publications in which the results of research and original thought could find expression in harmony with the religious and national characteristics of our country' before announcing that 'it is with this object that some University Professors and Graduates have undertaken to conduct an Irish Quarterly Review, which, under the general name of *STUDIES*, will publish contributions in various departments of Letters, Philosophical subjects, and Science'. By contrast with its predecessors, the journal was to be controlled by a committee chaired by Tom Finlay and would appear in the months of March, June, September and December. Although the founders may have been somewhat shy about their Catholic religious provenance, they were not afraid to say that the principles of treatment in philosophy, sociology, and education 'will be based on the traditional philosophy of the Christian world, which has even in recent years shown itself far superior to any of its temporary rivals in organising the proved results of modern research'.[45]

The fledgling journal might well have foundered in the first two years as Corcoran showed himself to be an obdurate colleague and poor manager.[46] The minute book notes that the first two years' financial losses were such that 'the question of ceasing publication was considered'. A 'confidential memorandum' from early 1914 opens with a litany of complaints against the editor (Fr Corcoran), ranging from a failure to solicit articles to lack of supervision

45 Foreword to first issue of *Studies*, 1 (Spring 1912), 3–4.   46 For more on the troubled early years of *Studies*, see Declan O'Keeffe, '"Time, energy and brass": why *Studies* did not fail', *Studies*, 106:422 (Summer 2017), 209–20.

over the production process, resulting in shoddy work. It also questions the 'mistaken policy' of the journal whereby, despite the aspiration to publish a review of letters, philosophy and science, 'the articles were largely historical'. The memorandum then recalls that the Jesuit world had been told of the launch of the periodical 'to keep up the standing of our University professors in Dublin' (shades of *Atlantis*) and warns of the disgrace that would befall the province, and the 'severe discouragement [it would be] to the hopes of the younger generation', should it fail 'after only two and a half years'. The report suggested that a change of editor might solve the problem and made a strong case for Patrick Connolly, SJ, citing his work as editor of *The Clongownian*.[47]

The provincial seems to have been persuaded by the memorandum, as Connolly replaced Corcoran as editor in July. The effect of the change was immediate – a deficit of £35 14s. 4d. in September 1914 was eliminated within a year and circulation figures rose steadily from 258 copies in September 1914 to 2,200 copies in March 1920. In March 1921 the annual subscription, which had remained at 10s. since the foundation, was raised to 15s. and two years later Connolly was able to write confidently that '*Studies* has now, March 17 1923, paid off all debts incurred since Sept. 1920 and is financially sound'.[48] Connolly was 'convinced that what was required was a series of articles written by specialists, but with a general interest', to which he added book reviews, which comprised from 36–40 pages of each 176-page issue of the journal. This radical change in approach in December 1914 ensured that he 'soon had a very successful and influential periodical [which he] edited until his death in 1950' (by far the longest serving of the nine editors to date).[49] The journal caught the eye of its English peer, *The Month*, which noted that 'it seems to be admirably adapted to meet the needs of the country that produces it, a country old in history [whose] scholars ... are preparing to make their country once again a centre of enlightenment for the West'.[50] *America*, after which it was fashioned, called it 'remarkable', as it treated 'of every subject of the day ... with a clearness and comprehensiveness we have witnessed in no other publication'.[51] Praise also came from without the Jesuit world, with the *Times Literary Supplement* writing that 'this Irish Quarterly ... has won a good position ... [as] is proved by the singular variety and ability of its September issue',[52] and the *Freeman's Journal* remarking that '*Studies* now ranks among the great quarterlies in interest'.[53]

47 Confidential memorandum on *Studies* (IJA: CM/LEES/87). 48 Fr P.J. Connolly, Note to a file of statements of accounts for *Studies*, Sept. 1914–June 1920 (IJA: ADMN/27/7). 49 O'Donoghue, 'Irish Jesuit publications', 325–6. 50 *The Month*, Jan. 1915. 51 P.J. Connolly, SJ, 'Studies – An Irish Quarterly Review' in 'Irish Jesuit periodicals', The Irish Jesuit Directory and Year Book (Dublin, 1930), 2. 52 *Times Literary Supplement*, 20 Sept. 1917. 53 *Freeman's Journal*, 18 Oct. 1924.

Accounting for his first sixteen years of stewardship in 1930, Connolly quotes many such 'flattering appreciations [which] call attention to the wide range of subjects treated and to the high standard of scholarship shown'. In a thoughtful and reflective piece, he restates the philosophy behind the journal and how it has been delivered since his advent in 1914. He remembers the change of emphasis on his watch, which led to 'the contributors to *Studies* [who] are all specialists in some department of knowledge [writing] for the general reader rather than for the specialist'. He explains that 'practically eve-rything published in *Studies* is commissioned' and that 'if the problem is of national importance, other experts are invited to comment on [the] article'. This method results in 'a symposium of views', which has sometimes 'called for government action to solve the problem [and] action has followed in due course'. Connolly goes on to explain that

> The guiding principle in the management of *Studies* is the common good of Ireland – moral, intellectual, social, economic. Each article is expected to forward, directly or indirectly, this object. Its ambition is to expound and defend Catholic principles in the domains of religion, philosophy, ethics, sociology, history, science, literature … For centuries European thought and culture have come to us filtered through the Protestant mind of England. The Reformation broke down the bridge between Europe and Ireland. It is the ambition of *Studies* to contribute in some small way to the rebuilding of this bridge.[54]

Bryan Fanning, who assembled a compendium of thirty-one essays drawn from over 3,000 published in 400 issues, says that 'a strong distaste for any of the authoritarian political experiments of the twentieth century … char-acterised the early decades of *Studies*' and that the journal was 'very much preoccupied with economics' from the start, which was unsurprising as 'its behind-the-scenes founder, Thomas Finlay', became professor of political economy at UCD – as did his protégé and successor, George O'Brien, who asked John Maynard Keynes to deliver the first Finlay Memorial Lecture.[55] In 1953 Connolly's successor as editor, Roland Burke Savage, SJ (following a three year stint at the helm on the *Irish Monthly*), published 'The Economist and Public Policy', a defence of Keynesian planning and state activism. This had been the keystone of one of Connolly's much-vaunted symposia – on

54 Connolly, SJ, 'Studies – An Irish Quarterly Review', p. 2.   55 Bryan Fanning, *An Irish century: Studies, 1912–2012* (Dublin, 2012), pp 6, 8.   56 Patrick Lynch et al., 'The economist and public policy [with comments]', *Studies*, 42:167 (1953), 241–74.

economics and public policy – and was penned by Patrick Lynch, erstwhile private secretary to John A Costello, who would succeed Finlay and O'Brien as professor of political economy in UCD.[56]

Reflecting on the journal in the seminal year of 1966, Burke Savage observed that '*Studies* over the past fifty years has been a quiet force and influence in intellectual life in Ireland.' Citing the founding fathers' ambition to 'give publicity to work of a scholarly type … to a wider circle of cultured readers', he notes how 'Mass Media … have made it deceptively easy to feel that one knows all about a particular … problem from a snappy attractively presented programme on Radio or Television'. By contrast, he wrote, '*Studies* … sets out to provide a mature well-considered presentation … that will enable [readers] to reach their own conclusions'. In addition, the large book-review section (with a nod to Aristotle's Golden Mean) means that 'the layman is enabled to keep abreast of current thought [while] the specialist is often given valuable direction in areas outside his own special field but within his general interest'. The editor concluded by quoting erstwhile Taoiseach Sean Lemass' tribute to the journal when he applauded its 'significant contribution to the development of public opinion in Ireland … which has sometimes determined the future of our country [as well as contributing] to the democratic process'.[57] Nonetheless, and despite this liberal approach, Francis Shaw, SJ's controversial savaging of Pearse's interpretation of Irish history, 'The Canon of Irish History: A Challenge', had been refused publication in the same year as the editor 'considered it too controversial for what was meant to be a commemoration'. The essay would appear (under a new editor, Peter Troddyn, SJ) in 1972, by which time the troubles in Northern Ireland were beginning 'to preoccupy *Studies* to a considerable extent'.[58]

Concern about Northern Ireland and the notion of a united Ireland had surfaced as early as 1957 in response to the IRA's border campaign of the previous year. Articles by Donal Barrington ('Uniting Ireland') and Conor Cruise O'Brien ('A Sample of Loyalties')[59] 'argued that prevalent nationalist thinking was impoverished'.[60] In the same year that Shaw was jilted, future taoiseach (and protegé of the editor), Garret FitzGerald, questioned the sacred text of the Proclamation of 1916 'as a great source of political and social doctrines', claiming that the leaders of the Rising 'did not regard themselves [as] – nor were they in fact – great thinkers … with few clear cut ideas of political or social philosophy … beyond the wish to secure freedom'.[61] Barrington's

57 Fr R. Burke Savage, 'Studies' in *Irish Jesuit*, 1:14, 2 (IJA). 58 Fanning, *An Irish century*, pp 11, 13. 59 Conor Cruise O'Brien, 'A sample of loyalties', *Studies*, 46:184 (1957), 403–10; Donal Barrington, 'Uniting Ireland', *Studies*, 46:184 (1957), 379–402. 60 Fanning, *An Irish century*, p. 10. 61 Garret FitzGerald, 'The significance of 1916', *Studies*, 55:217 (1966), 31–2.

argument that if there were to be unification it would have to be by consent was added to by John Brady, SJ, director of the Jesuit-founded College of Industrial Relations, in an essay in 1978 on pluralism and Northern Ireland. The essay addressed the thorny issue of divorce, which would convulse the country eight years later, with the view that 'a carefully framed divorce law would be for the common good … where definitive marital breakdown is proven'. Rejecting 'the argument that this would have bad social consequences', he notes that 'consequential morality is almost always bad morality'. The piece also addressed the problem of identity, church-state relations and inter-denominational education before concluding that 'it is important that those of us who … would welcome an all-Ireland dimension to economic, social and political life, should say so frequently'.[62]

Fanning notes a radical change in editorial policy in 1982 that had been developing since the late 1970s when '*Studies* had misplaced its raison d'etre'. The winter editorial ran: 'We aim be non-academic in future, reacting more to the problems of the day, while maintaining the traditional interest of *Studies* in general Irish culture.'[63] This contrasted with the *Lyceum*, which had avoided the burning issues of the day, while the *New Ireland Review* had provided a forum for them. Social justice, poverty, inequality and liberation theology were the watchwords as 'a 1985 editorial by Brian Lennon, SJ urged the church to position itself to the left of the political mainstream', and immigration would be added to the list in the new century.[64] The journal marked its centenary in 2012 (at 400 not out), and the eighth editor, Fergus O'Donoghue, SJ, reflected on the circumstances of its birth 'on the brink of major upheaval [as] a world war and revolution … would radically transform the rules of engagement with the culture [the original board] had set out to address'. Its survival and 'rare longevity … has been [in] a time of extraordinary change, of which the magazine … has continued to keep track'. O'Donoghue restates their commitment to the 'founding purpose of commenting on Irish political, cultural and economic issues in the light of Christian values'. Accepting that 'the national conversation has moved on', he argues that 'the need for commentary from a thoughtful, informed Christian perspective has arguably become all the more urgent as the 21st century unfolds'.[65]

In the century and more that has passed since its foundation, *Studies* has borne witness to the progress of a state that was not yet in existence when it commenced and that would have quite a different complexion to the 'new

---

62 John Brady, 'Pluralism and Northern Ireland', *Studies*, 67:265/6 (1978), 88–99.   63 Bryan Fanning, 'A century of *Studies*', *Studies*, 100:400 (2011), 397–405 at 402.   64 Fanning, *An Irish century*, pp 14–15.   65 'Editorial: Winter 2011', *Studies*, 100:400 (2011), 396.   66 James Murphy, *Ireland: a social, cultural and literary history, 1791–1891* (Dublin, 2003), pp 9, 162–3.

Ireland' envisaged by the editorial committee that oversaw its gestation and birth. The Catholic Church was resurgent in late nineteenth-century Ireland and the Jesuits were in the vanguard of the revival, mainly through their works in education but also in publishing. Periodicals such as *Studies* and the *Irish Monthly* were put in place to influence and shape society at a key period of transition for the Irish social order and the modernization of Catholicism. They were important weapons in the propaganda war that was being waged by the Catholic middle class within British politics, and especially for the heart of Liberalism.[66] *Studies* was a product of the periodical culture of its time in an age when the Catholic Church in Ireland was resurgent. Much has changed since then in both of these regards and neither that church nor reflective journals have the dominant position of yore – thus posing the question 'where now?' for each of them. For the former a period of much needed reflection is both timely and salutary, while the future for the latter may lie in embracing the possibilities offered by modern technologies and reinventing itself as 'a kind of metablog'[67] whereby it may continue to act as a mirror and a searchlight in an Irish society that is in sore need of both.

THE LITTLE RED BOOK

The *Irish Messenger of the Sacred Heart*, to give it its full title, was one of a number of Sacred Heart Messengers modelled on the original, which had been founded in France by Henri Ramiére, SJ in 1844. It arose out of the devotional Apostleship of Prayer (League of the Sacred Heart), which was designed to offer an antidote to Jansenism, and was imitated in several countries, including England and Australia, both of which had strong connections to the Irish province.[68] The founder of the Irish version of the *Messenger*, James Aloysius Cullen, was educated by the Christian Brothers in New Ross before moving to Clongowes at the age of fifteen. While there he was 'greatly taken by things religious and the notion of evangelisation', but not so impressed by the Jesuit teachers who were less concerned with the *aeterna* of '"saving souls" and spreading the Kingdom of God' and more taken with the relative *caduca* of saying Mass, teaching classes, organizing games and supervising dormitories. As a diocesan priest in his native Ferns (where he was first exposed to the results of excessive drinking among the boatmen on the Slaney), 'his copious personal diaries reveal a deep unease during the 17 years after his

---

67 Fanning, *An Irish century*, p. 18.   68 McRedmond, *To the greater glory*, pp 268–70. McRedmond observes that 'it is salutary to know that Father Ramiére, founder of the first *Messenger*, was also editor of *tudes*'.

ordination' and in 1881 he was received into the Society of Jesus, where he accepted the Jesuit thesis 'that very ordinary activities, if done for a good motive and with a right intention, could lead to the salvation of souls and the spread of the Kingdom'.[69]

Following his novitiate in Belgium, Cullen was posted to Dublin, where he replaced Russell as director of the Apostleship of Prayer for Ireland.[70] He approached his rector in Belvedere College about starting a new publication and received 'permission, a small room and a pound note'.[71] The first number was issued in January 1888, the circulation reached 9,000 by the end of the year and 73,000 copies a month were being published by 1904 when Cullen stepped down as editor – when his magazine was 'the most popular of all the Messengers'. His aim was 'to print nothing that could not be read and fully understood by even the simplest reader' and to ensure that the magazine 'would not only be welcome in every Irish home, but would be cherished by Irish exiles abroad as a welcome voice from their native land'.[72] The magazine strove to make a personal connection with its readers and even published their letters in addition to articles that 'were devotional rather than theological'. Significantly, 'it has always had a Catholic vision, looking at the global scene outside Ireland, reflecting the extraordinary interest of Irish people in the wider, universal church'.[73] The target market was the 'staunchly Catholic and desperately poor'. A 'hidden army of volunteer promoters' carried out the distribution and helped to keep costs down – and 'at a penny a copy [it] was affordable even to the poorest of the poor'.[74]

'One of the most startling phenomena of Irish life', the *Messenger*'s concerns have varied to reflect the times. Under Cullen's successor as editor, Joseph McDonnell, SJ (1904–28), 'the stress was on national self-sufficiency', while Paul Leonard, SJ 'reflected the wind of change that blew through the church windows opened by the Second Vatican Council' in the 1960s and '70s.[75] Over the years the *Irish Messenger* became part of the infrastructure of Irish social life, and not always for devotional reasons. The crossword puzzles and inspirational stories were very popular, as was the red cover among young women unable to afford rouge. Tarry Flynn is to be found reading it along with 'Old Moore's Almanac and the local newspaper [with which it] constituted

---

69 Bernard J. McGuckian, SJ, 'Roundabout route to the Jesuits', *The Clongownian*, 13 (2009). 'Aeterna Non Caduca' is the motto of Clongowes Wood College. 70 Thomas F. Ryan, SJ, 'The *Irish Messenger of the Sacred Heart*' in *The Irish Jesuit Directory and Year Book* (Dublin, 1930), p. 7. 71 John Looby, SJ, 'A *Messenger* of hope', Jesuits in Ireland, http://www.messenger.ie/News_-and-_Events_.aspx. 72 Ryan, 'The *Irish Messenger of the Sacred Heart*', 8. 73 Paul Andrews, SJ, 'A gift for reinvention' in *The Jesuits on Leeson Street, 1910–2010* (Dublin, 2010), p. 32. 74 John Looby, SJ, 'The *Sacred Heart Messenger*' in *The Jesuits on Leeson Street*, p. 78 75 Andrews, 'A gift for reinvention', pp 32–3.

the literature of Flynn's as of nearly every other country house'.[76] 'Touching the new market represented by the literate Irish Catholic at home and abroad', the magazine topped 300,000 copies a month in the 1920s, with a steady readership among emigrants. Continuity was assured by 'editors [who] normally spent decades … in office'.[77] In 1966 'copies of the *Messenger* [were] sent to every county in Ireland and to forty-one countries all round the world',[78] while it marked its centenary in 1988 with a circulation of 200,000 copies a month.[79] Sales began to decline as the century turned and in 2018 it could only claim a readership of some 50,000. The current editor, Donal Neary, SJ, explains that 'its popularity spread through the range of material in it, including religious articles, helpful advice, letters of petition, and praying with the Pope, [while] helpful articles in the early days offered advice ranging from how to iron a blouse to the good rearing of hens'. Such practical advice continues in today's issues, where it shares space with a more practical Christianity as it grapples with 'concrete issues that touch our lives … family problems, the refugee crisis [and] the challenge of middle age'.[80]

MADONNA

Ten years after its foundation (1898), the *Messenger* acquired a stablemate in the form of a 'quarterly of twenty-four compact double-columned pages' that aimed to 'bring into clearer light the history, nature, privileges and indulgences of the Primary Sodality of the Blessed Virgin Mary'. Like the *Messenger*, the *Madonna* had many counterparts in other Jesuit provinces but, while the *Messenger* took its being from the League of the Sacred Heart, the various imprints of the *Madonna* were the official organs of the Sodality of Our Lady, 'an association founded by the Society of Jesus and approved by the Holy See [which aimed] to help the neighbour (in all manner of spiritual and corporal works of mercy)'.[81] This would harmonize with Vatican II's *Constitution on the Church in the Modern World*, which focused attention on the whole human family and the realities in which it lives.[82] Writing in 1930, the editor notes that 'it was principally to further … intercommunication of ideas amongst the Irish Children of Mary, in Ireland and beyond the seas … that the *Madonna*

76 Patrick Kavanagh, *Tarry Flynn* (London, 1978), pp 18–19.   77 O'Donoghue, 'Irish Jesuit publications', p. 325.   78 Fr Paul Leonard, 'The *Irish Messenger*', *Irish Jesuit*, 1:14 (Dec. 1966), 3 (IJA).   79 O'Donoghue, 'Irish Jesuit publications', 325.   80 Donal Neary, 'Landmark for *Messenger* magazine', Jesuits in Ireland, https://www.jesuit.ie/news/messenger-magazine-130-years-old.   81 Michael Murphy, SJ, 'The *Madonna*' in *The Irish Jesuit Directory and Year Book* (Dublin, 1930), pp 12–13.   82 Fr P. Baggot, '*Madonna*', *Irish Jesuit*, 1:14 (Dec. 1966), 4 (IJA).

was founded' and that its success may be judged by the 'reports [received from] such far-away lands as India, China, Newfoundland', which led to the magazine being issued monthly from 1926.[83] Circulation peaked at 48,000, but change was afoot after Vatican II and sodalities began to decline in the early 1970s. Monthly sales dropped to 22,250, and the *Madonna*'s days were numbered. In 1974 the Irish Jesuit provincial, Cecil McGarry, SJ, wrote to his brethren to announce that 'from January 1, 1975, the *Madonna* will be incorporated in an enlarged *Messenger*'.[84] The die was cast, and the last issue of the *Madonna* appeared in December 1974 after seventy-six years of service to the Primary Sodality of the Blessed Virgin Mary.

AN TIMIRE

In 1910 the *Messenger* spawned another Jesuit publication, this time in the Irish language, when Cullen's successor, Joseph McDonnell, SJ, founded *An Timire* (*Irish Language Messenger*). Despite its title, the magazine is complementary to its companion and not a translation, although it published a similar variety of material. Although the Jesuits at the time did not have any policy on the movement for the restoration of the Irish language, they did encourage any of their members who were enthusiastic about the cause. These included Pádraig Ó Duinnín, SJ of dictionary fame and John C. Mac Erlean, SJ, anthologist of David Ó Bruadair. Initially a quarterly, the publication appeared monthly from 1932 to 1937, when it reached its peak circulation of 3,000 copies, before reverting to a seasonal timetable and a smaller readership.[85] Also an organ of the devotional Apostleship of Prayer, it concerns itself with the 'monthly intentions of the Holy Father [which it explains] to its Irish-speaking readers' and, like its English-speaking brother, it 'had a special application to our Gaeltacht exiles in Britain'. By the 1960s *An Timire* was moving with the times and, as the papal intentions were 'increasingly concerned with the implementation of the Vatican Council's Decrees', other articles were 'progressively dedicated to the same purpose', while progress in ecumenism was advanced by 'contributions from our separated brethren'.[86] In common with its companions in the Irish Jesuit publishing world, sales declined from 1,800 in 1988 to 450 a quarter over the next two decades until it experienced something of a revival under the stewardship of current editor, Frainc Mac Brádaigh, SJ, and now issues 800

83 Murphy, SJ, '*The Madonna*', 11.   84 Cecil McGarry, SJ to the Irish Jesuit province, 27 Aug. 1974, IJA, ADMIN (3) 127 (67–8).   85 O'Donoghue, 'Irish Jesuit publications', p. 326.   86 An tAth Seosamh Ó Mhuirthuile, SJ, '*An Timire* (*Irish Language Messenger*)', *Irish Jesuit*, 1:14 (Dec. 1966), 7 (IJA).

copies and is by some distance the oldest Irish-language magazine continually in print.[87]

THE *PIONEER*

James Cullen not only wrote for the underprivileged but also set about addressing a key issue among the working classes in Ireland, the abuse of alcohol. The Pioneer Total Abstinence Association of the Sacred Heart was founded by him in stages between 1898 and 1904, and numbered more than 277,000 adult members by 1919.[88] Through its meetings and supported by the *Messenger*, it addressed 'a major social evil in rural and urban Ireland alike'.[89] In 1948 the association marked its golden jubilee by launching a monthly magazine 'to explain the meaning and work of the Pioneer Association and to help keep members in touch with the Association and its activities'.[90] Like the *Messenger*, the *Pioneer* found a wide audience among the diaspora, with a high-water mark of some 60,000 copies twenty years later in 1968. Readership has declined since then and now numbers 7,000 to 8,000, while control has moved from the Society of Jesus to that of the diocesan clergy and laity. Links with the founders continue, with contributions from several Jesuits, and 'the influence of Jesuit spirituality remains prominent, especially in the insistence on promotion of Devotion to the Sacred Heart of Jesus', while the Society's publishing arm – Messenger Publications – continues to print the magazine.[91]

JESUIT COMMUNICATIONS

Studies and the *Irish Messenger* (and *An Timire*) are the great survivors of the Irish Jesuit publications that are considered in this chapter. They appealed to different readerships (that, however, sometimes overlapped) and have chronicled both the devotional and intellectual missions of the Society in Ireland over time. Whether giving 'publicity to work of a scholarly type, extending over many important branches of study, and appealing to a wider circle of cultured readers',[92] or printing 'nothing that could not be read and fully understood

87 Frainc Mac Brádaigh, SJ, *An Timire* editor, in conversation with the author, 30 Nov. 2020.   88 Michael Viney, *The Jesuits in Ireland, 1542–1974* (Dublin, 1974), p. 22. Cullen had begun to form temperance sodalities as early as 1884.   89 McRedmond, *To the greater glory*, pp 227–8.   90 Revd D. Dargan, '*Pioneer*', *Irish Jesuit*, 1:14 (Dec. 1966), 8 (IJA).   91 Fr Bernard McGuckian, SJ, *Pioneer* editor, 1976–2018, in correspondence with the author, 30 Nov. 2020.   92 Foreword to first issue of *Studies*, 1 (Spring 1912), 3.

by even the simplest reader',[93] they are 'still following editorial policies which their founders would recognise [and] together with the *Irish Monthly* and the *Madonna*, their back numbers are a fascinating record of Irish preoccupations over many generations'.[94] When Ignatius of Loyola began to send his companions around the world in 1541, just a year after the foundation of the Society of Jesus, his watchword was communication and communications have been a mainstay of Jesuit life over the centuries. He enjoined his fellow missionaries to stay in touch with him and each other by letter, albeit by means of the painfully slow postal system of the sixteenth century. He took care over what he committed to paper, noting – in words that ring true down through the centuries and are particularly relevant in today's mire of social media – that 'what one writes must be considered more carefully than what one says, because the written word remains and is a witness for all times'.[95]

93 Ryan, 'The *Irish Messenger of the Sacred Heart*', p. 8.   94 O'Donoghue, 'Irish Jesuit publications', p. 326.
95 Brian Grogan, SJ, *Alone and on foot: Ignatius of Loyola* (Dublin, 2008), p. 218.

Index

Abrahamson, David, 155
Adams, Gerry, 89, 93, 95, 115–16
Agnew, Paddy, 196
Ahern, Bertie, 116
Aiken, Frank, 42, 46, 49, 50–1
Akenson, Donald Harman, 29, 30, 34
Amárach, 254
An Iris, 241
An tUltach, 240, 241
Anderson, Perry, 98
Arensberg, Conrad, 270
Armstrong, John, Archbishop, 151
Armstrong, Robert, 159, 162
Arrigan, Mary, 196
Arthur, Paul, 91
Atkenson, Robert, 270
Atlantis, 281, 282, 284, 285, 286

Ballin, Malcolm, 20, 104
Banville, John, 91
Barnes, Monica, 170, 190, 193
Barrington, Donal, 288–9
Barry, John, Canon ('Cromlyn'), 137, 141–2, 145, 146, 151
Barry, Norman, 233
Bates, Maire, 190
Beasley, Caroline, 196
Beattie, Robert, 141
Beaumont, Caitriona, 206
Beckett, Samuel, 69, 74, 100
Bell, Robert, 101
Bell, The, 11, 15, 16, 18–35, 60, 65, 67, 70, 71, 72, 73, 74, 75, 76, 79, 80, 142
Belloc, Hilaire, 271, 279
Bennett, Louie, 68, 205, 210
Benson, Rodany, 112
Bentley, Michael, 41, 57
Beresford, David, 89
Bew, Paul, 96
Bielenberg, Kim, 102
Binchy, Daniel, 270
Blackwell, Annette, 192

Blaney, Neil, 106
Blanshard, Paul, 258–9
Bodkin, Thomas, 268
Boggs, Richard, 91–2
Boland, Bridget, 228
Boland, Frederick, 39, 42, 43, 44–5, 46, 47, 51, 54–5
Bono, 116
Booth, Arthur, 23, 63
Bouch, Joseph J., 125
Bourdieu, Pierre, 111–13
Bowman, Jonathan Philbin, 160
Boylan, Clare, 197, 233, 234
Boyle, Kevin, 84, 85, 86, 89–90, 96
Brady, John, 289
Breen, Joe, 7, 12, 16, 102–21
Breen, Suzanne, 96, 98
Breen, T.C., 182
Brennan, Pat, 7, 13, 104, 190–202
Brennock, Mark, 160
Briscoe, Ben, 114–15
Brown, Stephen, SJ, 25, 269, 275, 284
Brown, Terence, 70, 91
Browne, Noel, 173, 176, 212–13, 244
Browne, Nora, 218
Browne, Vincent, 106, 167, 168, 171, 190, 198, 201
Bryan, Dan, 39, 41–2, 45, 48, 55–6
Bulbulia, Katharine, 199
Burbage, Thomas H., Fr, 261, 263
Burke, Helen Lucy, 196
Burns, Jimmy, 96
Butler, Arthur, Bishop, 145–6
Butterfield, Herbert, 39, 40–1, 42, 52–3, 54, 57–8, 59
Byrne, Al, 231
Byrne, Anne, 196
Byrne, Catherine, 210
Byrne, Máiread, 160, 162, 164, 167, 170

Cafferkey, Maurice, 182
Caffrey, Cissy, 182

Caldwell-Myers, John, 79
Capuchin Annual, 60, 65, 67, 68, 73, 74, 75, 78, 80
Carlson, Matt, 111
Carr, Bunny, 234
Casement, Roger, 269
Catholic Bulletin, 14, 258–76
Catholic Penny Magazine, 32
Chambers, John, 117
Chenevix, Helen, 210
Chesterton, G.K., 271
Chichester-Clark, James, 145
Church of Ireland Gazette, 12–13, 16, 135–54
Clark, Norman, 136, 141
Clarke, Harry, 269
Clear, Caitríona, 7, 14, 208, 220–36
Cleary, Michael, Fr, 117
Clery, Arthur, 283
Clissmann, Helmut, 43–5, 53, 54
Clongownian, The, 286
Clune, Anne, 216, 241
Cole, Roger, 159, 166
Collins, Aongus, 159
Collins, Bill, 186
Collins, Eddie, 199
Collins, Liam, 102
Collis, Robert, 203
Colum, Padraic, 66, 69
Colvin, Ian, 58
Comerford, Maire, 231–2
Comhar, 14, 237–57
Commentary, 60, 65, 71, 72, 74, 80
Commonweal, 32
Conboy, Martin, 11, 12, 15
Condell, Frances, 142, 231
Conlon, Audrey, 193
Connolly, James, 124
Connolly, Patrick, SJ, 286–7
Connolly, Sybil, 226, 229
Cooke, Emma, 196
Cooper, Cecil, Recd, 141
Corcoran, Timothy, SJ, 258, 259, 262–76, 284, 285–6
Cork Examiner, 253
Corkery, Daniel, 66, 266
Corrigan, Mairead, 87

Cosgrave, W.T., 126, 259, 268, 270, 272–3
Costello, John A., 212, 218, 244, 288
Coulter, Carol, 198
Coveney, Simon, 114
Cox, Pat, 116
Coyne, Sabina, 234
Coyne, W.P., 283
Cronin, Anthony, 80, 161
Crowley, Des, 107
Crozier, John, Archbishop, 144
Cullen, James, SJ, 278, 290–1, 294
Cullen, Kevin, 96
Curran, Michael, Fr, 260, 264
Curtayne, Alice, 224

Daiken, Leslie, 80
Daily Mail, 25–6, 252
Dalton, Annie, 228
d'Alton, Ian, 7, 12–13, 15, 135–54
Daly, Brendan, 193, 194
Daly, Cathal, Cardinal, 89
d'Arcy, Charles, Archbishop, 144, 148–9
Dawe, Gerald, 91
Dawson, Kevin, 160
Day, Maurice, Bishop, 143–4
de Valera, Éamon, 27–8, 36, 38, 43, 44, 45, 46, 49, 52, 76, 77, 126, 151, 213, 245, 258, 264, 265, 273, 274, 275, 276
de Valera, Sinéad, 228–9
de Valera, Vivion, 49
de Vere, Aubrey, 265, 278
Deane, Seamus, 97
Deasy, Austin, 199
Deevy, Teresa, 224
Delany, William, SJ, 279, 284
Dervan, Michael, 160, 168
Desmond, Dermot, 109
Devilly, Simon, 160
Devlin, Bernadette, 83
Devlin, Paddy, 91
Digby, J.P., 76
Doheny, Edward, 269
Doherty, Seán, 117
Donnelly, Catherine, 196
Dorman, Sean, 71
Dowling, Aiden, 117

Doyle, Avril, 119

Doyle, John, 156–9, 160, 162, 163–4, 165–6, 167, 171

Drumm, Maire, 86

Dublin Magazine, 60, 65, 66–8, 74, 75, 79, 81

Dublin Opinion, 15, 19, 20, 21–3, 61, 63–5, 108, 142

Dublin Review, 265

Dudgeon, Jeffrey, 179

Duffy's Fireside Magazine, 32

Duignan, Clare, 192

Duke, Kenneth, 52–3

Dukes, Alan, 245

Dunbar, Wendy, 97

Dunbar-Harrison, Letitia, 272, 273

Dundalk Examiner, 241

Dunleavy, J.P., 60

Dunne, Aiden, 160, 168

Dunne, Ben, 107, 117

Dunne, Derek, 160

Dwyer, Michael, 160

Eason & Son, 61–3, 65, 66, 68, 69, 70, 71–2, 182, 184

Edwards, Hilton, 68, 185, 203

Edwards, Robin Dudley, 36, 40–1, 42, 55, 57, 274

Egan, Larry, 75

Emerson, Newton, 101

Emerson, Peter, 96

English, Richard, 101

Enright, Anne, 96

Envoy, 60, 65, 67, 68, 71–2, 73, 74–8, 79, 80

Ewart-Biggs, Jane, Lady, 88–9

Fahy, Denis, Fr, 263

Fairclough, Norman, 109–10

Fallon, B.P., 233

Fanning, Bryan, 15, 287, 289

Fanning, Ronan, 59

Farrell, Michael, 96

Farrell, Paul, 118

Faulkner, Brian, 85

Fay, Liam, 106

Feasta, 240

Feehan, Matt, 43

Feely, Julie, 80

Fennell, Nuala, 170, 192, 194, 200

Ferriter, Diarmaid, 207

Finan, Mary, 196

Fingleton, Michael, 117

Finlay, Peter, SJ, 282–3

Finlay, Thomas, SJ, 263, 267, 270, 277, 278, 281, 282–3, 284, 285, 287, 288

Finucane, Marian, 190–4, 195, 197–8, 199–200

Fisk, Robert, 96

Fiske, John, 185

FitzGerald, Alexis, 52

Fitzgerald, Barbara, 192, 195–6

Fitzgerald, Frank, 186

FitzGerald, Garret, 89, 96, 106, 116, 165–6, 169, 192–3, 194, 196, 245, 288

Fitzgerald, George Francis, 265

Fitzgerald, Thomas Aloysius, OFM, 260

Fitzsimmons, Jean, 182

Flaherty, Mary, 194, 196

Flanagan, Oliver J., 50

Flynn, Declan, 178

Flynn, Leontia, 97

Flynn, Roddy, 106–7

Fortnight, 12, 13, 16, 82–101

Foster, Roy, 96, 97

Freeman's Journal, 253, 286

Friel, Brian, 97

Frost, Stella, 214–15

Fullerton, Lady Georgiana, 278

Gaelic Athlete, 124

Gageby, Douglas, 89

Gallagher, Frank, 28, 49

Gallagher, Patrick, 164

Gannon, Sean, 119

Gay Community News (*GCN*), 13, 186–9

Gay News, 174, 175

Geary, Roy, 271

Gellner, Ernest, 276

Giff, William, Revd, 150

Gilbert, Irene, 225, 226, 229

Gillespie, Elgy, 174–5, 190, 197

Gogarty, Oliver St John, 270

Goldsmith, Rudy, 101

Gonne, Maud, 217

Gore-Booth, Eva, 217

Gorman, Ed, 96

Grace, Sylvia, 232

Grace, Tom, 159

Greening, Ernest, Revd, 141

Gregg, John, Archbishop, 135, 137, 151, 153, 154

Gregory, Padraig, 69

Gregory, Tony, 106, 166, 183

Griffin, Victor, Dean, 142

Griffith, Arthur, 123, 125, 128, 253–4, 266

Groarke, Vona, 97

Guardian, The, 25, 89, 98

Guelke, Adrian, 94–5

Gwynn, Aubrey, 40–1

Hackett, Francis, 66, 69, 74

Hadden, Tom, 82–3, 84, 85, 86–7, 89, 90, 92, 93, 94, 96, 97, 100, 101

Hagan, John ('Scotus'), Fr, 260, 264, 266

Haines, Francis, 170

Hall, Frank, 231

Haller, Kurt, 45

Halliday, Fred, 96–7

Harcup, Tony, 111, 113

Harmon, Maurice, 35

Harney, Mary, 116

Haugh, Irene, 69

Haugh, Kevin, 52, 56

Haughey, Charles, 106, 107, 111, 115, 116, 117, 118, 121, 165–6, 192, 218, 245

Haverty, Anne, 196

Hayden, Mary, 268

Hayes, Jimmy, 194

Healy, T.M., 31, 144, 263, 264

Heaney, Shemus, 82, 91, 92, 96, 97

Hempel, Edouard, 43, 46

Hermon, John, 89

Hewitt, John, 91, 100

Hibernia, 15, 86, 102, 104, 105, 106, 107, 142

Higgins, Michael D., 99, 246, 255

Hilliard, Stephen, Revd, 119

Hillman, James, 71

Hobson, Valerie, 228

Hogan, Patrick, 259, 271

Holland, Mary, 89, 166, 168

Holmquist, Kate, 160

Hone, Evie, 214–15

Honesty, 12, 16, 122–34

Horgan, John, 15, 16, 106–7

Horizon, 33, 34, 65

Hot Press, 15, 106, 119

Hourican, Bridget, 215–16

Hourihane, Ann-Marie, 160

Housewife's Voice, 206, 218

Hume, John, 89, 94, 95, 249, 256,

Hutcheson, Francis, 100

Hutton, Will, 96

Hyde, Douglas, 211, 238, 244, 255, 257, 283

Identity, 13, 182, 184–6

Image, 192, 197

In Dublin, 13, 155–72, 182

In Touch, 13, 179–81, 184–6

Inniu, 241

Ireland To-Day, 60, 65, 69–70, 73, 74, 75, 78, 79, 80

Ireland's Own, 74, 223

Iremonger, Valentine,

Irish Arts Review, 102

Irish Catholic, 19, 29–31, 253

Irish Churchman, The, 135, 141

Irish Citizen, 13–14, 205, 210

Irish Ecclesiastical Record, 32

Irish Homestead, 277

Irish Housewife, 13–14, 203–19

Irish Independent, 19,20, 25–7, 29, 31, 102, 103, 181, 207, 241–2, 253, 262

Irish Messenger, 14–15, 32, 61, 261, 277, 278, 280, 290–2, 293–5

Irish Monthly, 14, 32, 263, 277–81, 287, 290, 295

Irish Press, 19, 21, 25, 26, 27–9, 36–59, 86, 125, 169, 181, 198, 241

Irish Statesman, 15, 142, 258, 260, 268–9

Irish Tatler and Sketch, 65, 223–4

Irish Times, 19, 23–5, 27, 84, 85, 87, 89, 92, 96, 102, 103, 104, 107, 110, 119, 153, 160, 174, 175, 181, 183, 190, 199, 209, 216, 240, 253, 259, 272, 273

Irish War News, 124, 125

Irish Writing, 21, 81

Jacob, Rosamond, 215, 258
Jellett, Mainie, 69, 215
Johnstone, Robert, 87, 91
Joyce, James, 23, 92, 269

Kajermo, Arja, 159, 171, 200
Kavanagh, Ann, 193
Kavanagh, Patrick, 37, 66, 68, 71, 72, 77, 78
Kavanagh, Peter, 72
Kavanagh's Weekly, 72
Keane, E.T., 123–4
Keane, Paul, 117
Keane, Terry, 115
Keating, Anthony, 7, 12, 122–34
Keating, Justin, 261
Keating, May, 261
Kelly, Charles E., 23, 63
Kelly, Gerry, 101
Kelly, Maeve, 192, 196
Kelly, Veronica, 231
Kenna, Colm, 160
Kennedy, Mary, 175–6
Kennedy, Michael, 8, 11, 36–59
Kennedy, Patricia, 224
Kennedy, Stanislaus, Sr, 190
Kenny, Colum, 128
Keogh, Dermot, 59
Keohane, Patrick, 260
Kernan, Alvin, 111
Kerney, Leopold, 37–8, 43–5, 47–59
Kerr, W.S., Revd ('Shebna the Scribe' & 'Boreas'), 141, 145, 148
Kerrigan, Gene, 168
Kerrigan, Páraic, 185–6
Kettle, Tom, 283
Keynes, John Maynard, 271, 287
Keys, Graeme, 117
Kiberd, Declan, 19, 20, 32, 34, 91
Kilkenny Journal, 123–4
Kilkenny People, 123
King-Hamilton, Alan, 175
Kingston, Lucy, 217
Kinsella, Catherine, 195
Kirrane, Máire, 187–8
Knox, Ian, 88

Laffan, Michael, 59
Laing, Carole, 182
Lambert, Margaret, 53
Langer, William, 42
Larkin, Celia, 116
Larkin, Felix M., 8, 11, 18–35, 108
Laverty, Maura, 228, 230, 231
Leader, The, 11, 36–59, 264, 276
Lee, J.J., 41, 59
Lehane, Una, 232
Leland, Mary, 231
Lemass, Seán, 218, 288
Lennon, Brian, SJ, 289
Lennon, Denis, 174, 175
Lennon, Sean, 117
Leonard, Anne, 196
Leonard, Paul, SJ, 291
Leslie, Shane, 264
Levin, Bernard, 175
Levine, June, 197, 200
Lewis, Sheelagh, 231
Liddell, Cecil, 48
Liddell, Guy, 41–2, 48
Lockyer, Sharon, 110–11
Longley, Edna, 91, 97
Longley, Michael, 91
Looney, Fiona, 171
Lord, Miriam, 117
Loughran, Seamus, 86
Lukes, Heather, 231
Lunney, Linde, 206
Lyceum, 277, 281, 282–3, 284, 285, 289
Lynch, Declan, 160
Lynch, Edmund, 181, 182, 183
Lynch, Jack, 192, 218, 245
Lynch, Paricia, 215, 224
Lynch, Patrick, 288
Lyons, F.S.L., 258, 259

Mac a'Bhaird, Proinsias, 250
Mac Aonghusa, Proinsias, 252–4
MacAnna, Ferdia, 171
Macardle, Dorothy, 212
Mac Brádaigh, Frainc, 293–4
Mac Cába, Anton, 246–7, 255
MacCurtain, Margaret, 190

Mac Erlean, John C., SJ, 293
Mac Gabhann, Séamas, 254
MacIntyre, Tom, 160–1
Mac Liammóir, Micheál, 69, 185, 203
MacManus, Francis, 258
Macnamara, Angela, 232–3, 235
MacNeill, Eoin, 241, 265, 283
Mac Réamoinn, Seán, 241
MacRory, Joseph, Cardinal, 153
MacWhite, Michael, 39
Madden, Martina, 8, 13, 155–72
Madonna, 277, 292–3, 295
Magennis, Peter Elias, O.Carm, 260, 264
Magennis, William, 283
Magill, 15, 97, 163, 167, 168, 171, 190–1, 196, 197, 199, 201–2
Mag Shamhráin, Antain, 250
Maguire, Anne, 96
Mahaffy, John Pentland, 259
Maher, Mary, 218
Mahon, Derek, 91
Mandy, W.J.K., 69
Manning, Mary, 68–9, 72
Manning, Maurice, 170–1
Manning, Susan, 205
Mansfield, Thelma, 234
Mara, P.J., 166
Markievicz, Constance, 217
Marshall, Douglas, 87
Mathews, Tom, 117
Maume, Patrick, 8, 14, 258–76
McAdoo, Henry, Bishop, 152, 181
McAleese, Mary, 99, 182
McAughtry, Sam, 91
McCafferty, Nell, 160, 162, 168–9, 170, 194, 195
McCann, Eamonn, 91, 160
McCann, James, Archbishop, 138
McCartan, Patrick, 78, 79
McCarthy, D.F., 278
McCartney, Robert, 88
McClean, Tom, 181, 182
McCormack, Inez, 190
McDonald, Frank, 161
McDonald, Mary Lou, 116
McDonnell, James, SJ, 291, 293

McDowell, R.B., 258
McEnroy, Monica, 231
McGarry, Cecil, SJ, 293
McGinley, Ciaran, 156
McGrath, Joseph, 78–9
McGrath, William, 87
McGuckian, Medbh, 91
McGuinness, Catherine, 170, 171, 190
McGuinness, Frank, 182
McGuinness, Martin, 101
McInerney, Tony, 79
McIntyre, Anthony, 95, 98
McKearney, Tommy, 98
McKenna, David, 159–63, 164, 167–71
McKenna, Lambert, SJ, 280–1
McKenna, Siobhán, 228, 251–2
McKeown, Ciaran, 84, 86–7
McKeown, Michael, 87
McKitterick, David, 87, 94
McKnight, James (pseudonym of Andy Pollak), 87–8
McLaughlin, Hugh, 104
McNamara, Kevin, Archbishop, 182
McQuaid, John Charles, Archbishop, 212
McWilliam, Herbert, 177–8, 181
Meagher, William, SJ, 278
Meehan, Sylvia, 193
Meenan, James, 259
Mercier, Vivian, 20–5, 27–9, 32–5
Meredith, Fíonola, 100
Meyer, Rolf, 98
Michell, Caroline, 231
Milk, Harvey, 180
Millet, Kate, 162
Mills, Rosaleen, 207
Miss (later *Young Woman*), 233–5
Mitchell, Charles, 231
Mitchell, Rob, 176
Model Housekeeping, 62, 64, 65, 208, 223, 224–5, 227, 233
Modern Girl, 63–5
Moffat, Chris, 84, 100
Moloney, Ed, 87, 89, 92
Moloney, Helena, 217
Moloney, William, 269
Molyneaux, James, 89

Monaghan, Paddy, 187–8
Monroe, Harriet, 67
Montague, John, 91
Montessori, Maria, 267
Montgomery, Hugh de Fallenberg, 143
Moore, Brian, 88
Moore, George, 283
Moore, Phil, 178
Moran, D.P., 37, 264, 276, 283
Moran, Nuala, 37
Morash, Christopher, 107
Morrison, Danny, 89, 98
Morrissey, Betty, 225
Morrissey, Sinead, 97
Motley, 60, 65, 68–9, 71, 72
Moynihan, Maurice, 52
Moynihan, Senan, Fr, 67, 68, 73–4, 75, 80
Ms, 201
Muinzer, Louis, 83
Mulcahy, Aengus, 120
Mulcahy, Elizabeth ('Budge'), 43, 44
Mulcahy, John, 102–6, 107, 108, 109–10, 117,
    118–19, 120, 121
Mulcahy, Neilí, 226, 229
Mulcahy, Richard, 272
Mulcahy, T.J., SJ, 281
Muldoon, Paul, 91
Mulholland, Rosa, 263, 279
Murphy, Blackwood, 211
Murphy, Brian P., OSB, 259
Murphy, David, 111
Murphy, Denis, SJ, 265
Murphy, Dervla, 197
Murphy, Eileen, 234
Murphy, Niall, 117
Murphy, Noel, 93
Murphy, William Martin, 25–6, 31, 262
Murray, Donal, Bishop, 181
Murray, Ruby, 228
Murray, Tony, 159

Nagle, Deirdre, 196
Namier, Lewis, 58
Nationality, 253–4
Naughton, Lindie, 158
Neary, Donal, SJ, 292

Nelson, Sarah, 87
Neveu, Erik, 112
New Ireland Review, 263, 277, 281, 283–4, 289
Newman, Dolly, 196
Newman, John Henry, Cardinal, 264, 266–7,
    281, 283, 284, 285
News Letter, The (Belfast), 92, 137, 253
Newspaper and Periodical Forum of
    Ireland, 16–17
Ní Bhriain, Doireann, 200
Ní Chiaráin, Póilín, 249
Ní Chléirchín, Caitríona, 250
Ní Chuilleanáin, Eiléan, 91
Ní Congáil, Ríona, 250
Ní Dhonnchadha, Aisling, 251
Ní Dhuigneáin, Cláir, 242
Ní Fhoghlú, Siobhán, 251
Ní Gearbhuigh, Ailbhe, 250
Ní Ghrianna, Deirdre, 246
Ní Scolaí, Máire, 228
Nic Pháidín, Caoilfhionn, 238, 248
Nolan, Jim, 198
Nolan, Patrick, OSB, 271
Norris, David, 162, 173, 175, 176, 177–9, 180,
    181, 182, 183, 186, 187
Noyk, Michael, 128
Nua-Aois, 243
Nugent, Barbara, 197
Nunan, Seán, 46, 47–8, 54

Ó Brádaigh, Ruairí, 115
O'Brien, Conor Cruise, 20–1, 25–7, 29–32,
    34–5, 39, 45, 89, 91, 157, 288
O'Brien, Frank Cruise, 20
O'Brien, George, 259, 287, 288
O'Brien, Ignatius, 261–2
O'Brien, Kate, 215–16, 228
O'Brien, Mark, 8, 13, 18, 106–7, 173–89
O'Brien, Sophie Raffalovich, 263
Ó Brolcháin, Fionnbarra, 245–6
Ó Bruadair, David, 293
O'Byrne, Patrick, 182
Ó Cadhain, Máirtín, 237–8, 248
O'Callaghan, Gary, 161
O'Callaghan, Margaret, 259
O'Callaghan, Tanis, 234

Ó Caoimh, Ian, 238
O'Carroll, Maureen, 229
O'Clery, Conor, 96
O'Connell, Daniel, 264, 266
O'Connell, Maura, 200
O'Connor, Franks, 66, 69
O'Connor, Kathleen, 229
Ó Cuív, Éamon, 246
Ó Direáin, Máirtín, 249–50
O'Doherty, Malachy, 92, 99–100, 101
Ó Doibhlin, Breandan, 250
O'Donnell, Donat, *see* Conor Cruise O'Brien
O'Donnell, J.F., 278
O'Donnell, Peader, 70, 76, 78, 79, 80
O'Donoghue, Fergus, SJ, 289
O'Donovan, James (Jim), 69–70, 72–3, 78–9, 80
O'Donovan, Mary E.M., 224
Ó Drisceoil, Fachtna, 255
O'Duffy, Eoin, 273
O'Duffy, Molly, 170
Ó Duinnín, Pádraig, SJ, 293
O'Faoláin, Eileen, 76
O'Faolain, Nuala, 196
O'Faoláin, Seán, 18–21, 27, 28, 32–5, 66, 68, 69, 70, 78, 81, 215
O'Farrell, Audrey, 232
O'Farrell, John, 82, 98–9, 100
O'Farrell, Patrick, 259
Ó Fiach, Tomás, Cardinal, 89, 91
Ó Fionnaile, Deasún, 244–5
O'Flaherty, Liam, 74
Ó Flaitheartaigh, Máirtín, 237
O'Flanagan, Cathal, OFM, 176
O'Flanagan, Michael, Fr, 262
Ó Flatharta, Peadar, 255
Ó Gallcobhair, Eamonn, 69
O'Hagan, Martin, 90, 93
O'Hara, Mary, 228
O'Hara, Maureen, 225–6
O'Hegarty, W.R., 213–14
Ó hÉigeartaigh, Seán Sáirséal, 238
Ó hEithir, Breandáin, 249, 254
O'Keeffe, Declan, 9, 14–15, 277–95
O'Kelly, J.J. ('Sceilg'), 258, 260, 262, 264
O'Kelly, Phyllis, 226

O'Kelly, Seán T., 226, 272–3
O'Laoghaire, Liam, 69
O'Leary, Joe, Fr, 182
O'Leary, Olivia, 190
O'Malley, Desmond, 116
O'Malley, Padraig, 89
Ó Móráin, Dónall, 238
Ó Muirí, Pól, 240–1, 248
O'Neill, Joseph, 273–4
Ó Néill, Séamus ('Bricriú'), 241–2
O'Neill, Terence, 145
O'Nolan, Brian, 216, 241
Ó Nualláin, Ciarán, 241
O'Rahilly, Alfred, 31
O'Reilly, Emily, 96
Ó Riagáin, Dónall, 246
O'Shea, Tony, 159
Ó Snodaigh, Aengus, 246
O'Sullivan, John Marcus, 40
O'Sullivan, Sean (artist), 77
O'Sullivan, Seán, 229, 231
O'Sullivan, Seumas (James Sullivan Starkey), 66–8, 73, 74, 79
O'Toole, Fintan, 96, 160, 163, 164, 166, 167, 168
Oakeshott, Michael, 52–3
Oldmeadow, Ernest, 265
Opsahl, Torkel, 94, 95
Oram, Hugh, 18
Orr, Lawrence, 83
Out, 13, 182–6

Paisley, Ian, 83, 87, 90, 92, 116, 150
Paisley, Ian, Jnr, 88
Parker, Stewart, 100
Parker, Tony, 93
Passant, E. James, 53–4, 55
Paulin, Tom, 91
Pearse, P.H., 124, 258, 288
Pereira, Lisa, 170
Perkins, Sonya, 9, 11–12, 15, 60–81
Phoenix, The (Mulcahy) 12, 16, 102–21
Phoenix, The (Upton) 125
Pioneer, The, 294
Plunkett, Grace, 217
Plunkett, Horace, 263, 270–1, 283

Pollak, Andy (see also James McKnight), 9, 12, 82–101
Prendiville, Paddy, 103–4, 105–6, 108, 111, 113, 115, 117, 118, 119–20, 121
Price, Dolores, 101
Price, K. Arnold, 196
Private Eye, 104, 107–8, 110, 111, 114
Publicity, 122–3, 127–8, 131–4
Purcell, Deirdre, 192
Purcell, Mary, 229

Quigley, George, 95
Quinn, Bob, 255
Quinn, Helen, 192
Quinn, Ruairí, 171

Rabbitte, Pat, 246
Raftery, Mary, 160, 163, 164, 167, 170–1
Ramaphosa, Cyril, 98
Ramiére, Henri, SJ, 290
Rea, Stephen, 97
Redmond, Jennifer, 206
Redmond, John, 261
Reynolds, Lorna, 215–16
Robertson, Nora, 148
Robinson, Lennox, 69, 71
Robinson, Mary, 99, 115, 179, 189, 190
Robinson, Peter, 89, 101
Robinson, Sue, 111, 112–13
Roche, Eamonn, 77
Rockett, Dolores, 234
Ronan, Myles, 266
Rooney. Maude, 206, 217
Roscommon Herald, 213
Rose, Kieran, 187–8
Rosenstock, Gabriel, 256
Rowe, Jim, 198
RTÉ, 103, 171, 183, 191, 192, 198
Russell, Bernice, 234
Russell, Charles, 278
Russell, George (Æ), 74, 258, 263, 269
Russell, Matthew, SJ, 263, 267, 277–80, 281, 291
Russell, Sheila, 234
Ryan, Agnes, 76–7
Ryan, Dermot, Archbishop, 181

Ryan, Frank, 45
Ryan, John (*Envoy*), 60, 71, 73, 76–8
Ryan, John (IGRM), 180
Ryan, Liz, 200
Rynne, Michael, 51
Rynne, Stephen, 224

Salkeld, Blánaid, 69
Savage, Roland Burke, SJ, 15, 287, 288
Scanlon, Moire, 244
Scissors and Paste, 124
Self, Charles, 178
Shan Van Vocht, 15, 142
Shatter, Alan, 170
Shaw, Francis, SJ, 288
Shaw, Helen, 160, 170
Shawn, William, 160
Shea, J.B., Canon, 142
Sheridan, Monica, 231, 236
Sherwin, Frank, 214
Shirlow, Peter, 99
Silver, Carol Ruth, 180
Simmons, James, 91
Simmons, Nancye, 204
Situationists International, 114
Skeffington, Andreé Sheehy, 204, 205–6
Skeffington, Francis Sheehy, 205
Skeffington, Hanna Sheehy, 205, 207–8, 210, 217
Skeffington, Owen Sheehy, 69, 205
Skelton, Marguerite, 204
Smith, Anthony D., 276
Smith, Constance, 228
Smith, Sam, 160
Smurfit, Michael, 109
Smyth, Damian, 97, 100
Spare Rib, 158, 201
Spark, The, 124
Speirs, Derek, 195
Spence, Gusty, 89
Spiker, Ted, 114
Spring, Dick, 108–9
Standard, The, 16, 19, 29–30, 31, 213
Stanley, C.O., 76
Stanley, Joseph, 122, 124, 125, 129, 131
Status, 13, 14, 190–202

Stephens, James, 66
Stephenson, Jonathan, 87
Strong, Eithne, 196
Stuart, Francis, 161, 167
Studies, 14–15, 32, 81, 259, 263, 264, 269, 270, 277, 280, 281, 284–90, 294–5
Sullivan, T.D., 30–1
Sunday Business Post, 103, 197
Sunday Independent, 102–3, 188, 199, 223, 242
Sunday Press, 43, 189, 223
Sunday Tribune, 102, 104, 106, 107, 168, 171, 197
Sunday World, 90, 104
Sweeney, Maxwell, 229
Sweetman, Rosita, 197
Synge, J.M., 283

Tablet, The, 32, 265
Taylor, Cliff, 107
Taylor, Peter, 89
Thackaberry, Frank, 186
Thatcher, Margaret, 89–90
Thompson, George, 83
Tiernan, Sonja, 9, 13–14, 203–19
Tierney, Michael, 40, 242–3, 270
Timire, An, 15, 293–5
Titley, Alan, 251
Tóibín, Colm, 160, 162, 163–7, 168
Toner, Eddie, 69
Treber, Michael, 185
Trench, Brian, 104, 160
Trimble, David, 90, 96
Troddyn, Peter, SJ, 288
Troughton-Smith, Michael, 217
Troy, Una, 225
Turner, Martyn, 84, 85–6, 92, 101
Turton, Ted, 156
Tweedy, Hilda, 193, 203, 204–5, 206, 208, 209, 212–13, 216, 218, 219
Tweedy, Robert, 209
Twohig, David, 182
Tynan, Katherine, 279, 280
Tyrie, Andy, 89

Uí Chollatáin, Regina, 9–10, 14, 237–57
Uíbh Eachach, Vivian, 248
Upton, James W., 12, 122–34

van Hoek, Kees, 40
Van Slyke, Leslie, 92
Varadkar, Leo, 114
Veesenmayer, Edmund, 43–5, 47, 49, 51, 52, 54, 55, 59
Veil, Simone, 200
Vellacott, Paul, 39
Viney, Michael, 148

Wall, Frank, 199
Walsh, Caroline, 104–5
Walsh, Paul, Fr, 266
Walsh, Tonie, 186
Walsh-Atkins, Leonard, 56
Walshe, Joseph, 44, 45, 46, 47–8, 51
Ward, Brian, 259
Warke, Roy, Revd, 181
Waterford Standard, 134
Waterford Star, 134
Waterford Whispers, 121
Waters, John, 171
Watkins, Kathleen, 228
Watson, Katherine, 210–11
Waugh, Evelyn, 265
Wells, Warre B., 141, 143, 144
Whelan, Aoife, 10, 14, 237–57
Whelan, Leo, 261
Whitaker, T.K., 246, 255
White, Dan, 180
Whitehouse, Mary, 175
Whitty, Robert, SJ, 282
Whyte, Barry J., 103, 121
Whyte, John, 91
Wilde, Oscar, 174, 185, 259, 279
Williams, Betty, 86–7
Williams, Sheila, 229
Williams, T. Desmond, 36–59
Willis, Andy, Canon, 137, 141, 142
Wilson, Gilbert, Revd, 137
Wilson, Robin, 92–8, 99, 100, 101
Wilson, Sammy, 89
Windle, Bertram, 264
Wiskemann, Elizabeth, 52–3, 58
Wogan, Terry, 234
Woman's Life, 223, 226, 227–31
Woman's Mirror, 223, 225–7

Woman's Realm, 230–1
Woman's Way, 14, 192, 223, 229, 231–3, 234,
    236
Women's Illustrated, 225
Woods, Tommy, 39
Wright, Frank, 91

Yeates, Padraig, 160
Yeats, Anne, 215
Yeats, Jack B., 68, 77
Yeats, W.B., 66, 92, 215, 263, 268, 269, 279,
    280, 283
Young Woman, see *Miss*